History of the Order of the Eastern Star

With an authentic biography of the founder
Rob Morris, LL.D.

By Jean M'Kee Kenaston, M.E.
Past Worthy Matron, Rosebud Chapter No. 12, Bonesteel, S. D.
Past Grand Marshal of the Grand Chapter of South Dakota

1917 Edition
Restored and Edited by
Jonathan K. Poll

"History, to be above evasion or dispute, must stand on documents, not opinions." —Lord Acton

A Cornerstone Book

History of the Order of the Eastern Star
by Jean M'Kee Kenaston
Restored and Edited by Jonathan K. Poll

A Cornerstone Book
Published by Cornerstone Book Publishers
Copyright © 2024 by Cornerstone Book Publishers

All rights reserved under International and Pan-American Copyright Conventions. No part of this book may be reproduced in any manner without permission in writing from the copyright holder, except by a reviewer, who may quote brief passages in a review.

Cornerstone Book Publishers
Hot Springs Village, AR

First Cornerstone Edition - 2024

www.cornerstonepublishers.com

ISBN: 979-8-3304-9077-6

"I shall pass this way but once. If therefore, there be any kindness I can show, or any good that I can do to my fellow human beings, let me do it now. Let me not defer or neglect it, for I shall not pass this way again."

"We cannot understand the actual of a character or system, without in some degree, entering into its ideal."

"Truth is a divine attribute and the foundation of every virtue."

Here is a story of the grand, old time,
A tale of virtues, tender, yet sublime,
Inscribed on sacred page to give us faith
In woman's constancy, in life and death;
Here, in God's book, the bright narration see,
And five brave hearts make up the history.

Adah, great Jephthah's daughter, soul of truth,
Ruth, flower of Moab, humble, pious Ruth,
Esther, the crowned, and worthiest of a crown,
Martha, His friend, whom saints and angels own,
Electa, strong the martyr's cross to bear—
These are the heroines of the Eastern Star.

Fairest among ten thousand deathless names,
How altogether lovely do they glow!
Time's annals yield no brighter, nobler themes,
No purer hearts the ranks of heaven know;
Here, then, Oh! Sisters, sister-virtues trace,
And light from these your lamps of truth and grace.

—Rob Morris, LL.D.

Foreword

The history of Masonic and Masonic affiliated Orders is all too often a hazy, confused, and disordered mess. Often knowing and keeping these histories is like grasping dry sand in our clenched fists. While it has our focus, most of it can be kept from slipping through our fingers, but one lapse of inattention and so much is lost to the wind.

The Eastern Star is blessed with a gift that so many other Orders lack. A clear history, a concise story from creation that can be kept and passed from generation to generation. Keeping and holding these histories is a duty for all who truly care about their Order. The Eastern Star holds a special place among those bodies affiliated with Freemasonry. It serves as a unifying force, strengthening bonds of Masonic families and pulling them together in a way other organizations are ill-suited to do.

Mrs. Jean M'Kee Kenaston went to great lengths to collect and preserve the history of the early days of The Eastern Star. She Interviewed family and acquaintances of the founder Dr. Rob Morris to have their personal accounts preserved. She extensively collected names, dates, and old records from very early Eastern Star bodies. Despite all her efforts, this book was in danger of falling out of the public mind. It has been out of print and difficult to acquire for many years prior to its re-publishing by Cornerstone Book Publishers. It was in this effort to preserve and protect this history and make it more widely accessible that this book was selected for restoration.

The restoration of this 1917 edition was done with care and attention to detail. The original text was scanned and digitized so that a new typeset could be applied for ease of reading. The text was painstakingly examined to ensure the accuracy of the conversion. The original artwork was preserved where possible and appropriate.

The formatting of prose and poems was preserved as closely to the original author's style as possible.

It is our pleasure and honor to present this restored edition of *History of the Order of the Eastern Star*. We hope you find its contents illuminating and informative as we continue our mission to find and preserve as many of these historical texts as possible.

Jonathan K. Poll
September 2024

Preface

N presenting for the consideration of the Fraternity, this volume, embracing the origin, together with a history of the Order of the Eastern Star, the author has endeavored to perform two duties: first, that of entertaining and interesting the reader in the records of the achievements of those honored women and men, whose acts have combined to make this the greatest fraternal organization of women extant; second, to produce some evidence of the value and useful character of the Institution, that its claims for Charity, Truth, and Loving Kindness may be the more readily seen and appreciated.

Such a book is not easy to write for the reasons that it is the history of a secret Order, much of whose lore is not to be made public; and the facts concerning its history are more or less difficult to obtain.

All writers on the Order of the Eastern Star appear to have been influenced by a desire to impress upon the Fraternity a love for its science and philosophy. Every line of this book has been written in the conviction that the real history of the Order of the Eastern Star is great enough, and its simple teachings grand enough, without further embellishments.

The bonding powers of the Sisterhood are manifest to the world by its five adorning virtues: obedience, constancy, fidelity, faith, and love. The entire ritual has been prepared in wisdom and beauty. It is only as the Eastern Star member of the present seeks true light — teaches genuine truth — that it proves itself deserving of a future.

From my early experience in Eastern Star work, I learned that the character of the institution was elevated in one's opinion just in proportion to the amount of knowledge that had been acquired of its teachings, history, symbolisms, and philosophy. The difficulty of obtaining this knowledge of the Eastern Star — what it is, whence it came, what it teaches and what it is trying to do — and an earnest desire to obtain a more extensive knowledge of the Order, has prompted the compilation of this book.

Keeping this purpose always in mind, the effort has been to prepare a brief, simple, and vivid account of the origin, the development, the mission, the ideals, and the teachings of the Order, so written as to incite a deeper interest in and a more earnest study of its story and of its service to mankind.

To this end, the various sources of the Order of the Eastern Star records have been liberally explored and the highest authorities have been consulted; and cited when necessary to substantiate the statements made, and also to guide the reader into further and more detailed research. The author is richly indebted to the many Grand Secretaries who have so generously aided in this work; also to many women and men prominent in the development of the Order, whose achievements are recalled by a humble student who would gladly pay the honor belonging to those whose earnest labors and great results have wrought the glorious fruition which the Order has attained at the present day.

To every Eastern Star student, in fact to every Eastern Star member, a knowledge of its purposes and achievements is an absolute essential in the attainment of that perfection upon which depends the full realization of its usefulness and beauties and toward which we should ever strive with unceasing effort.

When we comprehend our position in this earthly career — its pathos and its wonderful extent, — and our duty in retaining and beautifying the inheritance of the race, a deep sense of the fraternal tie that binds us to our co-workers, especially those to whom must soon be entrusted these sacred legends, duties, obligations, and principles, at once comes a feeling of awe and we stop to consider. Shall we not then do our part to have the younger members of the Order earnestly strive to preserve and more fully realize the faith, the spirit, and the character, of the beautiful lessons our Order teaches;

at the same time presenting to those who will follow, the latent powers for the advancement of womanhood through this the greatest fraternal Order for women. Each can do her part faithfully and well, and by so doing we shall impress this great truth, that our Order has helped to make its members, and through them the world, more prompt in obedience, more firm in constancy, more devoted to kindred and friends, richer in faith and wiser in love and pity.

With an earnest hope that more light may result to every inquiring member of the Order of the Eastern Star from the study and perusal of these pages, I have the honor to present this compilation of its history.

Mrs. Jean M'Kee Kenaston
Bonesteel, South Dakota
June 1, 1916

Contents

FOREWORD ix
PREFACE xi
CHAPTER I - *Origin of the Order of the Eastern Star* 1
CHAPTER II - *Biography of Rob Morris, LL.D.* 33
CHAPTER III - *Other Degrees, Minor Rituals, etc.* 62
CHAPTER IV - *Organization of the General Grand Chapter* 99
CHAPTER V - *Officers of the General Grand Chapter* 142
CHAPTER VI - *Brief Histories of the Several Grand Chapters* ... 163
    Grand Chapter of Alabama 163
    Grand Chapter of Alberta 167
    Grand Chapter of Arizona 170
    Grand Chapter of Arkansas 173
    Grand Chapter of British Columbia 178
    Grand Chapter of California 183
    Grand Chapter of Colorado 194
    Grand Chapter of Connecticut 198
    Grand Chapter of District of Columbia 203
    Grand Chapter of Florida 207
    Grand Chapter of Georgia 213
    Grand Chapter of Idaho 219
    Grand Chapter of Illinois 224
    Grand Chapter of Indiana 245
    Grand Chapter of Iowa 249
    Grand Chapter of Kansas 252
    Grand Chapter of Kentucky 256
    Grand Chapter of Louisiana 259
    Grand Chapter of Maine 262
    Grand Chapter of Maryland 265
    Grand Chapter of Massachusetts 268
    Grand Chapter of Michigan 271
    Grand Chapter of Minnesota 275

Grand Chapter No. 2 Minnesota 278
Grand Chapter of Minnesota (Reorganized) 279
Grand Chapter of Mississippi 282
Grand Chapter of Missouri 287
Grand Chapter of Montana 291
Grand Chapter of Nebraska 293
Grand Chapter of Nevada 297
Grand Chapter of New Hampshire 299
Grand Chapter of New Jersey 301
Grand Chapter of New Mexico 306
Grand Chapter of New York 307
Grand Chapter of North Carolina 319
Grand Chapter of North Dakota 322
Grand Chapter of Ohio 325
Grand Chapter of Oklahoma 328
Grand Chapter of Ontario 336
Grand Chapter of Oregon 339
Grand Chapter of Pennsylvania 343
Grand Chapter of Puerto Rico 348
Grand Chapter of Rhode Island 350
Grand Chapter of Saskatchewan 352
Grand Chapter of Scotland 353
Grand Chapter of South Carolina 358
Grand Chapter of South Dakota 363
Grand Chapter of Tennessee 369
Grand Chapter of Texas 372
Grand Chapter of Utah 378
Grand Chapter of Vermont 381
Grand Chapter of Virginia 386
Grand Chapter of Washington 389
Grand Chapter of West Virginia 393
Grand Chapter of Wisconsin 398
Grand Chapter of Wyoming 404
Chapters under the Immediate Jurisdiction of the
    General Grand Chapter 408

Alaska 408
Canal Zone — Panama 409
Hawaiian Islands 410
Philippine Islands 412
Canada 412
    Manitoba 413
    New Brunswick 413
    Quebec 414
Cuba 414
Delaware 415
India 416
Mexico 417
Yukon 418

CHAPTER I

Origin of the Order of the Eastern Star

THE Masonic Order symbolically dates its origin back to the reign of King Solomon, who ascended the throne 1015 years before the Christian era, and had, in its inception, three great men termed Grand Masters. In the Holy Bible, the recognized great light of Freemasonry, we read that Solomon, King of Israel, in his great wisdom, erected a temple at Jerusalem and dedicated it to Jehovah. In the execution of this great work, he sought the assistance of Hiram, King of Tyre, who sent the wonderful and gifted architect, Hiram Abif, whose skill and experience were utilized in superintending the labors of the craft, and in adorning and beautifying the building. These three, according to traditions and records, are termed the first Council of Grand Masters.

The Order of the Eastern Star can trace a portion of its symbolic traditions and history to, and in consequence has the privilege of dating its origin back to RUTH, the great-grandmother of King Solomon. This Order also had three Master Workmen; our distinguished brother, Dr. Rob Morris, who wrought out the degrees, contemplated the themes incorporated, culled from the pages of antiquity the heroines and names upon which the beautiful work is built, established the signs and passes, communicated the esoteric mysteries of the Order and promulgated the fundamental principles which have remained unchanged; Robert Macoy, who, with the consent and assistance of Dr. Rob Morris, devised and arranged the Chapter system, developed a broader field of labor and a grander organization, vitalized the impressive ceremonials and symbolisms of the Chapter work; the master builder and architect, Rev. Willis D. Engle, first Secretary of the General Grand Chapter and Past Most Worthy Grand Patron, who, by his keen foresight, persistent effort, indefatigable and unselfish labors, is recognized as the great organizer of this fraternal Order.

One of the most valuable records now in possession of the Order of the Eastern Star, is that of the "Origination of the Eastern Star," written under date of August 1, 1884, by its founder, Dr. Rob Morris, a complete copy of which is herewith presented:

The Origination of the Eastern Star

In these last years of my earthly pilgrimage I have been importuned by friends, old and new, to commit to paper, while memory is clear and documents accessible, all the facts concerning the origination of the Eastern Star. "What would we not give" has often been said, what would we not give for a history of the origin of the Royal Arch System, of the Cryptic System, the Commandery Orders, the Scottish Rite, all of which are as truly *Modern* and *American* as the Order of the Eastern Star itself. But their authors are dead, and the history of their origin died with them.

From the period of my initiation into Masonry I had entertained the desire of introducing the female relatives of Masons into closer relationship with the Order. Through the immense influence of women so much might be done to bring the *performances* of Freemasons nearer their *professions*. If the wife and mother would but become interested in the workings of the Lodge, the husband and father dare no longer introduce into "the tyled precincts" such caricatures of men — drunkards, gamblers, brawlers, rogues — as I saw, forty years since, walking familiarly in Masonic processions. If committees of charitable women, female members of the families of Freemasons, would but undertake our charitable disbursements, the widow, the orphan and the destitute need no longer suffer neglect upon the plea that "such oversight is not the proper work of men." If the sharp eye of the domestic housekeeper were but cast occasionally over the Lodge rooms, its furniture, aprons, jewels, etc., cleanliness and order would become the *law* there instead of the *exception.*

Again, if the gratitude of the Craft were once fairly awakened toward their female relatives for such benevolence as I have suggested many methods would be opened to women for self-support that are now sealed up. Many a clerkship, many a copyist's desk, many a situation in post office, library, public bureau, etc., now filled by men alone, would be equally available to women, and so the circle of female occupations would be vastly enlarged. All this I had pondered for several years in my mind, and I was fast coming to the initial step of sitting to weave the warp and woof which now constitute the Order of the Eastern Star.

Bowing now to the expression of a wish, widespread and urgent, I proceed to overhaul my Diaries, to tease my sluggish memory, and now (1884) sit down, through quiet summer hours, to rescue from oblivion, the facts connected with the origin of the Eastern Star. One witness, Mrs. Morris, still survives to substantiate the statements I am about to make.

In the winter of 1850, I was a resident of Jackson, Mississippi. For some time previous I had contemplated, as hinted above, the preparation of a *Ritual of Adoptive Masonry*, the degrees then in vogue appearing to me poorly conceived, weakly wrought out, unimpressive, and particularly defective in point of motive. I allude especially to those degrees styled *The Mason's Daughter*, and the *Heroines of Jericho*. But I do expressly except from this criticism, *The Good Samaritan*, which, in my judgment, possesses dramatic elements and machinery equal to those that are in the

Templar's Orders, the *High Priesthood*, the *Cryptic Rite*, and other organizations of Thomas Smith Webb. I have always recommended *The Good Samaritan*, and a thousand times conferred it in various parts of the world.

About the first of February 1850, I was laid up for two weeks with a sharp attack of rheumatism, and it was this period which I gave to the work in hand. By the aid of my papers and the memory of Mrs. Morris, I recall even the trivial occurrences connected with the work; how I hesitated for a *theme* how I dallied over a *name*, how I wrought face to face with the clock that I might keep my drama within due limits of time, etc. The *name* was first settled upon, the Eastern Star. Next the number of points, *five*, to correspond with the emblem on the Master's carpet. This is the pentagon, "the signet of King Solomon," and eminently proper to Adoptive Masonry.

From the Holy Writings I culled four biographical sketches to correspond with my first four points, viz., Jephthah's Daughter (named "Adah" for want of a better), Ruth, Esther, and Martha. These were illustrations of four great congeries of womanly virtues, and their selection has proved highly popular. The fifth point introduced me to the early history of the Christian Church, where amidst a "noble army of martyrs" I found many whose lives and death overflowed the cup of martyrdom with a glory not surpassed by any of those named in Holy Writ. This gave me Electa, "the Elect Lady," friend of St. John, the Christian woman whose venerable years were crowned with the utmost splendor of the crucifixion.

The colors, the emblems, the floral wreaths, the esotery proper to these five heroines were easy of invention. They seemed to fall ready-made into my hands. The only piece of mechanism difficult to fit into the construction was the *cabalistic motto* known as * * * * *; but this occurred to me in ample time for use.

The composition of the *lectures* was but a recreation. Familiar from childhood as I had been with the Holy Scriptures, I scarcely needed to look up my proof texts, so tamely did they come to my call. A number of odes were also composed at that time, but the great part of the three score odes and poems of the Eastern Star that I have written were the work of subsequent years. The first Ode of the series of 1850 was one commencing "Light from the East; 'tis gilded with hope."

The theory of the whole subject is succinctly stated in my *Rosary of the Eastern Star*, published in 1865: To take from the ancient writings five prominent female characters, illustrating as many Masonic virtues, and to adopt them into the fold of Masonry. The selections were: I. Jephthah's Daughter, as illustrating respect to the binding force of a vow; II. Ruth, as illustrating devotion to religious principles; III. Esther, as illustrating fidelity to kindred and friends; IV. Martha, as illustrating undeviating faith in the hour of trial; and V. Electa, as illustrating patience and submission under wrong. These are all Masonic virtues, and they have nowhere in history more brilliant exemplars than in the five characters presented in the lectures of the Eastern Star. It is a fitting comment upon these statements that in all the changes that the Eastern Star has experienced at so many hands for thirty-four years, no change in the names, histories, or essential lessons has been proposed.

So, my Ritual was complete, and after touching and retouching the manuscript, as professional authors love to do, I invited a neighboring Mason and his wife to join with my own, and to them, in my own parlor, communicated the Degrees. They were the first recipients — the first of twice fifty thousand who have seen the signs, heard the words, exchanged the touch, and joined in the music of the Eastern Star. When I take a retrospect of that evening — but thirty-four years ago — and consider the abounding *four hundred* Eastern Star Chapters at work today, my heart swells with gratitude to God who guided my hand during that period of convalescence to prepare a work, of all the work of my life the most successful. The greatest number of Stellar Lights that shine with so much splendor in the Grand Chapters of America will read this passage, I think, with similar sentiments. *L'homme propose, Dieu disposes.* How little could I anticipate such a harvest from such a scanty sowing!

Being at that time, and until a very recent period, an active traveler, visiting all countries where lodges exist — a nervous, wiry, elastic man, unwearying in work — caring little for refreshments or sleep, I spread abroad the knowledge of the Eastern Star wherever I went. Equally in border communities, where ladies came in *homespun*, as in cities, where ladies came in *satins*, the new degree was received with ardor, and eulogized in strongest terms, so that every induction led to the call for more. Ladies and gentlemen are yet living who met that immense assemblage at Newark, New Jersey, in 1853, and the still greater one in Spring Street Hall, New York City, a little earlier, where I stood up for two hours or three, before a breathless and gratified audience, and brought to bear all that I could draw from the Holy Scriptures, the Talmud, and the writings of Josephus, concerning the five "Heroines of the Eastern Star."

Not that my work met no opposition. Quite the reverse. It was not long until editors, report writers, newspaper critics, and my own private correspondents began to see the evil of it. The cry of "innovation" went up to heaven. Ridicule lent its aid to a grand assault upon my poor little figment. Ingenious charges were rung upon the idea of "petticoat Masonry." More than one writer in Masonic journals (men of an evil class, we have had them, men who know the secrets, but have never applied the *principles* of Masonry), more than one such expressed in language indecent and shocking, his opposition to the Eastern Star and to me. Letters were written me, some signed, some anonymous, warning me that I was periling my own Masonic connections in the advocacy of this scheme. In New York City the opponents of the Eastern Star even started a rival project to break it down. They employed a literary person, a poet of eminence, a gentleman of social merit, to prepare rituals under an ingenious form, and much time and money were spent in the effort to popularize it, but it survived only a short year and is already forgotten.

But the Eastern Star glittered steadily in the ascendant. In 1855 I arranged the system of "Constellations of the Eastern Star" of which the *Mosaic Book* was the index and established more than one hundred of these bodies. Looking over that book, one of the most original and brilliant works to which I ever put my hand, I have wondered that the system did not succeed. It must be because the times were not ripe for it. The opposition to "Ladies' Masonry" was too bitter. The advocates of the plan were not sufficiently influential. At any rate it fell through.

Four years later I prepared an easier plan styled "Families of the Eastern Star" intended, in its simplicity and the readiness by which it could be worked, to avoid the complexity of the "Constellations." This ran well until the war broke out, when all Masonic systems fell together with a crash.

This ended my work in *systematizing* the Eastern Star, and I should never have done more with it, save confer it in an informal manner as at first, but for Brother Robert Macoy of New York, who in 1868, when I had publicly announced my intentions of confining my labors during the remainder of my life to Holy Land Investigations, proposed the plan of Eastern Star Chapters now in vogue. He had my full consent and endorsement, and thus became the instigator of a third and more successful system. The history of this organization, which is now disseminated in more than four hundred chapters, extending to thirty-three states and territories, I need not detail. The annual proceedings of Grand Chapters, the indefatigable labors of the Rev. Willis D. Engle, Grand Secretary of the General Grand Chapter, the liberal manner in which the Masonic journals have opened their columns to the proceedings of the Adoptive Order, the annual festivals, the sociables, concerts, picnics, etc., which keep the name of the Society before the public, make a history of their own better than I can write.

It is sufficient to say that the largest anticipations I ever had concerning the Eastern Star are fast realizing. Masonic opposition has ceased, or so nearly so that it has become merely a whine. Already there is an Eastern Star Chapter in one out of every twenty-five Lodges in America, and there are persons living, I apprehend, who will see twenty of the other twenty-four equally favored. Internal contentions, which seem the doom of all societies in their youth, have died away, leaving but a murmur and an echo. The orphan has come into a closer relationship with Masonic charities. The widow has discovered that her claim upon the brothers of her dead one is real and genuine. Masonic Halls have lost their dust and cobwebs, and a spirit of purity (astonishing to Tylers) broods in whiteness over gloves and aprons. In the cemeteries, gravestones rise frequently, displaying the mystic star with its cabalistic motto.

And there is another practical result of the Eastern Star movement, the credit of which I am in no wise inclined to give to others; this is the broader opening that is offered to females for self-support. The deadly needle, the unwomanly washtub, the unwholesome country school, the sinew-wearying kitchen, are not now the only fields on which women, old and young, who are wrestling with the perplexities of human life, can win bread. Thousands and tens of thousands of places, cleanly, womanly, easy, and fairly profitable, have been opened to them since the story of the "Five Heroines of the Eastern Star" was first disseminated in 1850. In almost every post office and courthouse throughout the land — in a great number of banks and libraries — at the desk of cashiers of mercantile houses — behind counters — but the catalogue need not be extended. Long as it is, it is daily lengthening, and every year the salaries of women are brought more nearly to those of men, as it is found they are equally accurate and expert in business, and that the defalcations, forgeries, and general rascalities with which our morning papers are defiled are commonly the work of *men*, rarely of *women*.

In conclusion, I may call to witness the thousand groups of men and women who, in all these years, have sat under my voice while communicating the instructions of the Eastern Star, that no greed of money has actuated me in this work. How often have I refused fees offered me! how often forbidden collections to be made for my benefit! Monitors of the Eastern Star have been published by twenties of thousands, but the money profits were enjoyed by others, not by me. It is with honest pride that I make, as I have so often made, these declarations.

Rob Morris.
La Grange, Kentucky, August 1, 1884.

As indicated by Dr. Morris, he found that the Constellation form with its dramatic ritual was too complicated and difficult of rendition to be popular, demanding more dramatic skill than was readily available in many places. Because of this, together with the fact that the conditions of the country were negative, and the minds of the people not prepared to accept secret Orders conducted by women, the Eastern Star under the Constellation system did not flourish as had been hoped for by its originator. Consequently, as he relates, Dr. Morris prepared a ritual in 1859 which was very simple in arrangement, unpretentious in ceremony, and free from dramatic elements. This he styled "Families of the Eastern Star," and immediately organized under this name. The aim of the Families was the same as that of the Constellations, and all who had been members of the first system retained their privileges under the second, the officers remaining the same with changes only in the names.

Dr. Morris, in explanation of the change, said that charters would be issued in the old form: "The use of the old form of charter is continued, although the association governed by the Supreme Constellation, has ceased to exist. This is done to show that the two systems of 'Constellations' and 'Families' are identical in spirit, the latter having taken the place of the former. It serves further to show that the thousands of ladies who were introduced to the advantages of Adoptive Masonry under the former system retain their privileges under the latter."

The Supreme Constellation, which had been inaugurated by Dr. Morris in 1855, had been organized with the powers as stated in the *Mosaic Book*. Of this Supreme Constellation, Dr. Rob Morris was Most Enlightened Grand Luminary, Joel M. Spiller, Delphi, Indiana, Right Enlightened Deputy Grand Luminary and Grand Lecturer; Jonathan R. Neill, New York, Very Enlightened Grand Secretary; and Very Enlightened Deputy Grand Luminaries were appointed as follows:

New Jersey and *pro tem.* for New England — James B. Taylor, Newark.

New York — Thomas C. Edwards, Elmira.

Indiana — Joel M. Spiller, Delphi.

Iowa — L. D. Parmer, Muscatine.

Kentucky — John Scott, Flemingsburg.

Georgia — M. B. Franklin, Atlanta.

Missouri — M. J. F. Leonard, at large.

Right Eminent Deputy Grand Luminaries were also named:

Illinois, Fourth District — Harmon G. Reynolds, Knoxville.

Kentucky — James G. Gorsuch, Portland; W. C. Munger, Covington.

The following Constellations were granted charters under the Supreme Constellation system, and for convenience are given by States in alphabetical order:

Alabama — Venus No. 11, New Market.

Arkansas — Evening Star No. 16, Morristown.

California — Morning Star No. 44, Grass Valley; Orion No. 57, Mariposa.

Connecticut — Morning Star No. 48. Fair Haven; Alpha No. 1, New London.

Florida — Electa No. 11, Tallahassee; Flora No. 21, Uchee Anna.

Georgia — Virgo No. 4, Woodstock; Magnolia No. 5, Hillsboro; Rose No. 39, Whitesville; Electa No. 58, Cedartown.

Indiana — White Rose No. 3, Crown Point; Jessamin No. 8, Moore's Hill; Cassiopeia No. 28, Cambridge City; North Salem No. 36, North Salem; New Albany No. 160, New Albany; Newman No. 161, Milton.

Illinois — Griggsville No. 10, Griggsville; Orion No. 15, Sycamore; Flora No. 18, Pecatonica; Pittsfield No. 56, Pittsfield; Friendship No. 65, Knoxville; Rose of Sharon, No. 67, Tipton.

Iowa — Electa Morris No. 66, Muscatine; Violet No. 68, Iowa City.

Kansas — Mendias No. 1, Wyandotte.

Kentucky — Purity No. 1, Lodgeton;[1] Vesta No. 7, Burlington; Covington No. 60, Covington.

Louisiana — Cassiopeia No. 32, Lisbon.

Maine — Moriah No. 19, Denmark; Corona No. 22, Waterville.

Michigan — Buchanan No. 20, Buchanan; Western Star No. 61, Litchfield.

Missouri — Flora No. 13, New Madrid; Hesperus No. 17, Charlestown; Lyra No. 24, Arcadia; Morning Star No. 25, Caledonia; Cassiopeia No. 26, Potosi; Eastern Star No. 30, Frederickstown; Evening Star No. 31, Franklin; Western Star No. 33, Pauldingville; Prudence No. 34, Marthasville; Pleides No. 37, Mexico; Mary Washington No. 38, Florida; Martha No. 40. Madison; Robert Burns No. 42, Fulton; Astrea No. 43, Fayette; Rob Morris No. 45, Spring Hill; Esther No. 46, Pattonberg; Ruth No. 47, Gallatin; Nannie No. 49, Windsor City; Mary Anna No. 50, Roanoke; Mary Washington No. 52, Haynesville; Martha Washington No. 54, Richmond; Rose No. 59, Clinton; Louisa No. 162, Dekalb; Lucinda No. 164, Ridgeley; Hebe No. 167, Rochester; Lafayette No. 168, Palmyra; Hannah No. 169, Trenton.

Mississippi — Concordia No. 6, Tallaloosa; Ripley No. 41, Ripley; Hebron No. 55, Hebron.

New York — Orion No. 9, Evans; Purity No. 27, Spencer; Speedsville No. 29, Speedsville.

North Carolina — Hookerton, No. 63, Hookerton.

Pennsylvania — Towanda No. 166, Towanda.

Tennessee — Acacia, Clifton.

Texas — Lavacia No. 23, Hallettsville; Lily No. 35, Sabine Pass; Pleiades No. 51, Texana; Mount Horeb No. 165, Gabriel Mills.

Vermont — Irene No. 53, Swanton Falls.

Wisconsin — Lake Mills No. 171, Lake Mills.

---

[1] This is the first Constellation which was organized under the new ritual and was organized under the direct supervision of Dr. Rob Morris at his hometown in Lodgeton, Kentucky.

Dr. Rob Morris continued to hold the office of Most Enlightened Grand Luminary, and in 1857 Brother James B. Taylor was elected Very Enlightened Grand Secretary. In all, nearly three hundred Constellations were organized, and charters were granted.

According to the *Mosaic Book*, which was the ritual of the Supreme Constellation, "the inherent right which Master Masons possessed to communicate the degree remains forever unchanged, nor does the Supreme Constellation presume to interfere with it."

The Supreme Council was a self-perpetuating body, with its membership unknown to any but a very few, and all communications with it had to be through the Grand Secretary of the Supreme Council, who would not even disclose the number and location of its subordinate bodies. This body maintained an organization until about 1876 when it ceased to exist.

In 1859 Dr. Morris simplified the ritual into what was published under the title of *Morris' Manual*.[2] This was prepared for the communication of the degrees and opened with an explanation of Freemasonry and its benefits to women, the obligation administered being one of secrecy only. The signet was explained, also the signs, followed by the lectures which were simplified and adapted from the *Mosaic Book*. Each was followed by an explanation of the appropriate signs, emblems, and colors, which were fully described in a manuscript that was issued at the same time and accompanied the *Manual*. Early in 1860 Dr. Morris began organizing and issuing charters under the Family System, extending to all Constellations the privilege of changing to the Family System.

LODGES OF ADOPTION OR ADOPTIVE MASONRY

An organization which bears a very imperfect resemblance to Freemasonry in its forms and ceremonies, and which was established

---

[2] See *Manual of the Eastern Star*

in France for the initiation of females, has been called by the French *"Maconnerie d' Adoption"* or Adoptive Masonry, and the societies in which the initiations take place have received the name of "Loges d' Adoption" or Adoptive Lodges. This appellation is derived from the fact that every female or Adoptive Lodge is obliged, by the regulations of the association, to be, as it were, adopted by, and thus placed under the guardianship of some regular lodge of Freemasonry.

As to the exact date which we are to assign for the first introduction of this system of female Masonry, there have been several theories, some of which, undoubtedly, are wholly untenable, since they have been founded, as Masonic historical theories too often are, on an unwarrantable mixture of facts and fiction — of positive statements and problematic conjectures. Mons. J. S. Boubee, a distinguished French Mason, in his *Etudes Maconniques*, places the origin of Adoptive Masonry in the seventeenth century, and ascribes its authorship to Queen Henrietta Maria, the widow of Charles I of England; and he states that on her return to France, after the execution of her husband, she took pleasure in recounting the secret efforts made by the Freemasons of England to restore her family to their position and to establish her son on the throne of his ancestors.

This, it will be recollected, was once a prevailing theory, now exploded, of the origin of Freemasonry — that it was established by the Cavaliers, as a secret political organization, in the times of the English civil war between the King and the Parliament, and as an engine for the support of the former. M. Boubee adds, that the Queen made known to the ladies of her court, in her exile, the words and signs employed by her Masonic friends in England, as their modes of recognition, and by this means instructed them in some of the mysteries of the Institution, of which, he says, she had been made the protectress after the death of the King. This theory is so full of absurdity, and its statements so flatly contradicted by well-known historical facts, that we may at once reject it as wholly apocryphal.

Others have claimed Russia as the birthplace of Adoptive Masonry; but in assigning that country and the year 1712 as the place and time of its origin, they have undoubtedly confounded it with the chivalric Order Saint Catherine, which was instituted by the Czar, Peter the Great, in honor of the Czarina, Catharine, and which, although at first it consisted of persons of both sexes, was subsequently confined exclusively to females. But the Order of Saint Catherine was in no manner connected with that of Freemasonry. It was simply a Russian order of female knighthood.

The truth seems to be that the regular Lodges of Adoption owed their existence to those secret associations of men and women which sprang up in France before the middle of the eighteenth century, and which attempted in all of their organization, except the admission of female members, to imitate the Institution of Freemasonry.

Clavel, who in his *Histoire Pittoresque de la Franc-Maconnerie*, an interesting but not always a trustworthy work, adopts this theory, says that female Masonry was instituted about the year 1730; that it made its first appearance in France, and that it was evidently a product of the French mind. No one will be disposed to doubt the truth of this last sentiment. The proverbial gallantry of the French Masons was most ready and willing to extend to women some of the blessings of that Institution from which the churlishness, as they would call it, of their Anglo-Saxon brethren had excluded them.

But the Masonry of Adoption did not at once, and in its very beginning, assume that peculiar imitative form of Freemasonry which it subsequently presented, nor was it represented as having any connection with the Masonic Order until more than thirty years after its first establishment. Its progress was slow and gradual. In the course of this progress it affected various names and rituals, many of which have not been handed down to us. It was evidently convivial and gallant in its nature, and at first seems to have been only an imitation of Freemasonry, inasmuch as it was a secret society, having a form of initiation and modes of recognition. A specimen of one or two of these secret female associations may not be uninteresting.

One of the earliest of these societies was that which was established in the year 1743, at Paris, under the name of the "*Ordre des Felicitaires,*" which we might very appropriately translate as the "Order of Happy Folks." The vocabulary and all the emblems of the order were nautical. The sisters made symbolically a voyage from the island of Felicity, in ships navigated by the brethren. There were four degrees, namely, those of Cabin-boy, Captain, Commodore, and Vice Admiral, and the Grand Master, or presiding officer was called the Admiral. Out of this society there sprang in 1745 another, which was called the "Knights and Ladies of the Anchor," which is said to have been somewhat more refined in its character, although for the most part it preserved the same formulary of reception.

Two years afterwards, in 1747, the Chevalier Beauchaine, a very zealous Masonic adventurer, and the Master for life of a Parisian Lodge, instituted an androgynous system under the name of the "*Ordre des Fendeurs,*" or the "Order of Wood-Cutters," whose ceremonies were borrowed from the well-known political society of the Carbonari. All parts of the ritual had a reference to the sylvan vocation of wood-cutting, just as that of the Carbonari referred to that of coal-burning. The place of meeting was called a "wood-yard," and was supposed to be situated in a forest; the presiding officer was styled Pere Maitre, which might be idiomatically interpreted as Goodman Master; and the members were designated as cousins, a practice evidently borrowed from the Carbonari. The reunions of the "Wood-Cutters" enjoyed the prestige of the highest fashion in Paris; and the society became so popular that ladies and gentlemen of the highest distinction in France united with it, and membership was considered an honor which no rank, however exalted, need disdain. It was consequently succeeded by the institution of many other and similar androgynous societies, the very names of which it would be tedious to enumerate.

Out of all these societies, which resembled Freemasonry only in their secrecy, their benevolence, and a sort of rude imitation of a symbolic ceremonial — at last arose the true Lodges of Adoption, which so far claimed a connection with and a dependence on Masonry as that Freemasons alone were admitted among their male members — a regulation which did not prevail in the earlier organizations.

It was about the middle of the eighteenth century that the Lodges of Adoption began to attract attention in France, whence they speedily spread into other countries of Europe — into Germany, Poland, and even Russia; England alone, always conservative to a fault, steadily refused to take any cognizance of them. The Masons embraced them with enthusiasm as a practical means of giving to their wives and daughters some share of the pleasures which they themselves enjoyed in their mystical assemblies. And this, at least, may be said of them, that they practiced with commendable fidelity and diligence, the greatest of the Masonic virtues, and that the banquets and balls which always formed an important part of their ceremonial were included numerous acts of charity.

The first of these lodges of which we have any notice was that established in Paris, in the year 1760, by the Count de Bernouville. Another was instituted at Nimeguen, in Holland, in 1774, over which the Prince of Waldeck and the Princess of Orange presided. In 1775, the Lodge of Saint Antoine, at Paris, organized a dependent Lodge of Adoption, of which the Duchess of Bourbon was installed as Grand Mistress, and the Duke of Chartres, the Grand Master of French Masonry, conducted the business, In 1777, there was an Adoptive Lodge of La Candeur, over which the Duchess of Bourbon presided, assisted by such noble ladies as the Duchess of Chartres, the Princess Lamballe, and the Marchioness de Genlis; and we hear of another governed by Madame Helvetius, the wife of the illustrious philosopher; so that it will be perceived that fashion, wealth, and literature combined to give splendor and influence to this new order of female Masonry.

At first the Grand Orient of France appears to have been unfavorably disposed to these pseudo-Masonic and androgynous associations, but at length they became so numerous and so popular that a persistence in opposition would have evidently been impolitic, if it did not actually threaten to be fatal to the interests and permanence of the Masonic institution. The Grand Orient, therefore, yielded its objections, and resolved to avail itself of that which it could not suppress. Accordingly, on the 10th of June 1774, it issued an edict by which it assumed the protection and control of the Lodges of Adoption. Rules and regulations were provided for their government, among which were two: first, that no males except regular Freemasons should be permitted to attend them; and, secondly, that each Lodge should be placed under the charge and held under the sanction of some regularly constituted Lodge of Masons, whose Master, or, in his absence, his deputy, should be the presiding officer, assisted by a female President or Mistress; and such has since been the organization of all Lodges of Adoption.

A Lodge of Adoption, under the regulations established in 1774, consists of the following officers: a Grand Master, a Grand Mistress, an Orator (dressed as a Capuchin), an Inspector, an Inspectress, a male and female Guardian, a Mistress of Ceremonies. All of these officers wear a blue watered ribbon over the shoulder, to which is suspended a golden trowel, and all the brothers and sisters have aprons and white gloves.

The Rite of Adoption consists of four degrees, whose names in French and English are as follows: 1. Apprentice or Female Apprentice; 2. Compagnone or Craftswoman; 3. Maitresse, or Mistress; 4. Parfaite Maconne, or Perfect Mason.

It will be seen that the degrees of Adoption, in their names and their apparent reference to the gradations of employment in an operative art, are assimilated to those of legitimate Freemasonry; but it is in those respects only that the resemblance holds good. In the details of the ritual there is a vast difference between the two institutions.

There was a fifth degree added in 1817 — by some modern writers called "Female Elect" — "Sublime Dame Ecossaise," or "Sovereign Illustrious Dame Ecossaise;" but it seems to be a recent and not generally adopted innovation. At all events, it constituted no part of the original Rite of Adoption.

The first, or Female Apprentice's degree, is simply preliminary in its character, and is intended to prepare the candidate for the more important lessons which she is to receive in the succeeding degrees. She is presented with an apron and a pair of white kid gloves. The apron is given with the following charge, in which, as in all the other ceremonies of the Order, the Masonic system of teaching by symbolism is followed: "Permit me to decorate you with this apron; kings, princes, and the most illustrious princesses have esteemed, and will ever esteem it an honor to wear it, as being the symbol of virtue."

On receiving the gloves, the candidate is thus addressed: "The color of these gloves will admonish you that candor and truth are virtues inseparable from the character of a true Mason. Take your place among us and be pleased to listen to the instructions which we are about to communicate to you." The following is a part of the charge then addressed to the members by the Orator:

> *My dear Sisters:* Nothing is better calculated to assure you of the high esteem our society entertains for you, than your admission as a member. However, whatever pleasure these sentiments have enabled us to taste, we have not been able to fill the void that your absence left in our midst; and I confess, to your glory, that it was time to invite into our societies some sisters who, while rendering them more respectable, will ever make of them pleasures and delights. We call our Lodges Temples of Virtue, because we endeavor to practice it. The mysteries which we celebrate therein are

the grand art conquering the passions and the oath that we take to reveal nothing is to prevent self-love and pride from entering at all into the good which we ought to do.

The beloved name of Adoption tells you sufficiently that we choose you to share the happiness which we enjoy, in cultivating honor and charity; it is only after a careful examination that we have wished to share it with you, now that you know it we are convinced that the light of wisdom will illumine all the actions of your life, and that you will never forget that the more valuable things are, the greater is the need to preserve them; it is the principle of silence that we observe, it should be inviolable. May the God of the universe who hears us vouchsafe to give us strength to render it so.

It will be seen that throughout this charge there runs a vein of gallantry, which gives the true secret of the motives which led to the organization of the society, and which, however appropriate to a Lodge of Adoption, would scarcely be in place in a Lodge of the legitimate Order.

In the second degree, or that of Compagnone, or "Craftswoman," corresponding to that of Fellow-Craft, the Lodge is made the symbol of the Garden of Eden, and the candidate passes through a mimic representation of the temptation of Eve, the fatal effects of which, culminating in the deluge and the destruction of the human race, are impressed upon her in the lectures or catechism. Here is presented a scenic representation of the circumstances connected with that event, as recorded in Genesis. The candidate plays the role of our common mother. In the center of the Lodge, which represents the garden, is placed the tree of life, from which ruddy apples are suspended. The serpent, made with theatrical skill to represent a living reptile, embraces in its coils the trunk. An apple plucked from the tree is presented to the recipient, who is persuaded to eat it by the promise that thus alone can she prepare herself for receiving a knowledge of the sublime mysteries of Freemasonry. She receives the fruit from the tempter, but no sooner has she attempted to bite it, than she is startled by the noise of thunder; a curtain which has separated her from the members of the Lodge is suddenly withdrawn, and she is detected in the commission of the act of disobedience. She is sharply reprimanded by the Orator, who conducts her before the Grand Master. This dignitary reproaches her with her fault, but finally, with the consent of the brethren and sisters present, he pardons her in the merciful spirit of the institution on the conditions that she will take a vow to extend hereafter the same clemency to the faults of others.

All of this is allegorical and very pretty, and it cannot be denied that on the sensitive imagination of females such ceremonies must produce a manifest impression. But it is needless to say that it is nothing like Masonry.

There is less ceremony, but more symbolism, in the third degree, or that of "Mistress." Here are introduced, as parts of the ceremony, the tower of Babel and the theological ladder of Jacob. Its rounds, however, differ from those peculiar to true Masonry, and are said to equal the virtues in number. The lecture or catechism, is very long, and contains some very good points in its explanations of the symbols of the degree. Thus, the tower of Babel is said to signify the pride of man — its base, his folly — the stones of which it was composed, his passions — the cement which united them, the poison of discord — and its spiral form, the devious and crooked ways of the human heart. In this manner there is an imitation, not of the letter and substance of legitimate Freemasonry, for nothing can in these respects be more dissimilar, but of that mode of teaching by symbols and allegories, which is its peculiar characteristic.

The fourth degree, or that of "Perfect Mistress," corresponds to no degree in legitimate Masonry. It is simply the summit of the Rite of Adoption, and hence is called the "Degree of Perfection." Although the Lodge, in this degree, is supposed to represent the Mosaic tabernacle in the wilderness, yet the ceremonies do not have the same reference. In one of them, however, the liberation, by the candidate, of a bird from the vase in which it has been confined is said to symbolize the liberation of man from the dominion of his passions; and thus a farfetched reference is made to the liberation of the Jews from Egyptian bondage. On the whole, the ceremonies are very disconnected, but the lecture or catechism contains some excellent lessons. Especially does it furnish us with the official definition of Adoptive Masonry, which is in these words:

> It is a virtuous amusement by which we recall a part of the mysteries of our religion; and the better to reconcile humanity with a knowledge of its Creator; after we have inculcated the duties of virtue, we deliver ourselves up to the sentiments of a pure and delightful friendship by enjoying in our Lodges the pleasure of society — pleasures which among us are always founded on reason, honor, and innocence.

Apt and appropriate description of an association, secret or otherwise, of agreeable and virtuous well-bred men and women, but having not the slightest application to the design or form of true Freemasonry.

Guillemain de St. Victor, the author of *Manuel des Franches-Maconnes, ou La Vraie Maconnerie d'Adoption* (which forms the third part of the *Recueil Precieux*), who has given the best ritual of the Rite and from whom the preceding account has been taken, thus briefly sums up the objects of the Institution:

> The first degree contains only, as it ought, moral ideas of Masonry; the second is the initiation into the first mysteries, commencing with the sin of Adam, and concluding with the Ark of Noah as the first favor which God granted to men; the third and fourth are merely a series of types and figures drawn from the Holy Scriptures, by which we explain to the candidate the virtues which she ought to practice.

The fourth degree, being the summit of the Rite of Adoption, is furnished with a "table-Lodge" or the ceremony of a banquet, which immediately succeeds the closing of the Lodge, and which of course, adds much to the social pleasure and nothing to the instructive character of the Rite. Here, also, there is a continued imitation of the ceremonies of the Masonic institution as they are practiced in France, where the ceremoniously conducted banquet, at which Masons only are present, is always an accompaniment of the Master's Lodge. Thus, as in the banquets of the regular Lodges of the French Rite, the members always use a symbolical language by which they designate the various implements of the table and various articles of food and drink, calling, for instance the knives "swords," the forks "pickaxes," the dishes "materials," and bread a "rough ashier;" so, in imitation of this custom, the Rite of Adoption has established in its banquets a technical vocabulary, to be used only at the table. Thus, the Lodge room is called "Eden," the doors "barriers," the minutes a "ladder," a wineglass is styled a "lamp," and its contents "oil" — water being "white oil" and wine "red oil." To fill your glass is to "trim your lamp," to drink is to "extinguish your lamp," with many other eccentric expressions.

Much taste and in some instances, magnificence, are displayed in the decorations of the lodge rooms of the Adoptive Rite. The apartment is separated by curtains into different divisions, and contains ornaments and decorations which of course vary in the different degrees. The orthodox Masonic idea that the Lodge is a symbol of the world is here retained, and the four sides of the hall are said to represent the four continents — the entrance being called "Europe," the right side "Africa," and left "America," and the extremity in which the Grand Master and Grand Mistress are seated, "Asia." There are statues representing Wisdom, Prudence, Strength, Temperance, Honor, Charity, Justice, and Truth. The members are seated along the sides in two rows, the ladies occupying the front one, and the whole is rendered as beautiful and attractive as the taste can make it.

The Lodges of Adoption flourished greatly in France after their recognition by the Grand Orient. The Duchess of Bourbon, who was the first that received the title of Grand Mistress, was installed with great pomp and splendor in May 1775, in the Lodge of St. Antoine, in Paris. She presided over the Adoptive Lodge Le Candeur until 1780, when it was dissolved. Attached to the celebrated Lodge of the Nine Sisters, which had so many distinguished men of letters among its members, was a Lodge of Adoption bearing the same name, which in 1778, held a meeting at the residence of Madame Helvetius in honor of Benjamin Franklin, then our ambassador at the French Court. During the Reign of Terror of the French Revolution, Lodges of Adoption, like everything that was gentle or humane, almost entirely disappeared. But with the succession of a regular government, they were resuscitated, and the Empress Josephine presided at the meeting of one at Strasburg in 1805. They continued to flourish under the imperial dynasty, and although less popular, or less fashionable under the Restoration, they subsequently recovered their popularity and are still in existence in France.

Illustrative of the work of these Lodges, it may not be improper to insert two accounts, one of the installation of Madame Cesar Moreau, as Grand Mistress of Adoptive Masonry, in the Lodge connected with the regular Lodge La Jerusalem des Vallees Egyptiennes, on the 8th of July, 1854, and the other, of the reception of the celebrated Lady Morgan, 1819, in the Lodge La Belle et Bonne, as described by her in her Diary.

The account of the installation of Madame Moreau, which is abridged from the *Franc-Macon*, a Parisian periodical, is as follows:

> The fete was most interesting and admirably arranged. After the introduction in due form of a number of brethren and sisters, the Grand Mistress elect was announced, and she entered, preceded by the five lights of the Lodge and

escorted by the Inspectress, Depositress, Oratrix, and Mistress of Ceremonies. Mons. J. S. Boubee, the Master of the Lodge La Jerusalem des Vallees Egyptiennes, conducted her to the altar, where, having installed her into office and handed her a mallet as the symbol of authority, he addressed her in a copy of verses, whose merit will hardly claim for them a repetition.

To this she made a suitable reply, and the Lodge then proceeded to the reception of a young lady, a part of the ceremony of which is thus described:

Of the various trials of virtue and fortitude to which she was subjected, there was one which made a deep impression, not only on the fair recipient, but on the whole assembled company. Four boxes were placed, one before each of the male officers; the candidate was told to open them, which she did and from the first and second drew faded flowers and soiled ribbons and laces, which being placed in an open vessel were instantly consumed by fire, as an emblem of the brief duration of such objects; from the third she drew an apron, a blue silk scarf, and a pair of gloves, and from the fourth a basket containing the working tools in silver gilt. She was then conducted to the altar, where, on opening the fifth box, several birds which had been confined in it escaped, which was intended to teach her that liberty is a condition to which all men are entitled, and of which no one can be deprived without injustice. After having taken the vow, she was instructed in the modes of recognition, and having been clothed with the apron, scarf, and gloves, and presented with the implements of the Order, she received from the Grand Mistress an esoteric explanation of all these emblems and ceremonies. Addresses were subsequently delivered by the Orator and Oratrix, and an ode was sung, the poor or alms box was handed around, and the labors of the Lodge were then closed.

Madame Moreau lived only six months to enjoy the honors of presiding officer of the Adoptive Rite, for she died of a pulmonary affection at an early age, on the 11th of the succeeding January.

The Lodge of Adoption in which Lady Morgan received the degrees at Paris, in the year 1819, was called *La Belle et Bonne*. This was the pet name which long before had been bestowed by Voltaire on his favorite, the Marchioness de Villette, under whose presidency and at whose residence at Fauberg St. Germaine, the Lodge was held, and hence the name with which all France, or at least all Paris, was familiarly acquainted as the popular designation of Madame de Villette.

Lady Morgan, in her description of the Masonic fete, says that when she arrived at the Hotel de Villette, where the Lodge was held, she found a large concourse of distinguished persons ready to take part in the ceremonies. Among these were Prince Paul of Wurtemberg, the Count de Cazes, elsewhere distinguished in Masonry, the celebrated Denon, the Bishop of Jerusalem, and the illustrious actor, Talma. The business of the evening commenced with the installation of the officers of a sister Lodge, after which the candidates were admitted. Lady Morgan describes the arrangements as presenting, when the doors were opened, a spectacle of great magnificence. A profusion of crimson and gold, marble busts, a decorated throne and altar, an abundance of flowers, and incense of the finest odor which filled the air, gave to the whole a most dramatic and scenic effect. Music of the grandest character mingled its harmony with the mysteries of initiation, which lasted for two hours, and when the lodge was dosed, there was an adjournment to the hall of refreshments which was opened by the Grand Mistress with Prince Paul of Wurtemberg. Lady Morgan, upon whose mind the ceremony seems to have made an impression, makes one remark worthy of consideration: "That so many women," she says, "young and beautiful and worldly, should never have revealed the secret, is among the miracles which the much-distrusted sex are capable of working." In fidelity to the vow of secrecy, the female Masons of the Adoptive Rite have proved themselves fully equal to their brethren of the legitimate Order.

Notwithstanding that Adoptive Masonry has found an advocate in no less distinguished writer than Chemin Dupontes, who, in the *Encyclopedie Maconnique*, calls it "a luxury in Masonry, and a pleasant relaxation which cannot do any harm to the true mysteries which are practiced by men alone," it has been very generally condemned by the most celebrated French, German, English, and American Masons.

Gaedicke, in the *Freimauer Lexicon*, speaks slightingly of it as established on insufficient grounds, and expresses his gratification that the system no longer exists in Germany.

Thory, in his *History of the Foundation of the Grand Orient*, says that the introduction of Adoptive Lodges was a consequence of the relaxation of Masonic discipline; and he asserts that the permitting of women to share in mysteries which should exclusively belong to men is not in accordance with the essential principles of the Masonic Order. The Abbe Robin, the author of an able work entitled *Recherches sur les Initiations Anciennes et Modernes*, maintains that the custom of admitting women into Masonic assemblies will perhaps be, at some future period, the cause of the decline of Masonry in France. The prediction is not, however, likely to come to pass; for while legitimate Masonry has never been more popular or prosperous in France than it is at this day, it is the Lodges of Adoption that appear to have declined.

Other writers in other countries have spoken in similar terms, so that it is beyond a doubt that the general sentiment of the Fraternity is against this system of female Masonry.

Lenning is, however, more qualified in his condemnation, and says, in his *Encyclopadie der Frcimaurerei*, that while leaving it undecided whether it is prudent to hold assemblies of women with ceremonies which are called Masonic, yet it is not to be denied that in these female Lodges a large amount of charity has been done.

Adoptive Masonry has its literature, although neither extensive nor important, as it comprises only books of songs, addresses, and rituals. Of the latter, the most valuable are: 1. *La Maconnerie les Femmes*, published in 1775, and containing only the first three degrees, for such was the system when recognized by the Grand Orient of France in that year. 2. *La Vraie Maconnerie de Adoption*, published in 1787. This work, which is by Guillemain de St. Victor, is perhaps the best that has been published on the subject of the Adoptive Rite, and is the first that introduces the fourth degree, of which Guillemain is supposed to be the inventor, since all previous rituals include only the three degrees. 3. *Maconnerie de'Adoption pour les Femmes*, contained in the second part of E. J. Chappron's *Necessaire Maconnique*, and printed in Paris in 1817. This is valuable because it contains the fifth degree. 4. *La Franc-Maconnerie des Femmes*. This work, which is by Charles Monselet, is of no value as a ritual, being simply a tale founded upon circumstances connected with Adoptive Masonry.

In Italy, the Carbonari, or "Woof-Burners," a secret political society, imitated the Freemasons of France in instituting an Adoptive Rite attached to their own association. Hence, an Adoptive Lodge was founded at Naples in the beginning of this century, over which presided that friend of Masonry, Queen Caroline, the wife of Ferdinand II. The members were styled Giardiniere, or Female Gardeners; and they called each other Cugine, or Female Cousins, in imitation of the Carbonari, who were recognized as Buoni Cugini, or Good Cousins. The Lodges of Giardiniere flourished as long as the Grand Lodge of Carbonari existed at Naples.

The Rite of Adoption as practiced on the continent of Europe, and especially France, has never been introduced into America. The system does not accord with the manners or habits of the people, and undoubtedly never would become popular. But Dr. Rob Morris introduced in 1850 the "Eastern Star" which he had invented. No trace of the existence of the "Eastern Star" as now practiced, and the history of which we now are trying to bring before the individual members of this Order, can be found to exist before that originated by Dr. Morris during the period of his convalescence from an attack of rheumatism, the early part of February 1850, while residing at Jackson, Mississippi. This elegant and attractive system, after varied fortunes, dissensions, oppositions, rivalries, and detractions through this entire period of sixty-six years, has outlived calumny and abuse, and stands today one of the great successes of the Masonic theory.

The portion of the Bible upon which the theory of the first degree is founded points to Judges xi: 29-40. The impressive history of that excellent woman instructs us in Obedience, the virtue of which is particularly cultivated in this degree, it being the degree of Obedience or Jephthah's Daughter — called for want of any special name, Adah.

The first lesson taught in this Order is Obedience. We are bade to remember the poor and afflicted. The most encouraging sign that the Order is growing is the interest and aspiration among the members. It is indeed delightful to know that today our ambitions blend in a desire to be mutually helpful to each other; that we stand together in offensive and defensive alliance, actuated by purest motives, to do good to the largest number of men and women. Its organization has in every way been beneficial to Masonry. Why should it not? Who are eligible to membership in this Order? Your brother Masons; your mothers who gave you birth; your sisters, companions of sweet childhood days; she who left father and mother and knelt with you at matrimony's altar; and the daughters who brought joy to your hearts and sunshine to your homes.

The Order of the Eastern Star is full of intrinsic excellence, and it will eventually work its way through the entire universe. Astronomically speaking, the most remarkable conjunction of planets —

that of Jupiter and Saturn in the constellation Pisces, which occurs only once in 800 years — did take place no less than three times in the year 2 B.C., or two years before the birth of Christ (in May, October, and December). This conjunction is admitted by all astronomers. It was not only extraordinary but presented the most brilliant spectacle in the night sky, such as could not but attract the attention of all who watched the sidereal heavens, but especially of those who studied astrology. In the year following, 1 B.C., another planet, Mars, joined this conjunction. The great astronomer Kepler observed a similar conjunction in 1603-1604, also noticed that when the three planets came into conjunction a new, extraordinarily brilliant and peculiarly colored evanescent star was visible between Jupiter and Saturn. A Star of this Order is a visible ornament to society and to humanity, provided the member is a devout worshiper of the principles of her profession. It is pleasing to note that the animated Stars who have been admitted to membership at this date (1913) now number 665,246, and we believe that they are all sincere to their vows and that their lives are made pleasant and their opportunities for doing good are enhanced through their associations.

There is one point, however, that deserves specialization, and that is the interest manifested. To be a brilliant Star we must be enthusiastic in the belief that our cause is a just one, then we must implicitly follow the regulations, so that our record may entitle us to the appellation of a Star. Where there is a lack of interest the significance of the Star is disregarded, but where followed up in a career of usefulness, in a constant desire to upbuild the Order, and in a system of self-improvement leading to the desire to be a zealous Star, then is the benefit apparent. Let the word Star, so commonly used as referring to the members of the Eastern Star, be one of power as representing a vast concourse of people, all actuated by the same desire to add pleasures and advantages, with a firm determination to scatter seeds of kindness and helpfulness through all the walks of life.

During the period which intervened from 1850, the date of the origination of our Order by Dr. Rob Morris, until the year 1855, it would appear that the degrees of the Order had been communicated, in lecture form, to those entitled to receive them. Dr. Morris was a great traveler and wherever he attended Masonic meetings, he invited, at least once, the Masonic brethren with their wives together in a joint meeting and conferred the degrees of the "Eastern Star" to all those desiring to receive them.

In 1855 Dr. Morris published his ritual, which he called *The Mosaic Book of the American Adoptive Rite*, which appeared in three parts. Part I was given to the general instructions for the conducting of the "Constellations" as they were termed by this book. Part II, the Ritual, which is given elsewhere. Part III, which gives the constitution and by-laws for the guidance of the Constellations and was published by the authority of the Supreme Constellation of the American Adoptive Rite.

The original object of the Order was to enable the female relatives of Master Masons to make themselves known as such, communicating to them secret signs and passes by which they would be enabled to make themselves known to each other. But it has far outgrown this original idea, having acquired a much broader view of the usefulness to which the Order may be developed and has become a vast army of co-laborers with the great brotherhood in its work of beneficence and to pay the tribute of love and labor at the shrine of loving effort in the direction of helpfulness to the orphan and helpless. Often are the Stars found leading in movements to establish Eastern Star and Masonic homes, uniting with the Masonic Craft or caring alone for its sick and needy, burying with touching ritualistic services the bodies of its dead, as well as remembering with flowers and loving ceremonies the names of the departed. In some of the States the principal object toward which they are striving is an Eastern Star home, in others they are working in a cooperating manner with the Masonic Fraternity for the erection and maintenance of homes open to both Orders. All this establishes, without the possibility of a doubt, the value of one great army of women and men, united in this work of benevolence, to promote the higher development of humanity within the territory where this work is established, which will be well-nigh universal within the next decade.

CHAPTER II

Biography of Rob Morris, LL.D.[1]

THE effort to give a true history of the Order of the Eastern Star has many times been attempted by those who wish this story retained in its perfection, and these articles have differed so much in the essential facts, that using the words of St. Luke, "I too, set forth my declaration as a living witness" as from the first inception of the Eastern Star to its now crowning glory. As St. Luke says: "It seemed good to me also, having had perfect understanding of all things from the very first, to write unto thee," etc.

So little is known by the majority of the members of the Eastern Star as to its origin and early history, that to give all the facts, though appearing trivial to many readers, it is essential to add the early life and character of its founder, Rob Morris, LL.D.

As the son of this illustrious author, Rob Morris, Jr., passed through every event in the history of the Eastern Star. He served as his father's amanuensis for many years, handling the most of his correspondence on this as well as other matters.

Dr. Rob Morris, the author and founder of the Order of the Eastern Star and its rituals, was born near Boston, Massachusetts, August 31, 1818. His parents were teachers and for the first ten years of his earlier manhood he followed the same profession. His mother was left a widow with a young family, of which he was the oldest. As was the tendency of many, he drifted from the New England States to the South. Being wholly dependent on his own efforts for a scant living, his first misfortune met him on this new field of adventure, early in life.

While enroute to his southern home, the steamer on which he was traveling was burned and though many lives were lost, Dr. Morris

---

[1] From official data furnished by Rob. Morris, son of the founder of the O. E. S., Past Grand Patron of Kentucky.

escaped with his life, but lost all his books, papers, and his additional wearing apparel. Making his way to Memphis, after a hard struggle and weeks of travel which was attended by difficulties that would have caused many of a less determined character to turn back, he reached Oxford, Mississippi, and after a short time secured a position in a school near that city. There he met Miss Charlotte Mendenhall, whose parents resided near that place, and they were married August 26, 1841. In 1860 Dr. Morris removed to La Grange, Kentucky, where he passed his remaining years until his death in 1888.

It was but a short time after he arrived at Oxford that Dr. Morris was elected president of the Mount Sylvan Academy, near Oxford, which responsible position seemed to be the beginning of his brilliant career.

Through the means of the great amount of labor done by him and the excellence of that work, Dr. Morris's name became familiar to all Masons throughout this country and to distant parts of the Masonic world.

He was a very large contributor to many Masonic periodicals, and a number of newspapers and magazines. Throughout the world the name of the second Poet Laureate of Freemasonry is known and loved next to the Order itself.

Among the members of the Masonic Order who were poets, were Thomas Moore, Sir Walter Scott, James Hogg, Ferguson, George P. Morris, Percival, Robert Burns, Duganne, Shilliber, Lamartine, Cowper, and others, yet all together they have written very few Masonic poems. Percival and George P. Morris wrote two each, Robert Burns, one, the greatest of them all except Rob Morris's poems, while all the others named did not write any.

Over one hundred years ago, in the year 1787, Robert Burns was crowned with the laurel wreath in Cannongate, Kilwilling Lodge No. 2, of Edinburgh, Scotland, which crowning signified his elevation to the station of the first Poet Laureate of Freemasonry. This was for one poem he wrote, and he was the first to be so crowned. Upon his death, no one was deemed worthy to assume the high station until Dr. Rob Morris was so selected through the expressed wish of over 500,000 Masons throughout all the world, as the second Poet Laureate of Freemasonry.

The coronation took place in New York City on December 17, 1884, in the presence of several thousand Masons who attended, many of them from distant points of the compass, merely to witness the event. It was, in a double sense, the crowning point of a wondrous and useful life.

Following the death of Dr. Morris in 1888, the vacancy caused by his death was not filled until Right Worshipful Brother Fay Hempstead, of Little Rock, Arkansas, was coronated the third Poet Laureate of Freemasonry on Octobers 5, 1908, in Ravenswood Lodge No. 777, at Medinah Temple, Chicago, Illinois.

It was the prediction of the venerable and learned Salem Towne, LL.D., a Mason of great prominence and an expounder of its grandest themes, that "Brother Morris's fame as a poet will outlast his memory as a writer in prose."

Dr. Rob Morris began his Masonic career at Oxford, Mississippi, under the tutelage of Hon. J. M. Howry, Grand Master of that State, a thorough Mason and learned in Masonic lore, and a man who took a special interest in Dr. Morris, and up to the time of his death was numbered as a true friend and adviser. Often in my boyhood days I met Brother Howry at father's home and listened to his wise counsels with more than an ordinary interest. On one occasion, after arriving at manhood, Brother Howry made it a point to call on me at my home in Nashville, Tennessee, and reminded me of many events in the life of my father, which are to be made a portion of this article.

From Brother Howry, I learned much of the opposition in many of the States to the introduction of the Eastern Star, and the censure heaped upon Dr. Morris by many Masons. Brother Howry always took the part of Dr. Morris, and his influence aided in counteracting the storm of abuse which from its beginning was condemned by the Craft in general.

Many were the sneers Dr. Morris received from what they termed "Morris's Petticoat Masonry." Disapproval was manifest, critics were severe, and threats were made to bring the author before his Lodge and warn him against further presenting his female Masonry.

Notwithstanding all this, Dr. Morris continued to write, lecture, and confer his favorite "Star" on all who desired it when some were eligible. Being Grand Lecturer of Kentucky and Tennessee, this gave him vast opportunities which otherwise he would not have enjoyed, to lead his favorite Eastern Star to success.

Dr. Morris was a man of the most sensitive temperament and many a cruel cut from the Masonic Brotherhood pained him severely; yet, feeling he was right, his faith in the justice of his claims never forsook him, but only spurred him on to greater exertions, determined that the Masonic world would yet recognize the great good to the wives, mothers, daughters, and sisters of the many left to their charge.

After a few years spent in Mississippi, Dr. Morris moved to Lodgeton, Fulton County, Kentucky. There he commenced the publication of *The American Freemason*, which was a magazine of wide circulation, both in this and foreign countries. Though strictly a Masonic paper, it gave him a large field for promoting the Eastern Star by placing it fully before the Craft and using arguments in this paper to an incredulous Brotherhood. He often remarked that it was the most tedious work of his life trying to convince the Masons that it, in the end, would work for their good. In all his labors for the Eastern Star he never accepted any form of remuneration, having resolved from the start that it should be given "without money and without price" to the female members of the families of the great Masonic Order.

Out of more than three hundred pieces that make up his poetical collections, there are many of rarest delicacy and beauty. His poetical labors extended over every class of thought proper to the theme. Very many were written to be accompanied by music, and so have entered into festival, funeral, and work meetings; some to be recited with emblematic accompaniments. The greater portion were composed while going in stagecoach, railway carriage, on steamboats, on horseback, and at Low XII hours after lodge meetings.

It would seem that no man could perform the amount of labor accomplished by Dr. Morris, unless he preserved all his faculties intact and attained nearly the number of years allotted to Methuselah. Yet that work was all done, unassisted, by Dr. Morris, and the spring of inspiration which promoted it lay in the one source, "ambition."

When this ambition was gratified with his coronation as Poet Laureate, he ceased his labors and dwelt nearly four years in the quiet lull before death came to claim him for its own. In speaking of him, a number of Masons, among the most eminent in the land, said that he was one of the greatest Masonic Poets and prose writers and also one of the greatest Masons that had ever lived.

In fact, there have been few men who ever lived who have done more work with the pen for publication than Dr. Morris. The work he has done would seem too stupendous for any one man to perform in a lifetime, yet he has done it, and well. He has not only written all these works, songs, hymns, poems, addresses, and essays, but furthermore he has done such other minor literary work as would require a couple of columns additional merely to enumerate.

It is of course chiefly as a writer that Dr. Morris is known to the Masonic world. He was not only the universally accepted Poet Laureate of Masonry, but in addition to this his prose works are of the first rank in Masonic literature. He wrote extensively on the subject of Masonic jurisprudence, produced several rituals and handbooks, many fugitive pieces, edited some Masonic journals, and published an important book of travel and research, *Free Masonry in the Holy Land*, which appeared in 1872.

The Masons of this country raised between $9,000 and $10,000 as a fund to enable Dr. Morris to make his journey to the original seat of Masonry. He went to the Orient in 1868 and traveled very extensively there and in Europe. His research confirmed many traditions as to Masonry and enabled the author to contribute much valuable evidence as to the truth of what was before then little more than conjecture. Being learned in Masonic lore, the inscriptions, coins, and customs of the people among whom he journeyed often had a meaning for him which was not apparent to others. His trip to the Holy Land discovered abundant testimony as to the great age of Masonry. His book is dedicated to His Excellency, Mohammed Raschid, Governor-General of Syria and Palestine, who was an eminent Mason.

A profound admiration for the Bible, as the only inspired book in Masonry, led Dr. Morris early in his career to propose the exploration of the lands of the Bible in the interests of the Order. In 1854 the Grand Lodge of Kentucky entered into the plan, and proffered a loan sufficient for the cost, but circumstances at that time forbade the journey. It was still, however, a favorite theme in his lectures and writings, and in 1867 he visited one hundred and thirty lodges, chiefly in the northern States, and proposed to them that he would donate the necessary time and labor if they would undertake the cost. The response was a practical one, for 3,782 brethren clubbed together to supply the necessary means.

He set out February 2, 1868; addressed the lodges at Smyrna, upon the way, on February 25th, and reached Beyrout, Syria, March 3rd. At Damascus, through the influence of Brother E. T. Rodgers, H. B. M. consul there (and Master at the time of Lebanon Lodge at Beyrout), he made the Masonic acquaintance of the governor-general and of General Abdel Kader. He delivered addresses before the members of the Masonic Fraternity in Damascus, Beyrout, Joppa, and Jerusalem. In the latter city he opened a Lodge of Instruction, May 13th, which, five years afterwards, culminated in the Royal Solomon Mother Lodge, No. 293, of which he was first Master. He reached home early in August. The results of his industrious research are seen in the large volume entitled *Freemasonry in Holy Land*. At Jerusalem he made the personal acquaintance of that learned and zealous explorer, Captain Warren, himself a member of the Masonic Brotherhood. This oriental lodge has maintained a distinct and honorable existence and has become the mother of a group of lodges in Palestine and the center of a Grand Lodge in Jerusalem.

Dr. Morris made a second trip to Europe in 1878, at which time he was especially noticed by the Prince of Wales, who, being a Mason, departed from his habit of non-attendance so far as to attend lodge in London, and then to follow him to Oxford to attend lodge there, while Dr. Morris was at those places lecturing.

Dr. Morris was "brought to Masonic light" as the phrase is, in Oxford, Mississippi, March 5, 1846, when he joined Gathright Lodge No. 33. At that time, he was principal of the Mount Sylvan Academy, near Oxford. He at once became deeply interested in the subject of Masonry, and his progress thereafter was notable.

He was exalted to the degree of Royal Arch in Lexington, Mississippi, in 1848; accepted as Royal and Select Master in 1849; made a Knight Templar at Jackson, Mississippi, in 1850; received the Scottish Rite degrees to the thirty-second degree in 1854. He received the Rite of Memphis, so far as the ninetieth degree, in New York, in 1864, and the Encampment Order of English Templary in Canada, in 1857. He also received a very large number of the honorary appendages to Masonry, such as the three official orders of Royal Arch Masonry, Past Eminent Commander, Past Grand Commander, Grand High Priest, Past Grand Commander-in-Chief 32°. The Masonic and Military Orders of the Knights of Rome, and the Red Cross of Constantine were communicated to him in 1857, and afterwards in 1873.

The Order of Past Grand Master was given to him at his installation as Grand Master of Kentucky, in 1858, the Hon. Henry Wingate, Past Grand Master, presiding. Among his honorary degrees and complimentary memberships, which were nearly one hundred and fifty in number, that of Past Deputy Grand Master of the Grand Lodge of Canada was chiefly prized.

Dr. Morris was a member of Fortitude Lodge No. 47, at La Grange, Kentucky, and of the Eminence Royal Arch Chapter. He was also a member of the Louisville Commandery No. 1, Knights Templars, and was Past Grand Commander-in-Chief of the Grand Consistory of Kentucky, 32°.

He was the originator of a large number of special features, among them the most superior degrees of "Ladies' Masonry." The most popular of these is the Order of the Eastern Star, composed and communicated by him in 1850.

In 1847 the degree of the "Heroine of Jericho," which is a degree conferred only on Royal Arch Masons, their wives and daughters, was conferred upon Dr. Morris and his wife by William H. Stevens, and from that ceremony Dr. Morris acquired his taste for androgynous degrees. He says: "From the period of my initiation into Masonry I had entertained the desire of introducing the female relatives of Masons into closer relationship with the Order. Through the immense influence of women, so much might be done to bring the performances of Freemasons nearer their professions."

Among a certain class of mankind an opinion prevails, somewhat prejudicial to the character of women, which should be refuted by every liberal and high-minded Mason who wishes to give justice where it is merited. The opinion disseminates the false and erroneous views that their minds are not as susceptible of cultivation and improvement as man's — that woman is deficient in intellectual powers and does not possess those acute perceptions which man boasts and claims as being inherently his by nature.

Who among us who have witnessed the deliberations in the Grand Chapters, and the General Grand Chapter of the Order of the Eastern Star, where woman presides in all her strength and beauty, with tact and knowledge, but will refute this idea as one entirely absurd and unjust. In some respects, it may be said that man is woman's superior; in others, he is unquestionably her inferior; and when the claims of each are summed up and weighed in the scale of impartial justice, very little difference will be found to exist between them. Her feelings are more acute, her sensibilities are more refined, and she shines resplendent with luster as a beacon light on the lofty pinnacle of virtue. She shines as conspicuous in her private and domestic places as she does in the public walks of life, and next to the supreme excellency of the Christian religion, the example and softening influence of female virtue restrain and in a great measure regulate man's conduct in leading him to right and truth.

Dr. Rob Morris, the founder of the Order of the Eastern Star, had all this in view when he realized the wrongs placed upon women, and in the formation of this beautiful Order he could see in the distant future his hopes realized, and women could then be placed in that sphere of beauty and grandeur to which she of right belongs.

Women cannot be made Masons. This is a rule that has been handed down with other rules of Masonry for thousands of years. All Masons are pledged to this, therefore they cannot invite women to their lodges, but they can and do and will share in all the solid privileges and benefits of Masonry, and thus in "Our Star" practically unite in this great, this glorious, this heavenly work of doing good.

Dr. Rob Morris built better than he knew. Genial, earnest, faithful Rob Morris. To have known him was a pleasure long recalled; to have listened to his folklore of Masonry in prose and verse, was delightful beyond comparison. Just such a gentle spirit, and only such as he, could have originated the "Eastern Star." There remains no shadow of a doubt but that to Dr. Rob Morris the American women — and women in general — owe a debt of gratitude for an Order founded upon the Holy Scriptures and Jesus Christ, to whose Star none other ever shone so bright.

The oldest daughter of Dr. Rob Morris painted the first signet and at this writing (1916) that signet now adorns the parlor of Mr. Robert Morris, Jr., Past Grand Patron of Kentucky, in his home at

Franklin, Kentucky. It had the five-pointed star, the cabalistic word and motto, and also titles applied to Jesus from the beginning of Genesis to the end of Revelations. She also painted a set of plates in a similar manner, which are still in the possession of the Morris family.

While the Morris family were residents of Jackson, Mississippi, in 1850, while ill with an attack of rheumatism, Dr. Rob Morris produced the beautiful system of the Order of the Eastern Star. A complete statement of the details of the work is given elsewhere in this volume in Dr. Morris's own words left by him to be handed down to the world after he was gone.

On March 6, 1854, Dr. Rob Morris purchased eighty acres of land at Lodgeton, Fulton County, Kentucky, upon which he proceeded to erect a dwelling for his family. This house was built of substantially hewn logs. On either side of a wide hall there is a spacious room, both up and down stairs. A portico with pillars ornaments and enhances the comfort of the front portion, while an L adds to the size and convenience of the rear. The house has since been weather boarded. It stands on a slight eminence that gradually slopes to the highway that was intended for the principal street of Lodgeton. Stately oaks and elms tower above the cedars, with creepers running at random over the fences and bodies of trees and adding to the picturesqueness of the home where "the Poet Laureate of Freemasonry," originator of the "Eastern Star," penned those immortal lines, "The Level and the Square." This beautiful Masonic poem which was written while he was living in this home at Lodgeton, has been published by the million copies, and is recognized as one of the brightest gems of Masonic poetry that has yet been given to the Masonic world. This poem has been compared to Robert Burns' production, "Farewell to Tarbolton Lodge," which poem was the one production of his pen which won for Robert Burns the honor of having conferred upon him the laurel wreath which crowned him "Poet Laureate of Freemasonry" many years previous to the time that Dr. Rob Morris was so honored.

On the upper side of this house, at the end of a shady avenue of forest trees, stood the neat little office where all the business was transacted with his numerous callers. A post office and several stores, together with a blacksmith shop and a few dwellings, completed the visible portion of Lodgeton. Ever an advocate and a promoter of culture, the part of the enterprise nearest Dr. Morris's heart was the establishment and thorough equipment of a first-class school; the necessary means, however, not being at command, the plan ever remained in embryo.

A half mile away from Lodgeton stands Union Church, where Sunday after Sunday Dr. Morris lectured to an admiring audience and devoted congregation of Kentucky and Tennessee citizens. He was never regularly installed as pastor but filled the pulpit at the solicitation of his numerous friends of various denominations. The Masonic Lodge that he organized met in the second story of the church building and to this Lodge room Dr. Morris carried his family organ, which was then the only one in the neighborhood. The instrument was placed in his buggy, where his wife took her seat to hold it steady, while Dr. Morris led the horse to ensure an even gait and avoid jostling. In this Lodge room, his conferring the Eastern Star degrees on the ladies and brethren entitled to them, was always a pleasing part of the program.

Many years have passed since Dr. Morris preached in Union meeting house. The old church has given place to a neat white frame house of worship that stands in the same spot. A few of those who as elderly men and women sound forth God's promises in song, recall with a sense of unforgotten pleasure the days when as youths and maidens, or youthful maidens and young men, they listened to Rob Morris.

"I would have ridden ten miles any day," said one old man, "to hear Dr. Rob Morris read a chapter from the Bible. I have never heard a man read Scripture as Dr. Morris read. There," said he, pointing to a country burying ground, "is the cemetery Rob Morris dedicated.

When we saw the funeral lamps burning, which he said represented life in death, and heard him speak of the resurrection of these frail bodies, some of us, at least, felt that we could well-nigh face death itself with him nearby to encourage us with his hopeful and trusting words."

A man of fewer years, who had heard the last words of this aged speaker, added: "Dr. Rob Morris may not have been considered an accomplished and magnetic speaker by the world at large, but to us he was an interpreter and prophet of good things. My judgment at the time was immature, but I do not believe I overestimated him in saying that in general knowledge, in nobility and expression of features, in voice, and in all the requirements for fascinating an audience, Dr. Morris had few superiors. His memory was a storehouse of historical facts, of anecdotes and stories, and he was instructive and fascinating. His power over the minds of the people in this section was unquestionably greater than any other man's has ever been within my memory."

A few years after leaving Fulton County, Dr. Morris started on his great Eastern tour, at which time he visited almost every lodge in Europe and Asia. No stronger proof of the love and trust reposed in him by his fellow Masons could have been given than the promptness and unanimity with which they responded to his appeal for raising the necessary funds for his journey. Dr. Morris proposed, upon his return, to publish an account of his travels and research, which was published under the titles of *Travels in the Holy Land* and *Freemasonry in the Holy Land*. In addition to a copy of this work, he volunteered to furnish every person assisting him to the amount of ten dollars, a certain number of curios from the Holy Land. These conditions were faithfully fulfilled.

Dr. Morris honored Freemasonry, also the Order of the Eastern Star by his pure life, his learning, and his piety. He well merited the honor conferred upon him by the Masons of America and the Masonic world, at the Masonic Temple, New York, on Wednesday,

December 17, 1884, when he was crowned "Poet Laureate of Freemasonry." Robert Burns, Dr. Rob Morris, and Fay Hempstead are the only individuals upon whom this honor has ever been conferred.

A former Grand Master, who witnessed the coronation of Dr. Morris as Poet Laureate of Freemasonry, said: "The laureation with its ceremonies and exercises constituted one of the most beautiful and impressive episodes in the modern history of the Craft." In this laureation the New York Grand Lodge, which is the largest Grand Lodge in the world except that of England, took the initiative. This was the crowning event of the long and useful life which Dr. Morris had spent so laboriously in the interests of Masonry and the Eastern Star. He had given to the world over three hundred Masonic lyrics and seventy-four volumes of Masonic literature, more than fifty Eastern Star poems and a number of volumes designed to perfect the Order which he had originated.

Dr. Morris wrote the original ritual of the Order of the Eastern Star while living at Jackson, Mississippi, in the early part of the year 1850. Upon completing the same, he invited a neighboring Mason and his wife to join them and he communicated the degrees to those three — Mrs. Morris and the Mason and his wife — who were the first recipients of the degrees which have since been given to many thousand persons who have seen the signs, heard the words, exchanged the touch, and joined in the music of the Eastern Star. Early in the history of the Order, it was communicated to a great many persons and a number of "Constellations," as the original organization was called, established in different States. The ritual was afterwards re-written and simplified.

Coming now to the middle of "The Constellations," as was then given, the first era of the Eastern Star beginning to shine with feeble light, encouraged Dr. Morris to the point of organizing a chapter, which he did and styled it Purity Chapter No. 1, near his residence at Lodgeton, Fulton County, Kentucky.

Forming a little company of some ten or fifteen of his Masonic neighbors and the female members of their families, they proceeded to the old Union Church, one-half mile distant, to the Lodge room in the second story of this building. The meeting was opened by a most fervent prayer, asking the aid of heaven in all their undertakings, and blessings on their present convocation, and all future acts to meet with the approval of the Grand Architect of the Universe, until "time shall be no more." Thus, we have the records of the first chapter of the Order of the Eastern Star.

As the author of the system, and by virtue of this fact, the office of Grand Patron belonged to him; this office he conveyed to Brother Robert Macoy of New York in 1868, prior to taking his trip to the Holy Land in the interests of Masonry.

To advance and elevate humanity was the controlling motive in everything that Dr. Rob Morris did. It seems very natural, therefore, that he should be unwilling to preach the gospel of brotherly love, relief, and truth to but one-half of mankind. To enlarge the privileges and usefulness of women and to raise her to a higher plane, was an idea that early took deep root in his mind, and to the consummation of this work he applied himself.

In the progress of human events, the Order of the Eastern Star has been and will continue to be an important factor. An Order professing the tenets taught in the lectures of the Eastern Star, with its vast membership, could not help but be a power for good, and its influence has been such. This beautiful Order stands as a monument to female secrecy and fidelity; and may it ever shine to illumine woman's pathway until time shall be no more. History has finally settled itself and become a written page — Dr. Rob Morris stands without a peer in Masonic and Eastern Star work. That he was the author of various standard books of Freemasonry proves his capability to originate an Order to be auxiliary to the Masonic body, and it is a great joy and blessing that he brought the Order of the Eastern Star into a living and lasting possibility. Every member of the Order should especially cherish his memory, for it is to him they owe the very existence of the Order. His fertile brain, fluent tongue, and ready pen brought this Order into being, and sent it forth upon the grand mission in which it is now actively engaged. The mighty influence of his life and work, who can estimate! While he has gone to dwell with the tender Savior whom he loved so well, and so reverently worshiped, the ennobling influence of his work shall be felt in an ever-widening circle, as the years roll on; and wherever the Order of the Eastern Star shall be known, the name of Dr. Rob Morris shall be held in loving remembrance.

Let us emulate his virtues, his unfeigned piety and noble Christian character, and be guided in our lives by those pure principles which he enunciated, and which he learned from the teachings of the blessed Jesus.

We cannot re-kindle the morning beams of childhood; we cannot recall the noontide glory of youth; we cannot bring back the perfect day of maturity; we cannot fix the evening days of age in the shadowy horizon; but we can cherish this goodness which is the sweetness of childhood, the joy of youth, the strength of maturity, the honor of old age, and the bliss of saints.

In addition to the Eastern Star, Dr. Morris also was the author of "The Queen of the South," "The Cross and Crown," and several other degrees, none of which gained the popularity which has been accorded to the Eastern Star.

Of Masonic rituals and handbooks, the following is a list of his works: *Free Mason's Monitor*, three degrees; *Miniature Monitor*, three degrees; *Eastern Star Manual, Rosary of Eastern Star, Guide to High Priesthood, Special Help for Worshipful Master*, same for Senior Deacon, same for the Secretary, *Funeral Book of Freemasons, Prudence Book of Freemasons, Masonic Ladder, Dictionary of Freemasonry, Guide to the Consecration of Masonic Cemeteries, Discipline of Masonic Offenders*. He was the first writer, according to very high authority, in

Masonic belles-lettres, his *Lights and Shadows of Freemasonry* being the pioneer work in that line.

His rule of life, from the commencement of labor as a Masonic journalist, was borrowed from Addison: "I promise never to draw a faulty character, which does not fit at least a thousand people, or to publish a single paper that is not written in the spirit of benevolence, and with a love of mankind."

By many, Dr. Morris was considered the leading numismatist in America. In the science of historical numismatics in America he was one of the pioneers, his monograph, entitled *The Twelve Caesars, illustrated by Readings of 217 of their Coins and Medals*, being the first issue of its class west of the Atlantic. He also published the *Numismatic Pilot*, devoted to the explanations of ancient coins. He was secretary of the American Association of Numismatists, honorary member of the Numismatic and Antiquarian Society, of Montreal, Canada; also of the Boston Numismatic Society and the New London, Connecticut, Historical Society, and an active member of the American Numismatic and Archaeological Society, of New York.

Dr. Morris gave us altogether, as from a perennial fountain, more than three hundred effusions in form of odes and poems; but none wear so well with old admirers, none secure so speedily the favor of the newly initiated, as his conception of August, 1854, composed while living in the house described above as his residence at Lodgeton, Fulton County, Kentucky, which has gone out through all the earth under the name of "The Level and the Square." It is the Masonic song of the age, tending to the immortal. Brother George Oliver, D.D., eminent above all others in English Masonry, and the Masonic writer for all time, said of this piece: "Brother Morris has composed many fervent, eloquent, and highly-poetic compositions — songs that will not die — but in "The Level and the Square" he has breathed out his depth of feeling, fervency, and pathos with brilliancy and vigor of language, and expressed his faith in the immortal life beyond the grave." Periodically published in Masonic journals, quoted in a thousand orations, seen in fragments in innumerable epitaphs, musically wedded to sixteen airs, declaimed by traveling performers, and embodied in many "Gems of Reading," this effusion deserves best of all to live in memory as one of his grandest efforts.

Of Masonic belles-lettres, he wrote *Life in a Triangle*, 1853; *The Two St. Johns*, 1854; *Tales of Masonic Life*, 1860; *Lodge at Mystic*, 1863; and *Masonic Poems*, 1864 and 1876. In Masonic history and biography he wrote *Freemason's Almanacs*, 1860, 1861, 1862, 1863, 1864; *Masonic Reminiscences*, 1857; *History of Freemasonry in Kentucky*, 1859; *Life of Eli Bruce*, 1859; *Freemasonry in the Holy Land*, 1872. He also published in thirty octavo volumes, under the general title of *Universal Masonic Library*, fifty-six distinct works, including writings of Oliver, Mackey, Town, Portal, Preston, Hutchinson, George Smith, Morris Anderson, Harris, Calcott, Ashe, Lawre, De Vertot, Gourdin, Taylor, Creigh, Brown, Morton, Arnold, and Towne. In addition to these, he published the *American Freemason*, 1853-1858; *Voice of Masonry*, 1859-1867; *Light in Masonry*, 1873, and *Kentucky Freemason*, 1853. His copious and original notes and manuscripts, taken when secretary of the "American Holy Land Explorations," have been made available in the study of Freemasonry.

In addition to these he has given to the Sunday school literature of the world scores of odes, sketches, addresses, and songs. In 1884 he published a new edition of his poems entitled the *Poetry of Freemasonry*, which was a compilation of his best poetry. He also wrote a series of sketches for the *Courier Journal*, entitled "Jesters with whom I have Jested," published in 1886. One of his most famous songs was called "Blind Bartemus."

The beginning of official work of this zealous veteran was that of Grand Lecturer, first in the State of Tennessee; afterwards in Kentucky. On horseback, before the days of railways, he visited the Lodges of those jurisdictions to the number of a hundred or more and communicated to them rituals and general instructions in Masonry. The originality and thoroughness of his teachings are best described by a gentleman who accompanied him for a week or more in the spring of 1851:

> Brother Morris's marked trait was *industry*. He made little pretentions to genius or talent of high order, but he always made the *best use of his time*. I never saw him idle for a moment. In the lodge or out of it he was ever *seeking* or *communicating* Masonic light. He visited sick brethren, if there were any, at their houses, and imparted comfort. He inquired for destitute brethren and tendered them aid. He looked up the graves of departed Masons and suggested better care of them. He set the secretary to making lists of the widows and orphans of the craft, that if any were needy, they might not be overlooked by the brotherhood in future. His appearance in those days was very peculiar. Lank as a rattlesnake, and as swift at a witty stroke; nervous to the last degree; frightfully dyspeptic; extremely fond of nature, and an indefatigable collector of shells, arrowheads, and eccentric stones; a glutton for reading books; fluent as the river and generous as the sea; speaking in all things from the heart; amiable and generous.

In Dr. Morris's Lodge lectures a beauty, grandeur, and significance were apparent that impressed even the doltish mind. At that period, American lodges were at a low ebb of information. The ceremonials were often wretchedly burlesqued by ignorant pretenders, and Rob Morris came among them as a reformer. Instead of an unmeaning tragedy the Craft acquired a sublime symbol, and if the neophyte had a soul at all able to appreciate a grand thought, he received a permanent impression. On Sabbath days Dr. Morris addressed communities, wherever he might be, in their churches and schoolhouses, upon *Freemasonry as identified with Bible truth*. Once, at least, in every village, he invited a union of the ladies with their husbands, fathers, and brothers in the Lodge room, and to the united assembly gave his beautiful system entitled the Eastern Star. Though the country was wild with political and sectarian strife (the mutterings of civil war) he talked of nothing but Freemasonry and for all this service he accepted a compensation so meager that the poorest lawyer or physician who sat in any of his audiences would have spurned it.

The growth of skepticism among American Masons has been too marked to escape the notice of any. Leading men among the Craft have at one time and another publicly attacked the old principle of "faith in an inspired word as a fundamental belief in Masonry." To counteract this, the most' dangerous foe that Masonry can have, Dr. Morris early made himself the champion of Biblical faith. To unsettle the minds of the Craft as to *the object* their fathers. venerated has been the first aim of the Masonic skeptic, and we see that while casting the Holy Scriptures out of the Lodge room was the first step of the French infidel, ignoring faith in God was the second and easier step. Dr. Morris said in an oration in 1853: "I repeat, with the great moralist Johnson, that there is no crime that a man can commit so great as poisoning the sources of eternal (Masonic) truth. Faith in God tends, in the only high and noble sense, to make Freemasons *one*.

So many of Dr. Morris's diplomas and official jewels were destroyed in the burning of his 'bouse, "The Three Cedars," at La Grange, Kentucky, November 1861, and in the terrible conflagration of Chicago, October 1871, that no accurate list can now be given of them. It is within bounds, however, to assert that the number of honorary degrees and complimentary memberships with which his signal services were recognized in America and abroad exceeds one hundred. Dr. Morris at one time recalled a list of one hundred and forty-three regular degrees and orders in Masonry, whose covenants he had assumed. In 1856 he made this summary of them in a symbolic strain of thought:

> I have been *around, under* and *through* the temple of
> Masonry, searching out its foundations, its builders and its

trestle boards. With its builders I have handled, in turn, each of its implements; with the *Entered Apprentice*, trimming the rough ashier on the checkered pavement; with the *Fellow Craft*, moralized upon the pillars of the porch, and the fifteen grades of the winding stairs; with the *Master Mason*, smoothing the indissoluble cement with silent awe; with the *Mark Master* I have penetrated the quarries, found my own best block, brought it up for a place in the walls, and claimed my penny with the rest; for I never have received, of salary or official emolument, to the value of one Jewish half shekel of silver. I have shared the responsibilities of the *Past Master*, seated in the Oriental Chair of King Solomon. As a *Most Excellent Master*, my hands have aided to rear the capstone to its place, while my lips have sung the triumphant strain, *All Hail to the Morning*, of Thomas Smith Webb, and my face was bowed to the pavement in acknowledgment of the descent of fire and cloud. As a *Royal Arch Mason*, returning from exile in Babylon, my feet have entered, weary and sore, over rough and rugged ways, seeking the Sacred Hill. As a *Select Master*, I have wrought in silence, secrecy and darkness, upon the mystic arches within the Holy Mountain. I have stood as a *Knight Templar* with companions loyal and brave, wielding my brand, Excalibur, two-edged and cross hilted, while guarding the Shrine where the body of My Departed Lord was laid. In all my career as a Mason I have ever held that excellence is granted to man only in return for labor, and that nothing is worth having that is not difficult to acquire: My life has been, thus far, a contest with obstacles; but no man would be what he is, had he tamely suffered the *difficulties* of life to overcome him.

It has been claimed that Dr. Morris was the first to ever write a book upon the subject of Masonic jurisprudence. The work upon that subject was published in 1855 and was entitled the *Code of Masonic*

Law. Doubtless there has been too much legislation among American Grand Lodges, too much of the whimsical, special, and ephemeral, yet he conceived that there is a *basis of legal principles* to which all questions may be referred, and this is what he undertook to point out in his *Code of Masonic Law*. All thoughtful Masons admit that Law should speak Seldom, and never but as wisdom prompts, and equity. The spirit of his writings upon jurisprudence is suggested by Hooker: "It is easier a great deal for men to be taught by laws what they *ought* to do, than entrusted to judge as they *should*, of law; for the wisest are ready to acknowledge that soundly to judge of law is the weightiest thing he can take upon him."

The custom of giving honors to our Masonic dead has become so intimately incorporated into our American Masonry that many continue their attachment to the Order "even down to old age" that so they may not forfeit the funeral honors due the faithful departed. On the other hand, it is an attraction to a certain class of minds to unite themselves with a fraternity which follows its members lovingly to the grave's brink and lays them gently back upon the bosom of mother earth. In honoring this custom, the practice of Dr. Morris was supplemented by his writings. His *Funeral Book of the Freemasons*, a work of widespread celebrity, contains, in addition to copious and easy instructions, a long catalogue of epitaphs and forms of obituary notices, also of funeral songs suitable to such occasions; while no one was so often called upon to attend in person and preside over such ceremonials.

This passage was first published by Dr. Morris in 1852, and expressed his views upon the subject with much vigor:

> In all ages the bodies of the Masonic dead have been laid in graves, dug due east and west, with their faces toward the east. This practice has been borrowed from us, and adopted by others, until it has become nearly universal. It implies that when the great day shall come, and He who is death's conqueror shall give the signal, *His ineffable light*

shall first be seen in the east; that from the east He will make His glorious approach; will stand at the eastern margin of these graves, and with his mighty power — that grasp irresistibly strong which shall prevail, — will raise the bodies which are slumbering therein. We shall have been long buried, long decayed. Friends, relatives, yea, our nearest and dearest, will cease to remember where they have laid us. The broad earth will have undergone wondrous changes, mountains levelled, valleys filled. The seasons will have chased each other in many a fruitful round. Oceans lashed into fury by the gales of today will tomorrow have sunk like a spoiled child to their slumber. Broad trees with broader roots will have interlocked them, hard and knobbed as they are, above our ashes, as if to conceal the very fact of our having lived; and then, after centuries of life, they, too, will have followed our example of mortality, and, long struggling with decay, at last will have toppled down to join their remains with ours, thus obliterating the last poor testimony that man has ever lain there. So shall we be lost to human sight. But the eye of God, nevertheless, will mark the spot, *green with the everlasting verdure of faith*; when the trumpet's blast shall shake; the hills to their very bases, our astonished bodies will raise, impelled upward by an irresistible impulse, and we shall stand face to face with our Redeemer.

Dr. Rob Morris closed his earthly career at LaGrange, Kentucky, on July 31, 1888. He had been in poor health for a year or more but was not seriously ill until about six weeks before his death, when he was stricken with paralysis, and after that time he steadily declined. For twenty-four hours preceding his death he was unconscious. His immediate family of six children and their mother were present during his last moments. The surviving children were John A. Morris, Charlotte F., married to Hon. H. J. Goodrich, Dr. Alfred W. Morris,

Robert Morris, Jr., Sarah M., married to Mr. Latimer Hitt, and Ruth E., married to Mr. John Mount.

The Grand Master of Kentucky, upon receipt of the intelligence of the death of Dr. Morris, at once caused the issuance of the following circular letter:

Grand lodge of Kentucky, F. and A. M.
Lexington, KY., July 31, 1888.

To the Free and Accepted Masons of Kentucky:

It becomes my painful duty to announce to you the death of our venerable and learned, P.G.M. Rob Morris, which occurred at his home in LaGrange, on the 31st day of July, 1888, after an illness of short duration, following years of ill health.

The fame of our eminent brother was not confined to oar continent — he was a citizen of two hemispheres; for his learning and zeal made him known to Masons everywhere as a chieftain among the clans, a master builder among the workmen. His mark is upon the most beautiful stones of our Masonic edifice, and his designs remain upon our trestle board, for he both conceived and executed.

It is my order that this announcement be read in every lodge at its next regular meeting, that proper respect may be shown to the memory of our deceased brother until the Grand Lodge of Kentucky can, in ample form, testify its appreciation of his many excellencies.

J. Soule Smith, Grand Master.
H. B. Grant, Grand Secretary.

The funeral ceremonies took place at LaGrange, which had been his home for over thirty years, and was conducted by the Grand Lodge of Kentucky, Past Grand Master Hiram Bassett, an old and zealous Mason and an intimate friend of Dr. Morris, acting as Grand

Master. A special train carried the brethren of Louisville up to LaGrange on August 1st, the day of the funeral.

The Rev. H. Calvin Smith delivered the discourse from the text, Psalms lxviii: 13: "Though ye have lain among the pots, yet shall ye be as the wings of a dove covered with silver and her feathers with yellow gold." The Rev. Bro. H. R. Coleman followed with a few remarks and P.G.M. Eginton read a tribute prepared for Fortitude Lodge. P.G.M. James W. Hopper also read an original "song of Lamentations." Bro. H. B. Grant, Grand Secretary, being called upon, said: "About four years ago I received from Brother Rob Morris a paper containing these words, afterwards making verbal request that they be read at the first Masonic gathering after his death:

A Message From The Grave

To my dear friend, H. B. Grant:
I have composed this poem as under the shadow of impending death. I have made a few copies and sent them to particular friends only, asking that they 'should not be published, or any public use made of them, until I am gone.

Brothers in June or in December,
    Honoring the memory of the dear St. John,
Then let some kind participant remember
    The name of him who wrote this, *but is gone*;
Let some kind brother rise, while all are silent,
    And with deep pathos and fond friendship say:
He was a Mason, gentle, true, not violent,
    And loved old things that do not pass away.

He loved his friends; in them his heart found anchor,
    Bound in affection as with hooks of steel;
As for his foes, he gave few signs of rancor,

And bore their slanders patiently and well.
He loved to make in simple verse that rhyming
    Where ancient signs and emblems smoothly lie,
Where deeds of brother-love and truth are chiming,
    And Masonry is wed to poetry.

He loved the word of God; its hopes eternal
    Grew sweeter as the end of life drew nigh;
A sinful man, but saved by Grace supernal,
    Trusting in Christ, he dreaded not to die.
At times a cloud the promises disguising,
    And deep humility obscured the scene,
But the bright Son of Righteousness uprising
    Dispelled the gloom and warmed his soul again.

He gave the widows and the orphans duly
    A portion of his hard-earned scanty store,
And though the amount might seem but trifling truly,
    He gave so cheerfully it seemed the more.
His heart was in his work, to *Build the Temple*,
    In fervency he toiled through many years,
To "build the temple" spiritual and mental,
    He triumphs now — is freed from toils and tears.

He's gone; the problem that so long he studied,
    That mystery of "the world to come" profound
Is solved; his tree of life which only budded,
    Bears now full harvest in Celestial Ground.
In the Great Presence, with the wearied resting,
    He has his wages and is well content.
Brothers, in silence stand; your love attesting —
    This is the word your dying brother sent.

The Knights Templars commenced their beautiful service, which was concluded at the grave, Eminent Sir Frank H. Johnson, Commander, and Eminent Sir John Frank Lewis, Prelate, officiating. The procession filed out of the church and led by the band from Louisville, the Templars and the lodge were followed by the hearse and the mourning family and friends to the village cemetery.

Brother Bassett then took up the solemn Masonic services, which being concluded, Brothers J. H. Leathers and H. B. Grant placed upon the grave a floral design, representing a Masonic level, about three feet across the base, and a square, referring to the popular poem by Brother Morris, "We meet upon the Level, and we part upon the Square." This was surrounded by a laurel wreath, suggesting that the deceased had been crowned "Poet Laureate of Freemasonry." Another floral tribute by the Commandery was a very large Roman cross. Other very pretty designs were laid upon the grave. The attendance was very large and represented the brain and zeal of Kentucky Masonry.

> The harp which late so sweetly rang
>   Hangs stringless now and still;
> The Master wakes its chords no more,
>   Obedient to his will.

Biography of Rob Morris, LL.D.

THE LEVEL AND THE SQUARE [2]

We Meet Upon The Level, And We Part Upon The Square, —
What words of precious meaning those words Masonic are!
Come, let us contemplate them; they are worthy of a thought, —
With the highest and the lowest and the rarest they are fraught.

We meet upon the level, though from every station come—
The King from out his palace and the poor man from his home;
For the one must leave his diadem without the Mason's door,
And the other finds his true respect upon the checkered floor.

We part upon the square, for the world must have its due;
We mingle with its multitude, a cold, unfriendly crew;
But the influence of our gatherings in memory is green,
And we long, upon the level, to renew the happy scene.

There's a world where all are equal, — we are hurrying toward it fast, —
We shall meet upon the level there when the gates of death are past;
We shall stand before the Orient, and our Master will be there,
To try the blocks we offer by His own unerring square.

---

[2] From Poetry of Freemasonry, by Rob Morris, LL.D., by permission of his son, Rob Morris, Jr.

This is the original form in which the poem, "We Meet upon the Level," etc., was written. Its history, as often told, is simple enough, and has none of the elements of romance. In August, 1854, as the author was walking home from a neighbor's, through the sultry afternoon, he sat upon a fallen tree, and upon the black of a letter dashed off, under a momentary impulse and in stenographic character, the lines upon this page.

Eighteen years since, Brother George Oliver, D.D., eminent above all others in English Masonry, and the Masonic historian for all time, said of the poem: "Brother Morris has composed many fervent, eloquent and highly poetic compositions, songs that will not die, but in 'The Level and the Square' he has breathed out a depth of feeling, fervency and pathos, with brilliancy and vigor of language, and expressed due faith in the immortal life beyond the grave."

We shall meet upon the level there, but never thence depart;
There's a Mansion, — 'tis all ready for each zealous, faithful heart;
There's a Mansion and a welcome, and a multitude is there,
Who have met upon the level and been tried upon the square.

Let us meet upon the level, then, while laboring patient here, —
Let us meet and let us labor, tho' the labors seem severe.
Already in the western sky the signs bid us prepare
To gather up our working tools and part upon the square!

Hands round, ye faithful Ghiblimites, the bright, fraternal chain;
We part upon the square below to meet in Heaven again.
O what words of precious meaning those words Masonic are, —
We Meet Upon The Level, And We Part Upon The Square.

The Level, Plumb, And Square[3]

We meet upon the LEVEL, and we part upon the SQUARE:
What words sublimely beautiful those words Masonic are!
They fall like strains of melody upon the listening ears,
As they've sounded *hallelujahs* to the world, three thousand years.

We meet upon the Level, though from every station brought,
The Monarch from his palace and the Laborer from his cot;
For *the King* must drop his dignity when knocking at our door.
And *the Laborer* is his equal as he walks the checkered floor.

---

[3] From Poetry of Freemasonry, by Rob Morris, LL.D., by permission of his son, Rob. Morris, Jr.

This poem has been subjected to so many alterations in its thirty years of active use that it is deemed proper to give it here with the last emendations. It is likely that older readers will prefer it in its first draft.

We act upon the Plumb, — 'tis our Master's great command,
We stand upright in virtue's way and lean to neither hand;
The All-Seeing Eye that reads the heart will bear us witness true,
That we do always honor God and give each man his due.

We part upon the Square, — for the world must have its due,
We mingle in the ranks of men, but keep *The Secret true*,
And the influence of our gatherings in memory is green,
And we long, upon the Level, to renew the happy scene.

There's a world where all are equal, — we are hurrying toward it fast,
We shall meet upon the Level there when the gates of death are past;
We shall stand before the Orient and our Master will be there,
Our works to try, our lives to prove by His unerring Square.

We shall meet upon the Level there, but never thence depart.
There's a mansion bright and glorious, set for the pure in heart;
And an everlasting welcome from the Host rejoicing there,
Who in this world of sloth and sin, did part upon the Square.

Let us meet upon the Level, then, while laboring patient here,
Let us meet and let us labor, tho' the labor be severe;
Already in the *Western Sky* the signs bid us prepare,
To gather up our Working Tools and part upon the Square.

Hands round, ye royal craftsmen in the bright, fraternal chain!
We part upon the Square below to meet in Heaven again;
Each tie that has been broken here shall be cemented there,
And none be lost around the Throne who parted on the Square.

CHAPTER III

Other Degrees, Minor Rituals, etc.

A HISTORY of the Order of the Eastern Star may well include brief mention of some ancient ceremonies that have been re-arranged and adapted to the use of some of the Grand Chapters which are constituent members of the General Grand Chapter, also a number which have been adopted by and are now in use among the members of Grand Chapters not constituent members of the General Grand Chapter.

In an address to the General Grand Chapter, Mrs. Mary C. Snedden, Most Worthy Grand Matron, 1892-1895, said in reference to new degrees:

> During the past two years I have had several Rituals submitted to me for approval, the writers of which styled them "Higher Degrees to the Eastern Star." It is to be regretted that the writers have made a pre-requisite for petitioners to have a membership in the Eastern Star, as it gives the impression that our Order indorses the degrees. In some cases, members have printed upon their cards their Eastern Star standing and ranking this the "Higher Degree." We cannot prevent the gentlemen making degrees, but we feel they have no right to engraft them upon the Eastern Star as higher degrees. I have refused to give my approval to any of them.

On the same subject, before the next regular session of the General Grand Chapter, which met at Washington, D. C., in 1898, Mrs. Mary E. Partridge, Most Worthy Grand Matron 1895-1898, used the following language in her address:

> During my term of office, I have been repeatedly asked to endorse the so-called higher degrees to our Order and participate in their privileges; to all of which I have

courteously declined. I regret exceedingly that the name of the Eastern Star has been made one of the pre-requisites for petitioners, as it is often misleading, and some have joined in good faith believing it to be a higher degree to our Order. In reply to inquiries from several Grand Matrons and Grand Patrons, I have advised that while we cannot prevent any of our members from joining any lodge or society, they cannot in any manner connect them with the Ritual or hold their sessions in Chapter rooms on regular nights of meetings of the Chapter, referring them to the decision of my predecessor, Sister Mary C. Snedden, which was sustained by the General Grand Chapter.

The General Grand Chapter in 1895 approved the action of the Most Worthy Grand Matron in refusing to recognize any so-called higher degrees, and in 1898 resolutions were passed by the General Grand Chapter as follows:

Resolved, That there are no degrees connected in any way or manner with our Order other than those provided for and taught in the ritual.

Resolved, That any member willfully representing to anyone that there are side degrees, higher degrees, or any degrees other than those taught and provided for by our ritual, shall be guilty of conduct unbecoming a member of the Order, and, upon conviction thereof, shall be suspended or expelled from the Order.

There have been issued, at various times and on various occasions, works containing ceremonies to be used by the Eastern Star members, many of which have valuable lessons and beautiful ceremonies, all of which carry on in similar vein the thought embodied in the ritualistic work. Some of these are mentioned briefly below in the order of their appearance before the Fraternity, so far as the dates of issuance are obtainable.

The Ladies' Friend

This was published by G. W. Brown, M. A., in 1866, and contains the lectures and exoteric ceremonials as they are used in conferring the degrees of "The Mason's Daughter," "The Good Samaritan," "Heroines of Jericho," and "Kindred Degree;" also the "Eastern Star" as given in *Morris's Manual*, the secret work being given by initial letters, each of which was numbered. A vocabulary accompanied it, which when referred to by letter and number, indicated the word as it was intended to be used in rendering the work.

Macoy's Manual

A Manual of the Order of the Eastern Star, containing the symbols, scriptural illustrations, lectures, etc., adapted to the system of Adoptive Masonry, arranged by Robert Macoy, National Grand Secretary, and published in 1866. This was beautifully illustrated with pictures suggestive of the degrees. The edition published in 1904 increased the number of published copies to 71,000 and was practically a reprint of the first edition, with some additions and slightly enlarged. In it is contained a brief history of the Adoptive Rite or Female Masonry; rules for the government of the Order of the Eastern Star; hymns with the music to accompany same; address explanatory of the system and intended for communicating the degrees under a pledge of secrecy only; as well as a number of poems descriptive of the work. From the beautiful lessons of truth as presented we learn that "Ideal institutions are those organizations which, moved by a superior and creative inspiration, take the lead in the moral culture and civilization of the nations, and preside over their spiritual and intellectual development. Actual institutions are those organizations which spring from some thought, relation or inspiration to produce and establish a complete and perfect achievement; an existing and acting association for some benevolent, religious, political or social purpose; a genuine and positive reality, laboring to accomplish mutual and actual results.

"In the earlier periods of the world, the wisest and best of men withdrew from the imperfections of the exterior society, and in their secret temples sought to sound the mysterious systems of God, Nature and the Soul, and to live out their idea of a true life. The Mysteries of Egypt, of Eleusis, of the Cabiri, and those of India and of the North of Europe, had a widely extended influence; and so important were they that an investigation of them is necessary, if we would have an accurate view of the Theology, Philosophy, Science and Ethics of the past times."

A grip was introduced, the origin of which is given in the Masonic department of a New York weekly newspaper in 1877 as follows: "After diligent inquiry we learn that the grip was invented by accident at a meeting held in Concord, New Hampshire, when Brother W. S. Wolf, now of New York City, was conferring the degree as a lecture, in 1862, prior to which time there had been no grip. A lady whose husband was a Mason, 'rose in meetin' and said aloud, 'Brother Wolf, you have forgotten to give us the grip.' It was a dilemma, but Brother Wolf was equal to the emergency and gave the grip which is now so generally used, a council of Eastern Star lecturers having adopted it in 1863."

The above is not given as authoritative, lacking the records of the workers of the day by which the statement could be verified.

Adoptive Rite Ritual

The degrees were prepared by Brother Macoy and frequently read from the manuscript, to the members of Alpha Chapter No. 1, of New York City, during the year of 1868, and at the first meeting as a chartered Chapter, December 28, 1868, the degrees were conferred for the first time, Mrs. Eliza A. Macoy, wife of Robert Macoy, being the candidate. All the officers read their parts from a printed copy, this being the first ritual of the Adoptive Rite published in this form.

In it, the Sisters only were required to be initiated, brothers, if elected, being only required to pledge their honor as Master Masons, in open Chapter, to conform to the rules and regulations of the Order. The covenant of adoption provided for four conditions as obligated: to respect the secrecy of the Order; obey the laws; give advice, sympathy, and aid to the members; and refrain from any acts of injustice or unkindness.

The greater portion of the work was to be done by the Patron. Forms were arranged for the ceremony of installation, also provision and form for a Chapter of Sorrow, and funeral services.

A revised edition was published in 1874, followed by a more complete Adoptive Rite Ritual, in 1897, known as the New York Ritual.

NEW YORK RITUAL

This is a splendid compilation of ceremonies and directions for use in conducting the ritualistic work of the Order, containing the ceremonies for opening, closing, and initiation both for women and Master Masons.

The benefits of the Rite are mainly to the female sex; for them this temple has been reared, these walls set up. They are its crown and glory; and its value consists in the spirit in which they enter into and conduct it, and the grace they throw around it.

The form of petition used by Master Masons differs from that used by women, as does also the form used in the initiation, the brother, if elected, being required to pledge his honor as a Master Mason, in open Chapter, to conform to the rules and regulations of the Order. The Worthy Patron is required to pass upon the eligibility of the brothers to attend the Chapter ceremonies, obligating them when necessary, while the Conductress and Associate Conductress pass only upon the eligibility of the sisters present. The work is beautifully illustrated and the songs, with the music, are incorporated in the ritual.

Included with this edition are the ceremonies for the "Queen of the South" and "Matron's Administrative Degree"; ceremonies for the installation of the officers of the Grand Chapter and far the subordinate Chapter officers; constituting and inaugurating ceremonies; form of ceremony for the dedication of Eastern Star halls; Chapter of Sorrow and services at the grave of the deceased members.

THE ROYAL AND EXALTED ORDER OF THE AMARANTH

The word *amaranth* is derived from the Greek word meaning unwithering and is chiefly used in poetry, and applied to certain plants which, from not soon fading, typify immortality:

> Immortal amaranth, a flower which once
> In paradise, fast by the tree of life,
> Began to bloom; but soon for man's offence
> To heaven removed, where first it grew, there grows,
> And flowers aloft, shading the fount of life,
> And where the river of bliss through midst of heaven
> Rolls o'er elysian flowers her amber stream;
> With these that never fade the spirits elect
> Bind their resplendent locks

In ancient Greece the amaranth was sacred to Ephesian Artemis. It was supposed to have special healing properties, and as a symbol of immortality was used to decorate images of the gods and tombs.

In the connection which we wish to consider — the meaning of the word as it is used to express the highest degree of Adoptive Masonry — the original *Royal and Exalted Order of the Amaranth* was instituted by Queen Christina of Sweden in 1653, composed of fifteen knights, fifteen ladies, and the Queen as the Grand mistress. The insignia consisted of two letters "A" interlaced, one being inverted, within a laurel crown, and bearing the motto, *Dolce nella memoria*. The annual festival of this equestrian order was held at the Epiphany.

As the Order was instituted in Sweden in 1653, it was to honor the Lady Ammarranta, a woman of rare beauty, modesty, and charity, who was attached to the court of Sweden. For a long time, this knightly Order was immensely popular in Europe, and the most distinguished ladies and gentlemen considered themselves honored by being made members of it. The theory of knighthood and its orders, as applied to the citizens of a republican form of government, differs greatly in some respects, from that applied to the subjects of a monarchical state. In our great republic, where the people are all born equal, merit is the elevating standard of true nobility.

A society of a similar name, androgynous in its nature, was instituted in 1883, under the supervision of Robert Macoy, of New York, to supplement the Order of the Eastern Star, having a social and charitable purpose, the ritual of which, as well as its constitutional government, has met with much commendation.

The Amaranth degree as composed by Brother Macoy was intended by him to be used as the third and highest degree of Adoptive Rite. The illustration used upon the first page of the ritual shows the all-seeing eye of progress at the top, with graduated degrees typifying the road to progress with the Eastern Star upon the first step, Queen of the South as the second step, and Amaranth upon the third and top step. As arranged, the same number of officers are required as the Chapter but bearing more exalted titles — the Matron and Patron having the title "Royal" while all others were "Honored." The candidate was required to pledge confidence and hospitality by partaking of salt and bread as typical of a decision to make perpetual the mutual bond of friendship therein formed. The points of the star were each designated as exemplifying lessons — Truth, Faith, Wisdom, and Charity. At the fourth point, Charity, a legend, nautical in its references, is given as follows:

There is a beautiful thought conveyed in the legend, that on the shores of the Adriatic Sea, the wives of the fishermen, whose husbands have gone far off upon the deep, are in the habit, at eventide, of going down to the seashore and singing the first verse of a favorite hymn. After they have sung it they listen till they hear, borne by the winds across the desert sea, the second verse sung by their husbands as they are tossed by the gale upon the waves, thus rendering happiness to all. Perhaps, if we listen, we too may hear in the desert world, some whisper borne from afar to remind us that there is a heavenly home; and when we sing a hymn upon earth it may be we shall hear its echo breaking in sweet melody upon the sands of time, cheering the hearts of those who, perchance, are pilgrims and strangers, looking for a city that hath sure foundations.

(When possible to do so, a choir of ladies and gentlemen will sing two verses of a familiar hymn; the ladies, being in a distant part of the Chapter room, will sing the first verse and the gentlemen, in an adjoining room with the door ajar, will sing the second verse.)

The candidate arriving in the East the Royal Matron said: "The ceremony by which Knighthood is conferred is called the accolade. Conforming to this custom and by the authority vested in me, I receive you (places a sword on the left and right shoulders, and on the head of the candidate), and confer upon you the dignity of a Lady of the Royal and Exalted degree of the Amaranth; and as the Amaranthine flower is typical of undying friendship and eternal truth, so with this right hand accept our pledge of an abiding trust, and a cordial reception into our fellowship."

Conducted to the West she was crowned with a wreath: "This is no diadem of gold; no cincture of pearls; no regal tiara; no framework of gems, velvet lined, like that which so often presses upon the aching brows of royalty. That is a badge of power; frequently empty, unsubstantial and delusive. But our crown and our act of coronation have a higher and a nobler meaning. We crown you as being eminent for virtue, zeal and well-doing; showing charity to the destitute, and faithful in every walk of life. May all your footsteps fall upon flowers. May all your good intentions be fraught with success. May your last days be your best. We crown you in the hope of immortality. There is no death to the pure and loving. May your admission to the land celestial and everlasting be sure, and your entrance full of delight. And as the years roll along and bring about the great consummation for which we all hopefully wait, may your ransomed spirit be crowned with the never-ceasing favor of Almighty God."

The candidate was then made to bear the banner of the Order, which embraced the Eastern Star, within which was a circle bearing the letters S.H.E.B.A., while in the center was an amaranthine wreath.

The author says: "In introducing the elegant formulas of the Amaranthine Order, our purpose, therefore, is to inquire only for noble deeds, knowing and caring nothing for noble birth. The present form of the Royal and Exalted Degree of the Amaranth is adapted to the demands of those who are seeking light and advancement in this popular and sublime system. It is made to form the apex of the Rite of Adoption, and to establish a Court of Honor, wherein the highest grade of instruction, culture, and usefulness may be imparted in symbolical guise to the advanced members of the Rite; for the dissemination of mutual aid and the bestowal of the largest charity. It is therefore offered in the spirit of the beautiful sentiments of

Rome's greatest orator: '*Haac primo lex in amicitia Sanciator ut neque rogamus res turnes, nec faciam rogate.*' This is the first law to be established in friendship, that we neither ask of others that which is dishonorable, nor ourselves do wrong when asked."

The honorable and exalted purposes that Brother Macoy had in view when disseminating these degrees, can have no opposition worthy the name. Their effects in winning to the advocacy of charity the virtuous, intelligent, and influential female members of the nation are truly encouraging and stimulate its friends to persevere in a general promulgation of the ceremonies.

The degrees of the various Orders, dependent upon the Masonic Fraternity for the eligibility of those seeking its benefits, has been framed and established for a more extended diffusion of the principles of morality and friendship by positive and significant emblems; for inciting the influence of women toward the purposes of the Masonic institution; for ameliorating the connection of the destitute widows and helpless orphans; and for affording increased facilities in relieving worthy distressed women travelers.

The wives, mothers, widows, sisters, and daughters of Masons cannot, from the immutable laws of the Fraternity, be permitted to share in the grand mysteries of Freemasonry; but there is no reason why there should not be a society for them, which may enable them to make themselves known to Masons, and so obtain assistance and protection, and by means of which, acting in concert through the tie of association and mutual obligations, they may cooperate in the great labors of Masons by assisting in some respects, such as directing its charities, etc. As these privileges greatly depend upon the good standing and affiliation of the brother through whom she is introduced, this system will be a strong inducement, it is believed, to keep a brother, otherwise inclined to err, within the bounds of morality.

Rose Croix of the Dames

This degree, called also the Ladies of Beneficence (Chevalieres de la Bienfaisance), is the sixth capitular or ninth degree of the French Rite of Adoption. It is not only Christian but Roman Catholic in its character and is derived from the ancient Jesuitical system as first promulgated in the Rose Croix Chapter of Arras. (Rose Croix means Rose Cross.)

Heroines of Jericho

This androgynous degree is said to have originated with Brother David Vinton, a lecturer of considerable eminence, about 1815 to 1820, and is conferred in America, on Royal Arch Masons, their wives and daughters. Brother Vinton published *The Masonic Minstrel*, a large and elegantly printed volume of Masonic and miscellaneous music and is well known to the Masonic world through his beautiful Masonic hymn, "Solemn Strikes the Funeral Chime."

The degree is intended to instruct the female recipients in the claims which they have upon the protection of their husbands' and fathers' companions, and to communicate to them an effectual method of proving those claims. An instance of friendship extended to the entire family of a benefactress by those whom she had benefited, and of the influence of a solemn contract in averting danger, is referred to in the case of Rahab, the woman of Jericho, from whom the degree derives its name; and for this purpose the second chapter of the Book of Joshua is read to the candidate. When the degree is received by a man, he is called a Knight of Jericho, and when by a woman she is termed a Heroine.

From the fact that some lecturers have attached the name of William Wallace to an incredible legend and connected the same with this degree, some have been ready to ascribe to it a date far more remote, but it seems to be a settled fact that Brother Vinon instituted it.

It is a side or honorary degree and may be conferred by any Royal Arch Mason on a candidate qualified to receive it. It is known in every section of the United States, especially among the older members of Royal Arch Chapters. Nearly all Royal Arch Masons who were exalted before 1830, have the degree. In 1877 the Grand Chapter of Mississippi authorized its subordinates to confer the "Mason's Daughter," "Heroine of Jericho," "Queen of the South," and "Cross and Crown."

In the hands of some it is beautiful and effective. Lessons of vigilance; attention to the sick and imprisoned; the inviolability of moral obligations; the scriptural duty of prayer, etc., are conveyed and conferred in the lectures and exemplified by the traditionary personage whose name is cited therein. The Rev. Brother Leigh, P.G.M. of Alabama, enlarged and adorned this degree and added a monitorial part in a little publication of his issued in 1852, styled *Ladies' Masonry*, and the production was accepted as one of rare impressiveness.

So far as can be determined, no organization has been equal to the degree of the Heroine of Jericho, though the means of recognition are ample and more practical in their nature than any other except the degree of the Eastern Star. The signs are practical and can be given without detection in a public assembly. The lectures are singularly appropriate and ingenious.

The medals are variously made and lettered. One is an oval figure engraved on a plate of gold about one inch in its transverse direction, having on one side the lady's name, residence, the date of presentation, and the name of the donor; on the other side are these letters in four partitions: B.O.T., N.U.Y.I., Y.F., L.O. — the whole curiously interloped with a cord. The letters R.A.H.A.B. are in the center.

Three Buds of the Sweet Brier

This is an adoptive degree originated in 1850, the author being unknown. Its lady recipients are the wives, widows, mothers, sisters, and daughters of Master Masons in good standing; its emblems correspond with what its name denoted.

Holy Virgin

The degree of the Holy Virgin is an adoptive degree composed by the Rev. William Leigh, Past Grand Master of Alabama. This composition was instituted in 1852 and was accompanied by an ingenious monitor. Its lady recipients are the wives, widows, sisters, daughters, and mothers of Master Masons in good standing.

The Five Jewels of the Orient

Written by Juliette T. Burton and published in 1871. It was an effort to recount the lives of the five heroines of the Order of the Eastern Star in a romance which tended to bring these beautiful characters before the minds of the readers or listeners in a natural and very impressive manner. The story of the first four was greatly enlarged from the scriptural recording of the conditions surrounding their lives, though the story was not changed in fact. Adah was the Turquoise before Jephthah; Ruth the Topaz in the field of Boaz; Esther the Diamond before Ahasuerus, and Martha the Emerald before Christ; Electa the Ruby, which story differs widely from that portrayed by the ritual of the Eastern Star. The Rosary, as written by Morris, made Electa the wife of Gaius, while Sister Burton gives her in marriage to Adrian, and the mother of Gaius. Mary, the mother of Jesus, is here portrayed as the head of a large family. Electa is taken from Judea to Athens, and from there to Rome, where she suffers the death of a Christian martyr.

Good Samaritan

The authorship of this degree of androgynous Masonry is unknown. It is an honorary or side degree conferred in the United States with rather an impressive ceremony. The passages of Scripture upon which it is based are Luke X:30-37, inclusive. It is not connected with Masonic traditions but draws its allusions from the fate of Lot's wife, and from the parable of the Good Samaritan related in the Gospels. The passages of Scripture which refer to these events are read during the ceremony of initiation.

This degree is to be conferred only on Royal Arch Masons and their wives, and in conferring it two Good Samaritans must always be present, one of whom must be a Royal Arch Mason. Much dignity and importance has been given to this degree by its possessors; and it is usual in many places for a certain number of Good Samaritans to organize themselves into a regular, but of course independent, body to hold monthly meetings under the name of Assembly of Good Samaritans, elect officers and receive applications for initiation. In this manner the assemblies of the Good Samaritans, consisting of men and women members, bear a very near resemblance to the female Lodges which, under the name of "Maconnerie d' Adoption," prevail in France.

The medal or signet of the Good Samaritan is usually of a circular form, though an oval or shield is equally proper, having around its rim these letters: E.F.I.W.S.T.O.L. Eight curved lines are drawn from alternate letters on the rim, along which are the following sets of letters, including those above given: L.T.T.N., O.N.A.O.S., T.I.M.I.T.W.S.I.T.C., W.I.I.O.N., I.T.M.T.S.A.I.W.G.I.U., F.W.N.O.L.I.T.S.D., E.L.A.T.L., while in the center of the medal are the letters S. G. It is defective in its means of recognition and has no history on which to found a lecture.

The Queen of the South

This was an adaptation, by Brother Robert Macoy, of a degree arranged by Dr. Rob Morris and was incorporated in some editions of *Macoy's Ritual*, though apparently not rendered with any regularity in the Chapter rooms using the Macoy ritual. It is a degree designed to occupy an intermediate place in the Rite of Adoption and enlisted fourteen officers of a Chapter. It affords valuable instruction to the neophyte while passing from the first to the third degree and is calculated to inspire a greater desire to understand and appreciate the whole system. It was rendered on Mount Zion in the royal palace of King Solomon, who is "seated upon his great throne of ivory, overlaid with pure gold, surrounded with his officers and courtiers, and the kings of foreign nations, ambassadors, philosophers, and others who had come to gather wisdom from his lips."

When directing to the Court the following is used: "In this beautiful allegory we have considered the objections urged against the admission of ladies into the knowledge of Masonic principles. Those objections advanced by King Solomon were so easily answered and refuted by the Queen of the South, that it was impossible even for the wisest of men to maintain them."

The argument referred to above was carried on between King Solomon and the officers of the Chapter as proxies for the candidate, who represented the Queen of Sheba. This is one of the four degrees which the Grand Chapter of Mississippi authorized its subordinate Chapters to confer at its meeting in 1877. It illustrates, in dramatic form, that ancient and renowned visit of the Queen of Sheba (Queen of the South) to the court of King Solomon at Jerusalem more than three thousand years ago. Sheba (the Sabaea of profane history) formed a province of the southern part of Arabia. In the commercial intercourse of the people of Jerusalem with the inhabitants of her country, the Queen had often heard of the inspired wisdom, of the immense wealth, great power, and vast dominions of Solomon; she undertook a journey from what was then deemed to be "the uttermost parts of the earth" to see and converse with the King, and obtain some of the knowledge he possessed.

The magnificence of the Queen's audience with King Solomon and her convincing arguments in favor of the right of women to be instructed in wisdom, are fully set forth in this degree.

True Kindred

This is an adoptive degree, formerly much practiced in the south and west. Its authorship is unknown and its lady recipients are the wives, widows, mothers, sisters, and daughters of Master Masons in good standing. It is founded upon the touching record of the piety, submission, and filial tenderness of Ruth, as recorded in the Gospel by that name. As mentioned at the beginning of this chapter, the Eastern Star does not recognize any degrees claiming to be independent Orders, and this one is not recognized in any jurisdiction, unless possibly New Jersey and New York. Several Grand Chapters have forbidden Eastern Star members to belong to them and at the meeting of the Grand Chapter of Wyoming, 1909, an order was issued declaring "All Orders, or so-called Orders, which base their membership, in whole or in part, upon membership in the Order of the Eastern Star, which have or may hereafter, invade the jurisdiction of this Grand Chapter, are hereby declared to be clandestine, and all Eastern Star members, holding membership in said Order or so-called Orders of 'The True Kindred of Masonry,' are hereby required to cease membership therein within sixty days from the date hereof, or be subject to expulsion for conduct unbecoming a member of this Order, in refusing or failing to obey the above mandate of the Grand body."

Ark and Dove

An adoptive degree formerly much practiced in the United States. Its emblems are the Dove; Olive Branch, Rainbow, and Ark. As to the origin of this degree, nothing is known.

The Cross and Crown

It was the original plan of Brother Robert Macoy to make the Queen of the South the second and the Cross and Crown the third degree in the Adoptive Rite, and to this end he worked out, in 1875, a carefully arranged degree, but it failed to enlist the interest of the intelligent members. It was to be worked out by Chapter officers in a body called a Court, the point officers forming a cross instead of a star. The degree consisted of the brief mention of five American women who had been foreign missionaries; the presentation of five objections to Masonry on behalf of the women and their refutation by the Patron; the mention of four great crosses in human life; and the application of five religious graces — piety, friendship, resignation, truth, and constancy. The ritual was illustrated with banners for the five divisions of the degree, which covered the baptism, temptation, agony, crucifixion, and ascension of the Savior. It would require a great amount of ingenuity to take this disconnected material and work it all into one harmonious degree which could invite the favorable decision of the intelligent members. It might therefore have been expected that failure would result.

At the Grand Chapter meeting of Mississippi in 1877, it authorized its subordinate Chapters to confer this degree, "The Cross and Crown."

STAR AND CROSS, OR PREPARATORY WORK

This is a composition consisting of scriptural recitations and marches, written by Brother S. Clark, Past Patron of Radiant Chapter No. 35, of New York, and was published in 1876. The purpose is best expressed in the language used in its preface as follows:

With the restoration of the Adoptive Rite under the names of the Eastern Star the figure of the Savior was presented in the symbol of the Star of Bethlehem, but the teaching of the Great Master was omitted. It resembled the clay image ere immortal breath had quickened it. This little work which is added are the words and teachings of Him of whom the Star is the Symbol and is calculated and intended to prepare the mind of the initiated for a proper reception of the ritual. It not only, by due solemnity, prepares the mind for a proper reception of the main work, but is also calculated to impress it with the beauty and truth of the sacred scriptures, by planting the germ, which will only require culture, to ultimate in purity of life, by leading the votary the true path to heaven and a blessed immortality.

CROMBIE'S RITUAL

John Crombie, at one time an active Mason and Grand Warden of the Grand Lodge of Scotland, published a blue lodge ritual, which he was ordered to recall, and not doing so he was suspended from the Fraternity. Subsequently he issued rituals of other rites, including *Crombie's Ritual of the Order of the Eastern Star*, and under the title of the Supreme Council of Rites he chartered Chapters, first at Aberdeen, Scotland, and subsequently at other points, but it is believed that none survived except at Aberdeen and Dundee.

Crombie's *Ritual* was an arrangement of the work for the use of the Order of the Eastern Star in Scotland and was compiled from Dr.

Rob Morris's *Manual of the Adoptive Rite* and was not well adapted to the work in an organized body. In it provision was made for the Worthy Patron at the left of the Worthy Matron except when presiding at the ceremonies of the rite, when he is on her right. The prayer is offered by the Worthy Matron, who continues with a portion of each star point as it was given in the *Manual* intended for the lecture form of the degrees and poorly adapted to use in organized Chapters. Upon entering the room the first time the Conductress escorts the candidate directly to the Worthy Matron and when seated in front of the Worthy Matron's station, the Worthy Patron gives a lecture which includes much of the address that was contained in the *Manual* which was written solely for the communicating of the degrees in lecture form; and since the other portions of the work were arranged to be rendered by the star officers, this lecture was not well adapted to the communicating of the degrees. At each of the star points, the candidate is caused to be seated while the lecture is given by the star officer and closes with a poetical tribute to the one whose life is exemplified in the lecture. This is the tribute to Jephthah's Daughter:

> See 'midst the multitude the victim stands!
>   Dauntless, serene, though terror palsies them!
> And she must die by her own father's hand!
>   And she must die a sacrifice of shame!
> Of shame! ah, no! she flings the veil abroad,
> Once, twice, yea thrice: looks hopefully to God;
> Fixes the noonday sun with earnest eyes,
> Then crowned with innocence, the maiden dies!
>
> Lament for Jephthah, ye who know his fate,
>   Weep and lament: "Broken the beautiful rod,
> And the strong staff; Mizpeh is desolate!"
>   But for the sweet Adah weep not; let the word
> Be: "joy to the Captive, freed from earthly dust

Joy for one witness more to woman's trust,
And lasting honor, Mizpeh, be the strain
To her who died in light without a stain!"

The lecture of Martha follows more nearly and completely the account as given in the Scriptures than other ritualistic versions of this degree, and in this particular is worthy of comment. The following is taken from the rendering of the lecture:

The family, composed of two sisters, Martha and Mary, with their brother Lazarus, seem to have possessed all things needful for a happy life. Bound up in the love for each other and blessed with the friendship of Him whom to know is everlasting life, the little group was distinguished from their neighbors by a name that proved how thoroughly their hearts were occupied with divine things. They were "the beloved of the Master, the happy household of Bethany."

Upon an occasion when their Divine guest had gone out, beyond the Jordan, upon a mission of charity, Lazarus was taken suddenly and violently ill. The terrified sisters hastened to inform Jesus of the fact by a messenger, who was instructed to say, "Lord, behold he whom Thou lovest is sick!" They reasonably supposed that so tender a missive could not fail of success. But the Savior returned an ambiguous reply. The "Beloved at Bethany" died and was buried. Four days passed, days shrouded with mourning, still the Savior returned not. The sisters were abandoned in grief, not alone for the loss of their brother, their only earthly protector, but for the unkindness of Him upon whom they had leaned as the "Rock of their salvation." Yet Martha retained her faith and trusted in Him yet to come and restore the friend they had lost. . .. "Lord, if Thou hadst been here my brother had not died!" Looking a moment after into His face, animated by the God-like benignity with which He looked down upon her, she added: "But I know, that even now, whatsoever Thou wilt ask of God, God will give it Thee!"

Amazing faith! heroic spirit of confidence in her friend I though her brother had been four days in the embrace of death, and the subject of its corrupting influences — though the weight of watchfulness and sorrow rested heavily upon her spirit as she knelt, her hands wildly raised to heaven — there was a spirit of prophecy in her words which gave them a value altogether their own. . . .. The reward of such faith was soon rendered. Taking her by the hand, and passing by their dwelling, where they were joined by Mary, they went to the sepulchre, and there "Jesus wept." After ordering the stone to be taken away, He lifted up His eyes, and said: "Father, I thank Thee that Thou hast heard Me. And I knew that Thou hearest Me always; but because of the people which stand by I said it, that they may believe that Thou hast sent Me." And when He had thus spoken, He cried with a loud voice, "Lazarus, come forth!" And he that was dead came forth, bound hand and foot with grave clothes; and his face was bound about with a napkin. Jesus saith unto them, "Loose him and let him go."

The recognition work is given by the Worthy Matron and differs quite materially from that arranged by the General Grand Chapter for the use of its members, and which is by that body directed to be given by the Worthy Patron.

Tatem's Monitor of the Eastern Star

This is a ritual compiled by John H. Tatem for the use of the Order in Michigan and was arranged largely from Morris's *Mosaic Book* and Morris's *Manual* with some additions and variations of giving the lectures. The title of female members of this rite is Stellae; that of male members, Protectors. In the chapter relating to the object, it is stated that "The business of the Lodge is to act upon petitions; to initiate; to dispense charity and sympathy; to confer the degree of the Eastern Star and communicate the lectures of the same; to exercise discipline; likewise to take all proper measures for cultivating peace and harmony, and extending the Christian principles of morality and love among the members. Finally, to aid in the important work of extending the benefits of the American Adoptive Rite to every community where there are persons entitled to receive it."

The officers were named Worthy President (Matron), Vice President (Patron), First Patron (Adah), Second Patron (Ruth), etc., Secretary, Treasurer, Conductor, Guard, and Sentinel.

Tatem's Monitor was first to introduce the manner of communicating the Cabalistic Motto and word in the manner used, with very little change, as it is used at the present time. Much of the work was given by initial letters only, without any other key as to what the matter intended was, and it was necessary to have long instruction from the enlightened in order to make proper use of this ritual. The dialogues as used in the Mosaic Book were retained, also the vacant chairs, but the dialogues were somewhat abbreviated. The instruction is given that "a Mason, on seeing one of these signs given, shall write his name on a card, or slip of paper, together with the pass belonging to the sign given." Introductory remarks for the initiation contain the following:

> The ceremonial of initiation into the American Adoptive Rite is not reckoned a Degree, but rather a mental preparation and trial of the temper and spirit of the applicants, preparatory to their being favored with the full light of the adoption. One week's time must be given between the initiation and the degree, save whereby a vote of the lodge, permission for a more rapid advancement is given. . ... The applicant, if a lady, being elected and in waiting, a communication to that effect is made by the Sentinel, the Vice President [Patron] then retires to the anteroom with the

petition in his hand, introduces himself to the candidate as an official member of the lodge and thus addresses her: . . . The Society of Adoptive Masonry is a society of Christians. None enter our ranks save those who believe that Jesus Christ is the Son of God, the Redeemer of the World, and the Almighty Savior. We teach no lessons, but such as relate to Him. We make no prayers but through His holy name. We entertain no religious hopes but those which are founded upon His Birth, Life, Death, Resurrection and Ascension. . . . As a large portion of our work as Adoptive Masons lies in acquiring the doctrines and temper of Jesus Christ, whom truly to love is everlasting life. We often unite to address the Heavenly Throne and to plead with God that the very spirit of faith and wisdom may descend upon us and make our meeting place a place like Heaven.

The beautiful Masonic tradition which has left for our benefit the story of Electa is quoted from *Tatem's Monitor* in part as follows:

The last of these five female characters, whose virtues and misfortunes make up the glory of the Eastern Star, is Electa. No account of this celebrated woman is given in the scriptures; we are entirely indebted for what we know of her to Masonic tradition. Her husband's name was Gaius, and he was long *Grand Master of Masons,* in which situation he was succeeded by the illustrious John the Evangelist. Electa had been reared up amongst a heathen people, and like the rest, had been taught to worship idols, in which faith she had reared her children. But happening by good chance to hear a discourse from the Christian missionary, Paul, she, with her husband and all her family, yielded their faith in Him whose gospel was so powerfully imparted to them, and they became Christians. . . . The Masonic influence which her husband so largely shared, made friends amongst those who would otherwise have persecuted them; and although they were often scourged and pointed at as the followers of a crucified Savior, yet no other evil befell them.

In adopting the Christian religion, Electa adopted all the virtues and graces that flow out of it. To spend her large income in relieving the poor; to devote much of her time to the care of the sick; to keep an open house for indigent and hungry travelers — she was ripening daily for a better world. Her children growing around were hers as well by faith in Christ as by the ties of blood. . .. A band of soldiers soon found their way through those doors so long opened for the entrance of the poor and distressed; but the captain of the band was a Freemason, and most loth to injure one of whose good deeds he had heard so much.

The Michigan Ritual

The Grand Lodge of Michigan had a revision of the *Tatem's Monitor* printed, about 1875, for the use of its subordinate Chapters. Much of the work represented by initials in the *Monitor* was represented by asterisks in the ritual, while the lectures of the five heroines were a reproduction of the former publication, which was, at that time, out of print. "The benefits of this rite are mainly to the female sex. For them this temple has been reared, and these walls set up. They are its glory and crown; and its value consists in the spirit with which they enter it, and the grace they throw around it."

The California Ritual

The Grand Chapter of California was organized in 1873, at which time a committee was appointed and very soon prepared a ritual giving ceremonies for opening the Chapter, conducting its business, forms of initiation, closing the Chapter, and installing the officers of subordinate Chapters. In 1875 a committee was appointed to revise the ritual and abbreviate the ceremonies of initiation so far as it can be done and retain the sense or value of the work. The responses of the Star Point officers found in the New York Ritual of the Adoptive Rite revised were adopted for the use of the subordinate Chapters.

In the revised edition the special form for the initiation of Master Masons was omitted. The following is taken from the revised ritual of 1877: "All the lady officers wear collars consisting of the five colors of the star — blue, yellow, white, green, and red; the red on the outer edge. The five officers of the star should wear sashes and aprons, corresponding in color with that of the point represented by them. The aprons (worn by the sisters only) are five-sided, each side measuring twelve inches, the upper one cut out to fit the waist. The point of the bib reaches to the center of the apron, and both are trimmed with the five colors. The color of the apron is white and the braid for trimming is worsted, one-quarter inch wide. The color on the outer edge is red, then green, white, yellow and blue."

The password was required to be given to the Conductress or the Associate Conductress as the case may be, by all visiting members. "The password is changed annually and can only be given to Sisters by the Worthy Matron, and to Brothers by the Worthy Patron of the Chapter, or such persons as they may authorize to communicate it. But such officers can ONLY communicate it, or cause it to be communicated, to members of their own Chapter, and must satisfy themselves that the Sister or Brother is in good standing before investing them or causing them to be invested with it. No other member is permitted to give it to another, in any place, and under any circumstances, the possession of the password being the proof of a member's good standing."

Five blows of the gavel are directed to call up the Chapter instead of the number directed by the General Grand Chapter *Ritual*.

The beautiful charge given to the Treasurer in the installation ceremony may well be quoted: "My Sister, the proper preservation of our funds demands the utmost honesty and care upon the part of the

Treasurer. In the eye of God the money that is in your hands represents so much food, clothing and medicine, which belong to the widows and orphans whom God may, at the most unexpected moment, send us as objects of our bounty."

After the Marshal has presented the five rays of the central star, for the installation by the retiring Worthy Patron, the Marshal is directed to cause the sisters to form the floral center of the bright star. This is done by causing each sister to stand on her appropriate color and facing the altar. The five sisters then place their right hands together over the altar, raising them to the height of their heads. Each sister should have a bouquet of flowers of the appropriate colors, which, when placed together, form the floral star. While this position is retained, the installing officer says: "My Sisters, you are the floral center of this Chapter, and as the various flowers which your colors represent, illuminated by that great light, the Holy Scriptures, teach us the lessons of undying love, unending possession, heart purity, undeviating sincerity, and unfading beauty, so are represented in you the most charming, the most pathetic, and the most instructive lessons of the Old and New Testament. . ... The truly sublime virtues exemplified in the lives of those you represent are worthy of all imitation, and as you teach those virtues *in* the Chapter, so I trust will you practice them *out* of it."

MEMORIAL SERVICE — CHAPTER OF SORROW

This addendum, designed for public use and intended to create the best impression upon non-members, was published in 1888 by Mrs. Addie C. S. Engle, Past Grand Matron of Connecticut. The author dedicated this volume to Rob Morris, LL.D., Patriarch of the Eastern Star, in the following impressive lines:

> The harp which late so sweetly rang
>   Hangs stringless now and still;
> The master wakes its chords no more
>   Obedient to his will.
>
> Oh, who shall strike again that lyre
>   And sing our Order's weal?
> Who follow in his steps, and to
>   Our vows be ever leal
>
> The cause he loved he honored well,
>   Its light he followed far;
> Death's gloomy vale was all illumed
>   By Bethlehem's Holy Star.
>
> To chant with joy Redemption's song
>   May voice to him be given,
> The song of Moses and the Lamb,
>   The melody of heaven

At the assembly of the General Grand Chapter in 1889 the Most Worthy Grand Patron included in his address the following:

    I call your attention to a recently published memorial service, entitled Chapter of Sorrow of the Order of the Eastern Star, composed and arranged by Sister Addie C. S. Engle. As indicated by its name, it is intended as a service, supplemental to the prescribed funeral ceremonies, in commemoration of those who, year by year, are taken by the stem reaper, Death, and is designed for use in the Chapter room. It is a very beautiful form of service and is worthy of being used in every Chapter when it is desired to do honor to the memory of our deceased members. I most heartily commend it to you and recommend its use in every Chapter of the Order.

During the progress of the business of the 1889 assembly, the report of the committee on revision of ritual was adopted as follows:

> We have reviewed the memorial service, Chapter of Sorrow of the Order of the Eastern Star as arranged by Mrs. Engle. We do most heartily indorse it as being all we could desire, both in beauty and expression, and take pleasure in recommending its use to the Order.

The service has been officially adopted by many Grand Chapters both for their own use and by such of the subordinate Chapters as may desire to do honor to their deceased members. It provides for the opening ceremony for each officer, differing from the ritual and especially calling the attention of the listener to the intention of the meeting, eulogies, prayers, the forming of a floral star surrounded by a wreath, which, with a number of other appropriate emblems, are deposited upon a memorial shrine during the progress of the ceremony.

> The weary labyrinth of earth
>   Has fewer hopes than fears.
> Our path, e'en from our very birth,
>   Is crowded oft with tears.
> We clasp the warm fraternal hand
>   Of friends we love and trust,
> And lo! they've reached the shadow land,
>   Leaving with us but dust.
>
> Have we but Martha's earnest faith
>   To lo! the funeral gloom,
> We gain the victory over death
>   Through Him who burst the tomb.
> Christ points us to that city fair,

High walled, with pearly gate,
Within the many mansions there
His ransomed children wait.

We then will trust, for His dear sake—
Till faith be lost in sight—
That those who sleep in Jesus, wake
In God's eternal light.
His Star we see, Lord, let us come
With those who've gone before,
To worship Him and rest at home,
Where partings are no more.

MEMORIAL SERVICE

Sister Elvira Adams Atwood, Grand Chaplain of Michigan, arranged an elegant and impressive memorial service for the Grand Chapter of Michigan in 1909, which has been used by more than twenty States:

They are no more! No more shall we hear the voices of the Sisters and Brothers who have fallen in life's battle during the year that is past. They have entered upon the sleep that knows no waking. Let us, with loving reverence, assemble around our altar to pay honor to their memory; and from the borne wherein they know no travail, may they be conscious of the esteem in which we hold them.

• • • • • • • •

Let us, dear Sisters, in loving remembrance, place these evergreens around our Altar, emblematical of our trustful faith and hope of the immortality of the soul, and the realization of our everlasting happiness beyond the grave. May these ferns remind us that where "dust to dust returneth," arises the beautiful earth flowers with their delicate perfume;

> "Emblems of our great resurrection,
> Emblems of the bright and better land!"

for death is but the initiation into an eternal life, where the soul into perfection blossoms.

As arranged, this service embraces prayers, hymns, responsive parts for all officers, directions for draping the Altar, and diagram of floor work as intended to be rendered.

The Floral Work

Brother Alonzo J. Burton, of New York, arranged a beautiful ceremony under this title, designed to be rendered by ten officers, which includes some of the secret work; if given in public, this portion of the composition is omitted. Many appropriate vocal selections are included. The work was rearranged by John N. Bunnell, Past Grand Patron of New Jersey, and was further revised and arranged and published by Sister Lorraine J. Pitkin, Past Most Worthy Grand Matron and now Right Worthy Grand Secretary, and since this publication it has been adopted by many Grand Chapters and has been widely used. The floral march usually accompanies the rendering of the work, as also the candidate is presented with appropriate flowers from each of the star officers and from the Associate Conductress. The floral emblems of the Eastern Star are nature's smiles, wrought from her own hues and materials, and are monitors of truth and loving kindness. They delight the eye, gratify the sense, and are eloquent teachers of purity and love. In the ritual of our Order, they suggest, through their graceful forms and beautiful colors, fragrance and beauty, the womanly graces and brave lessons of our heroines.

The blue takes its tint from the cerulean sky beneath which the mountain maid spent the happy days of her youth. The yellow borrows its golden tint from the glowing sun above, and the ripening grain beneath, between which throbbed the faithful heart of the Widow of Moab. The white suggests that dignity which the heroic Queen so cheerfully laid aside to preserve God's chosen people from extinction. The evergreen leads the chastened spirit through and beyond the grave, to all that is animating in the thought of a glorious resurrection. The red directs our thoughts to the charity and hospitality inculcated in all teachings of the Order.

> In virtue's path my way shall be,
>   Among the flowers rarest;
> And all I am and all I be,
> A sister's love shall prove in me,
> By yon bright star that reigns above
> Through weary labyrinth I rove,
> I'll faithful be, and strive to prove,
>   Among the thousand fairest.

The Star Of Bethlehem — A Christmas Service

This is a service compiled by Mrs. Helen H. Stires, Past Grand Matron of Nebraska. As originally intended, it was for the use of her local Chapter during her official work as Worthy Matron and gave interest and enthusiasm to the work of the year. Having been rendered by a number of Chapters on the first Sunday following Christmas and found worthy of the attention and use of the Fraternity, it was adopted by the Grand Chapter of Nebraska and published in 1896. It contains a responsive exercise, elegant and well adapted to the season intended, as recognition of the original "Star in the East"; a number of hymns and prayers. One of the most beautiful passages occurs in the "Commemoration of our Order":

O Lord, our Heavenly Father, we beseech Thee to look upon the members of our Order, wherever they may be throughout the world. Bless us in our going out and coming in. Help us to be faithful, constant, pure, trustful, and fervent, and to have love and charity among ourselves. Enable us to follow the teachings of the Star of Bethlehem, and grant that it may shine upon our pathway through life and be a light to guide us through the dark valley of the shadow of death. Give unto us the blessed hope of immortality, that we may look for the general resurrection of the last day, and the life of the world to come, through our Lord Jesus Christ; at whose second coming in glorious majesty to judge the world, the earth and the sea shall give up their dead, and the corruptible bodies of those who sleep in Him shall be changed and made like unto His own glorious body.

The Vocal Star

Though the title selected by Sister Addie C. S. Engle would indicate this to be a musical production, it is an attempt to give the star of our Chapter a voice by types and symbols and emblems and flowers. It was written for the Past Grand Matrons of Michigan and was first rendered by them before that Grand body in 1890. The author outlines the object sought in her introductory as follows:

In the inception of the Order of the Eastern Star some imagery was used in its ritualistic work which has not been retained in the present initiatory ceremony. Those who remember the well-loved symbolism, and regret its omission, will welcome this attempt to preserve some of it from oblivion, and the author cheerfully acknowledges her indebtedness to the old Mosiac work; to the ritual of Adoptive Masonry as formerly used in Michigan; to the Connecticut Addenda, and to the first ritual of the General

Grand Chapter, whose explanation of the resemblance between the language of the emblematic flowers and the heroines they represent had been too carefully made to be entirely lost. The balance is original with her who, being earnestly engaged in the work when these various figures were used, has treasured them in her heart through many changes, and with a simple arrangement of her own, now offers them for the enjoyment of others.

In connection, the "Vocal Star March" is usually rendered, wherein a number of beautiful figures and appropriate letters are formed. The closing is a poem given as follows:

> Accept now, dear friends, as we part here tonight,
>   Our wish that the bright Vocal Star
> May cheer you through life with its radiance bright;
>   And pierce every gloom from afar.
> The Star in the East with its lesson fraught ray,
>   If taken at once for our guide,
> Shall lighten each lab'rinth we meet on life's way,
>   And comfort, whatever betide.
>
> Its five radiant beams earth's dim pathway shall gild,
>   Its blue shall combine with its gold,
> Its red and its green with rich treasures be filled,
>   All teaching the same Gospel old;
> And when their rich lessons, our spirit shall con,
>   We then learn this truth (strangely odd)
> That all the colors our souls must put on,
>   To make up the white light of God!

Magic Lantern and Monitor

Brother Kimball Sedgwick, of Sunbury, Ohio, published a monitor which was indorsed by the Grand Chapter of Ohio in 1898. This was a beautiful lecture, formed largely from extracts taken from the poetical compositions of Dr. Rob Morris, Sister Addie C. S. Engle, Sister Susanna C. Russell, and other hymns of the Order, and is used in explaining the lantern slides illustrating the work of the Order. In 1899 the degrees were conferred upon the superintendent of the Masonic Home and his wife, at the Grand Chapter meeting in Ohio, at which time the monitor lectures were given by the author while there were shown by magic lantern slides illustrations of the different scenes of the degrees. The portraits of many of the leading members of the Order were included in the publication.

Souvenir Star Songs

This is a collection of O.E.S. songs, composed by Sister Elvira Adams Atwood, published in 1911, each one arranged for some special occasion and dedicated to various prominent members of the Order.

Many were written by request, to be sung upon a special occasion, and the beauty of sentiment expressed, together with the rare poetic value of this series of songs, has given them a much-deserved recognition throughout the O.E.S. fraternity.

> Wise men in far Judea,
>   Saw in the sky,
> Lo! there the Star appear,
>   Glowing on high.
> Bring now the myrrh and gold,
>   For they the sign behold,
> That leadeth them afar;
>   Lo! there the Star!

The Guiding Star and Floral Offering

Mrs. Mary T. Molyneau, Past Grand Matron of Minnesota, first published this ceremony in 1903. In its poetical responses are arranged for each officer, combining in an impressive and elegant manner with the flowers emblematic of each of the heroines of the Order.

The Blue is spoken by the Conductress as she holds a bunch of violets in her hand, as follows:

Tell me why; when I lift these blossoms, blue —
They still seem to whisper — be true! be true!
Perhaps when Heaven — to them their color brought —
With its reflected hue — it bestowed the thought.

At night, when the cloud veil is lifted on the wings of the breeze—
And I — the auspicious moment, do most eagerly seize,
To direct my gaze through the azure depths — afar — afar
Beyond the seeming limit — of the rays of the guiding star —
I find nothing there to obstruct my sight —
And I inwardly cry — More light! More Light!
But the failure to win, lies not above,
When Divinity within, seeks its source, of love;
'Tis found in this mortal cage, and the spirit, like the captive dove —
When the earthly bars are broken, will soar to its home — above.

As the gaze finds no obstruction, on its way through the azure blue,
These flowers seem to say to me — neither will you —
If while this earthly pathway-you are striving to pass through —
You take to heart, the lesson — unto thyself — be true.

God chose the Star to point out "the Way — the Truth — the Life" — the Christ, and ever since, to all those who catch a ray of its light, comes the desire to follow its guiding. It is fitting that this symbolic Star should point to the way to be traversed — the truths to be learned — in seeking the inner life.

The ceremony also includes a drill in which the point emblems are formed with elaborate marches, etc., and tableau scenes connected with the heroines of the Order.

Draping the Altar is a memorial service written by Sister Addie C. S. Engle, published in 1908, to be used as a brief ceremonial in Grand and subordinate Chapters.

Chapter of Sorrow is the title given to a publication by Brother Charles C. Dike, Past Grand Patron of Massachusetts, published in 1886.

Funeral Ceremony, Golden Gate Chapter No. 1, of San Francisco, published a funeral ceremony in which the principal part was given to the Worthy Matron. The first portion was arranged to be given in the Chapter room and concluded at the grave, where the floral star was deposited in the grave.

The Mystic Tie is the title of a ceremony arranged by Sister Addie C. S. Engle, designed to be used for the reception of Grand officers and other distinguished guests. In the rendition of the work, the teachings of the jewels of the Order are impressively indicated and a series of beautiful marches by sixteen officers shows the formation of the star, cross, and square.

The Sisterhood Degree is a degree adopted by the Grand Chapter of New York, as written by Alonzo J. Burton. It was intended to follow the degrees of the Eastern Star. The life of Mary, the mother of Jesus, was taken as the foundation of the degree, with symbolic teachings of Faith, Hope, and Charity.

The Matron's Administrative Degree, written by Brother Robert Macoy, is so arranged that it properly is conferred upon Worthy Matrons before installation or very soon after installation, in an administrative council composed of Past Patrons and Past Matrons. The story, as taken from the Scriptures, is to symbolize the value of strong faith in a single woman as it may benefit a nation, as shown by the narrative of Deborah and Barak.

The Floral Tribute was published in 1903 by Sister Hattie C. Derthick, P.G.M. of Michigan, to be used in presenting flowers to candidates after initiation.

The Star of Light was published by Sister Lizzie C. Beller in 1898. Each of the star points is given impressively — the first a poetic composition entitled "The Blue Veil" developing the sublime lesson of Fidelity; the second poem gives the example of Constancy as "Ruth, the Gleaner"; the third or wife's lesson of faithfulness to kindred and friends is given in the poem, "The Signet of Solomon"; the sister's faith is a prose composition, "If a Man Die, Shall He Live Again?"; followed by the — last symbol of a mother's love in a wonderful poem, "The Red Rose."

The Pilgrims is a ceremony published by Sister Ella A. Bigelow and so arranged that it can be rendered publicly. It is to be presented by seven pilgrims clothed in black and five officers. It is in poetical form, beautified by a number of musical numbers.

The Guiding Light is a poetical composition by Sister Julia C. Tenney, presenting the impressive lessons of the Order in a different form, with a special part for the various officers.

Decoration Ceremony, by Sister Julia C. Tenney, is designed as a memorial to be given at the graves of the beloved dead and is written in a poetical manner.

CHAPTER IV

Organization of the General Grand Chapter [1]

THE preliminary steps leading to the organization of the General Grand Chapter of the Order of the Eastern Star are fully explained in the following:

The Grand Chapter of Mississippi, at its session held in Tupelo, July 15, 1875, adopted the following:

Whereas, We deem uniformity of rituals and lectures essential to the present and future prosperity of the Order; therefore we respectfully recommend that a committee, consisting of seven members of this Grand Chapter, of which committee the Grand Patron and Grand Matron shall be members, shall be appointed to confer with like committees that may hereafter be appointed by other Grand Chapters of the Order in the United States, or elsewhere, whose duty it shall be to take under advisement, and present, if practicable, some feasible and judicious plan for the organization of a Supreme Grand Chapter; which said Supreme Body shall, when organized and recognized by two-thirds of the Grand Chapters in the United States, have absolute and supreme control over the Ritual and lectures of the Adoptive Rite. We also recommend that said committee shall be the accredited delegates from this Grand Jurisdiction to a convention of the Order wheresoever and whensoever convened, and they shall have all power and authority to do any and all acts necessary and lawful to be done in the premises; and they shall report their doings to this Grand Chapter at each Annual Grand Convocation.

---

[1] John M. Mayhew, president; John R. Parsons, secretary; Rev. John D. Vincil, chaplain.

The delegates then appointed were: Mrs. Annie T. Clark, Grand Matron; Mrs. Laura L. Burton, P.G.M.; Mrs. Mary I. Hunter, P.G.M.; Mrs. C. M. Barton, P.G.M.; J. L. Power, G.P.; A. H. Barkley, D.G.P.; P. M. Savery, G.L.

At its session, held in Vallejo, October 19, 1875, the Grand Chapter of California adopted the following:

Resolved, That the Grand Chapter constitute a committee of seven, of which the Worthy Grand Patron and Worthy Grand Matron shall be members, to confer with like committees that may hereafter be appointed by other Grand Chapters of the Order in the United States. It shall be their duty to take under advisement, and present, if practicable, some feasible and judicious plan for the organization of a Supreme Grand Chapter, which Supreme Body shall, when organized and recognized by two-thirds of the Grand Chapters of the Order in the United States, have absolute and supreme control over the Ritual and lectures of the Order.

Resolved, That said committee be the accredited delegates from this Grand Jurisdiction to a convention of the Order wheresoever and whensoever convened, have power to do any and all acts necessary and lawful to be done in the premises, and report their doings to this Grand Chapter at each Annual Communication.

Resolved, That the Grand Patron be requested to submit, or cause to be submitted, the action of this Grand Chapter to each and all sister Grand Chapters in the United States, and respectfully solicit their zealous co-Operation.

At the session of the same body, held in San Francisco, October 17, 1876, it was

Resolved, That this Grand Body cordially accept the invitation of the Grand Chapter of the State of Indiana to send seven delegates to a Supreme Grand Chapter to be holden in the city of Indianapolis in November next.

Resolved, That the retiring Grand Patron, Bro. J. E. Whitcher, the retiring Grand Matron, Sister Emily Rolfe, the Grand Patron-elect, Bro. Jerome Spaulding, the Grand Matron-elect, Sister Ada A. Libbey, the Grand Secretary-elect, Abbie E. Wood, the Grand Associate Patron-elect, John C. Marsh, and the Grand Associate Matron-elect, Elizabeth Sweasey, be such delegates.

Resolved, That the delegates present at such Grand Council cast the votes of absentees.

The Grand Chapter of Indiana, at its session in Greencastle, April 6, 1876, took the following action:

Whereas, Uniformity of work, modes of recognition, and regulations governing eligibility to membership are not only desirable, but absolutely necessary to the permanent growth and prosperity of our Order, now so rapidly increasing in numbers, and advancing in the estimation of the Masonic Fraternity; and

Whereas, Several Grand Chapters recognizing this necessity, have appointed committees to represent and act for them in a convention to be thereafter called to organize such a body, but have failed to take any steps which will lead to the calling of such a convention, and this Grand Chapter, realizing the importance of speedy and definite action which will lead to so desirable an end; therefore, be it

Resolved, That all Grand Chapters of the Order, be invited and requested to appoint seven delegates, of which the Grand Patron and Grand Matron shall be, ex-officio, two, with full power to do any and all acts necessary to be done in the premises for and in behalf of their respective Grand Chapters, to meet in convention, for the purpose of organizing a Supreme Chapter, at Indianapolis, at 10 o'clock on Wednesday, the eighth day of November next.

Resolved, That the Grand Patron appoint a committee of three brothers and two sisters to act in conjunction with the Grand Patron and Grand Matron, as delegates from this Grand Chapter to such convention.

Resolved, That the said delegates be appointed the committee of this Grand Chapter to submit a copy of the foregoing preamble and resolutions to all sister Grand Chapters and request their prompt and zealous co-operation.

Resolved, That said committee be instructed to make all preliminary arrangements necessary for the accommodation of said convention.

Resolved, That the necessary expenses of the said convention, not to exceed one hundred dollars, be paid out of the Grand Treasury: Provided no part thereof shall be expended for mileage.

Mrs. Mary A. Comstock, G.M., Mrs. Sallie J. Evans, Mrs. Mary E. M. Price, James S. M'Nutt; G.P., James A. Thompson, P.G.P., James Crooks, and Willis D. Engle were appointed as delegates.

The Grand Chapter of Missouri, at its session in St. Louis, October 9, 1876,

Resolved, To accept the invitation of the Grand Chapter of Indiana, and to appoint a committee of seven to represent this Grand Chapter in the proposed meeting at Indianapolis, November 16th.

Rev. John D. Vincil, Mary J. Wash, Mattie A. Yost, Frances E. Holden, Thomas C. Ready, P. D. Yost, and John R. Parsons were appointed as such committee.

The Grand Chapter of New Jersey, on October 13, 1875.

Resolved, That five delegates be selected to represent this Grand Chapter at any meeting or convention that may be called for the purpose of organizing a Supreme Grand Chapter of the Order of the Eastern Star.

Organization of the General Grand Chapter

At the session October 11, 1876, of the Grand Chapter of New Jersey, the resolutions of the Grand Chapter of Indiana were received, the invitation accepted, and the following delegates were elected: John M. Mayhew, G.P., Mrs. E. D. Tilden, G.M., George Haskins, W. V. W. Vreeland, Mrs. Anna M. Mayhew, P.G.M., Mrs. E. A. Graul, and Mrs. M. C. Dobbs.

The Grand Chapter of Illinois, at its session October 4, 1876, accepted the invitation of the Grand Chapter of Indiana, and elected Daniel G. Burr, P.G.P., H. R. Kent, G.P., Mrs. Elizabeth Butler, P.G.M., and Mrs. Laura N. Young, G.M., as delegates.

The Grand Chapter of Arkansas, on November 8, 1876, decided that it was not expedient for it to send delegates to the Convention but that it would cooperate in the movement.

Pursuant to the arrangements as set forth in the above resolutions and in accordance with the call of the Grand Chapter of the Order of the Eastern Star in the State of Indiana, the delegates from the Grand Chapters of California, Illinois, Indiana, Missouri, and New Jersey assembled in the Masonic Temple at Indianapolis, on November 15 and 16, 1876.

Brother James S. Nutt, Grand Patron of Indiana, called the convention to order, and Brother John M. Mayhew, of New Jersey, the Senior Grand Patron present, was chosen President, with Brother John R. Parson, of Missouri, Secretary. A committee, consisting of one member from each Grand Jurisdiction represented at the convention, reported a form of constitution which was adopted and the General Grand Chapter organized. Thus, was launched forth, in this assemblage, the beginning of the General Grand Chapter, which has now assumed proportions so great that the respect and love of its members, and the recognition of the world is tendered.

A committee consisting of seven members was appointed to prepare a ritual, which report was submitted at the second session of the General Grand Chapter held in Chicago, May 8-9-10, 1878, and the several Grand Chapters were instructed to continue the use of the rituals then in use until another had been adopted by the General Grand Chapter.

The Most Worthy Grand Patron was authorized to issue dispensations to all subordinate Chapters holding charters, purporting to emanate from a Supreme Grand Chapter, without expense, upon proper application from said Chapters.

The meeting closed with a public installation of officers. The Most Worthy Grand Patron-elect, the Rev. John D. Vincil, was installed by the Most Worthy Grand Patron *pro tem.*, and the Most Worthy Grand Patron then installed Mrs. Elizabeth Butler, M.W.G.M., and the remaining officers.

The Most Worthy Grand Patron was made the executive head; the name of the organization as adopted at the meeting is "The General Grand Chapter of the Order of the Eastern Star." The officers with their titles are: Most Worthy Grand Patron, Most Worthy Grand Matron, Right Worthy Associate Grand Patron, Right Worthy Associate Grand Matron, Right Worthy Grand Treasurer, Right Worthy Grand Secretary, all of whom shall be elected by ballot and shall hold their offices until their successors are elected and installed. All the other officers who are brethren shall be appointed by the M.W.G.P. and all who are sisters shall be appointed by the M.W.G.M.

The powers and authority of the body are given in articles III, IV, and VII of the constitution, quoted below:

> ARTICLE III. — Section 1. The General Grand Chapter shall possess no other power than is expressly delegated to it. It can exercise no doubtful authority or power, by implication merely. All Eastern Star authority not hereby granted to it, is reserved for the Grand Chapters, subordinate Chapters, and their members individually.
>
> Section 2. It shall have and maintain jurisdiction over all Chapters established by itself in any section of any country where there is no Grand Chapter established and have disciplinary power over such Chapters until a Grand

Chapter shall be legally organized and recognized by this General Grand Chapter, and no longer.

Section 3. It shall have power to decide all questions of Eastern Star law, usage and custom which may arise between any two or more Grand Chapters or in any subordinate Chapter under its own immediate jurisdiction, and all that may be referred to it for its decision by any Grand Chapter, and its decision so made shall be regarded as of the Supreme tribunal of the Eastern Star in the last resort

Section 4. It shall be the judge of the qualifications of its own members.

Section 5. It shall adopt and prescribe a uniform Ritual of work, and formula for installation of its own officers, as well as the officers of Grand and subordinate Chapters.

Section 6. All amendments, alterations or additions to the Ritual that shall be promulgated by this General Grand Chapter, must be submitted in writing at a stated meeting, when, if approved by a majority of the members present, shall lie over until the next stated meeting, when if adopted by a two-thirds vote, shall become a part of the same.

ARTICLE IV. — Section 1. The General Grand Chapter shall meet at least once in three years, but may meet oftener if it so orders, at such time and place as shall be fixed upon at its previous meeting.

Section 3. Representatives from a majority of the Grand Chapters under its jurisdiction shall be necessary for a quorum to transact business.

ARTICLE VII. — Section 2. The General Grand Chapter may levy such contributions as in its judgment shall be required, which shall always be uniform in proportion to membership, and which shall not exceed five cents per annum from each paying member.

It is a pleasant thought in this connection, that no tax has yet been levied by the General Grand Body, except that the five jurisdictions which were represented at the organization advanced to the General Grand Chapter treasury two and one-half cents for each member of its subordinates, the same to be applied on their dues, which amount was very cordially paid, amounting to a total of $148.43.

Second Assembly, Chicago, Illinois, May 8-10, 1878 [2]

At the second meeting of the General Grand Chapter, seven Grand Chapters were represented — Illinois with two delegates, Indiana four, Kansas two, Massachusetts one, Michigan two, Missouri one, and New Jersey one, with two past Grand officers entitled to recognition; also, Past Grand Matrons of New York and Connecticut were present as visitors.

The report of the Right Worthy Grand Secretary shows that ten Chapters had been added to the number — five of them having been organized and five Macoy Chapters having exchanged their charters.

The committee, consisting of Thomas M. Lamb, John M. Mayhew, and Willis D. Engle, appointed to prepare a ritual for the use of the members of the Eastern Star, reported their work finished. The result of their strenuous and arduous labors was accepted and their ritual was adopted as the work to be used and adopted in all Grand and subordinate Chapters owing allegiance to the General Grand Chapter; the same to be in full force and operation so soon as printed, and its use enjoined by edict of the Most Worthy Grand Patron.

Let the amended ritual adopted at this meeting be prefaced with a deserving tribute to him whose regard for the welfare of humanity suggested a theory which has developed to be world-wide in its

---

[2] Thomas M. Lamb, M.W.G.P. pro tem.; Mrs. Elizabeth Butler, M.W.G.M.

practice, and unlimited in its results. For more than a century previous to this time, efforts had been made from time to time, by eminent Masons, to establish an order, kindred in design to the Eastern Star; but only partial or temporary success attended their efforts. It remained for Rob Morris to successfully initiate a system of so great promise, not only to the families of Masons, but to the great Brotherhood from whose generous impulses it sprung. May his name be tenderly cherished by all who recognize in this Order a movement for the betterment of the condition of the human family. His efforts were supplemented and largely made successful by the zeal and executive ability of Brother Robert Macoy, of New York, whose labors have brought to him an abundant reward. The Order of the Eastern Star will ever gladly hold these distinguished brothers in grateful remembrance.

The tenets and teachings of the Order of the Eastern Star imply standard virtues and are calculated to lead the initiated to look on his fellow with all the kindliness which charity, in its fullest sense, could suggest. Thank God there are many, very many, strong, noble, devoted souls, who shrink not from labor or sacrifice in their efforts to promulgate principles which incite the human heart to a more perfect love and trust in each other and hasten the fulfilment of the divine mandate, "Love thy neighbor as thy self."

Those who arranged the duties of the M. W. G. Matron were most unwise when they assigned no duty whatever to her during the vacation of the General Grand Chapter, her position during the three years' interval being merely an honorary one. This was an unfair provision, since where both sexes are to be governed, both should have concurrent supervisory duties. The natural keen intuition of woman, her quick perceptive qualities, combined with her strict sense of justice should fit her to be man's equal in this particular at least.

Third Assembly, Chicago, Illinois, August 20-21, 1880 [3]

The third stated meeting of the General Grand Chapter was held in Chicago on August 20-21, 1880. The delegates who were in attendance were the representatives of eleven Grand Chapters and visitors were present from fourteen States. Eleven Chapters had been organized, one Macoy charter had been changed, and two charters issued by the Grand Chapter of New York to Chapters in Maryland and Wyoming had been exchanged, making a total of fourteen Chapters added. There were fourteen Chapters released to form two Grand Chapters, Minnesota on June 28, 1878, and Iowa on July 30, 1878.

Brother Rob Morris was unanimously invited to be present and take part in the proceedings of this session, and he was made an honorary member of the General Grand Chapter. A committee of two was appointed to inform Dr. Morris of the action taken by the General Grand Body, and this action was unanimously concurred in by vote.

Most Worthy Grand Patron, Brother Thomas M. Lamb, in his address, said in part: "I have informally invited to be present upon this occasion, one whom the Order will ever remember as the founder of the Order of the Eastern Star — Brother Robert Morris, LL.D., of La Grange, Kentucky. Our brother is not a Chapter member, nor is he in the ordinary sense a member of the Order; but as its founder he *alone* may occupy the exceptional position of membership in the Order universal. I am assured by the brother that he has watched with deep interest the progress of the Order through the several stages of its growth and regards the organization and success of the General Grand Chapter as evidence of the Eastern Star's ultimate complete triumph. He bids us God-speed and assures me that he will be only too glad to aid us in any way in his power. Such being the case, I am sure that time will only increase the honor with which a grateful Order will remember its founder."

---

[3] Thomas M. Lamb, M.W.G.P.; Mrs. Elmira Foley, M.W.G.M.

Organization of the General Grand Chapter

Accordingly, at the session of the General Grand Chapter held on Saturday afternoon, August 21, 1880, upon the motion of Sister Emily Rolfe, it was ordered that the natal day of Brother Morris, whose birthday is August 31st, be appointed as a festal day of the Order. During the forenoon session of that same date, Brother Morris was invited to a seat in the East, introduced and saluted with the Grand Honors, whereupon he made an address which is of sufficient interest to the members of the Order to be well worthy publication in full, and it is given below:

> *Most Worthy Grand Matron, Officers and Members of the General Grand Chapter:*
>
> I am too tired after my arduous labor in connection with the Triennial Conclave to speak to you as I would like to of the Order as it is, for my heart is full of interest for it. I will say a word of my personal connection with the origin of the Order. Many of the present leading members have expressed surprise at the little interest I seem to have taken in the Eastern Star of late years. For this there have been two reasons: First — My life has been a very active, though not always a successful one; for twelve years I have devoted my time to explorations in the Holy Land, having been abroad twice, and having sent an agent almost every year. This and other things have kept me poor and prevented me giving my time to the Eastern Star. If I had been rich, or my time unoccupied, I would cheerfully have put in practical shape the interest I have always felt for it. The Ritual of 1868 was the last active effort I made for it.
>
> As I have written Brother Lamb, I am satisfied with what has been done by the officers of this Body in the last three years, and that the basis on which the Order now rests is a permanent one.

Second — I have always felt the warmest friendship for Brother Macoy and friendship is a thing not to be broken for slight causes. This friendship has existed for thirty years, and it would take a great deal to break it. I disapprove the course he has taken, and have labored unavailingly, to restrain him. I would never suffer a hard word to sever true friendship, which is of inestimable value, but would bear many things from friends. Others have borne with my faults, and I will bear with theirs. Brother Macoy's course I have. disapproved from the first, although I do not think that he was properly treated at first; yet that does not justify him in the course he has since pursued.

When I was informed of the unexpected honor you have conferred upon me, by electing me an honorary member of your Body, I felt very much complimented. I knew how such a motion was rather outside the law, and I appreciate the delicateness which must have been felt about electing a non-affiliate to honorary membership. In the future you can command me to the extent of my ability.

The idea of forming an *Eastern Star Degree* came to me when I was confined to my house from the effects of an accident, in 1850. For several years I had felt the necessity of some system of what was then called "Lady Masonry." There were several degrees then in existence — such as the Good Samaritan, Heroine of Jericho, the Master Mason's Daughter — but they did not prove successful and the ladies slighted them. In talking the matter over with my wife, she thought these degrees of little value. I thought that as I had been traveling for several years, and had considerable experience and observation, I could do better. So, I set to work and wrought out the whole system, not as it now is, but the basis of what is now. This I first conferred upon my wife and a couple of neighbors, and they pronounced it a success. I see plainly now that if I had given my life to the work, it could have been made a great and world-wide institution. I conferred it for many years and upon many thousand people, but it needed some thorough organization to make it more successful; and to that end, in 1855, Constellations were organized upon a Ritual gotten up at great expense, but it was found that the work was too heavy, it being almost impossible in an average town to get ability to render it properly, so that the movement resulted in utter failure. In two or three years Families were organized, the Manual being used as the Ritual thereof. Though several hundred of these were organized, they very soon failed from exactly the opposite cause that ruined the Constellations. There was not enough of a dramatic nature to make the work interesting. In 1868, Brother Macoy made me a proposition that if I would assist him in getting up a Chapter Ritual, he would furnish the necessary money to make it a success. This was accepted and carried out. Those here from all parts of this broad land need not be told that it is a grand success. I well remember when there were not, in the whole United States, as many Knights Templars as are now embraced in the membership of one Commandery of Chicago. Not until the Triennial meeting at Hartford in 1856, did people look upon Knight Templarism as a success. And what is written of it in the events of the last week! It has passed through difficulties and strifes until it is now a perfect success. If any Grand Chapter has any idea of withdrawing from your Body, as Grand Commanderies did from the General Grand Encampment, I would say to them. "Don't do it. I beg of you." Wait fifteen or twenty years and let the General Grand Chapter have a chance to demonstrate the good that I am sure is in it, and which will result in such a grand success that the Masonic Fraternity will accept it as a helpmeet for it, and be surprised that it did not take it up sooner; for, properly worked out, it will form a grand attachment to Freemasonry. This I felt years ago, and I trust the day will come when every Lodge will have in connection with it, a Chapter of this Order. The more there are the cheaper they can be run, and the more good they can accomplish. I am sorry today that I have not given my own personal attention for thirty years to this matter, and it is with sincere regret that I realize it is too late for me to do the good in it that I could have accomplished if I had begun years ago, but I am glad to know that younger men and women have taken hold of the work with a zeal and wisdom which will assure success; and I say to you: Preserve the Order in unity, frown down all secession; keep the Grand Chapter in rank, for in union there is strength.

When a sister dies, she receives the same honor from the Eastern Star that a brother does from the Fraternity, and the little ones are assured of care from kind friends. It is ridiculous to attempt to exclude women from this good work. For forty years the exclusiveness that kept women out of almost every avenue whereby she might gain a livelihood, has been passing away. Because that in Jerusalem and its vicinity three thousand years ago women were excluded from participating with men in good works is no reason why women today should be kept in exclusion. In the Holy Land no woman goes to school or church. I never saw anything more degrading than a woman's condition in that land. Shall *we* treat woman thus? We educate our daughters better than we do our sons. Shall Masonry push them aside? No, a wife is just as interested in it as a husband and is entitled to rights and privileges to which the Eastern Star enables her to prove her claims.

Now, my kind friends, accept from an old brother and friend his cordial good wishes for the Order's welfare and prosperity; for what it is in my power to do for it you can command me to the utmost. May the blessing of God rest upon you, and hereafter — not in, but beyond the Eastern Star — in those celestial mansions, may we all meet, a united family.

Well may Dr. Morris look with pride upon the result of his noble conception of founding an Order whereby women might become co-workers in the grand aims of their brothers of the Masonic Fraternity, and as it spreads its rays to the uttermost parts of our land, it is well to gratefully celebrate his natal day. The mission of the Order is to relieve distress, administer to the suffering, and carry healing balm to the sorrowing and disconsolate. May the glorious Star, as the life-giving beams of the morning, shining alike through life's vicissitudes in every State of our Union from the Orient to the Occident, from the ice-bound caves of Boreas to the flower-wreathed groves of Auster, glow brighter and brighter to a perfect day — to guide the tempest-tossed as with a beacon light, and gild with ambient luster the very portals of the tomb.

Fourth Assembly, San Francisco, California, August 17-23, 1883 [4]

The fourth meeting of the General Grand Chapter was held in the city of San Francisco, August 17-23, 1883, when twelve Grand Chapters were represented. Twenty-seven Chapters had been organized and two Macoy charters had been exchanged, making a total of twenty-nine. Five Chapters of the jurisdiction of Ontario had been released to form the Grand Chapter of Ontario on May 3, 1882. The withdrawal of the Grand Chapter of New Jersey in October 1880, and its return in 1881, were reported. At this date (1883) the Order was

---

[4] Willis Brown, M.W.G.P.; Mrs. Lorraine J. Pitkin, M.W.G.M.

established in thirty-seven States, Provinces, and Territories, in thirty of which the General Grand Chapter Ritual is the only one used or recognized. With seventeen Grand Chapters and the Order firmly established in thirty-three States and Territories and with the members numbering over 25,000, it was recommended by the Most Worthy Grand Matron that a fund to be known as "Widows' and Orphans' Fund" be established. "Let us increase our revenue, elevate our standard, erect a living monument of charity; contention and strife will be strangers among us; peace and harmony and prosperity will reign supreme. Let us exercise our prerogative as members of the Order for its general good. Let us protect our sisters and brothers as far as truth, honor, and justice shall warrant. Let us watch our words that they may speak evil of none; our actions, for they speak louder than words; our thoughts, for with purity of thought our words and actions must be justice, tempered with charity; our conduct, that example may clasp hands with precept; our hearts, for a pure and contrite heart is beyond the tongue of reproach. Let us watch our words, actions, thoughts, conduct, and hearts, proving our fidelity to convictions of right and duty; our obedience to the demands of honor and justice; our loyalty to kindred and friends; our faith in the hour of trial, and our zealous advocacy of the Truth."

A committee was appointed whose duty it was to receive all proposed amendments to the *Ritual* and report upon the same at the next regular meeting of the General Grand Chapter. Two amendments were made to the Constitution at this meeting, which referred to the legally appointed proxies and named the four officers who are entitled to such proxy representation.

The Fifth Stated Assembly, St. Louis, Missouri, September 23-25, 1886 [5]

The fifth meeting was held in St. Louis, Missouri, September 23-25, 1886, ten Grand Chapters being represented. Twenty-nine Chapters had been organized and one Macoy Chapter reorganized, making a total of thirty, while thirteen Chapters had been released to form the Grand Chapter of Texas on July 20, 1884. The address of the Most Worthy Grand Matron includes her report of a visit to Queen Esther Chapter No. 1, at Louisville, Kentucky, which chanced to be the regular meeting at which the presentation of Dr. Rob Morris's name for membership was made, and Dr. Morris was duly accepted and initiated.

At this meeting, the fifth of the General Grand Chapter, Dr. Morris was conducted to the Grand East and saluted with grand honors, after which he addressed the General Grand Body as follows:

> I have no language that will fitly express my thanks for the complimentary introduction you have given me. It is by the favor of Almighty God that I am permitted once more to meet the General Grand Chapter. Ever since the organization of this honorable body in 1876, I have followed its progress with profound interest and ardent prayers for your success. I cannot deny that I was surprised, perhaps mortified, that I was not consulted in the original organization of this Body, seeing that the Eastern Star was strictly a matter of my own conception, it seemed strange to me and to my friends, that when the subject was deemed worthy of a national recognition, that I was not invited to the convention in 1876, though living only four hours distant from the place. This is my answer to the question, a thousand times asked me, why I did not take an interest in the movements

---

[5] Rollin C. Gaskill M.W.G.P.; Mrs. Jennie E. Matthews, M.W.G.M.

of the General Grand Chapter during the first four years of its existence.

But when at Chicago, in 1880, you welcomed me with such honor, made me a life member and even adopted my birthday as the day of your annual festival, then you rolled away the reproach from me. Then you awakened every sentiment of gratitude in my heart. Then I promised you my best efforts in the promotion of the great work in which you are engaged.

I think there are but few delegates present who have not received letters from me in reply to inquiries upon the laws and usages of the Eastern Star. You will bear witness that I always urged you to obey the laws of your Grand and General Grand Chapter, to respect the decisions of the officers set above you and to perform strictly the duties which you voluntarily assumed when you became members of the Eastern Star. When complaints have been made to me I have answered that I am not the executive and have no power to decide questions referred to me. If I have been of any service to you since you elected me a life member six years ago, it has been in the interest of peace, harmony, and submission to law.

As a token of respect, I beg to offer a brief poem written for this occasion: [6]

> If to our world dear lost ones would descend,
> If Ruth and Martha would in kindness bend,
> With Esther and Electa from the sky
> And sanctify our harmony and joy,
>   I think while in these roseate bonds we meet,

---

[6] Lines composed for the convocation of the General Grand Chapter, O.E.S., September, 1886, by Rob Morris, LL.D., Patriarch of the Order.

Our happiness this morning was complete.

So hard is life, so anxious and unsure,
So much there is to combat and endure,
We need a greater than an earthly hope,
To buoy our dull, despondent spirits up;
    Oh God, Thou fountain of all-perfect love,
    Send messengers of comfort from above.

So shall this Conclave of the Eastern Star,
Be like the gatherings where the angels are;
So shall one purpose occupy each heart
And give full consolation e'er we part;
    While every evil thought shall fade away
    And naught remain but one perpetual day.

Brother Morris asked that a committee be appointed to define the power and duties of a life member, which committee reported as follows and the report was adopted:

Your committee to whom was referred the question of the power and privileges of Brother Robert Morris in this General Grand Chapter, respectfully report that the life membership heretofore conferred on Brother Morris by this Grand Body, was honorary alone and did not confer on the said brother the right to vote in this General Grand Chapter. We would recommend that the following resolution be adopted:

> *Resolved*, That Brother Robert Morris be accorded membership in this General Grand Chapter, so far as to allow him to present resolutions and other written documents for its consideration, and also to participate in all discussions.

Jurisdiction was assumed over Mississippi by the Most Worthy Grand Patron, in behalf of the General Grand Chapter, it having developed that the Grand Chapter of that State had become dormant and ceased to exist.

Recognition had been withdrawn from the State of Minnesota, on account of gross violations of Eastern Star law, and a new Grand Chapter had been organized and recognized. This was a matter that provoked much controversy and occupied the attention of the General Grand Chapter for three consecutive meetings and was a disturbing element in the progress of the work in the State of Minnesota for a period of ten years.

The address of the Most Worthy Grand Patron in 1886, was largely devoted to a statement of the Minnesota troubles and his action in the premises, which attempted the abolition of the old Grand Chapter and the assumption of jurisdiction over the Order in that State and the subsequent organization of another Grand Chapter. The first official manifestation of the trouble was in a criticism by the Grand Patron, in his address to the Grand Chapter in 1883, of the work as exemplified in Minneapolis Chapter No. 9, which resulted in a declaration by the Grand Chapter that the work was not an infraction of the Ritual, which was the only action in the matter ever taken by the Grand Chapter. The following year the matter was presented by the Grand Matron in her address, but before action was taken and before the election and other routine business had been disposed of, the Grand Chapter adjourned without appointing a day or date upon which to again reassemble. Then an edict was issued by the Grand Matron dated March 30, 1885, suspending all the officers and members of the Minneapolis Chapter from all the rights and privileges of the Order until the next meeting of the Grand Chapter. The Grand Secretary being a member of No. 9, Minneapolis, on April 7th the Grand Matron issued a notice relieving her of the duties of that office and appointing another sister to fill the vacancy.

Following this came a call for a special meeting of the Grand Chapter, which was held May 13, 1885, and at which all the acts of the Grand Matron were approved and a new corps of officers elected.

At this stage the Most Worthy Grand Patron issued an edict, and when the matter was presented to the General Grand Chapter, it took action as follows:

> *Resolved*, That in his edict of withdrawal of recognition of the Grand Chapter of Minnesota the Most Worthy Grand Patron was justified by the exigencies of the case, and this General Grand Chapter confirms his action.
>
> *Resolved*, That the Most Worthy Grand Patron be authorized to call a convention of all the Chapters in Minnesota claiming to work under the authority of both the so-called Grand Chapters of the State, and that he, in person or by deputy, proceed to that convention and organize a new Grand Chapter, consisting of all the Chapters willing to become members of this new Grand Chapter, and that no other body but the one thus organized be recognized by this General Grand Chapter.

The newly elected Most Worthy Grand Patron accordingly, on October 21st following, issued the call as directed, fixing the time for the meeting November 3, 1886, but before that time he cancelled the same, and later, finding it to be for the best interests of all concerned to do so, issued an edict requiring all Chapters to recognize the original Grand Chapter, and restoring recognition to the same on March 25, 1887, to take effect within ninety days thereafter.

At the meeting of the General Grand Chapter in 1889 this action was confirmed, and all Chapters in the State were ordered to make report and pay dues to said Grand Chapter under penalty of forfeiture of all rights, and in compliance herewith, on the 25th day of June, 1887, full recognition was effected and this action was confirmed. The Minnesota Grand Chapter was ordered to receive such Chapters as made reports and paid dues into full membership, under penalty of a withdrawal of recognition of the Grand Chapter. The Grand Chapter failing to comply with these conditions, recognition was withdrawn April 14, 1891, and at the meeting of the General Grand

Chapter in 1892 what was known as Grand Chapter No. 2 was recognized as the only Grand Chapter of Minnesota. By the tactful and conservative administration and the support of the leading members of the Order in both divisions, a consolidation of all bodies under one head and the recognition thereby of all Chapters and past Grand Officers, was effected May 10, 1894, since which time peace and harmony have prevailed.

At this meeting it was ordered that "The jewels of a Grand Chapter be the emblems within a star, or triangle, within a pentagon. That the jewels of the General Grand Chapter be the emblems within a star, or a triangle, within a circle." At a later meeting by the adoption of the Revised Ritual in 1889, the jewels of the General Grand Chapter were made like those of a Grand Chapter, with the addition of an outer circle.

SIXTH ASSEMBLY, INDIANAPOLIS, INDIANA, SEPTEMBER 25-27, 1889 [7]

The sixth meeting of the General Grand Chapter was held at Indianapolis, Indiana, September 25-27, 1889, at which time twelve Grand Chapters were represented, including two delegations from Minnesota, and one subordinate Chapter. Twenty-eight Chapters had been organized and twenty-seven had been released to organize four Grand Chapters: Grand Chapter of Washington, organized March 26, 1889; Grand Chapter of Ohio, organized August 8, 1889; Grand Chapter of Indian Territory, organized August 19, 1889; Grand Chapter of South Dakota, organized July 11, 1889. On August 8, 1889, jurisdiction was resumed over the territory of Ontario because of the Grand Chapter having become dormant.

For the second time, New Jersey declared her withdrawal from the General Grand Chapter and has since remained without the jurisdiction of this body. The Most Worthy Grand Matron was made the

---

[7] Jefferson S. Conover, M.W.G.P.; Mrs. Mary A. Flint, M.W.G.M.

executive head of the General Grand Body, the business of organizing Chapters and granting charters still remaining the duty of the Most Worthy Grand Patron. The committee on revision of the *Ritual* reported and it was adopted that all *Rituals* now in use be exchanged, free of charge, for the revised edition as adopted.

It was during the year preceding the sixth meeting of the General Grand Chapter that the Order was called upon to mourn the loss of one who was present at the last meeting as an honored guest, Dr. Rob Morris. It is to his inspired genius that the Order owes its existence, and the entire membership recognizes him as its author and founder. The death of this venerable patriarch occurred at his home in La Grange, Kentucky, July 31, 1888, he having nearly completed the three-score and ten of life's allotted span. Immediately following his death, the following notice, under date of August 3, 1888, was sent to the members of the Order throughout the world, giving the intelligence of the mournful event:

Once more the grim reaper, death, has wielded the sickle; this time gathering into the great gamer of eternity, grain fully ripe. Our beloved friend, the venerable Patriarch of our Order, Robert Morris, LL.D., has been called from this world, where his labor was so active, to that rest in Paradise of which he so loved to speak and write. He died of paralysis at his home in LaGrange, Kentucky, on Tuesday, July 31st, aged seventy years.

Brother Morris made Masonry his lifework and all members of the Order of the Eastern Star should especially cherish his memory, for to him we owe the very existence of our Order. His fertile brain, fluent tongue and ready pen brought our Order into being and sent it forth upon the grand mission in which it is now actively engaged.

Brother Morris was made an honorary member of the General Grand Chapter in Chicago, on August 20, 1880. At the last meeting in St. Louis, his words of wisdom were intently listened to. He has gone from our midst; but the mighty influence of his life and work, who can estimate? They cease not with his mortal life, but while he rests in the arms of the tender Savior, whom he loved so well and so reverently worshipped, the ennobling influence of his work shall be felt in an ever widening circle as the years roll on; and wherever the *Order of the Eastern Star* shall be known, the name of Rob Morris shall be held in loving remembrance.

Let us emulate his virtues, his unfeigned piety and his noble Christian character, and be guided in our lives by those pure principles which he enunciated, and which he learned from the teachings of the blessed Jesus.

It is requested that this letter be read in all Chapters at the first meeting after the receipt thereof, and that all the Chapter rooms and jewels be draped in mourning for the space of sixty days, in memory of our distinguished brother.

It is also suggested that Brother Morris' birthday anniversary (August 31) which was made the Festal Day of the Order, by action of the General Grand Chapter in 1880, be this year observed as a Memorial Day by the Order generally, in such appropriate manner as may be found practicable by the different Chapters.

Jefferson S. Conover, M.W.G.P.
Mary A. Flint, M.W.G.M.
Willis D. Engle, R. W. Grand secretary.

SEVENTH ASSEMBLY, COLUMBUS, OHIO, SEPTEMBER 15-17, 1892 [8]

This meeting will ever stand as a monument to the ability of woman to preside with the same degree of competency as is shown

---

[8] Mrs. Nettie Ransford, M.W.G.M.; Benjamin Lynds, M.W.G.P.

Organization of the General Grand Chapter

by man. Most Worthy Grand Matron, Mrs. Nettie Ransford, demonstrated to the Eastern Star world that in the change of the executive head to the Most Worthy Grand Matron, the business of the three preceding years had been carried forward in the same degree of perfection, and with the greatest possible tact and discretion that could be exercised. It was here acknowledged that the added responsibility given to the Most Worthy Grand Matron by the change in the constitution, making her the chief executive during the recess of the General Grand Chapter, conveyed not only a position of honor and trust, but duties that would require time, thought, and wisdom, and that these demands were within her ability to perform with credit.

Added to the change in the executive arrangements of the two highest officers, for the first time in history the office of Right Worthy Grand Secretary had been filled by a sister—Mrs. Lorraine J. Pitkin, of Chicago, Illinois, who has continued to perform the duties of this office uninterruptedly, from her first election in 1889; she was reelected 1892, 1895, 1898, 1901, 1904, 1907, 1910, and 1913. Twenty-four years of official service has made the name of Lorraine J. Pitkin familiar in every country where there exists a Chapter of the Eastern Star. It is impossible at this time to see the far-reaching effect of her influence or appraise the full value of her counsel and advice to the thousands of members and officers.

Sixteen Grand Chapters and two subordinate Chapters under the immediate jurisdiction of the G. G. C. were represented at the seventh assembly. Fifty-four Chapters under the jurisdiction of the General Grand Chapter, with a membership of 2860, had been released to organize Grand Chapters in Oregon, Montana, Wisconsin, New Hampshire, Colorado, and Maine. As the years pass it is demonstrated that wherever the principles of the Order find a lodgment, the prejudice arising from lack of knowledge is speedily removed, and worthy men and women from every vocation in life become earnest seekers after the true light and knowledge of the Eastern Star.

EIGHTH ASSEMBLY, BOSTON, MASSACHUSETTS, AUGUST 29-30, 1895 [9]

At the eighth meeting, twenty-one Grand Chapters and nine Chapters under the jurisdiction of the General Grand Chapter were represented; fifty-eight Chapters had been organized and eighteen had been released to organize two Grand Chapters — one on June 14, 1894, at Valley City, the Grand Chapter of North Dakota, and one November 22, 1894, the Grand Chapter of Pennsylvania, at a meeting held at Scranton.

The Right Worthy Grand Secretary gave a most excellent report of the work done during the World's Fair, giving in detail the efforts put forth by the Order to spread abroad the valuable aims and purposes of the Order. The result of maintaining this "Corner" for the Order of the Eastern Star in the organization room of the Woman's Building was far-reaching. It did much to bring the Order to the attention of Masons and their relatives.

The Right Worthy Grand Secretary also reported a very successful program on Eastern Star Day at the World's Congress of Women held in Chicago, May 16, 1893.

By action of this General Grand Body, the officers to be elected were made to include the Worthy Grand Conductress and the Worthy Grand Associate Conductress. These two officers had previously been appointive.

The address of the Most Worthy Grand Matron affectionately mentioned the death of Sister Charlotte Morris, wife of Rob Morris, the founder of the Order of the Eastern Star, and recommended that a page be set apart in the Proceedings in memory of her, which request was most cordially approved.

The name of Robert Macoy will ever stand associated with that of the founder of the Order, Dr. Rob Morris. For many years they worked together, the one originating the Order, the other with his

---

[9] Mrs. Mary C. Snedden, M.W.G.M.; James R. Donnell, M.W.G.P.

executive ability putting it into an organized system, without which it would have been a failure. Robert Macoy was born October 4, 1816, and died January 9, 1895. It is fitting to accord to his memory the honor due for his many years of earnest labor for, and love of the Eastern Star, and the Most Worthy Grand Matron at this meeting asked that a suitable page be set apart in the Proceedings in memory of Brother Robert Macoy, as well as Charlotte Morris and other honored dead.

The report of the committee on necrology contained the following:

> Sister Charlotte M. Morris, widow of the Patriarch of our Order, Brother Rob Morris, was the first person upon whom the degrees were conferred and was a helpmeet for him throughout all her subsequent years, which were so actively devoted to Freemasonry.

• • • • • • • •

> Robert Macoy, Past Grand Patron of New York, although never connected with this body, but rather opposed to it, rendered most valuable service to the Order by his talent and great executive ability, giving it the Chapter form of organization which has resulted in its present highly prosperous condition. We gladly then cover what we deem his failings, believing that he honestly held and battled for his views, with the broad mantle of charity, and express the sense of loss we must feel as an Order, and inscribe his name upon the General Grand Chapter memorial roll.

NINTH ASSEMBLY, WASHINGTON, D. C., SEPTEMBER 27-30, 1898 [10]

The ninth assembly of the General Grand Chapter was held in Washington, D. C., September 27-31, 1898. Sixty-five Chapters had been organized and eleven Chapters released to form two Grand Chapters. The Grand Chapter of Rhode Island was organized August 22, 1895, and the Grand Chapter of the District of Columbia was organized April 30, 1896. This infant Grand Chapter of less than two years of life assumed the delightful and responsible duty of entertaining the General Grand Chapter, officiating as hostess to that honorable body at its Ninth Triennial Assembly, and though the youngest of the sisterhood of Grand Chapters, she received as her guests the most distinguished company of sisters and brothers within this great fraternity.

Twenty-six Grand Chapters were represented, together with representatives of the Grand Chapters of Connecticut, New Jersey, and New York, not members of the body. At the Eighth Triennial Assembly held in Boston three years previous, the Right Worthy Grand Secretary was instructed to invite the four Grand Chapters which had not yet become constituent members of the General Grand Chapter (Connecticut, New Jersey, New York, and Vermont) to send representatives to the next assembly with the result that all were represented except Vermont at the same assembly. A committee was appointed to confer with them and subsequently a report was submitted opening the way for the affiliation of the Grand Chapters above mentioned with the General Grand Chapter.

The opening ceremony for the General Grand Chapter, also the closing ceremony were adopted and included with the printed Proceedings of the 1898 assembly. They provide the manner of conducting that portion of the assemblage of this honored body, with provisions further for exercises both elegant and becoming, though

---

[10] Mrs. Mary E. Partridge, M.W.G.M.; H. H. Hinds, M.W.G.P.

differing slightly from that prescribed for the subordinate Chapters and for the Grand Chapters.

The Right Worthy Grand Secretary reported that a copy of the "Test Oath" had been sent to all Chapters under the jurisdiction of the General Grand Chapter at the time the report blanks were sent, December 1, 1895, with full information for its use.

Several Grand Chapters having requested the secret work in cipher, the Right Worthy Grand Secretary had same prepared and supplied to such Grand Chapters as preferred to have it in this manner.

By the organization of seven Chapters in the State of Virginia, more territory engaged actively in the O.E.S. work was recognized, where "steadily the Star shines brightly on, increasing in brilliancy with each added Chapter, to eventually become one more Grand Jurisdiction."

Tenth Triennial Assembly, Detroit, Michigan, September 24-27, 1901 [11]

The Tenth Triennial Assembly was held in the Masonic Temple in the city of Detroit, Michigan, September 24-27, 1901, with representatives present from thirty-one Grand and one subordinate Chapter. Sixty-four Chapters had been organized, eighty-seven Chapters had been released to organize the Grand Chapters of Maryland, Arizona, Louisiana, Tennessee, Georgia, and Alabama, and recognition of the Grand Chapters of Connecticut and Vermont as constituent members of the General Grand Chapter had been declared; jurisdiction had been resumed over the Chapters in Nevada which Chapters had, at a previous meeting of the General Grand Chapter, been placed under the jurisdiction of the Grand Chapter of California.

---

[11] Mrs. Hattie E. Ewing, M.W.G.M.; Nathaniel Gearhart, M.W.G.P.

The committee on ritual to which was referred the question concerning the proper position of the five-pointed star, reported, and the report was adopted, that:

> Your committee finds, according to the oldest authentic Ritual of the Order extant, the Tessara, which was an emblem to be used by members, was made with one point down, and that in every subsequent Ritual in which reference is made to badges or jewels containing a star, it was to be thus worn. It finds that in the various signets used in the Order's history, from the Morris signet of about 1860 down, the star has been represented with the white point down. There can be but one opinion as to what is the proper position of the star, so far as established both by its Ritual and by practice of the Order. In Masonry the five-pointed star is represented with two points down, and in the teachings of ancient mythology the five-pointed star with one point down was an emblem used to represent the goat of Mendes — a God of Lust — but it does not consider that this Order is compelled to conform to the Masonic custom in the use of this emblem, much less to the heathen practice, feeling, as it does that, even if its mythological significance was one of evil, it has been redeemed from the domain of Satan and converted into an emblem of good by its half century of use by this Order, so beneficial to humanity.

It is worthy the attention of all members of the Order, that the decision of the Most Worthy Grand Matron, that "gross and confirmed habits of intoxication proved against a member of the Order of the Eastern Star, man or woman, are sufficient cause for expulsion," was concurred in at this session and therefore is our guide in this particular. In performing their fraternal duties members of the Order must regard their acts as the connecting links which are to bind the past to the future. Devotion to the principles of the Order should be uplifting and soul-inspiring and with the Master's touch upon their acts, lives will be more earnest, with a desire to uplift all mankind until they shall stand in the presence of Him whose Star they have seen in the East.

The organizing of Chapters in India, British Columbia, Hawaiian Islands, and Scotland was reported, with active interest in each place mentioned.

ELEVENTH TRIENNIAL ASSEMBLY, ST. LOUIS, MISSOURI, SEPTEMBER 19-21, 1904 [12]

The Eleventh Triennial Session assembled in Scottish Rite Cathedral, St. Louis, Missouri, September 19-21, 1904, thirty-nine Grand and one subordinate Chapter being represented. Fifty-nine Chapters had been organized, seven in Nevada transferred from the jurisdiction of California to that of the General Grand Chapter, and one hundred fifteen had been released to form eight Grand Chapters: Grand Chapter of Oklahoma, organized February 14, 1902; Grand Chapter of New Mexico, April 11, 1902; Grand Chapter of Idaho, April 18, 1902; Grand Chapter of Kentucky, June 9, 1903; Grand Chapter of Florida, June 7, 1904; Grand Chapter of Virginia, June 22, 1904; Grand Chapter of Scotland, August 20, 1904.

Reports showed that the Order had been extended to the Philippine Islands and a petition for charter had been received from Manila; Mayon Chapter No. 1 was organized August 29, 1904, with thirty-two petitioners.

During the year the Most Worthy Grand Matron visited Scotland and on August 20, 1904, at a convention of the Chapters of the Order in Scotland, held in Glasgow, the following Concordat, in the form of resolutions, was passed:

    A. That all the Chapters of the Order of the Eastern Star in Scotland here represented, or declaring their adherence

---

[12] Mrs. Laura B. Hart, M.W.G.M.; L. Cabell Williamson, M.W.G.P.

thereto, shall be and are hereby united under one jurisdiction; and the representatives of such Chapters now present or adhering, not only bind themselves to sign this resolution in token of their acceptance thereof but also bind and oblige themselves and the Chapters which they represent to ratify and confirm the same and to support and further said procedure as may be requisite to carry this resolution into effect.

B. That the body formed by this resolution shall be known at present as the Grand Chapter of Scotland, but shall have supreme and exclusive jurisdiction over Great Britain, Ireland, and the whole British dominions (excepting only, those upon the Continent of America) and that a Supreme or General Grand Chapter of the British Empire shall be formed as soon as Chapters are instituted therein and it seems expedient to do so.

C. That the Constitution and the laws of the late existing Supreme Grand Chapter of the Order of the Eastern Star in Scotland shall, with some slight alterations, be, and are hereby adopted as the Constitution and Laws of the Grand Chapter now formed.

D. That the Ritual to be used by all the Chapters under this Constitution shall be that now issued by the General Grand Chapter of America.

E. That this Grand Chapter as now constituted shall take over all Assets and Liabilities of the preceding Supreme Grand Chapter of the Order in Scotland.

F. That all Grand office bearers and Past Grand office bearers of the preceding Supreme Grand Chapter of the Order in Scotland shall be and are hereby accorded Past Grand Rank and shall be entitled to all privileges and precedence appertaining thereto.

G. That the office bearers of the Grand Chapter as now constituted be here and now nominated elected and installed to hold office till January 1906.

H. That the General Grand Chapter of America whose Ritual we have adopted will exchange with the late Supreme Grand Chapter of Scotland an official number (three) of said Ritual, in lieu of those the said body have been using, the same to be furnished free of charge.

A detailed report from the national chairman, O.E.S. World's Fair ways and means committee, showed that the Order contributed $5,742 to the maintenance of Eastern Star headquarters in the Fraternity Building during the St. Louis Exposition, and a home was maintained in the Temple of Fraternity, where a cordial welcome awaited all members, during the St. Louis fair.

Upon the invitation of the Grand Matron of Missouri, a visit was made to the Masonic Home of Missouri located in St. Louis.

It was voted that the General Grand Chapter shall meet every third year at such time and place as may be determined by a vote of the General Grand Chapter at its previous meeting — the first five officers of the General Grand Chapter to change the place of meeting in case of any extraordinary emergency.

Twelfth Triennial Assembly, Milwaukee, Wisconsin, September 4-6, 1907 [13]

The Twelfth Triennial Assembly convened in Milwaukee, September 4-6, 1907, with forty-three Grand Chapters and one subordinate Chapter represented. Twenty-five Chapters had been organized and fifty-nine Chapters had been released to form the following: Grand Chapter of North Carolina, organized May 20, 1905; Grand Chapter of Nevada, September 19, 1905; Grand Chapter of

---

[13] Mrs. Madeleine B. Conkling, M.W.G.M.; Dr. Wm. F. Kuhn, M.W.G.P.

Utah, September 20, 1905; Grand Chapter of Mississippi, May 29, 1906; Grand Chapter of South Carolina, June 1, 1907.

At this time the Order had extended into every State and Territory of our Union, except one, and into the continents and islands beyond the seas; into two hemispheres; into the tropics and into that beautiful "land of the midnight sun." They were bound together by the golden links of love, animated by purposes lofty and aspirations high, each following the STAR as it lights the way to that higher plane toward which the race has been toiling for centuries — a plane where the war of creeds will cease, the voice of selfishness be hushed, the contentions of unholy strife be forgotten — a plane where the people of each race and every clime will join hands as one great family, kneel at a common altar, and offer a common plea for the protective watchfulness and care and guidance from God the Father. Following the guiding light of our STAR, armed with the sword of Truth, the shield of Charity, and the armor of Loving Kindness, a victorious triumph will be the reward.

The Grand Chapter of Washington, which had withdrawn from the General Grand Chapter, resumed allegiance thereto. A German version of the Ritual — the translation as made by Brother August Torpe — was adopted and ordered printed.

Upon the filing of the official report of the chairman of the St. Louis Order of the Eastern Star headquarters fund, it was learned that a balance of more than a thousand dollars was in the hands of the Right Worthy Grand Secretary from this source. This amount, with sufficient added to increase the total amount to $2,738, was given to the maintenance of Eastern Star headquarters at the Lewis and Clark Exposition at Portland, Oregon, through the Right Worthy Grand Secretary.

For several triennial terms, the executive officers of the General Grand Chapter had felt that its constitution was deficient in many particulars. The organic law of 1876 had become, in 1907, incompetent, leaving the weightier matters of law and jurisprudence of the

Order of the Eastern Star to the individual opinion of the moment, and to the intelligence of whomsoever happened to be in office, both in the General Grand Chapter and in the Grand Chapters of its constituency. Therefore, a committee, consisting of five representative members from the east, west, north, south, and middle States, had been officially appointed by the Most Worthy Grand Matron, with instructions to formulate an instrument of organic law that would meet the requirements of the highest body of the Order, which body is the sole source of the ritual and its control. The Most Worthy Grand Matron incorporated in her address this new constitution, rules, and regulations to govern both the General Grand and the Grand Chapter deliberations, which were, after amendment, adopted. The powers of the General Grand Body as defined therein, give it exclusive sovereignty over the Ritual and government of the Order, but the words "and government" were stricken from the laws at the 1910 meeting.

It was adopted that the color appropriate to the office of Worthy Matron and Associate Matron shall be purple; for the points of the star, the color appropriate to the several degrees, and for all the remaining officers, the five colors combined.

The following poem was ordered printed in the Proceedings:

THE EASTERN STAr [14]

God bless our Eastern Star,
Thy praise we sing;
Our homage from afar,

To thee we bring.

---

[14] Adapted to the tune of "Nearer My God, to Thee."
To our loved Worthy Grand Matron, Sister Alice M. Metcalf, these lines are affectionately dedicated by Dr. S. M. M'Millan, Worthy Grand Patron, O. E. S., Maryland. Riverdale, Md., June 25, 1907.

We love thy precepts true;
Thy lessons ever new;
And to thee cling.

Oh, may we ever stand
In thy pure light,
To labor hand in hand,
For truth and right,
Our cause will not be vain,
For "Strength to strength" we'll gain,
To our loved "Golden Chain,"
By Thy great might.

We then should strive to prove
Our loyalty,
By our unselfish love
And "Charity."
Then we will surely find
Our lives with Thee entwined,
And teach to all mankind
Fraternity.

The three years administration which closed with the 1907 assembly, was marked by the great effort of the executive officer to bring about uniformity of ritual work, as well as law, and to the end that the Grand Chapters and the General Grand Chapter should maintain a mutual feeling of confidence one toward the other, thus uniting the interests and efforts into one harmonious whole, resulting in more beneficial effort than could otherwise obtain. Many of the Grand Chapters, in order to comply, gave up customs, some of which were very dear to them through long association. For the first time since its organization in 1876, the General Grand Chapter exemplified its own ritual work.

Thirteenth Triennial Assembly, Jacksonville Florida, November 8-10, 1910 [15]

The Thirteenth Triennial Assembly convened in Jacksonville, Florida, November 8-10, 1910, with forty-five Grand and seventeen subordinate Chapters under the immediate jurisdiction of the General Grand Chapter. Eighteen Chapters had been organized, as well as one Grand Chapter. On February 12, 1909, at Guthrie, the Grand Chapter of Oklahoma was organized from the territorial domain formerly representing the Territory of Oklahoma and Indian Territory, which were, by mutual consent of the two Grand Jurisdictions, consolidated and emerged on the date above named as the Grand Chapter of Oklahoma.

In the address of the Most Worthy Grand Matron, she called attention to the fact that all Grand Jurisdictions had either established a home for the care of its members or had some home interests; in many having united with the Masonic Order and assisting in the work of the Masonic Home. Others had established a home fund, looking toward the erection of a home at such a time as finances will render same practicable.

During her term of office, the Most Worthy Grand Matron had been the guest of the Grand Matron of the Grand Chapter of New Jersey, by invitation of Golden Link Chapter No. 1, with the official staff of Grand officers, and witnessed the work of the ritual of the Order beautifully rendered, followed by the *Floral Addenda*. She had also been invited to be the guest of the Grand Chapter of New York, to be present at the dedication of the Home at Waterville. Thoroughly appreciating the invitation, coming from this Chapter not a member of the body which she represented, yet showing their mutual interests to be identical in effort, she greatly regretted her inability to attend.

---

[15] Mrs. Ella S. Washburn, M.W.G.M.; William H. Norris, W.M.G.P.

Included in the Proceedings is a copy of the "Jewel of the General Grand Chapter," as designed by Sister Kitty Lee M'Clain, showing the various official positions of honor during the O.E.S. life of the Right Worthy Grand Secretary, Lorraine J. Pitkin, and presented to the General Grand Chapter at the meeting held in Jacksonville, Florida. "Twenty-one years of official service have made the name of Mrs. Lorraine J. Pitkin familiar in every country where there exists a Chapter of the Eastern Star. Who can see the far-reaching effect of her influence? Who can appraise the full value of her counsel and advice to the hundreds of members and officers? Who can fathom the great depth of her love for an Order which she has served from the days of her younger womanhood? But we all agree that among our vast collection of gems or jewels treasured in the hearts of our members there is no duplicate, there is none other just like Lorraine J. Pitkin, the Jewel of the General Grand Chapter."

We as a people need sunshine. We need bright things around us. We crave the affection of our fellow beings and aspire to such degree of excellence in our lifework that we may in return gain the approval of our associates. Our well-being is advanced when we look upon bright and happy faces. God has created us with these requirements and in order to best attain them, we must first look into our own hearts and cast out all bitterness and jealousy, and never let an opportunity pass for doing some kind act, be it apparently trifling at the time. If we go to our Chapter with a smile and a pleasant greeting and are ever ready to do our part toward making our Chapter among the very best in the jurisdiction to which we belong, then shall we reap a rich harvest of thoughts and deeds. Doctor Morris built well when he gave to us this Order founded upon the principles of charity, truth, and loving kindness, and may we today give to it our best thought and effort. Are we sowing the good seeds or are we careless about the little things that formed together make the great things of this life? The Order of the Eastern Star needs to be taught fraternalism as much as it needs constitutions, rules and regulations, or by-laws.

> He calleth us to words and deeds of love,
> As Spring calls forth from wintry crust the flowers,
> He breathes within us, spirit from above,
> As zephyrs breathe within the sunny bowers;
> He saith, "Arise, and forth you must go,
> Where duty calls, where sorrow hath its sway;"
> He points our feet the proper path, and Lo!
> He promiseth to be with us always

FOURTEENTH TRIENNIAL ASSEMBLY, CHICAGO, ILLINOIS, SEPTEMBER 23-25, 1913 [16]

The Fourteenth Triennial Assembly convened in Oriental Consistory Temple, Chicago, Illinois, September 23-25, 1913, with forty-eight Grand Chapters and eleven Chapters under the immediate Jurisdiction represented. Twenty-one Chapters had been released to form the Grand Chapter of Alberta, which was organized at Calgary, July 20, 1912, and the Grand Chapter of British Columbia, organized at Vancouver, July 23, 1912.

This vast army of workers assembled under the banner of charity, truth, and loving kindness, brought the records of labor performed during the past three years and counseled together for the good of the Order. By thus meeting, friendly relations are cemented; all are encouraged to further efforts for good, and cheered on their way, with the purpose in view of promoting peace and harmony and advancing all that is good and beautiful in the Order, which, numbering about 700,000 souls, tingles with thrift, and is riding on the high tide of prosperity. To these many co-workers is appointed the

---

[16] Mrs. M. Alice Miller, M.W.G.M.; Rev. Willis D. Engle, M.W.G.P.

work of carrying forward the torch, already lighted, that will illumine the dark places of men's souls. Because, with science-aided eyes, men have peered into the starlit vestibule of the Infinite and found no shape or form of God, they have denied His being. Engrossed in the present, they have thrown doubt on the future. The work of the Order is to stay and uphold the outstretched hand of Faith, and thus aid in bringing spiritual victory to mankind; to be so true to every friendship, so loyal to every trust, so faithful to every duty, that when the day breaks and the shadows fall, all may meet in a glorious reunion in the Grand Chapter above. A box of heather was sent from Maggie J. Foulds, Past Grand Matron of Scotland, and presented to the assembled members with greetings in part as follows:

> A sprig o' bonnie bloomin' heather,
>   Pu'ed frae Grampian Mountain's grand,
> A greetin' kind, to Sisters dear,
>   Frae Scotia's historic land.
>
> That a' the blessin's God can gie,
>   May be the gree o' ane an' a'
> Wha loe the "Star" an' lift the e'e
>   To "sacred symbol" shepherds saw.
> Whilk we hae seen, an' haud sae dear,
>   To worship come, frae far an' near.

This remembrance from members across the ocean was a most pleasant and gratifying recognition of the kindly interest of the absent ones, bound together by the strongest of fraternal ties.

Brother Rob. Morris, Past Grand Patron of Kentucky, and son of Dr. Rob Morris, the founder of the Order of the Eastern Star, was presented, made some very interesting remarks, and was the recipient of a pronounced ovation. Upon motion, the General Grand Chapter gave a rising vote of thanks to Brother Morris, with a Chautauqua salute. It was the vision of Dr. Rob Morris that made possible this great Order with its more than half a million members, who have for their guidance "His Star in the East" and in whose interests this meeting was held.

With the compliments of the Right Worthy Associate Grand Matron and Right Worthy Associate Grand Patron and in recognition of the Canadian delegates, a British flag was draped with the Stars and Stripes. Great enthusiasm was manifested by all present and the entire assembly arose and sang a medley composed of the national songs of both countries.

Pursuant to a condition that had come about from different and diverging interpretations of the Concordat with the Grand Chapter of Scotland, it was deemed expedient to adopt the following:

Resolved, That this General Grand Chapter do at this time, in 14th Triennial Assembly, deem it expedient and in the promotion of harmony, to again declare and reaffirm, in accordance with the aforesaid Concordat, the boundaries and confines of its jurisdiction to be as follows:

The entire civilized world outside the confines of the British possessions, except those located on the continent of America, which British possessions on said continent of America shall be under the jurisdiction of this General Grand Chapter; and be it further

Resolved, That no other body of the Order be permitted to organize Chapters or a Grand Chapter within the jurisdiction of this General Grand Chapter.

This meeting was strengthened by a large attendance, two members of which were present not only at the organization of the General Grand Chapter in 1876, but who also attended every one of the assemblies of this body. Thirty-seven years previous there gathered in Indianapolis, Indiana, fourteen members of the Order of the Eastern Star, eight brothers and six sisters, representing five of the twelve then existing Grand Chapters, two of which had been organized the previous month. The Order, at that time, numbered 228 Chapters, and 11,814 members. In addition to this there was a Grand Lodge of Adoptive Masonry in Michigan numbering 22 Lodges and 1,135 members, which organization antedated the organization of the first Grand Chapter of the Order by nearly three years. The Grand Chapters represented were: New Jersey, two delegates; California, one delegate; Indiana, five delegates; Illinois, one delegate, and Missouri, five delegates; Of the fourteen, ten have passed out of this life, leaving four surviving, only three of whom have maintained an interest in the Order: The Rev. Willis D. Engle, who presided as Most Worthy Grand Patron during this meeting and whose work for the organization exceeded any other one member, and further, who is the only brother who has been present at every assembly; Brothers John R. Parson, of Missouri, and James A. Thompson, of Indiana. There was also at the first meeting, one sister, Mrs. Nettie Ransford, who at that organization meeting and all the subsequent meetings has rendered most valuable assistance and who is the only sister who has been present at every meeting.

Considering the state of the Order at that time, the chaotic condition of the ritual work and jurisprudence, and the total lack of cooperation that had previously prevailed, it is evident that it required both energy and faith to organize a general body. The movement met with strenuous opposition from many of its most active members and workers, which required years and years of constant effort to eliminate and place the Order upon a prosperous and enduring basis.

It required fifteen years to reach the number of a thousand Chapters and fifty thousand members. Contrast the condition of the Order thirty-seven years ago and the condition today. Then we had 228 Chapters with 11,000 members; now we have 52 Grand Chapters, over 7,000 subordinate Chapters, and over 650,000 members, with absolute uniformity of ritual prevailing in every essential particular in the fifty Grand Chapters, with the Order making such progress that we have an average increase of 600 Chapters and 38,000 members annually.

Almost every Grand Chapter has a Home or is accumulating a fund for that purpose. Texas has two Masonic Homes and is planning for a distinctively Eastern Star Home in the near future. The new Grand Chapter of Alberta, Canada, has started a fund to be known as "The Masonic Home and School Fund." Hundreds of boys and girls are in training for good noble citizens, who, but for Masonic influence and their special care at these homes and schools, might have been vagabonds on earth — a menace instead of a blessing to society.

The Most Worthy Grand Matron prepared and embodied in her report, "Instructions to subordinate Chapters under the General Grand Chapter Order of the Eastern Star," which gives definite interpretation of the ritualistic work. The Eastern Star is a distinctive Order, with its own work and method of executing it. It needs no embellishment from other Orders; if well done, it is second to none in beauty, and its foundation principles are as enduring as truth, constancy, purity, faith, and love can make them. Enjoyment of every good is measured by the amount of interest we put into it, and that for which we sacrifice most seems of greatest value to us.

CHAPTER V

Officers of the General Grand Chapter

MRS. RATA ALICE MILLS [1]

A NATIVE-BORN Pennsylvanian who became a member of the Order of the Eastern Star in 1888, joining Keystone Chapter No. 2 which for six years was under the jurisdiction of the General Grand Chapter. At that time there were about sixty members in the State, now there are over 18,000.

From the beginning, Mrs. Mills manifested a most tender and earnest solicitation for the Order, promoting its interests in every way possible, and her activity was remarkable. When in 1894 the Grand Chapter was constituted, she was chosen on a committee to formulate the first Constitution of the Grand Chapter of Pennsylvania and was elected Associate Grand Matron and in the following year was advanced to Worthy Grand Matron. In 1898 she was elected Grand Secretary. By her untiring efforts and unselfish devotion, she did more than any other person to build up the O.E.S. in the great Keystone State.

Sister Rata A. Mills first attended the General Grand Chapter, which assembly was held in St. Louis, Missouri, in 1904, when she was elected Right Worthy Associate Grand Conductress; at Milwaukee, Wisconsin, in 1907, was elected Right Worthy Grand Conductress; at Jacksonville, Florida, in 1910, was elected Right Worthy Associate Grand Matron, and at Chicago, Illinois, in 1913, was elevated to Most Worthy Grand Matron. Her loyalty to the good of the Order was the strength of her leadership in the subordinate Chapter and the spirit of her success in the Grand Chapter. Wherever she visited the Chapters her presence was felt as an inspiration to

---

[1] Most Worthy Grand Matron, Order of the Eastern Star, 1913-1916. Died February 9, 1916.

better work and higher ideals. In addition to her zealous work in our beloved Order, she took an active interest in church work, being a lifelong attendant and member of the Methodist Episcopal church. Mrs. Mills was a charter member and an officer of the Woman's Club, organized in 1899, and a member of the Federation of Pennsylvania Women. Mrs. Mills came of Revolutionary stock. Her ancestor located in Boston and participated in the Battle of Bunker Hill; later settled near Philadelphia and enlisted in the Revolutionary War. Sister Mills was educated for the teacher's profession but early in life married and became the helpmate of John C. Mills, who has been an enthusiastic Mason ever since reaching his majority and is now a Knight Templar. With his wife he joined Keystone Chapter No. 2, serving as Worthy Patron for three terms. Sister Mills was a competent pharmacist and always took an active interest in business affairs, but never once forgetting or neglecting her home.

In honor of the first member of the Order in Pennsylvania to be elected to the most exalted position in the gift of the Order, Sister Margaret K. Griffith dedicated her composition, "Our Beautiful Eastern Star," to Sister Rata Alice Mills[2] In her letter of acceptance in

---

[2] Words and music by Mrs. Margaret K. Griffith, P. W. M., Brookline Chapter No. 117, Pittsburgh, Pennsylvania.

OUR BEAUTIFUL EASTERN STAR

When the angels sang on that first Christmas morn
To a waking world that a Saviour was born,
Whose birth was foretold by the prophets of old.
Our "Bright and Morning Star."

CHORUS

The way of the Star leads home,
The sign of the Star means life;
No more in sadness shall we roam,
No more in sorrow, no more strife —
But we'll walk with Him in white,

recognition of the honor conferred, she expressed the wish that the mission of this very expressive song could be further extended and that more benefits might accrue to the Order from this commendable effort of one of the splendid workers in Pennsylvania. Following this suggestion, after careful consideration, it was decided that the tenets of the Order would be most fittingly served by making this music a gift to the O.E.S. Home Association of Pennsylvania.

The Home Association had the song published and have offered it to the Fraternity anticipating the cordial support of the members of the Order in this noble work, knowing that it will assist them in this just and laudable cause, and that their splendid new home so recently acquired may be benefited by this work of charity and loving kindness.

Sister Rata Alice Mills, Most Worthy Grand Matron, passed to the higher life on February 9, 1916, after a brief illness. She had but recently returned from a three months' trip, extending as far as the Hawaiian Islands, in the interests of the O.E.S. and had mentioned to her friends that this trip was one of the most pleasing experiences of her life. The members of the various Grand Jurisdictions and

---

In. that City where all is light;
For we have seen His Star in the East,
And have come to worship Him,
Oh! Star, Shine on! For we have seen
His Star in the East,
And have come to worship Him.

Since that morn of morns countless voices still sing
That the manger of Bethlehem cradles a King,
Who is Jesus our Lord and whose Name we adore,
Our "Beautiful Eastern Star."

So today may we, like the shepherds of old.
And the wise men who traveled so wide and afar,
When we all reach Home we the face will behold.
Of our "Bright and Morning Star."

Chapters which she visited are fortunate in having had the opportunity to meet Sister Mills, whose inspiring personality won for her many friends. Her presence has ever been an incentive to higher ideals and nobler purposes, and her loss to the Order of the Eastern Star will be keenly felt throughout the General Grand Chapter jurisdiction. This is the first time in the history of the Order that the Most Worthy Grand Matron died during the term of her office.

"I HAVE SEEN HIS STAR"

BY MRS. RATA ALICE MILLS, M.W.G.M.

(Written for this volume)

When upon the mountain height,
    Piercing clouds, like dazzling snow,
Sparkling, glowing in the light —
    All around — above, below —
Far beyond the ethereal bar,
I have seen His shining Star.

When in vales of darkest gloom,
    Shadowed by the mountains vast,
Earth seemed buried in a tomb,
    Every ray of light o'ercast.
Still there gleamed, although afar,
Brightly beamed that glorious Star.

When the waves in breakers roll
    With the might of awful power,
Threat'ning wreck to every soul,
    And dark silence fills the hour,
Through the blackest clouds afar,

Still I see Thee, wondrous Star.

When wild storms sweep o'er the earth,
    Spreading desolation bare,
Bringing pestilence and dearth
    On the wings of blank despair,
Shining still, although afar,
Kindly beams that lovely Star.

Whatsoe'r the day shall be,
    Bleak as night or blessed with light,
Coming ages still shall see
    Over all, that Star so bright
Shining clear, through gates ajar,
Look beyond and see His Star.

GOD BLESS OUR STAR

BY MRS. RATA ALICE MILLS, M.W.G.M.

All the earth is clothed in splendor,
    Towering mountains lift their heads
O'er the tiny, fragrant blossoms,
    Springing from their mossy beds.
O'er head the sun is shining,
    Or the moonbeams softly fall,
Oh! this world is full of beauty,
    And the stars watch over all.

Sparkling streams and foaming torrents,
    Lakes, where mirrored landscapes lie,
Perfect in their tranquil beauty,
    'Neath the azure of the sky.

Gems of verdure clothe the branches
    Of the trees, so straight and tall,
Oh, this world is full of beauty,
    And the stars watch over all.

Hearts that throb with love's deep passion,
    Hearts that closely clasp our own,
Songs that thrill the soul with gladness,
    Beauty everywhere is shown.
And the STAR, our sacred emblem,
    In its glory seems to call
Us to join in the grand vigil,
    Sweetly watching over all.

God bless you! So I've wished you all
    Of brightness life possesses,
For, can there any joy at all
    Be thine, unless God blesses?
God bless you! So I breathe a charm
    Lest grief's dark night oppress you,
For, how can sorrow bring you harm,
    If 'tis God's way to bless you.

GREETING

BY MRS. RATA ALICE MILLS, M.W.G.M.

Greeting to Stars, the greatest and least,
    Whose radiance is not dim,
"For we have seen His star in the East,
    And are come to worship Him."

Charity, Truth and Loving Kindness,

Is our motto true,
Guiding each other through our blindness,
As is our duty to do.

A rich reward awaits you
If you but do your part,
To make the world grow better,
By cheering a weary heart

Yes, we love the Eastern Star,
With a Jove that naught can sever,
"Fairest among ten thousand, thou
Art lovely, altogether."

MRS. EMMA CRAGER OCOBOCK [3]

Mrs. Emma Crager Ocobock was born in Berrien County, Michigan, and has spent her entire life in the southwestern portion of the Wolverine State. She was married in 1890 to George W. Ocobock, a prominent merchant and an enthusiastic Master Mason of Hartford, Michigan, where she has since resided. From Mr. Ocobock came the inspiration which led to the subsequent interest which Mrs. Ocobock has ever had in Masonry, the Eastern Star, and all kindred subjects.

Being naturally imbued with the principles of charity, truth, and loving-kindness, and in order to enlarge her powers for doing good, Sister Ocobock was instrumental in organizing Benevolence Chapter No. 46, O. E. S., at Hartford, Michigan, and served as its first Worthy Matron in 1902.

Upon visiting the Grand Chapter of Michigan as a delegate, the unusual talents and charming personality of this sister made for her

---

[3] Acting Most Worthy Grand Matron, General Grand Chapter Order of the Eastern Star.
Written by Minnie Evans Keyes, P.G.M. of Michigan.

many friends who, in 1903, elected her to the office of Grand Conductress. She was advanced in office and in 1906 became the Worthy Grand Matron of Michigan. She at once entered upon a period of unselfish and beneficial effort for the Order. Her presence in the subordinate Chapters, where she so kindly directed and encouraged the officers in the work of the Order and inspired in the members everywhere a greater effort in dispensing real fraternity, made for the betterment and uplift of the Eastern Star.

As member of the Masonic Home board of control, where she served for three years on the finance committee, she again brought into play the spirit of benevolence and loving-kindness and the old friends in the Home will never forget her loving smile and kind words of comfort and cheer as she took occasion to visit them at each meeting of the board.

At present Sister Ocobock is a member of the board of control of the Masonic Home relief fund, Order of the Eastern Star, which fund is used to assist Chapters which are financially unable to maintain in the Home worthy sisters.

In all her Eastern Star affiliations Sister Ocobock has served with a distinction which has won for her the highest appreciation of the members of the Order throughout her State.

She was elected to the office of Right Worthy Associate Grand Conductress at the General Grand Chapter meeting in 1907 and was advanced to the office of Right Worthy Grand Conductress in 1910. At the Triennial Assembly in 1913 Sister Ocobock was made Right Worthy Associate Grand Matron and now, by the untimely death of our esteemed and beloved sister, Mrs. Rata A. Mills, Most Worthy Grand Matron, Sister Ocobock will assume her privileges and prerogatives. She will enter upon the duties of this new station with the same spirit of unselfish and generous devotion with which she served the Order in her own State.

Michigan is proud of this queenly woman, who possesses the love and esteem of every member of the Eastern Star in her State, and the large membership will follow her efforts into this larger field with the knowledge that reflected honors will be theirs as she carries out to fulfilment the plans of the General Grand Chapter.

GEORGE ATWOOD PETTIGREW, M.D.[4]

George Atwood Pettigrew was born in Ludlow, Vermont, April 6, 1858, the son of Josiah Walker and Susan Ann (Atwood) Pettigrew, natives of Ludlow and Londonderry, Vermont, respectively. He was educated at the Black River Academy, of Ludlow, Vermont, the Colby Academy, of New London, New Hampshire, and was graduated from the medical department of Dartmouth College, at Hanover, New Hampshire, with the class of 1882. He began the practice of his profession at Flandreau, South Dakota, February 2, 1883, and in June, 1884, entered into professional partnership with Dr. F. A. Spafford, which lasted until February, 1891, when he retired from the active practice and engaged in the real estate, loan, and banking business. He was the surgeon of the Chicago, Milwaukee and St. Paul Railroad for eight years; government physician to the Indians for eight years; surgeon of the Second regiment of Territorial Guards and their successors, from 1885 to 1893; surgeon-general of South Dakota under Governor Sheldon for two terms; member of the board of United States pension examiners from 1884 to 1901 with the exception of one year; surgeon of the First and Second regiments of South Dakota National Guard from organization to departure for the Philippines.

Dr. Pettigrew assisted in organizing the Flandreau State Bank in May, 1891, and was its president until July, 1903, when he resigned and moved to Sioux Falls, September 3d following. Until the fall of 1913 he was president of the Union Savings Association of Sioux Falls. He served as coroner of Moody County for many years and was the first to organize the movement to advance the interests of

---

[4] Most Worthy Grand Patron, Order of the Eastern Star, 1913-1916.

Flandreau and Moody County. He located hundreds of prosperous farmers in this county and lands have advanced from eight dollars per acre in 1891 to the present high and satisfactory prices.

He is a Mason, and has attained the thirty-third degree, Ancient and Accepted Scottish Rite, the Royal Order of Scotland, and the Red Cross of Constantine.[5]

---

[5] MASONIC RECORD OF DR. GEORGE ATWOOD PETTIGREW

King Solomon Lodge No. 14, New Hampshire: Entered Apprentice, July 2, 1879; Fellow Craft, June 14, 1880; Master Mason, June 14, 1880; dimitted, November '7, 1883.

Flandreau Lodge No. 11, South Dakota: Admitted, January 5, 1884; Secretary, 1884-1885; Senior Warden, 1886-1887; Worshipful Master, 1888-1889; dimitted, October 4, 1905.

Unity Lodge No. 130, South Dakota: Admitted November 3, 1905.

Minnehaha Lodge No. 5: Honorary member, April 8, 1908.

Grand Lodge of South Dakota A. F. and A. M.: Grand Pursuivant, 1889; Grand Secretary, June 13, 1894, to 1914.

King Solomon Lodge No. 14, New Hampshire: Entered Apprentice, July 2, 1879; Fellow Craft, June 14, 1880; Master Mason, June 14, 1880; dimitted, November '7, 1883.

Flandreau Lodge No. 11, South Dakota: Admitted, January 5, 1884; Secretary, 1884-1885; Senior Warden, 1886-1887; Worshipful Master, 1888-1889; dimitted, October 4, 1905.

Unity Lodge No. 130, South Dakota: Admitted November 3, 1905.

Minnehaha Lodge No. 5: Honorary member, April 8, 1908.

Grand Lodge of South Dakota A. F. and A. M.: Grand Pursuivant, 1889; Grand Secretary, June 13, 1894, to 1914.

Orient Chapter No. 18, South Dakota: Mark Master Mason, May 18, 1885; Past Master, May 21, 1885; Most Excellent Master, May 22, 1885; Royal Arch Mason, May 27, 1885; Secretary, 1885-1886; Principal Sojourner, 1887-1892; High Priest, 1893; dimitted, August 23, 1905.

Sioux Falls Chapter No. 2: Admitted, September 6, 1905.

Order of High Priesthood: Initiated, June 11, 1896, Huron; Grand Recorder, 1896 to 1914.

Grand Chapter of South Dakota, R A. M.: Grand Secretary, organization, 1890-June, 1906; Grand High Priest, June, 1906-1907; Grand Secretary, June, 1907-present.

Grand Chapter of Illinois: Grand Representative, 1890-present.

He served as Grand Secretary of the Grand Chapter of Royal Arch Masons of the State since 1889 with the exception of one year when

Royal and Select Masters, Koda Council, Flandreau, S. D.: Royal Master, December 18, 1894; Select Master, December 18, 1894; Super-Excellent Master, December 18, 1894; dimitted, December 2, 1896.

Alpha Council No. 1, Sioux Falls: Admitted, November 7, 1903; Thrice Illustrious Grand Master, 1896 and 1897; Deputy Illustrious Grand Master, 1903.

Cyrene Commandery No. 2 K. T., South Dakota: Red Cross, February 28, 1888; Knights Templar, February 28, 1888; Knights of Malta, February 28, 1888; dimitted, November 2, 1892.

Ivanhoe Commandery No. 13, Flaudreau: Charter member, November 15, 1888; Captain General, 1893, 1894, 1895; Generallissimo, 1896; Eminent Commander, 1897; dimitted, November 27, 1905.

Cyrene Commandery No. 2, Sioux Falls: Admitted, December 5, 1905.

Grand Commandery K. T., South Dakota: Grand Standard Bearer, 1892 and 1893; Grand Recorder, June, 1895-1906; Grand Commander, June, 1907-1908; Grand Recorder, 1909 to present.

St. George's Conclave No. 6, Red Cross of Constantine, St. Paul, Minnesota: April 25, 1911.

Grand Commandery of Iowa: Honorary Member, August 9, 1907.

A. A. A. Scottish Rite: Alpha Lodge of Perfection, Yankton, February 14, 1894; Mackey Chapter, February 15, 1894; Robert de Bruce Council No. 2, February 16, 1894; Oriental Consistory No. 2, February 17, 1894; Master of Ceremonies, 1897; Chancellor, 1899 and 1900; Preceptor, 1901; Khurum Lodge of Perfection, Sioux Falls, Charter Member; Albert Pike Chapter, Charter Member; Coeur de Leon Council, Charter Member; Occidental Consistory No. 2, Charter Member; K. C. C. H., Washington, D. C., October 19, 1897; Honorary 33d Degree, January 16, 1900; Deputy Inspector General for Sioux Falls, November 28, 1902; Royal Order of Scotland, October 19, 1903.

A. A. O. N. M. S., El Riad Temple, Sioux Falls, June 8, 1899; held all intermediate offices; elected Potentate, December 12, 1908; reelected Potentate, December 15, 1909; Grand Representative New Orleans, 1910; Rochester, July 11, 1911.

Masonic Veterans' Association, South Dakota, June 11, 1901; Secretary, June 14, 1911, to 1914.

Order of the Eastern Star: Beulah Chapter No. 2, Flandreau, February, 1885; Worthy Patron. 1885-1896.

Grand Chapter O. E. S., South Dakota: Second Grand Patron, May, 1890; Third Grand Patron, 1891; Fourth Grand Patron, 1892.

Jasper Chapter O. E. S., No. 4, Sioux Falls: Admitted, 1905.

General Grand Chapter O. E. S.: Chairman board of trustees, 1907-1910; Right Worthy Associate Grand Patron, November 1910-1913; Most Worthy Grand Patron, 1913 to 1916.

he served as Grand High Priest; has been Grand Secretary of the Grand Lodge since 1895, and Grand Recorder of the Grand Commandery since 1894 except one year when he served as Grand Commander; in 1896 was elected Grand Recorder of the Order of High Priesthood, and is also secretary of the Masonic Veterans' Association.

He is a member of the Order of the Eastern Star and was Grand Patron of the State from 1891 to 1893. In the General Grand Chapter of the Order he served as chairman of the board of trustees during the term 1907-1910; as Right Worthy Associate Grand Patron, 1910-1913; and at the session of 1913 was elected and installed Most Worthy Grand Patron of the Order.

He is a member of the Odd Fellows, Modem Woodmen of America, Elks, and the Association of Military Surgeons of America.

At Troy, New York, October 19, 1887, he was married to Eudora Zulette Stearns, who was born at Felchville, Vermont, July 28, 1858. This union has been blessed by the birth of one child, Addie Stearns, born September 17, 1890.

Greeting Song
By Eudora Z. Pettigrew, P. W. C. M.

We come from all over our beautiful State,
And join our glad voices in greeting elate.
We welcome you all, with right merry good cheer,
And thank Him, who kept us through all the glad year.

Chorus

"Happy greeting to all, happy greeting to all,
Happy greeting, happy greeting, happy greeting to all."

We hail with true pleasure, our bright "Eastern Star,"

Which shines on us all, and its beams scatter far,
It brightens our lives, fills each heart with pure love,
And praise, and thanksgiving, to our Father above.

CHORUS

Our chain has been lengthened by many links, bright;
Our lives have been strengthened, to enter life's fight,
We've sought to bring sunshine to sad hearts we know,
And "love" is our watchword, wherever we go.

CHORUS

Shine on may the light from our beautiful Star,
Its radiance shed o'er us, till we "cross the bar"
And sing the glad song on the bright, shining shore,
To dwell in the presence of "love" evermore.

CHORUS

NEW YEAR'S GREETINGS, 1902
BY EUDORA Z. PETTIGREW, P. W. C. M.

To the Sisters and Brothers of the O. E. S.:
    The bright New Year again has come,
        So full of joy and gladness;
    We bid "good by" to Nineteen One,
        With all its care and sadness.

    The year just past, to some brought joy,
        Increased their earthly treasure,
    And filled their hearts with peace and love,
        And life seemed only pleasure.

But others tell a sadder tale,
    The hopes of life seem ended;
A shadow rests upon their home,
    Despair and grief are blended.

What New Year work have we to do?
    To cheer our hearthstone only?
Our Eastern Star is full of love
    For all the sad and lonely.

Reflect the light from our bright star,
    Be each a faithful Martha,
And strive to lead the sad ones home
    To trust a loving Father.

I send you greetings one and all,
    My sister and my brother,
May peace and sunshine fill your hearts,
    Because you've helped another.

Be Bethlehem's star our guide this year
    To high and holy living,
And next New Year's day find our hearts
    O'erflowing with thanksgiving.

Faster and faster the years go by,
    How swiftly the time is fleeting.
A Happy New Year to everyone,
    To all, I send this greeting.

ORDER OF THE EASTERN STAR
By Eudora Z. Pettigrew, P. W. G.M.

The work is done, how well,
    Only the Master knows.
One never sees the fruit
    Of all the seed he sows.

It may be only our part
    To patiently turn the sod,
One plants, another waters,
    But the increase comes from God.

The golden fruit is ripening,
    With dew, the meadows wet,
The sheaves are few in number,
    The harvest is not yet.

We live, we. dream, we think,
    We hope, we love, we plan,
The future, with its mystery
    Is not revealed to man.

I give you back the gavel
    You trusted to my care,
To always use it wisely
    Has been my fervent prayer.

May Heaven's richest blessing
    Upon our labors rest,
And its glories meet our vision
    As the sun sinks in the west.

Mrs. Lorraine J. Pitkin [6]

In writing a sketch of the life of Mrs. Lorraine J. Pitkin, the Right Worthy Grand Secretary of the General Grand Chapter, O. E. S., and senior living Past Most Worthy Grand Matron, it is like writing a history of the Order of the Eastern Star to attempt anything that would be a true account of Sister Pitkin's fifty years of Eastern Star life. One who has illuminated the path in so many phases of O.E.S. history as has this honored and devoted member, is met with in every point of contact with Eastern Star affairs, and the task assumes such great and magnificent proportions that only a brief outline of her brilliant and well-rounded career can here be presented.

To chronicle the events of even an ordinary life and do justice to it, is not an easy task; but when an attempt is made to record the events which have combined to compose the well-spent years of the subject of this sketch, whose usefulness has been so far-reaching in its effects, then the impossibility becomes evident, the effort to be complete is a recognized failure, and only an approximate idea can be reached.

Lorraine J. Dickinson was born July 15, 1845, a farmer's daughter, in Waddington, St. Lawrence County, New York. Her parents, who were formerly of New England, removed west in 1849 and settled near Elgin, Illinois. At the age of eleven she was sent to Rutland, Vermont, to attend a young ladies' seminary at that place, and having returned home in 1861, she was married October 22, 1863, to Captain E. P. Pitkin, A. Q. M., U.S.A.

The call for volunteers brought a response from Captain E. P. Pitkin, who enlisted at Annapolis, Maryland, in the quartermaster's department. At the battle of Stone River, he had charge of an

---

[6] Senior living Past Most Worthy Grand Matron; Right Worthy Grand Secretary, 1883 to present.

ammunition train, and was captured, but by strategic measures he escaped his captors. He was soon after promoted to assistant quartermaster with the rank of captain. He entered the service when the first guns were fired on Sumter and was appointed colonel and chief quartermaster of the defense of New Orleans. Before his death, as a reward for his faithful service, his commission as colonel was issued, too late, however, to secure to his family a colonel's pension.

He spent about a year in Brazos, Texas, as master of marine transportation. While stationed in Chicago he met and married Miss Lorraine J. Dickinson, the marriage occurring on the date above mentioned, October 22, 1863. Very soon afterwards, the young husband was ordered to New Orleans. After an absence of seven months he returned on a month's furlough, going back to his post of duty on June 6, 1864. The good-bye spoken at that time was the final farewell, for on October 6th, just four months later, Captain Pitkin was called to journey to the home beyond. An escort brought the remains to the bereaved young wife, and they were taken to the family burying place in Cleveland, Ohio.

Before a twelve-month rolled by Sister Pitkin was a wife and a widow, and the following March, the day that Abraham Lincoln was, for the second time, inaugurated President of the United States, a little daughter was born to her.

The great sorrow which swept the joy from her young life when her lover-husband gave up his life for his country, so darkened the woof of life's web that many would have broken these delicate threads and have given up in utter despair; but not so with this courageous woman. Bravely clasping to her heart the little one, the sole pledge of her earthly love, she began the battle of life, determined that she could and would support herself and little child, dedicating herself to the widowhood she has ever held sacred.

How well she has woven the web of her earthly life with the bright and glorious filling of the blue thread of fidelity, the yellow thread of constancy, the white thread of light, purity, and joy, the

Officers of the General Grand Chapter

green thread of hope and immortality, and the red thread of fervency! These five beautiful colors of the Eastern Star have been exemplified and she has seen them honored in every State in the Union, with a respect second only to our glorious flag.

From the records of the Eastern Star life of Sister Pitkin, the following will suffice to establish her useful and honored service in the Order:

Mrs. Lorraine J. Pitkin joined the organization known as "Miriam Family No. 111," which was organized October 6, 1866, by D. W. Thompson, who conferred the Eastern Star degrees upon thirty members. In January 1867, she was elected Conductress. In the latter part of 1867, the Michigan ritual (as arranged by John F. Tatem) was adopted and Sister Pitkin was elected Worthy President. July 18, 1877, Sister Pitkin organized Queen Esther Chapter No. 41, and became its first Worthy Matron and still holds her membership in this splendid chapter. She was elected Worthy Grand Matron of the Grand Chapter of Illinois in 1878, and at the Grand Chapter session of 1879, her report or address, which contained her decisions, official acts, amendments to the by-laws, and recommendations, indicated a thorough knowledge of the workings of the Order and a recognition of the possibilities to be accomplished by the work of this organization of women. To her belongs the credit of first advocating practical charity, which has become the rallying cry of the Order in every Grand Jurisdiction. In her address she said: "If our Chapters had something to labor for, some little bare feet to clothe, there would be no time for contention and strife, the seeds of discord would never be sown, and a spirit of harmony and unity would prevail."

It can truthfully be said that to this devoted member the Order is indebted for much of the pioneer work, the ideas which have developed our laws of the present and the advancement of our principles, and its present position as the greatest secret organization among women, for now its strong arms of charity, truth, and loving kindness encircle the world and its beautiful story of fidelity to kindred and friends is told, not only in the English language, but also in the German and the Spanish languages as well.

Thus far, consideration has been given to Sister Pitkin as a local and State organizer and worker, but it is as a national worker in the Order that she shines as a bright jewel, eclipsing for years of service, diversity of experience, conservative judgment, thorough acquaintance with Eastern Star laws, as well as a full understanding of the usages, all of our grand galaxy of pioneer workers.

In August, 1880, in the city of Chicago, Mrs. Pitkin was elected Most Worthy Grand Matron of the General Grand Chapter, and her address and report at the session of 1883, held in San Francisco, California, evidenced the same indomitable energy and wise legislation that had characterized her previous services, and her election to the office of Right Worthy Grand Secretary at this assembly established the appreciation of her associates for her business ability. Circumstances seemed to warrant her resignation at this time, but at Indianapolis, in 1889, she was again elected to that honorable and responsible position, which she has filled continuously for nine consecutive terms of three years each, making a total of twenty-seven years, and is yet filling most creditably and acceptably to the Order.

During the thirty-eight years of uninterrupted service in the General Grand Chapter, many positions of honor and trust have been her reward for earnest and devoted services to duty. The World's Fair records of May 16, 1893, contain the work as accomplished by the O.E.S. The World's Congress of Women, with Mrs. Potter Palmer as its president, accorded to Sister Pitkin a day that should be given wholly to an O.E.S. program, and it was rendered in a manner that reflected great credit upon our Order, and obtained for us the respect and esteem of a large body of representative women. In 1902, Mrs. Pitkin was honored by an appointment on the board of directors of the World's Fair Fraternal Building Association, held in the city of St. Louis, and her experience and executive ability aided greatly in this important work. It was only fitting that she should be invited to give her assistance, also her presence, at the Lewis and Clark Exposition in Portland, Oregon, in 1905, where her large acquaintance and Eastern Star knowledge added much to the happiness of the visiting members of the Order.

For three years she had charge of the O.E.S. department in the American Home and in connection with Sister Jennie E. Matthews, P. M.W.G.M., she completed and published a collection of music for Chapter use entitled, *Gems of Song*. A more recent publication is *The Floral Work*, which is used extensively throughout the O.E.S. world. The membership badge, of which she holds the copyright, is the handsomest in use and is distinctively an Eastern Star badge.

She is an earnest and devoted member of the Women's Relief Corps in its great work of patriotism and relief and has been accorded the highest office in Illinois.

In her business life, Sister Pitkin served as postmistress of the House in the Illinois legislature, and such was her record that in the following year she was elected to a similar position in the Senate, receiving from the members of the Thirty-sixth General Assembly a beautiful gold watch and a recommendation for ability signed by every member of that assembly.

Sister Pitkin has agitated the question of an objective work for the Order of the Eastern Star almost the entire time of her membership, which is almost all the term of its existence. She has a money interest in nearly every Home or Home Fund in the United States and was one of the strongest factors in organizing the Masonic Orphans' Home and the Eastern Star and Masonic Home at Macon, Illinois. She also gave the first $100 to start the fund for the O.E.S. Home. In 1895 she saw the beginning of that splendid work and served on the Home board for two years.

Much more could be added without exhausting the subject. Mrs. Pitkin's record of fifty years' service in this, the grandest Order of women, and the greatest Order, except Masonry, in the world, has been productive of lasting and untold good. She has lived to see the

Order grow from a few scattering members, incompletely organized, to almost a million enthusiastic members; to see Homes for the aged and dependent members established in many States, and if not yet completed, a fund for this purpose created in every Grand Jurisdiction; to see the Order honored and respected wherever the five colors are known; to see the effect upon women of its influence for broadening and developing stronger characters, their lives sweetened and elevated by the memory of good deeds and kindly words.

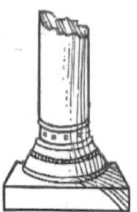

CHAPTER VI

Brief Histories of the Several Grand Chapters

GRAND CHAPTER OF ALABAMA [1]

AT THE organization of the Alabama Grand Chapter, there were no chapters holding charters of the Macoy system, so far as known, although quite a number of persons throughout the State had taken the degrees known as the Macoy degrees.

The first Chapter organized by the General Grand Chapter was Charity No. 1, located at Burlson, Franklin County, April 25, 1891, followed by Corona No. 2, Corona, July 24, 1895; Ruth No. 3, Lewisburg; Fellowship No. 4, Gordo, February 6, 1897; Florence No. 5, April 1, 1897; Golden Rule No. 6, Trussville, September 11, 1897; Temple No. 7, Marion, July 11, 1899; Ben Brecken No. 8, Rutledge, September 2, 1899; Columbia No. 9, Columbia, October 6, 1899; Elizabeth Armstrong No. 10, Montgomery, March 1, 1900; Julian No. 11, Berry Station, January 27, 1900; Adah No. 12, Birmingham, April 16, 1900; Julia Shelton No. 13, Fayette, August 24, 1900; Bertha Rubenstine No. 14, Andalusia, July 20, 1900; Green Hill No. 15, Green Hill, September 8, 1900.

The Grand Chapter was organized March 6, 1901, in the city of Birmingham, by Mrs. Hattie E. Ewing, Most Worthy Grand Matron, with nine chapters represented: Corona No. 2, Fellowship No. 4, Temple No. 7, Columbia No. 9, Julian No. 11, Adah No. 12, Julia Shelton No. 13, Bertha Rubenstine No. 14, Green Hill No. 15.

Mrs. Elizabeth Salter, of Birmingham, was elected Grand Matron, Daniel A. Gibson, Corona Chapter No. 2, Grand Patron, and William M. Cunningham, Corona Chapter No. 2, Grand Secretary.

---

[1] Data by Mrs. Elizabeth Salter, P.G.M., Grand Secretary, 1906 to present.

The first annual session of the Grand Chapter was held in Fayette, November 7 and 8, 1901; other sessions were held at Avondale, 1902; Montgomery, 1903; New Decatur, 1904; Ensley, 1905; Montgomery, 1906; Birmingham, 1907; Montgomery, 1908; Montgomery, 1909; Mobile, 1910; Anniston, 1911; Dothan, 1912; Montgomery, 1913; Birmingham, 1914.

At Ensley, 1905, a resolution was adopted to amend the constitution so as to allow ten cents per capita to be collected by the Grand Chapter to form a scholarship fund. This fund was lost sight of, nothing being done to carry out the objects of the resolution. At the meeting in Montgomery, 1906, a resolution was adopted, providing that twenty-five cents additional tax be made into a fund to be known as "The Eastern Star Widows' and Orphans' Fund," to be used in the erection of a home, either by the Eastern Star or in conjunction with the Masons of Alabama; to be decided as soon as the fund reached such proportions as to justify independent action of the Eastern Star, or the Masons of Alabama shall have made such progress towards building a home as shall justify cooperation. From this date began the Home fund which has continued to grow.

A Masonic Home in this Grand Jurisdiction was talked of-for a quarter of a century, but as it required a change of the constitution before any fund could be collected, the advocates of the Home were unable to accomplish anything until the year 1907, when Brother Ben M. Jacobs as Grand Master A. F. and A. M. of Alabama, began a campaign of education and kept it up until the desired change was accomplished. In the report of 1907 Proceedings of the Grand Lodge of Alabama, A. F. and A. M., we find: "There was no help, however, in reference to the Home movement more effective than that of the Order of the Eastern Star. Five thousand letters sent out by the Grand Secretary of this Order during the campaign had untold influence with the subordinate Lodges of the Grand Jurisdiction, while five hundred dollars contributed by the Grand Chapter last year, five hundred dollars this year, and one-half of the per capita tax of the Order will be a future contribution."

In 1908, the Masonic Grand Lodge began to collect a fund for the Home. The administration building was completed and dedicated in December, 1912; in November, 1912, the Grand Chapter, O. E. S., donated $2,500 to furnish the dining-room and lower hall; Elizabeth Armstrong Chapter No. 10, Montgomery, $100 to furnish a Matron's room; Brundridge Chapter No. 27, Wylam, $225 to furnish a sitting room; and Salter Chapter No. 21, Birmingham, $300 to furnish parlor; and the desired and necessary legislation was enacted by the State of Alabama, conveying the legal rights prayed for, which resulted in great benefit to the Order of the Eastern Star as well as to the Masonic Fraternity.[2]

---

[2] The petition for charter was addressed to the Hon. S. E. Greene, Probate Judge of Jefferson County, Alabama, as follows:

The undersigned would most respectfully certify unto your Honor that the "Order of the Eastern Star" is a fraternal and benevolent association, organized solely for fraternal and charitable purposes, with subordinate Chapters located at various places throughout the State and a Grand Chapter composed of representatives from such subordinate Chapters.

That said association is desirous of incorporating under the laws of the State of Alabama and in conformity to such laws have, within thirty days prior thereto, elected the following persons as Trustees: J. H. Edwards, Wylam, Alabama; Mary Camps, Wylam, Alabama; Elizabeth Salter, Flyton, Alabama.

Said above named persons have been elected as Trustees to hold office until the annual meeting of said Grand Chapter, to be held in November, 1908, at which three Trustees will again be elected whose term of office shall be for one year and until their successors shall be elected and qualified. The name of such corporation shall be: THE GRAND CHAPTER Of THE ORDER OF THE EASTERN STAR Of THE STATE Of ALABAMA.

Said corporation shall have and exercise all the rights, powers and privileges conferred on such corporations under the general laws of the State of Alabama as well as those granted to said Order of the Eastern Star under an act of the Legislature of Alabama at the adjourned session held in the year 1907.

Signed by those mentioned above as Trustees.

The charter granted provided:

In an act which was approved August 14, 1907, it was provided that all property, both real and personal, belonging to the Grand Chapter, O. E. S., or subordinate Chapters, be exempted from taxation.[3]

In 1913 the Grand Chapter donated money to build a hospital at a cost of $10,000, which building was dedicated December 2, 1914.

The Grand Lodge, A. F. and A.M., adopted a resolution authorizing the Grand Chapter to appoint a committee to act as advisory

---

(1) That the title to all real property, whether acquired by the Grand Chapter directly or by a subordinate Chapter, shall vest in the Grand Chapter, and no conveyance thereof can be made except by the properly constituted authorities of such Grand Chapter.

(2) When any real property is acquired by a subordinate Chapter the title thereto shall be taken in the name of the Grand Chapter of the Order of the Eastern Star of Alabama, but the use, income and privileges thereof shall remain and be wholly devoted to the benefit of said subordinate Chapter so long as its charter shall remain in force.

(3) The real property held by the Grand Chapter for the use of a subordinate Chapter may be conveyed in the same manner as the property held directly by the Grand Chapter, provided no conveyance thereof shall be made except upon a resolution of such subordinate Chapter adopted at a regular meeting thereof and duly certified to the Trustees of the said Grand Chapter under seal of the subordinate Chapter.

• • • • • • • •

(7) When any subordinate Chapter becomes defunct, either by a surrender, revocation or forfeiture of its Charter, any real property held by the Grand Chapter for its use and benefit, shall at once become unconditionally vested in the Grand Chapter, to be held or disposed of as said Grand Chapter may determine.

(8) The title of all furniture, regalia, jewels, and every form of personal property acquired by a subordinate Chapter becomes at once vested in the Grand Chapter; however, such subordinate Chapter has the exclusive right to the use of and the control of the said furniture, etc., so long as its Charter remains active and it may sell, exchange, convey or dispose of such property at will while holding such Charter, without the express consent of the Grand Chapter. In case any subordinate Chapter becomes defunct by non-use, surrender, forfeiture or revocation of its Charter, the Grand Chapter at once becomes entitled to the possession of all such personal property held by the Chapter at such time and if not surrendered, may take possession of same.

[3] An act to exempt from taxation all the property both real and personal belonging to the Eastern Star. Approved August 14, 1907.

committee with the board of control in the management of the Home and the following were appointed: Mrs. Elizabeth Salter, Birmingham; Mrs. Mattie W. Hand, Bay Minette; Mrs. Callie L. French, Columbia; and Mrs. Mary Youngs, Montgomery. This committee undertook to solicit donations to furnish the hospital and to date this committee has realized $2,000 from their efforts.

The Home has 236 acres of land; main building, three stories high with basement; two ten room cottages, and hospital; built of hollow tile and concrete tile floors, tile roof, with all modern improvements and conveniences, first class in every particular, at a cost of $135,000.

The Eastern Star is working in conjunction with the Masonic Order and members of the Eastern Star are admitted to this Home upon the same terms as the Masonic Fraternity.

> Think beautiful thoughts and set them adrift
>   On eternity's boundless sea!
> Let their burden be pure, let their white sails lift,
> And carry from you the comforting gift
>   Of your heartfelt sympathy.
> For a beautiful thought is a beautiful thing;
>   And out on the infinite tide
> May meet, and touch, and tenderly bring
> To the sick, and the weary and sorrowing
>   A solace so long denied.

GRAND CHAPTER OF ALBERTA [4]

The Order of the Eastern Star was introduced into the province of Alberta by Sister Rosetta West, a demitted member of Gloaming

---

[4] Organized July 20, 1912. Data by Brother Samuel J. Blair, P.G.P., Grand Secretary, 1913 to present.

Chapter No. 255, of Milford, Iowa, who after a great deal of trouble succeeded in getting the names of nineteen eligible persons on a petition for a new Chapter. Dispensation was granted by the General Grand Chapter on March 20, 1906, and on April 12 the Mountain View Chapter was instituted at Olds by Sister Rosetta West, acting Deputy for the Most Worthy Grand Patron.

On September 3, 1907, the second chapter, Venus, of Red Deer, was instituted by Brother John Duff of Mountain View Chapter. This Chapter started with a membership of twenty-three.

During his term as Most Worthy Grand Patron Brother W. H. Norris instituted in person, Chinook Chapter, Calgary, June 10, 1908; Alexandra Chapter, Lacombe, June 11, and Bow Valley, Calgary, August 6, 1909. The visit of Brother Norris in June 1908, was the first visit of any of the General Grand Chapter officers to the Province.

In 1910 Sister Beulah MacLaren of Chinook Chapter, represented Alberta at the assembly of the General Grand Chapter in Jacksonville and her report of that meeting was a source of great pleasure and profit to all who had the pleasure of hearing it.

In July 1911, Brother Willis D. Engle, Most Worthy Grand Patron, instituted the following Chapters: Mizpah, Maple Leaf, Connaught, Electa, Killam, Areme, and in July, 1912, Occidental. On both occasions he was accompanied by Sister Engle and a great amount of Eastern Star knowledge was obtained by the members of the young Chapters in this Province.

During the autumn of 1911 the Chapters of Alberta were honored by the Most Worthy Grand Matron, Sister M. Alice Miller, who visited a number of the Chapters and met representatives of nearly all. It would be difficult to estimate the amount of good resulting from this visit. Her ability to impart valuable information in a most impressive manner, together with a perfect knowledge of the requirements, made the visit of Sister Miller a treat that will long be remembered and appreciated. It was the beginning of an era of improvement, both of the work in the Chapter room and in the daily work of the members outside. To this visit the members in Alberta trace any degree of success which has attended their efforts, as from her came the inspiration to make the effort.

The initiatory steps in connection with the formation of the Grand Chapter of Alberta were taken by Mountain View Chapter No. 1, of Olds, in 1911, when their Secretary took the matter up with the Most Worthy Grand Patron and after considerable correspondence wrote to each Chapter asking for an expression of opinion as to the advisability of the plan. The result was a unanimous vote in favor of the movement. On June 28th the Most Worthy Grand Patron issued a summons requesting each Chapter to send representatives to attend a meeting to be held in the Masonic Temple, Calgary, on July 20, 1912. On that date the twelve Chapters (one only two days old) in the Province met and the Grand Chapter was formed. Sister Isabella Duff, of Mountain View, was elected first Worthy Grand Matron and Brother S. J. Blair, of Chinook Chapter, the first Worthy Grand Patron. Sister M. Alice Miller, Most Worthy Grand Matron, Brother Willis D. Engle, Most Worthy Grand Patron, and Sister Engle were made honorary life members.

In September 1913, the Worthy Grand Matron and Worthy Grand Patron attended the assembly of the General Grand Chapter in Chicago and very much enjoyed the entire proceedings. They were particularly impressed with the reception accorded visitors and the presentation of the Union Jack, to which the Worthy Grand Patron referred in his address to Grand Chapter in the following words: "One of the most pleasing events in which it has been my privilege to participate, was when the Right Worthy Associate Grand Matron and Patron presented the Canadian flag. All the visitors from Canada were invited to the Grand East and welcomed by the Most Worthy Grand Matron in a manner that left no doubt as to its sincerity. The Canadian flag was then entwined with the Stars and Stripes in the decorations of the Chapter room, while the Canadian visitors sang 'The Maple Leaf Forever.' This very thoughtful and courteous act was much appreciated by all the visitors from Canada, as I know it will be by you, to whom it is my pleasure to report it."

Since the formation of the Grand Chapter ten Chapters have been added and the membership more than doubled. The growth has not been rapid, but it has the appearance of health, and every Chapter reports considerable progress. The present great European War, in which Canada is participating, instead of dampening the ardor of the members, has inspired them with a desire to display, in tangible form, those beautiful teachings of our Order, charity and loving kindness.

It is pleasing to note that the Masonic Lodges have extended their approval and support to the O.E.S. and so long as this confidence is deserved there is a bright future for the Order in this Province.

Grand Chapter of Arizona [5]

By authority of the Most Worthy Grand Patron Brother Willis Brown, the Right Worthy Grand Secretary, Rev. Willis D. Engle, issued a commission to Brother Morris Goldwater, of Prescott, Arizona, as Deputy of the Most Worthy Grand Patron for the Territory of Arizona, 1880-1883, to organize Chapters. Consequently, on February 6, 1882, a charter was issued for Golden Rule Chapter No. 1, Prescott, which was organized by Morris Goldwater on March 9, 1882, with Mrs. G. W. Curtis as Worthy Matron and William H. Kelly as Worthy Patron. White Mountain Chapter No. 2, Globe, was chartered November 3, 1885, and organized by Alonzo Bailey, special Deputy of the Most Worthy Grand Patron. Alsap Chapter No. 3, Phoenix, was chartered April 30, 1887, and organized by H. B. Lighthizer, Deputy of the Most Worthy Grand Patron. Mount Frisco Chapter No. 4, located at Flagstaff, was chartered July 13, 1888, and

---

[5] Organized November 15, 1900.

Brief Histories of the Several Grand Chapters

organized by J. Guthrie Savage, Deputy of the Most Worthy Grand Patron, with twenty-six members.

White Mountain Chapter No. 2 at Globe, Alsap Chapter No. 3 at Phoenix, and Mount Frisco Chapter No. 4, at Flagstaff, had become dormant. White Mountain Chapter No. 2 surrendered its charter after having paid all dues to January 1, 1892, and members were given dimits. Alsap Chapter No. 3 never paid any dues to the General Grand Chapter and Mount Frisco Chapter paid dues for the year it was organized, but never paid any more. When a petition was received for a Chapter at Tucson, the Chapter was chartered November 19, 1898, as Arizona Chapter No. 2, and was organized by J. H. Langdon, Deputy of the Most Worthy Grand Patron, with forty-three charter members and with Mrs. Annie L. Tilton as Worthy Matron and Lanis Stanley Wilson as Worthy Patron.

A meeting of the Grand Lodge, Grand Chapter Royal Arch Masons, and Grand Commandery was to be held at Tucson in November 1899, and Arizona Chapter requested the privilege of conferring the degrees upon eligible members for the purpose of extending the Order in the Territory. On November 4, 1899, the Most Worthy Grand Patron granted a special dispensation to this Chapter to confer the degrees, November 16, 1899, upon members of the Grand Lodge not residing in Prescott, Tucson, Winslow, Phoenix, Flagstaff, or Globe. By authority of this dispensation, the degrees were conferred upon eight members of the Grand Lodge, of whom four were from Wilcox, two from Nogales, one from Florence, and one from Bisbee.

Ruby Chapter No. 3, Winslow, was chartered June 1, 1899, and organized June 24, 1899, by H. A. Simms, Deputy of the Most Worthy Grand Patron, with twenty-three charter members. Grand Canon Chapter No. 4, at Flagstaff, was chartered September 9, 1899, and organized October 27, 1899, by John Maurer, Deputy of the Most Worthy Grand Patron, with twenty-eight charter members. Phoenix Chapter No. 5, at Phoenix, was chartered November 3, 1899, and organized December 13, 1899, by Mrs. Annie L. Tilton, Deputy of the

Most Worthy Grand Patron, with fifty-one charter members. Pearl Chapter No. 6, at Bisbee, was chartered December 21, 1899, and organized January 5, 1900, by Mrs. Annie L. Tilton, Deputy, with forty-nine charter members. Diamond Chapter No. 7, at Jerome, was granted a charter February 21, 1900, and organized March 24, by Mrs. Annie L. Tilton, with thirty-four charter members. White Mountain Chapter No. 8, at Globe, was chartered May 23, 1900, and organized June 23, 1900, by Mrs. Annie L. Tilton, Deputy, with fifty charter members.

Of the eleven Chapters that had been organized, only eight were active at the time of the organization of the Grand Chapter, November 15, 1900. The convention was held at Phoenix and representatives of five Chapters participated in the organization in the reception room of the Commercial Hotel. The convention was presided over by Mrs. Annie L. Tilton, who was elected the first Grand Matron. A tax not to exceed twenty-five cents per capita was levied to meet the expense of organization.

The constitution adopted fixed the meeting at the same time and place as Masonic Grand Lodge. Past Grand Secretaries and Treasurers and Past Matrons and Past Patrons were made members of the Grand Chapter. All officers elected by ballot except the Grand Warder, Grand Sentinel, Grand Chaplain, Grand Marshal, and Grand Organist. Revenues are derived from the following sources: $30 for charter, if the $30 required for dispensation had not previously been paid; special dispensation, fifty cents; for affixing seal of Grand Chapter to any document not otherwise provided for, twenty-five cents; and the per capita tax, which was fixed at fifty cents, but in 1903 raised to seventy-five cents.

In 1905 the Territory was divided into districts, and in 1906 each Chapter was directed to give one entertainment each year to raise funds to be known as a Charity Fund, which could be used for the erection of a Masonic and Eastern Star Home, and in 1907 a per capita tax of twenty-five cents was levied for the same purpose. In 1908 it was voted to hold the next meeting February 10, 1910, which left 1909 without any session of the Grand Chapter. In 1911 Sister M. Alice Miller, Most Worthy Grand Matron, was the guest of honor and installed the Grand Officers elected. Sister Miller was presented with a handsome loving cup by the members of the Grand Chapter.

At every session of the Grand Chapter, it has met with the most courteous attention from the Masonic Fraternity, and the Grand Chapter and Grand Lodge have had social entertainments after the business sessions closed, at each annual meeting. Auto rides, receptions, card parties, and balls make the social life attractive. In 1905, a visit was made to the room known as "Lone Star Stope," deep underground and about 700 feet from the mouth of a tunnel-a room 50 feet from the floor to ceiling, 45 feet wide, and 110 feet long, brilliantly lighted. The Grand Lodge held its annual session in this room, which is near the City of Morenci, which place, by the way, has many interesting features.

The Grand Matron's address, 1912, contained a splendid O.E.S. thought: "We don't want to be theoretically good, but we do need to be more practically true. Our great trouble is we talk too much, and we do too little."

> The golden chain whose links of love,
> Forged by the hand that rules above,
> Will bind the race — Oh I that it would —
> Into one blessed brotherhood.

Grand Chapter of Arkansas [6]

During the existence of the Supreme Grand Chapter of the Adoptive Rite of the Order of the Eastern Star a number of charters were

---

[6] Organized October 2, 1876. Data furnished by Mrs. Nora G. Rushing, P.G.M., Grand Secretary, 1913 to present.

issued, including five Chapters in Arkansas, but of these the records are not complete. The first Chapter of the Order of the Eastern Star, as we now know it, organized in Arkansas, was Enola No. 1, Mount Vernon, in July 1870, though in the present roll of Chapters, the records show Witcherville Chapter as No. 1, which was organized in February 1906, and chartered in November 1906. This apparent imperfection is due to the fact that Enola Chapter No. 1 had become dormant and Witcherville was given the vacant place. The number indicates that it was the first Chapter organized and therefore the oldest, but it is not, for it was organized about thirty-six years after the Order had been in active existence, and it occupies the place of honor in preference to 170 Chapters organized before Witcherville No. 1.

In the order of organization, there were Martha Chapter No. 2, Jacinto No. 3, Carlton No. 4, Searchy No. 5, and Massey No. 6. These six Chapters, represented by their delegates, assembled at Searcy, October 2, 1876, in convention called by Brother W. B. Massey and organized the Grand Chapter. It is a peculiar condition and one to be regretted, that all of the six Chapters which participated in the organization of the Grand Chapter are now dormant and the statistics of the earlier meetings were not printed, rendering the particulars not accessible.

The first Grand Matron was Mrs. Kiddy A. Neal and the first Grand Patron was Brother J. M. Mallett. At the first regular meeting held in Searcy, November 8, 1876, at which time the original six Chapters were represented, the Grand Chapter decided that it was inexpedient for it to send delegates to the convention to be held at Indianapolis, Indiana, in November, 1876, for the purpose of organizing the General Grand Chapter, but that it would cooperate in the movement.

At the second regular meeting, which was in 1877, only four Chapters were represented. Legislation was enacted adopting the regalia of the Order: "A scarf of five colors, three inches wide, with a rosette on the shoulder, one on the breast, and one at the crossing, to be worn from the right shoulder to the left side." Past Matrons, Past Patrons, and Past Associate Matrons were made members of the Grand Chapter for one year after their term of office had expired; the Grand Matron was made the executive officer of the Grand Chapter; dues were fixed at ten cents per member but were raised to twenty cents in 1882 and to twenty-five cents in 1886.

Again, at the third meeting, 1878, only four Chapters were represented and but very little business was transacted.

At the session of 1879, a Grand Orator was elected, whose duty was to deliver an address at the installation of the Grand Officers, each year.

At the session of 1880, allegiance was acknowledged to the General Grand Chapter and its ritual was adopted. There were then seven Chapters and 304 members in the State. A committee was appointed to visit the Grand Lodge to present the claims of the Order before that Grand body and ask recognition of the Order by the Grand Lodge, A. F. and A. M.; and an edict was issued forbidding any member of the Order conferring the degrees in any other way than in the manner prescribed by the constitution.

In 1886 the State was divided into districts, and a Deputy Grand Matron and a Deputy Grand Patron appointed for each, which arrangement is still in force, and in 1891 district schools of instruction were inaugurated.

Immediately following the introduction of the Order of the Eastern Star into Arkansas, the Masonic Fraternity treated the organization with indifference, and in some instances, opposition was manifested. Many of the older Masons were disposed to an unfriendly feeling toward it, but as the years passed and the Order indicated its purposes and its principles, together with efforts to be in harmony with the best interests of the Masonic Fraternity, this condition gradually changed and in 1894 the Grand Lodge voted that the board of control of the Masonic Temple should provide rooms for the meetings of the Grand Chapter, if practicable. Leading Masons throughout the State became members of the Eastern Star, and there developed a beautiful harmony which resulted in the adoption by the Grand Lodge of 1904, of a resolution introduced by Brother John M. Oathout, Grand Lecturer of the Grand Lodge, as follows:

> *Whereas*, The Order of the Eastern Star is composed of Master Masons, their wives, widows, mothers, sisters, and daughters; and,
>
> *Whereas*, Said Order is engaged in works of charity and benevolence that merit our highest encouragement and approbation; therefore be it
>
> *Resolved*, That we commend the Order of the Eastern Star to the Masonic Fraternity of this Grand Jurisdiction as an institution worthy of their regard, and as such we wish the Order abundant prosperity and success.

At the session of the Grand Chapter of 1904, a committee, composed of Brothers George Thornburgh, T. J. Shinn, and E. E. Ammons, was appointed to secure passage by the legislature of a bill incorporating the Grand Chapter. The committee prepared the bill, which was introduced into the State Senate by Brother B. E. McFerrin, who at that time was a member of the Senate. It passed both houses and was approved by the Governor March 2, 1905.

The Order is proud of the fact that the first money contributed for the building of the Masonic Orphans' Home was by Esther Chapter No. 217, Little Rock. At its meeting February 4, 1904, it was voted to raise $100 toward the establishment of the Home. A social and literary entertainment was held in the Grand Lodge room at which $103.15 was raised, $100 of which was contributed to the purpose named.

At the session of 1904, the Grand Chapter sent the following communication to the Grand Lodge:

> The Grand Chapter Order of the Eastern Star, in session assembled, congratulates the Grand Lodge upon its

contemplated action relative to a Masonic and Eastern Star Home in Arkansas, and hereby tenders its assistance, both moral and financial, to bring about this great blessing to the Craft throughout the State.

At the same session the Grand Chapter adopted an amendment to its constitution, whereby it could and did levy an extra tax of twenty-five cents per capita for the building of a Masonic and Eastern Star Home. This action, together with the above, was taken the day preceding the 1904 session of the Grand Lodge. A beautiful Home has been erected upon the plat of one hundred acres near Batesville, in the dedication of which the Grand Chapter participated in 1909. The Grand Chapter is represented by two members upon the board of trustees of the orphanage at Batesville and has contributed liberally to its erection and support, having donated about $7,500 to the Home fund.

In 1911 the constitution was amended to permit the Grand Chapter by vote to order a regular session to be held at Batesville, in connection with the Orphans' Home, at such time of the year as the Grand Chapter might designate.

At the session of 1908, the Grand Chapter elected Mrs. Josie Frazer-Cappleman, Poetess Laureate of the Order in Arkansas. On the evening of February 4, 1909, in Esther Chapter, Mrs. Cappleman was crowned Poetess Laureate, using a wreath made of laurel gathered by Mrs. Lucy Thornburg, Past Grand Matron, from the Virginia mountains.

It has become an established custom for the Grand Lodge to invite the Grand Chapter O.E.S. to be present when the Grand Orator delivers his address, and the Grand Matron is invited to the East and also invited to address the assembly.

In 1914 the president of the board of trustees of the Albert Pike Consistory tendered the use of that building to the Grand Chapter O.E.S. for use during the annual meetings, which kindly courtesy is greatly appreciated by the Grand Chapter. This courtesy and valuable assistance from the Masonic Fraternity is greatly appreciated by the members of the Order in this State, with its 252 Chapters and 9,850 members all earnestly laboring to spread the cloak of charity, truth, and loving kindness over the entire State and to practice the principles of fidelity, constancy, light, purity, faith, and endurance.

GRAND CHAPTER OF BRITISH COLUMBIA [7]

In the beginning of the twentieth century the Most Worthy Grand Matron of the General Grand Chapter referred to the State of Massachusetts as being in the East and Indiana as in the west. Where then (in the north, the south, the east, the west, or out of the world) would one locate Ross land, British Columbia, at that time a thriving mining town with a population of some 10,000 people.

Here, on the western slope of the Canadian Rockies, on the 8th of June, 1899, John A. J. Moore, acting as Deputy for the Most Worthy Grand Patron, Nathaniel Gearhart, organized Alpha Chapter No. 1, with forty-two charter members and with Mrs. Kittie E. Bristow, Worthy Matron; J. A. J. Moore, Worthy Patron; Mrs. Eleanor Jacobs, Associate Matron. Thus, the seed of one of the noblest and most interesting of women's organizations was first planted on Canadian soil, and although nearly ten years passed before another Chapter was organized in British Columbia, yet this Chapter remained staunch and true to its teachings, ever ready to extend the hand of fellowship to the stranger, and today its past officers are active members of the Grand Chapter of the Province.

In the city of Vancouver on June 15, 1908, William H. Norris, Most Worthy Grand Patron, organized Vancouver Chapter No. 2, with twenty-five charter members, Mrs. Myra D. Heath, Worthy Matron; J. G. Elliott, Worthy Patron; Mrs. Stella Smiley, Associate

---

[7] Organized July 23, 1912. Data furnished by Mrs. Fannie N. Jones, Grand Secretary.

Matron. The next year, on August 10th, Brother Norris organized Burrard Chapter No. 3, of North Vancouver, with a membership of thirty-one, Mrs. Mary Frances Fugler, Worthy Matron; David J. Dick, Worthy Patron; Mrs. Mary Wheeler, Associate Matron. Two days later (August 12th) he organized Sharon Chapter No. 4, at Ladysmith, with sixty charter members, Mrs. Lilas Skilling, Worthy Matron; Hugh T. Fulton, Worthy Patron; Mrs. Mary Harries, Associate Matron.

Two years later, 1911, Brother Geo. M. Hyland, chairman of the board of trustees of the General Grand Chapter, and special Deputy for the Rev. Willis D. Engle, Most Worthy Grand Patron, organized in Victoria, on the 8th of March, Queen City Chapter No. 5, with a membership of 109, Mrs. Helen M. Richdale, Worthy Matron; Wm. H. F. Richdale, Worthy Patron; Mrs. Gertrude H. Preston, Associate Matron. On March 7, 1911, Alexandra Chapter No. 6 was organized by Brother Hyland with a membership of thirty-three, Mrs. Janie F. Jamieson, Worthy Matron; Charles F. Alston, Worthy Patron; Mrs. Alice M. Roberts, Associate Matron. A few months after the organization of this Chapter Sister Jamieson moved from the jurisdiction and Mrs. Mary M. Douglas was elected to fill the office thus made vacant. Sister Douglas has been a member of this Chapter since April 1911, and a member of the O.E.S. since May 31, 1887, having been initiated in Winona Chapter No. 141, of Winona, Minnesota. She has the honor and distinction of being the first Grand Matron of the Grand Chapter of the Province of British Columbia and has proved herself efficient in her work, impartial in her judgment, and at all times considerate of the opinions of others.

The same year (1911) the Most Worthy Grand Patron, the Rev. Willis D. Engle, on July 27th organized in New Westminster, Royal City Chapter No. 7, with thirty-nine charter members, Mrs. Annie F. Gilley, Worthy Matron; Samuel J. Ritchie, Worthy Patron; Mrs. Edith Laird, Associate Matron. On July 26th he organized Grandview Chapter No. 8, with thirty-four charter members, Mrs. Elizabeth Munro,

Worthy Matron; Wm. Coates Taylor, Worthy Patron; Mrs. Fannie N. Jones, Associate Matron. This Chapter has the honor of having its first Worthy Patron chosen as the first Grand Patron of the Grand Chapter of British Columbia and its first Associate Matron as the first Grand Secretary.

One year later, July 21, 1912, Princess Patricia Chapter No. 9 was organized by Brother Engle, Most Worthy Grand Patron, with thirty-two charter members, Mrs. Kate L. Greene, Worthy Matron; Rev. Chas. S. Rush, Worthy Patron; Mrs. M. Mabel Merkley, Associate Matron.

On July 23, 1912, the representatives of the nine Chapters of the Order of the Eastern Star of the Province of British Columbia having assembled in the city of Vancouver, the Rev. Willis D. Engle, Most Worthy Grand Patron of the General Grand Chapter, organized the Grand Chapter of British Columbia and the following officers were duly elected and installed: Mrs. Mary M. Douglas, Worthy Grand Matron; Wm. Coates Taylor, Worthy Grand Patron; Mrs. Elizabeth Bestwick, of Alpha Chapter No. 1, Associate Grand Matron; Hugh T. Fulton, of Sharon Chapter No. 4, Associate Grand Patron; Mrs. Katherin H. Irwin, of Burrard Chapter No. 3, Grand Treasurer; Mrs. Fannie N. Jones, of Grandview Chapter No. 8, Grand Secretary; Mrs. Anna D. Perry, of Vancouver Chapter No. 2, Grand Conductress; Mrs. Sarah Cody-Johnson, of Queen City Chapter No. 5, Associate Grand Conductress. The officers conducted the business of the Grand Chapter during this term in a very able manner. Peace and harmony prevailed throughout the year. One new Chapter was added, on October 1st, by the Worthy Grand Patron, that of Crescent No. 10, of Nanaimo, with a membership of thirty-one, Mrs. Margaret Langham, Worthy Matron; Dalton Alexander, Worthy Patron; Mrs. Margaret Cameron, Associate Matron.

The second session of the Grand Chapter was held in the city of Victoria June 17, 1913, and was royally entertained by Queen City Chapter No. 5. After a very pleasant and profitable session the following Grand Officers were installed to serve for the following year: Mrs. Anna D. Perry, Worthy Grand Matron; Wm. H. F. Richdale, Worthy Grand Patron; Mrs. Alice M. Roberts, Associate Grand Matron; B. E. Bears, Associate Grand Patron; Mrs. Katherine H. Irwin, Grand Treasurer; Mrs. Fannie N. Jones, Grand Secretary; Mrs. Myrtle Rees, Grand Conductress; Mrs. Viola Low, Associate Grand Conductress.

The following year seven new Chapters were added to our "Golden Chain." Robert Morris Chapter, of Eburne, named in honor of the founder of our beautiful Order, and having a membership of twenty-nine, with Mrs. Mina Commiskey, Worthy Matron; Robert. J. Roach, Worthy Patron; Mrs. Alice Lawrence, Associate Matron. This Chapter was organized by Wm. H. F. Richdale, Grand Patron, on the 17th of November 1913. Robert Morris Chapter has always been studiously devoted to the principles of our Order and has taken the initiative in establishing a fund to be used, at some future time, for a home for sick and indigent O.E.S. members. On December 20th Queen Esther Chapter was organized by Wm. Coates Taylor, Past Grand Patron, who acted as Deputy for the Worthy Grand Patron, this Chapter having a membership of forty, with Mrs. Christine S. Hosey, Worthy Matron; Nelson Jensen, Worthy Patron; Mrs. Marie Harvie, Associate Matron. On the 10th of March 1914, Maple Leaf Chapter, of South Vancouver, was organized by the Worthy Grand Patron, with a membership of twenty-eight, Mrs. Isabella Shirley, Worthy Matron; James A. Shirley, Worthy Patron; Miss Rose Campbell, Associate Matron. On the occasion of the organization of all of these Chapters the work was exemplified by the Grand Officers of the Grand Chapter.

On April 17th, Thomas Proctor, special Deputy for the Worthy Grand Patron, organized Merritt Chapter, Merritt, with Mrs. Margaret M. Grimmett, Worthy Matron; Sidney J. Solomon, Worthy Patron; Mrs. Louise M. Rankine, Associate Matron, this Chapter having a membership of thirty. On April 24th, Revelstoke Chapter, of

Revelstoke, was organized by Brother Proctor acting as Deputy for the Worthy Grand Patron. A membership of eighty-two was here enrolled and the officers appointed were Mrs. Fanny Howson, Worthy Matron; Thomas C. Rea, Worthy Patron; Mrs. Isabella Hopgood, Associate Matron. On April 25th, Brother Proctor organized Adah Chapter, at Kamloops, with thirty-three members enrolled, Mrs. Adelaide R. Johnstone, Worthy Matron; Charles Hirst, Worthy Patron; Mrs. Mabel A. Martin, Associate Matron. On the occasion of the organization of all of these Chapters the Deputy was accompanied by the Worthy Grand Matron, Mrs. Anna D. Perry, who had charge of the exemplification of the ceremony of initiation.

April 30th, the Worthy Grand Patron, Wm. H. F. Richdale, organized Victoria Chapter, of Victoria, with a membership of sixty-six, Mrs. Margaret Risser, Worthy Matron; Clarence B. Deaville, Worthy Patron; Mrs. Jewel Wallace, Associate Matron. Here again the work was exemplified by the Grand Officers. During the year over four hundred new members were added to our Order.

The third session of the Grand Chapter closed with the following Grand Officers installed: Mrs. Alice M. Roberts, Worthy Grand Matron; B. E. Beers, Worthy Grand Patron; Mrs. Myrtle Rees, Associate Grand Matron; James Wilby, Associate Grand Patron; Mrs. Katherine H. Irwin, Grand Treasurer; Mrs. Fannie N. Jones, Grand Secretary; Mrs. Viola Low, Grand Conductress; Miss Catherine McTavish, Associate Grand Conductress.

The Chapters in the city of Vancouver and immediate vicinity have established a fund for the relief of any members of the Order who may need assistance. This fund is placed in the hands of a general committee, elected from all the Chapters, and by this one charitable act, if no other could be attributed to the members in the Province, the Order of the Eastern Star in British Columbia have accomplished something "worthwhile."

GRAND CHAPTER OF CALIFORNIA [8]

A number of true and earnest men and women, endowed with sufficient power to direct and unite the blue ray of fidelity, the yellow ray of constancy, the white ray of charity, the green ray of hope and immortality, and the red ray of fervency and zeal into the illuminated Eastern Star in the State of California, organized Golden Gate Chapter No. 1, San Francisco, May 10, 1869. This was the first organization of the Order, though the degrees had been conferred in April 1860, and much interest in the Order had been manifested previous to the organization in Chapter form.

Ten Chapters were organized, only seven of that number being represented at the organization of the Grand Chapter in San Francisco on April 9, 1873, and six of the number remained in active condition throughout their entire history. By the constitution adopted, the Grand Patron was made the executive officer and has remained so until the present time. The first Grand Patron was Brother George J. Hobe, and the first Grand Matron was Sister Maria Anderson. No provision was made for Grand Officers at the star points, but at the October meeting in 1873 they were added to the corps of Grand Officers. Differing in their arrangements from almost all other Grand Jurisdictions, this State has continued the Grand Patron as the presiding officer and also the chief executive head.

In addition to the three principal officers and Past Matrons and Past Patrons, each Chapter was given an additional representative for each twenty-five members, and one for each fraction of twenty-five members more than seventeen, but this additional representation was, by vote of the Grand Chapter, annulled in 1875.

As was true of other Grand Chapters organized previous to the organization of the General Grand Chapter, necessity demanded that a committee be appointed to prepare a ritual, and when prepared,

---

[8] Organized April 9, 1873.

the report was accepted, the ritual adopted and published in 1873. In it, ceremonies were provided for opening the Chapter, conducting its business, form for initiation, closing the Chapter, and installation of officers. At the meeting in 1875 a committee was appointed to revise the Ritual with instructions to abbreviate the ceremonies of initiation so far as could be done without impairing the sense or value of same, and that the responses for the star points as given in the New York Ritual known as the Adoptive Rite revised, be adopted by subordinate Chapters. This committee reported in 1877, their report was adopted, and the California Ritual, revised, was published by authority of the Grand Chapter.

At its session, held in Vallejo, October 19, 1875, the Grand Chapter adopted a resolution "That the Grand Chapter constitute a committee of seven, of which the Worthy Grand Patron and the Worthy Grand Matron shall be members, to confer with like committees that may hereafter be appointed by other Grand Chapters of the Order in the United States. It shall be their duty to take under advisement, and present, if practical, some feasible and judicious plan for the organization of a Supreme Grand Chapter, which Supreme Body shall, when organized and recognized by two-thirds of the Grand Chapters of the Order in the United States, have absolute and supreme control over the Ritual and Lectures of the Order."

By resolution, at its session held in San Francisco on October 17, 1876, it was decided to accept the invitation of the Grand Chapter of Indiana to send seven delegates to a Supreme Grand Chapter to be held in Indianapolis in November 1876, and that delegates present at that time be authorized to cast the votes of the absentees.

After some discussion and deliberation it was resolved that the Grand Chapter of California should not recognize the authority of the General Grand Chapter until the Ritual be published and opportunity was given to examine the same; and further, that it would be proper to grant dispensations for the formation of Chapters in adjacent States or Territories where there was no Grand Chapter. In 1878 all resolutions and motions relating to the adoption of rituals and the form thereof were rescinded and the General Grand Chapter Ritual was adopted.

At the first session the use of a password was inaugurated and was continued until 1878.

In 1882 the State was divided into districts and a Deputy Grand Matron appointed in each district and this plan has continued in force. In 1898 and 1899 a system of schools of instruction was carried forward, with the Grand Matron directing same. They were very helpful and satisfactory and each year the work is continued along similar lines.

In 1880 a Chapter of Sorrow was held and in 1888 a memorial service was held by the Chapters of San Francisco in memory of Dr. Rob Morris, the founder of the Order, and the Grand Chapter attended the same. The same year the Grand Chapter adopted the following:

> *Resolved*, That while we recognize the lamented Rob Morris as the author and founder of the Order, we recognize Robert Macoy as the Master Builder, who systematized the work of the Order, and through whose instrumentality the Order has assumed its present grand proportions; and that we are proud to hail Brother Macoy as the Patriarch of the Order, and hope that his useful life may be spared many years to adorn and dignify the Order of the Eastern Star.

Referring to the efforts of some persons to introduce other degrees as higher or as dependent upon membership in the Eastern Star for eligibility, the Grand Chapter of California

> *Resolved*, That it is the sense of this Grand Chapter that it is not conducive to the upbuilding of our Order, and opposed to the well-established rules, regulations and edicts of the Fraternity, that any of the so-called side degrees not prescribed by the ritual of our Order, be conferred by our Chapters as such, at any time, or in the Chapter room during

the evenings of our meetings, or under the auspices or countenance of our Fraternity, but that it is the sense of this Chapter that all entertainments of an exclusively social nature be reserved for a time subsequent to the close of the Chapters, to the end that matters of a fraternal nature be not rendered secondary to social festivities.

In 1902 the Grand Patron's decision was approved as follows: "That persons visiting in the State, with no intention of making it their permanent home, although remaining more than six months, cannot be received into any Chapter in this Jurisdiction, nor can the Grand Matron grant special dispensation for such purpose." The total receipts for the Home fund were $1,216.55. This was to be given to the trustees of the Masonic Home for the benefit of the *girls only*, to educate them in music or any line of work which would assist them, when older, to be self-supporting. At this session $100 was appropriated for the purchase of a jewel for the retiring Grand Matron. It was also adopted "That it is the sense of this Grand Chapter that all alcoholic beverages be prohibited in serving refreshments at Subordinate Chapters." In 1904 the committee on finance was authorized to expend $100 annually for a gift for the Grand Matron, consulting her wishes in the matter.

In 1905 a resolution was adopted "That the use of flowers in the initiatory work is optional with Chapters, but if flowers are used, they must be the emblematic flowers of the several Degrees, designated in the explanation of the Signet." In 1903 regalia for the Grand Officers, consisting of jewels and collars, was purchased at a cost to the Grand Chapter of $270. In 1906 a relief fund of $16,673 was collected and wonderful help was rendered by the Grand Matron, Grand Patron, Grand Secretary, and Grand Treasurer, who personally superintended the distribution of clothing, bedding, and transportation to those made needy by the disastrous earthquake and fire. This Grand Chapter greatly appreciated the assistance so generously given by sister Grand Chapters.

In 1909 an official book of instructions to be used by subordinate Chapters was presented by the committee on ritual and adopted by the Grand Chapter. An amendment to the constitution was adopted authorizing the Grand Matron to preside during the opening and closing ceremonies and the reception of the representatives of other Grand Chapters and of Past Grand Officers; at all other times the Grand Patron continues to preside and also remains the highest authority in the Grand Chapter.

In 1910 the practice of issuing "Certificates of Qualification" to District Deputy Grand Matrons was inaugurated. That the true fraternal spirit richly abounds, is shown by the adoption by unanimous vote of the following: "There is hereby created the title Venerable Past Grand Patron, with all the rights and privileges of membership, to be conferred upon our beloved brother, William S. Moses, of Golden Gate Chapter No. 1, in view of the fact that he was the first Deputy Grand Patron, and as such organized the first Chapters in this State."

In 1901 memorial tiles were placed in the Masonic Home in loving remembrance of Brother George J. Robe, the first Grand Patron, and Sister Maria Anderson, the first Grand Matron.

In 1913 a resolution was adopted: "Desiring to show the love and esteem that we feel for thirty-one years of continuous active service as Grand Secretary, . . . we create Sister Kate Josephine Willats Past Grand Matron of the State of California, Order of the Eastern Star."

In 1912, Grand Matron Lena Walker Stannard recommended that an amendment to the constitution be made that would make the Grand Matron the first and the presiding officer of the Grand Chapter, but her recommendation did not meet with an approving vote and thus California remains as the only one of the Grand Jurisdictions now presided over by a brother. With the sisters in California vested with the highest prerogatives of citizenship — the right of the ballot — it must soon follow that her right to the highest position in the Order of the Eastern Star will be accorded the sisters of that Grand Chapter.

Although there are two Masonic Homes in the State, the demand is not fully supplied and a fund for an Eastern Star Home is now receiving very generous contributions, and this must soon result in the realization of the desired arrangements for the care of their dear ones. The sisters and brothers of this State appear to be observing the teachings of our Order, that justice at all times may prevail, making the Order of the Eastern Star the advance guard of a clean fraternity, and its ideals the standard of all womankind.

ORIGIN OF THE ORDER OF THE EASTERN STAR [9]

ROB MORRIS, LL. D.

Your kind welcome will bear testimony to the advocates of the Order throughout the world that the spirit which animates it — a spirit of tenderness, of gratitude, of respect to age, is not confined to any locality, but is co-extensive with the Order itself.

The gentlemen under whose tutelage I was made a Mason were warm advocates of what is often styled "Ladies' Masonry." One of them was making a practice of calling together the Masonic Craft with their wives and daughters, in every place he visited, and conferring upon them such degrees as the Mason's Daughter, the Good Samaritan, the Heroine of Jericho, and others of the class. But, truth to say, they made but little impression upon the mind and were soon forgotten. Like the numerous "side degrees" of Freemasonry there was no philosophy or system in them. No

---

[9] Extracts from an address prepared at the request of the Grand Chapter of the Order of the Eastern Star of California, and delivered at a called session of that body in San Francisco, April 1876. Published by request.

models of feminine character were presented, and there was little Biblical allusion. It was plain that the ladies regarded them but as trifles, only invented to amuse. They were far, therefore, from suggesting a correct idea of Freemasonry itself.

When I had determined upon consecrating my life to Masonic teaching, I gave careful reflection to this subject. I sought to understand the true relationship which woman sustains to Ancient Masonry. Surely the question is worthy the attention of the wisest. If it is so that a Mason's wife has an interest here, the fact should be explained to her before she becomes a widow. We have in our country one-half a million Freemasons. Multiply this by three to include all the ladies who enjoy the traditional relationship to them which Freemasonry recognizes, and the number is one and a half million I What a field of enquiry, said I. I will investigate it.

Now it demands but little knowledge of Masonry to perceive that its founders, whoever they were, never designed to separate husband from wife, father from child, etc., in the distribution of Masonic benefits. The ladies are secured in their full share by the strongest of our Masonic engagements, whatever *advantages* the Order presents to the man in his relations as husband, father, and brother, the same advantages accrue to the woman in her relations as wife, daughter, and sister. This is true, or else I must begin again to learn what is the purpose of Freemasonry.

The contrary theory has been very poorly maintained. "Because a woman cannot be a Mason, she has no interest in Masonry." "Because a woman cannot visit the lodge meetings, therefore she has no interest in the lodge meetings." Such arguments have no basis of truth. They who maintain them err radically in confounding the two ideas of *labor* and *wages*. "Because woman is not permitted to *labor* in partnership with her husband, therefore she cannot be permitted to share in the *wages paid* to her husband." See what such arguments tend to.

Now the contrary is true; the *man* labors in the work of Masonry, that the *woman* may share in the wages he receives. As the carpenter builds the house without female aid, but hands them his weekly wages; as the sailor braves the ocean voyage that his helpless ones at home may live in comfort upon his pay; as all who toil with head or hand do it that the household lamp may be kept alight and the fireside be made secure, so the Freemason attends his lodge and performs his part in the technical work without requiring aid from his family, but when the Masonic benefits ensure to him he appropriates a full share to the stay-at-homes who love him and are dependent upon him.

Do you ask, What is this *pay*, this *wages*, to which allusion has been made, this reward which is to compensate the loving wife for the occasional absences of him she best loves? The wages of Masonry, as you have often been told, are of three classes — relief in time of distress, sympathy in time of affliction, and protection in time of peril. The results of lodge-labor are to make the Mason a better husband, a better father, brother, and son. To make him better because more temperate, more industrious, kinder, more genial and amiable, more economical, more reverential to God and His law, more careful of the honor of his brethren and their families, more honest, virtuous, and truthful. A genuine *Mason* is a genuine *man*, having for his model and pattern the highest; drawing his rules of guidance from no earthly source; acting as in the presence of the Most High God; feeling that the All-Seeing-Eye inspects him; that an accurate record is kept in heaven of his earthly life and his *wages* in eternity will correspond with his *labors* in *time*. A Mason learns in the lodge teachings to be temperate, brave, prudent, and just. These, my sisters and brethren, are the deductions of my personal observations extended through many years.

Now, constituted as society is, the happiness of the *wife* must run parallel with the just behavior of her husband. If the man of the house is under a cloud, there can be no light and sunshine for the woman. The uprightness of the son makes the joy of the mother. The disgraceful life and death of the brother makes the misery of the sister. If, then, Freemasonry tends to promote the higher virtues of the man it is a thing to be exalted by the tongue of the woman.

And these were the views upon which I projected my lifework nearly forty years ago. This conception of Freemasonry led me to originate the Eastern Star. The degrees common at that time were unworthy of our Order. The system practiced in France cannot be modified to suit American ladies. I sat down to the work of originating an entirely new system, actuated by the belief that it would fill a place. Drawing to my aid the Holy Scriptures — a wealth of noble examples of women as well as men, I began in the winter of 1849-1850 to prepare the rituals.

First. I sought for a female character, willing to place her life in the scale of honor and found it in the history of *Jephthah's Daughter*.

Second. I sought for a female character willing to forsake all earthly attachments for the love of God and found it in the history of *Ruth*.

Third. I sought for a female character high in rank and position, willing to surrender them for the dear love she bore her nation and found it in the history of *Esther*.

Fourth. I sought for a female character, whose Christian faith was so strong and fervent that the most untoward event could not shake it and found it in the history of *Martha*.

Fifth — lastly. I sought for a female character, willing to surrender all life's allurements and even life itself for the great love she bore to Jesus and found it in one of the old legends of Holy Land in the history of *Electa*.

Having thus set up my five *Queens of Female Fame*, the rest was easy.

The emblems, the colors, the regalia, the lectures, the esoteric work, the odes and poems (more than forty) being composed and settled upon, the American Adoptive system was complete. The Eastern Star ascended the Masonic sky, shedding abroad a luster far greater than its author had ever anticipated.

The history of thirty-one years is before you. More than 100,000 ladies have received the degrees. A generation of our beloved, the virtuous and true, have accepted it. Its light is spreading further and further. I believe it will survive not only your aged brother, its founder, but all this large company, and will be cherished when we are in the dust.

Nothing that I have ever attempted for Masonry has given me so much pleasure as the origination of this degree. It was from the outset a labor of love. I have never made any pecuniary profit from it. The time, the research was given cheerfully under the belief that good would result from it.

It will appear strange to you, my sisters, that any Freemasons should be found to oppose this system. Yet to me, it is not strange. Freemasonry deals with the past. Its principles are fixed. There is a suspicion of all innovations. When Mr. Webb originated the Royal Arch System, ninety years ago, the opposition was so decided that had there been Masonic newspapers then as now, to warn the Fraternity, I think it could never have struggled into being. So, with what is called the Cryptic System; so, with the Templar Order. They are all modern and each in its day met a vigorous opposition. They outlived it because they were good things and supplied a want. So, with the Eastern Star, the opposition has become unworthy of notice. It has gone on with steady and ever-increasing momentum and its work has been useful. Freemasonry itself, the great oak whose branches have sheltered it, is the better for it. Humanity is the better for it. It must and will succeed.

May I say a word as to the attacks upon myself. I have been made the subject of ridicule, nay, of reproach for my attachment to "Ladies' Masonry." For many years there was a set of Masonic journals that made me a standing subject of invective. Some think that I might employ my time better. But have I not been industrious? Who has labored harder than I have? This right arm of mine, now suffering from paralysis — whose arm has been raised more frequently in teaching Masonic movements than this? These eyes of mine, so dim that I can scarcely read the notes that I have prepared for my guidance — whose eyes have been tried more frequently in Masonic research than mine? In what respect has my devotion to "Ladies' Masonry" interfered with my calling as a Masonic writer and lecturer?

A word of exhortation will close my address. The fraternal relationship I bear to all devotees of the Eastern Star justify me in offering you some counsel that may assist you in the future opening so pleasantly before you.

First. A Chapter of the Eastern Star to be useful must be made entertaining. All that charms and enlivens — music, poetry, recitations — must enliven its exercises. It must be the patron of social interests among its members.

Second. The officers of the Chapter should become skillful in the funeral ceremonies of the Order, so that when a sister, esteemed and respected, passes to that boundary to which we are all "nearer than we think," surviving sisters and brethren may hasten to bestow these loving honors, those marks of respect that prove to the world that our friendship does not cease at the grave.

Third. The Chapter should be prompt to attend the needs of the distressed widow and orphan who possess claims upon our charity. This is an indispensable duty, nor need we expect the blessing of God upon our labors if we neglect it.

Success, success long and lasting, success striking and brilliant follow all your doings as members of the Eastern Star! Thanks, grateful and many for the honors you have bestowed upon me. May great peace attend you. And when each in your turn shall be summoned by that call which is irresistible and cannot be denied, may your transit be glorious from this imperfect to that all-perfect, glorious and celestial Lodge above, where the Supreme Architect of the Universe presides!

GRAND CHAPTER OF COLORADO [10]

Though Brother Macoy had chartered Chapters at Black Hawk and at Silver Cliff some years previous (about 1877) to the Chapters chartered by the General Grand Chapter, those Chapters soon became inactive and the active work of the Order of the Eastern Star dates from the charter issued to Trinidad Chapter No. 1, at Trinidad, January 7, 1881, by Willis Brown, Most Worthy Grand Patron, M. Beshour being deputized to conduct the constituting ceremony. Mrs. M. Jaffa, Worthy Matron; Wilson L. Smith, Worthy Patron; Louisa Burnett, Associate Matron.

---

[10] Organized June 6, 1892.

Colorado Chapter No. 2, located at Leadville in Lake County, was granted a charter by Willis Brown, Most Worthy Grand Patron of the General Grand Chapter, on June 15, 1882, B. Fancher being deputized to constitute the Chapter, Mrs. A. E. Johnson, Worthy Matron; S. O. Hervey, Worthy Patron; Miss Maggie Braden, Associate Matron.

Eminence Chapter No. 3 was chartered by Rollin C. Gaskill, Most Worthy Grand Patron, at Salida, Chaffee County, April 19, 1884, and was constituted May 21, 1884, by James M. Bradbury, Deputy. The first officers were Miss Rose A. Slaughter, Worthy Matron; Sylvanus O. Harvey, Worthy Patron; Mrs. Vianette C. Lawrence, Associate Matron.

Adah Chapter No. 4, located at Aspen, Pitkin County, was granted a charter by Rollin C. Gaskill, Most Worthy Grand Patron, February 1, 1886, who deputized W. H. Bright to constitute the Chapter, February 15, 1886, Mrs. Julia A. Bright, Worthy Matron; J. W. Campbell, Worthy Patron; Mrs. Sarah M. Gillespie, Associate Matron.

Garden City Chapter No. 5, located at Greeley, was chartered February 22, 1886, by Rollin C. Gaskill, Most Worthy Grand Patron, who deputized W. B. Mason to constitute the Chapter March 1, 1886, Mrs. F. L. Childs, Worthy Matron; F. L. Childs, Worthy Patron; Mrs. C. H. Wheeler, Associate Matron.

Trinidad Chapter No. 1 having lapsed into a dormant condition and failed to pay dues for two or more years, thirty-nine petitioners asked for a new charter which was granted by Benjamin Lynds, Most Worthy Grand Patron, May 11, 1891, when M. H. Murphy was deputized to constitute the same and Chapter was reorganized June 4, 1891, Mrs. Alice Leslie, Worthy Matron; J. M. Baker, Worthy Patron.

Queen City Chapter No. 6, located at Denver, was chartered September 3, 1890, with 135 petitioners and organized September 9, 1890, by Rev. H. A. Guild, of Lincoln, Nebraska, who was deputized by the Most Worthy Grand Patron to constitute the Chapter, Mrs. E. E. Condit, Worthy Matron; W. H. L. Miller, Worthy Patron.

Queen Esther Chapter No. 7, located at Boulder, was chartered December 4, 1890, by Benjamin Lynds, Most Worthy Grand Patron, who deputized H. A. Baker, of Denver, to constitute the Chapter, December 20, 1890, Sarah Conwell, Worthy Matron; T. K. Carmack, Worthy Patron. There were sixty petitioners.

Electa Chapter No. 8, Durango, was chartered January 27, 1891, with twenty-seven signers to the petition. N. Nagengast was deputized to conduct the constituting ceremony in February 1891, Mrs. Charles Newman, Worthy Matron; Jethro C. Sanford, Worthy Patron.

Pueblo Chapter No. 9, located at Pueblo, was chartered August 1, 1891, and organized September 22, 1891, by H. D. Hathaway, of Pueblo, who was deputized by the Most Worthy Grand Patron. There were twenty-five petitioners, who chose Mrs. F. P. Wormley, Worthy Matron; H. D. Hathaway, Worthy Patron.

Twenty-nine petitioners, with John McCoach, of Colorado City, deputized to constitute the Chapter, were granted a charter by the Most Worthy Grand Patron September 4, 1891, and organized Glen Eyrie Chapter No. 10, Colorado City, September 12, 1891, with Hattie Stephens, Worthy Matron, and John McCoach, Worthy Patron.

October 30, 1891, a charter was issued to Ramona Chapter No. 11, Colorado Springs, and H. A. Baker of Denver was deputized by the Most Worthy Grand Patron to constitute this Chapter on November 4, 1891, with Mrs. Ella L. C. Dwinnell, Worthy Matron; Cassius E. Stubbs, Worthy Patron.

Ruxton Chapter No. 12, Manitou, was chartered February 9, 1892, and constituted by John McCoach, deputy of the Most Worthy Grand Patron, on February 27, 1892, with Mrs. Eva J. Aldrich, Worthy Matron, and Charles M. Elerick, Worthy Patron, having twenty-seven signers upon the petition.

Columbine Chapter No. 13, Longmont, was chartered March 17, 1892, by the Most Worthy Grand Patron, who deputized H. A. Baker, of Denver, to constitute the Chapter on March 28, 1892, with Mrs. Mary L. Carr, Worthy Matron, and E. J. Coffman, Worthy Patron.

The convention to organize the Grand Chapter was called by Romona Chapter No. 11 of Colorado Springs, and met at Colorado Springs, June 6, 1892, and there amidst the beautiful and sublime scenery of this magnificent stretch of nature's handiwork, ten of the thirteen Chapters in the State, represented by thirty-four representatives and past officers, organized the Grand Chapter. The Grand Matron was made the executive head and the per capita dues fixed at twenty-five cents per year. Past Matrons and Past Patrons were made permanent members and charters were issued to the Chapters working under the General Grand Chapter, numbering same according to date issued. Colorado Chapter No. 2 presented the new Grand Chapter with $50 toward paying the expenses of organization. Mrs. Carrie Reef, of Leadville, was elected Worthy Grand Matron, Henry D. Hathaway, of Pueblo, Worthy Grand Patron, and Mrs. Eliza S. Cohen, of Colorado Springs, Grand Secretary. With the completion of organization, the Order began a glorious field of labor, looking well to the noble purposes and loving kindnesses as framed by the solemn obligation, with their motto of their lives for the past, Charity, for the present, Hope, for the future, Faith, and in that spirit nobly entered upon the duties of the Order. In 1896 it was decided that "Members belonging to any of the independent States can visit Chapters if they can stand a thorough examination, and that they have the right of affiliation."

In 1901 the Grand Secretary reported the donation of $253.15 to the Galveston sufferers; seven Chapters pledged themselves to donate the sum of $320 toward a sinking fund for the purpose of starting a Home fund, and $180 annually toward its support; ten per cent of the receipts were set aside as a benevolent fund. In 1902 the sum of $50 was appropriated to the St. Louis Temple of Fraternity. During the National Encampment of the G. A. R., 1905, the Grand Chapter extended fraternal courtesies to all visiting O.E.S. members in the parlors of the Masonic Temple at an expense of $93.45, during which time more than eight hundred visitors were registered. In 1906 a relief fund was presented to the San Francisco sufferers amounting to $403.49. At the meeting in 1909, the *Floral Addenda* was exemplified by the Denver Chapter. A "System of Notice" was adopted in 1910, intended to protect the Chapters from visits by clandestines, also expelled or suspended persons, which notice was mailed by the Secretary to the home Chapter of the visitor. In 1909 the Grand Patron was' appointed as advisory trustee to cooperate with the trustees of the Masonic Benevolent Association as a representative of the O.E.S. The Grand Chapter relief fund was started in 1911, and contributions aggregated $4,602.15. An Eastern Star relief board was organized in Denver in 1907 with the object in view to more efficiently promote the charitable efforts of the Order.

Grand Chapter of Connecticut [11]

On Good Friday, March 26, 1869, at the home of Mrs. Mary Abigail Woodward, No. 25 Front Street, just opposite Potter Street, Hartford, Connecticut, there gathered eight Master Masons and nine wives of Master Masons "to devise some method for a social lodge of Master Masons, their wives, widows, and daughters, so that in a strange land they could be recognized by any Master Mason."

A committee was appointed on by-laws, which committee prepared a report which they presented at another special meeting held April 14, 1869, at the home of Mrs. Joseph Smith, No. 530 Main Street, Hartford, where the by-laws were considered, and the same committee was continued with the additional duty of preparing a ritual and secret work, and to report as soon as convenient.

They reported at another meeting called at the home of Brother George Giddings in West Hartford on May 12, 1869, where the by-laws, ritual, and secret work were discussed and adopted.

---

[11] Organized August 11, 1874. Data by Edward E. Fuller, P.G.P. of Connecticut.

They also decided upon a name for the Order, voting that it be called Giddings Lodge No. 1, A.M. (Adopted Masons). A committee was appointed to procure a suitable hall in which to hold their meetings. This committee secured the hall known as Stedman Hall in the building owned by Benjamin Bliss, corner of Main and Pratt Streets, Hartford, and the Lodge met there on Wednesday, December 8, 1869, and elected their officers, which consisted of a President, Vice President, Treasurer, and Secretary. At this meeting many applications were presented and referred to committees, much interest being shown.

At the annual meeting in December, 1872, in order to be in closer touch with the other bodies of like character in the State, the name, Ivanhoe Chapter No. 10, A.M., was printed on the ritual and during the year following, the Lodge and Chapter worked together as one body, after which time it ceased to be Giddings Lodge and became Ivanhoe Chapter No. 10, receiving its charter February 28, 1874.

Previous to its receiving its charter, there had been organized in Connecticut, through the efforts of Brother Rob Morris, and of Brother Chauncey M. Hatch, nine Chapters of the Order of the Eastern Star, and shortly afterward, one other Chapter was organized, making eleven in all, as follows: Orient Chapter No. 1, Bridgeport, April 22, 1869; Azalia No. 2, Stratford, May 9, 1869; Excelsior No. 3, New Haven, April 24, 1870; Grace No. 4, Danbury, May 27, 1870; Floral No. 5, Georgetown, April 18, 1872; Myrtle No. 6, Fairhaven, June 19, 1872; Unity No. 7, Guilford, November, 1872; Meriden No. 8, Meriden, December 4, 1873; Laurel No. 9, Northford, December 15, 1873; Ivanhoe No. 10, Hartford, February 28, 1874; Radiant No. 11, Willimantic, March 31, 1874.

On August 11, 1874, in Odd Fellows Hall, New Haven, a convention of the several chapters of the Order in the State was held, at the request of the several Chapters, to organize a Grand Chapter, a call having been issued for same by Brother Chauncey M. Hatch, of

Orient Chapter No. 1, of Bridgeport, by reason of his appointment (before the system of organized Chapters was instituted) by Brother Rob Morris, the Grand Patron of the Order in the United States, as Grand Patron of the Order in Connecticut.

At this convention the eleven Chapters were represented, a constitution was adopted, and officers elected, as follows: Grand Patron, Brother C. M. Hatch, No. 1; Grand Matron, Sister A. C. Thorpe, No. 3; Associate Grand Patron; Brother W. H. Ford, No. 10; Associate Grand Matron, Sister W. D. Weld, No. 7; Grand Treasurer, Addie C. S. Bario, No. 8; Grand Secretary, Kate L. Tuttle, No. 9; Grand Conductor, H. C. Holaday; Associate Grand Conductor, J. E. Gregory, No. 1; Grand Warder, M. J. Smith, No. 3.

All present, by vote of the convention, signed the constitution. The installation of officers was postponed until October 14, 1874, that being the time appointed by the Grand Chapter for its annual meeting in New Haven, to which date the convention adjourned. The Grand Patron was made the executive officer of the Grand Chapter, but this was changed in 1876 by placing the authority in the hands of the Grand Matron. Grand Chapter dues were arranged for by fifty cents for each member admitted during the year, with no per capita dues, but in 1878 dues were levied of two and one-half cents per capita, which was increased in 1880 to five cents, and in 1899 to ten cents, and later to twenty cents.

On October 14, 1874, the first annual meeting of the Grand Chapter, Order of the Eastern Star of Connecticut, was held in Grand Army Hall, New Haven, and was called to order by Grand Patron C. M. Hatch, representatives of each of the eleven Chapters being present. The Grand Patron was installed by M. W. Brother William Wallace Lee, who was present and who was then the Most Worshipful Grand Master of the Grand Lodge of Connecticut, assisted by Brother F. Turner De Bussy, of No. 3, as Grand Marshal, and the remaining officers were installed by Grand Patron C. M. Hatch, assisted by Brother S. T. Bartlett, of No. 1, as Grand Marshal. A petition for a charter for a Chapter in Thomaston was received, and it was recommended that it be granted and be known as Electa Chapter No. 12, and that it be allowed to participate in the doings of the Grand Chapter at this session.

At this session charters were granted, bearing date of October 14, 1874, to the twelve above named Chapters, whose total membership at this time numbered thirteen hundred and twenty-five.

All the Chapters used the ritual prepared by the committee appointed in 1874 and reported at a special session, held February 1, 1875, the ritual as usually practiced (Adoptive Rite), with some additions taken from the ancient ritual (*the Mosaic Book*) which was adopted and known as the Connecticut Addenda. Excelsior Chapter No. 3, of New Haven, exemplified portions of the dramatized work (Mosaic), and it was decided that Chapters in the jurisdiction of Connecticut might dramatize such portions of the work as they chose, provided the same be in accordance with the text and ceremonies as exemplified at this time. Brief exemplary dramatizations were printed by the Grand Chapter for the use of Chapters desiring to use them.

The Grand Matron's address in 1876 contained the following:

> In the brief time that the Chapter at Meriden has been in existence it has used three varieties of rituals, and I have seen a fourth, the revised work recently adopted by the Grand Chapter of New York (*Macoy Ritual*). The Grand Chapter of Connecticut adopted a ritual, and upon sending for more copies, are informed that they are not in print, thus compelling us to adopt the new ones for any new Chapters that may be formed.

In 1877 a resolution was adopted favoring the effort to offer a uniform ritual as was then in progress by the ritual committee of the General Grand Chapter and in 1878 the General Grand Chapter Ritual was adopted and the Grand Chapter of Connecticut, then an independent Grand Chapter, recognized the General Grand Chapter as a sister body, and expressed their willingness to cooperate with it in such matters as in their judgment will advance the interests of the whole Order. In the latter part of 1879, the new Rituals (General Grand Chapter Revised) was adopted as the Ritual of the Grand Jurisdiction of Connecticut.

In 1876, the Grand Chapter decided that the condition of the finances was such that they would be unable to bear their proportion of the legitimate expense attendant upon the formation of a Supreme Grand Chapter.

In 1897, a committee was appointed to visit the General Grand Chapter in 1898 in response to the invitation of the Right Worthy Grand Secretary and this committee reported in 1899, recommending affiliation with the General Grand Chapter, but action was indefinitely postponed. It was again taken up in 1900 and the recommendation of the committee adopted on October 10, 1900. On November 30, 1900, official notice from the Grand Secretary, Mrs. A. E. L. Stebbins, was sent to the Right Worthy Grand Secretary stating that the Grand Chapter of Connecticut had declared its desire to become a constituent part of the General Grand Chapter and the formal recognition notices which declared the Grand Chapter of Connecticut a constituent member of the General Grand Chapter were duly issued.

The Grand Chapter of Connecticut has now been in existence forty-one years. In these years, of the twelve original Chapters only two have relinquished their charters, and new Chapters have since been instituted in these same localities, while of the entire number of eighty-one Chapters, including the twelve original Chapters, only nine have surrendered their charters, and in almost every one, if not indeed every one of the localities in which these nine were located, new Chapters have since been instituted.

In these years also the Chapters have increased from twelve to seventy-three, with two others under dispensation, while the membership has grown from thirteen hundred and twenty-five to about ten thousand.

The generosity of the Order has been exhibited in a gift of $128 to the Eastern Star headquarters at the St. Louis fair, and the California earthquake sufferers were given $712 to assist in their relief.

The Sunday nearest June 12th is recognized as "Decoration Day" of the Order, while the Order unites with the Grand Lodge in celebrating "Grand Master's Day" at the Masonic Home at Wallingford. Over $5,000 has been contributed in cash to the Masonic Home and a fund for an Eastern Star Home has been started, which now is increasing rapidly, and the Grand Chapter is striving toward the erection of a Home at a date not far distant.

The Order in Connecticut, it can therefore be truly said, is prosperous, harmonious, and enthusiastic; growing in membership and in influence every year and looking forward toward still greater prosperity and influence in the years which are to come.

GRAND CHAPTER OF DISTRICT OF COLUMBIA [12]

The first Chapter chartered by the General Grand Chapter was Ruth No. 1, at Brightwood, July 16, 1892, with fifty-seven petitioners. As Deputy of the Most Worthy Grand Patron, John A. Becker constituted the Chapter August 11, 1892, with Mrs. Jennie Johnson, Worthy Matron, W. E. Nally, Worthy Patron, Mrs. Alcena Lamond, Associate Matron.

Electa No. 2, at Anacostia, was chartered July 12, 1894, with eighty-five petitioners; Naomi Chapter No. 3 was chartered January 25, 1895; Martha Chapter No. 4, Washington, chartered May 22, 1895; Esther Chapter No. 5, Washington, was chartered January 6, 1869; Adah Chapter No. 6, Washington, was chartered January 12, 1896.

---

[12] Organized April 31, 1896.

Brother H. H. Hinds, Most Worthy Grand Patron of the General Grand Chapter, called the convention that organized the Grand Chapter, April 30, 1896. For the third time Elmira Foley, Past Most Worthy Grand Matron, was given the distinction of assisting in the organization of a Grand Chapter, and all six Chapters, representing a membership of eight hundred and twenty-two earnest workers, assembled in the Scottish Rite Cathedral, Washington, by their representatives. The constitution adopted provided for two stated sessions each year, the annual session to be held in January and the second in June; the usual recognition was accorded to Past Matrons and Past Patrons, they being made permanent members of the Grand Chapter; the Grand Matron was made the executive officer and differing from the usual manner of filling offices in the Grand Chapter, all the Grand Officers were elected by ballot, but this was changed in 1901, making the point officers and Grand Organist appointive.

During the first year following organization, the Grand Chapter held its sessions as provided in the constitution, June 6, 1896; two special sessions, one October 6th to exemplify the degrees before the Grand Officers, and on December 26th for the purpose of granting charters to new Chapters.

During 1896 and 1897 the Matrons of the Chapters held monthly meetings in the interests of the charitable work of the Order. The accumulated funds for the National Masonic Fair in 1897 amounted to $1,435.96 as collected by the committee appointed for that purpose. Each Chapter was asked to appoint a committee annually, to communicate to members the secret work, and it was made mandatory that all new members especially be instructed in the obligation and impressed with the necessity of a faithful conformity to its requirements. At the June meeting in 1899 a committee on O.E.S. Home was appointed and reported at a special session held November 4th of the same year, the report requesting that the constitution be so amended as to provide for the establishment of a Home, its incorporation, etc., which report was adopted and the O.E.S. Home committee appointed. Continued care was given to orphan children and in 1900 a tea was held which brought in $303.30 for their support. A series of luncheons were also given, the proceeds amounting to almost $500 placed in the O.E.S. Home fund. In 1902, by an act of Congress, an Eastern Star Home for the District of Columbia was incorporated. In 1903 an O.E.S. Fair was held and $1,177.59 was realized to be added to the Home fund. With earnest effort and united consecration to the upbuilding of the beloved Order, determined to provide for their own who may need the assistance of the Fraternity, the Masonic and O.E.S. Home was completed and on October 16, 1905, it was dedicated free from encumbrance; after paying all bills, a balance of $2,945 was in the Home fund — a wonderful tribute to lay at the shrine of devotion to duty.

In addition to the charitable work mentioned, $175 was contributed to the relief of the Galveston flood sufferers; $162 was sent to the relief of the earthquake sufferers in San Francisco; 1,600 volumes of reading matter were sent to our soldiers in China and a Soldiers' and Sailors' Relief Association, formed for the purpose of assisting the Red Cross Society in the care of the sick and wounded United States soldiers and sailors in the Spanish-American War, furnished funds for carrying forward that portion of the charitable work. With the rising of each morning's sun come solemn responsibilities and obligations which must be discharged before the evening shadows shroud the day, or our record of life through time and eternity must remain clouded and defective. There is much work for the members of this greatest Order of organized fraternal charity to do, and this we can best accomplish by living the principles of our Order in our daily lives. Its purpose is to set before us a higher ideal, to give us greater inspiration toward good, and to teach us by precept and example the sacred duties which we owe to one another and to God.

In 1913 a new Masonic and Eastern Star Home was built, which was dedicated with the usual ceremonies and addresses and general rejoicing that the object sought had been attained. This home receives the hearty support of the Masonic Fraternity and continues its divine mission in the care of our sisters and brothers for whom fortune makes such an institution necessary. The review of the accomplishments of this Grand Jurisdiction must inspire, ennoble, and uplift all those who may have the opportunity to study this enduring monument and practical demonstration of the teachings of Masonry and its co-worker, the Order of the Eastern Star.

The history of the Grand Jurisdiction of the District of Columbia could not be written without giving special mention to Mrs. Alcena Lamond, Right Worthy Grand Treasurer of the General Grand Chapter. For nearly a quarter of a century she has continued, without intermission, her work for the good of the Order and, judged by the results, it places her in the front rank of those who have toiled and sacrificed to build and make our Order useful in the District of Columbia. A charter member of Ruth Chapter No. 1, its second Worthy Matron, first Worthy Grand Matron of the Grand Chapter of the District of Columbia, the first president of the board of directors of the Masonic and Eastern Star Home and continuing in that capacity each year since that time, one of the members of the first board of trustees of the General Grand Chapter, she continuing in such office until appointed by the Most Worthy Grand Matron, Mrs. Rata A. Mills, to the office of Right Worthy Grand Treasurer of the General Grand Chapter to fill the vacancy caused by the resignation of Sister Harriette A. Ercanbrack.

Sister Lamond is fully competent to discharge the important duties which this appointment has placed upon her and the members are deeply grateful for the honor conferred upon one of their number as well as the recognition accorded the jurisdiction of the District of Columbia.

Grand Chapter of Florida [13]

By authority of the Supreme Grand Chapter of the Adoptive Rite, a Chapter of the Order of the Eastern Star was organized in Florida, though little is known further than the fact that a charter was issued.

The first Chapter of the Order of the Eastern Star in Florida having authentic records was organized in Jacksonville, December 17, 1872, by the wife and daughters of Judge D. C. Dawkins, Mrs. O. P. Knapp, Mrs. J. H. Abbott, Mrs. David Jones, Mrs. E. Wasgate, Mrs. O. L. Keene, and others. This Chapter was named Evergreen No. 1 and held its meetings the first and third Tuesdays of each month. The first Worthy Matron was Mrs. O. P. Knapp; Worthy Patron, Judge Dawkins; Associate Matron, Mrs. David Jones.

The first ritual used by this Chapter was the *Macoy Ritual* of the Adoptive Rite published in 1871, which is now in possession of Sister Cora R. Franz, P.G.M. She also has the *Macoy Ritual* used by this Chapter published by Brother O. L. Keene in 1880. This Chapter existed for a few years and then from deaths, removal, and lack of funds, suspended, but some of its members are still residents of Jacksonville.

Evergreen Chapter No. 2 was chartered by the General Grand Chapter June 18, 1880, by Brother R. B. Thomas, special deputy of the Most Worthy Grand Patron, with Mrs. Mary E. Mitchell, Worthy Matron, R. B. Thomas, Worthy Patron, Mrs. Mary E. Randolph, Associate Matron. It was reported dormant in 1886, sent no report to the General Grand Chapter in 1889, and never paid any dues.

Magnolia Chapter No. 3, Palatka, was organized by Brother W. E. Ransom, special Deputy of the Most Worthy Grand Patron, on June 30, 1882, the charter having been issued by the General Grand Chapter on June 13, 1882, with Mrs. Martha A. Bowen, Worthy Matron, W.

---

[13] Organized June 7, 1904. Data by Brother Arthur H. Carter, P.G.P., Grand Secretary from 1907 to the present.

E. Ransom, Worthy Patron, Mrs. Adeline D. M'Leod, Associate Matron. This Chapter did not report to the General Grand Chapter in either 1886 or in 1889 and upon recommendation of the Right Worthy Grand Secretary the two Chapters (No. 2 and No. 3) were stricken from the records.

At the seventh assembly of the General Grand Chapter in 1892 a record was given of Electa Chapter No. 1, Green Cove Springs, which was granted a charter December 24, 1889, and organized December 29, 1889, by Dewitt C. Dawkins, of Jacksonville, special Deputy of the Most Worthy Grand Patron; Worthy Matron, Miss L. Dova Greer; Worthy Patron, A. W. Monroe; Associate Matron, Miss Jane L. Moss; with twenty petitioners. This Chapter paid dues in 1891, 1892, 1894, and 1895.

The Charter of Magnolia Chapter No. 2 (reorganized), located at Palatka, was dated October 23, 1893, with forty petitioners, and was organized by W. H. Hancock, special Deputy of the Most Worthy Grand Patron, with Mrs. N.C. Clark, Worthy Matron; B. T. Flowers, Worthy Patron; Miss Maude V. M'Kenzie, Associate Matron; paying dues in 1893, 1894, and 1895. In 1896 Magnolia Chapter No. 2 was represented in the General Grand Chapter assembly by Sister Alice H. Haskell, who served upon one of the committees at that session. She further had the distinction of being the first representative of the Order from Florida to attend the Triennial Assembly. Again, in 1899, Magnolia Chapter No. 2, of Palatka, became dormant and was not revived again until May 25, 1909, when it was chartered by the Grand Chapter of Florida as Palatka Chapter No. 33. The original "Star Floor Carpet or Cloth" of the first Chapter of Palatka was kept as an heirloom by the Masonic Lodge of Palatka; it was among its properties in 1886, and was used when Magnolia Chapter No. 2 was organized in 1895. It is now used by the members of Palatka Chapter No. 33 in their meetings.

Tropical Chapter No. 3 was organized at Bartow on December 15, 1894, by James Harden as Deputy for the Most Worthy Grand

Patron, with fifty-one petitioners. They selected as their first Worthy Matron, Mrs. Beulah R. Stevens; Worthy Patron, James Harden; Associate Matron, Mrs. Bessie E. Johnson, and did not pay dues after 1896.

Inverness Chapter No. 4 was organized April 12, 1895, by Dr. J. F. Miller, Deputy of Most Worthy Grand Patron, with sixty-two petitioners. Worthy Matron, M. Lottie Wells; Worthy Patron, Dr. J. F. Miller; Associate Matron, Mrs. Louise Zimmerman. Dues were paid in 1895 for fifty members.

The charter for Live Oak Chapter No. 5, Daytona, was issued December 31, 1896. It was instituted January 15, 1897, by Jesse Oren, member of Lyra Chapter No. 129, Iowa, with twenty-five charter members. Worthy Matron, Mrs. Ida A. Peck; Worthy Patron, George H. Clark; Associate Matron, Mrs. Martha H. Carter; the last named being now a Past Grand Matron of Florida. This Chapter was rightly named Live Oak; it was the Chapter that lived and is now Chapter No. 1 of the Florida Stars. It is the home Chapter of three Grand Patrons and the present Grand Secretary, who is one of the Past Grand Patrons.

A charter was issued July 12, 1897, for Seminole Chapter No. 6, at Sanford. It was instituted July 20, 1897, by Rev. Harry Cassit, member of Fort Worth Lodge No. 148, Texas, with nineteen charter members. Worthy Matron, Mrs. Jennie Cassit; Worthy Patron, H. E. Munson; Associate Matron, Mrs. Annie B. S. Munson. Seminole Chapter gave to Florida her first Grand Matron, Mrs. Alice E. Robbins, who presided over the Grand Chapter for two years.

May 4, 1898, a charter was issued to Dolores Chapter No. 7, New Smyrna. It was instituted May 20, 1898, by Brother Jas. Carnell, with twenty charter members. Worthy Matron, Mrs. Minnie L. Moore; Worthy Patron, F. A. Barrett; Associate Matron, Miss Amelia Moeller. This is the home Chapter of Past Grand Matron Nettie V. Turner.

Queen Esther Chapter No. 8, Clearwater, was chartered June 12, 1899, with forty-five petitioners, and instituted August 8, 1899, by

H. L. Snyder as special Deputy. Worthy Matron, Mrs. Ella M. Padgett; Worthy Patron, John W. Williamson; Associate Matron, Mrs. Anna Williamson. This is the home Chapter of Past Grand Patron R. H. Padgett.

The charter of Eureka Chapter No. 9, at St. Petersburg, was granted December 27, 1899, and the Chapter was organized February 15, 1900, by R. H. Padgett, of Clearwater, with thirty-four charter members. Worthy Matron, Mrs. Virginia Ainslee; Worthy Patron, Jason L. Taylor; Associate Matron, Mrs. Kittie Holshouser.

To DeSoto Chapter No. 10, at Punta Gorda, a charter was granted April 27, 1899, and Chapter organized June 8, 1900, by J. M. Samuel, as special Deputy, with thirty-nine petitioners. Worthy Matron, Mrs. Bertha L. Johnson; Worthy Patron, John M. Samuel; Associate Matron, Mrs. Leonora G. Earnest.

A charter was granted to Friendship Chapter No. 11, Titusville, on May 16, 1901, and a Chapter was organized June 4, 1901, by Jas. Carnell, special Deputy, of Ormond, and member of Daytona Chapter. He was accompanied by several members of Live Oak Chapter and Dolores Chapter, who assisted in instituting Friendship. This is the home Chapter of Past Grand Patron George M. Robbins and was organized with a charter membership of twenty-seven. Worthy Matron, Mrs. Cora B. Schuyler; Worthy Patron, Dr. B. R. Wilson; Associate Matron, Mrs. Josephine M. Chaffee.

The first Most Worthy Grand Matron to visit Florida was Sister Hattie E. Ewing, who visited Dolores Chapter, New Smyrna, on February 11, 1901; Live Oak Chapter, Daytona, on February 12, 1901, and Seminole Chapter, Sanford, on February 15, 1901, which Chapter she reorganized. She held a school of instruction with Eureka Chapter, St. Petersburg, on February 16, 1901, and visited Queen Esther Chapter, Clearwater, on February 18, 1901. These are the first visits of any General Grand Chapter officer recorded.

Ruth Chapter, Fort Pierce, was granted a charter July 18, 1902, and organized July 23, 1902, by Frederick A. Morgan, special Deputy, with twenty-one charter members. Worthy Matron, Mrs. Frances S. Cross; Worthy Patron, Henry L. Klopp; Associate Matron, Mrs. Emeline R. Tyler.

A charter was issued to Grace Chapter No. 13, at Wellborn, September 17, 1903, to twenty petitioners, with Mrs. Laura J. Oliff, Worthy Matron; C. B. Oliff, Worthy Patron; Mrs. Jennie Spencer, Associate Matron.

Florida Chapter No. 14, Pensacola, was chartered July 2, 1903, with thirty-three charter members, and constituted by W. E. Anderson, special Deputy of the Most Worthy Grand Patron, L. Cabell Williams. Worthy Matron, Mrs. Marie S. Weeks; Worthy Patron, W. E. Anderson, a Past Master of Florida A. F. and A. M.; Associate Matron, Mrs. Eva Gibbs. This is the home Chapter of Sister Marie S. Weeks who served as Grand Matron of Florida 1906-1907. This Chapter observes with banquet and suitable literary and musical exercises, "Founder's Day" August 31, and has commenced to observe an annual "Chapter of Sorrow." At every meeting a March 15 led by the Worthy Matron and as the members pass the charity box on the altar by the open Bible, a contribution is dropped in. The Masonic Home fund is thus remembered at each meeting and an annual contribution is made. This Chapter has had, from the beginning, all requisite paraphernalia so that the degrees are given in a beautiful and impressive manner. The kindliest feeling exists between the Chapter and the Masonic bodies. The brethren of the Scottish Rite open their cathedral to the use of the Chapter as occasion demands.

A charter was granted to Bushnell Chapter No. 15, at Bushnell, March 10, 1904, with twenty-seven petitioners. Mrs. Katie Hooker, Worthy Matron; James De Witt, Worthy Patron; Miss Gertrude Pierce, Associate Matron.

A charter was granted to Evergreen Chapter No. 16, at Tampa, June 2, 1904, with twenty-two charter members. Miss Azeele Carruthers, Worthy Matron; Herman Glogowski, Worthy Patron; Mrs.

Maria G. Post, Associate Matron. This is the home Chapter of Past Grand Matrons Orpha D. Bruce and Miss Azeele Carruthers.

On June 4, 1904, a charter was issued for Keystone Chapter No. 17, at St. Augustine, with forty-one charter members. Worthy Matron, Mrs. Katherine J. Sineath; Worthy Patron, George A. Miller; Associate Matron, Mrs. Mary A. Corbett. This Chapter was organized by Brother John J. Sineath as Deputy of the Most Worthy Grand Patron and who also was Grand Patron of Florida in 1907-1908.

The Grand Chapter of Florida was organized in Sanford on June 7, 1904, by Mrs. Laura B. Hart, Most Worthy Grand Matron, acting as Deputy for L. Cabell Williamson, Most Worthy Grand Patron. The first officers were: Grand Matron, Mrs. Alice E. Robbins; Grand Patron, James Carnell; Associate Grand Matron, Miss Azeele Carruthers; Grand Secretary, Mrs. Cora H. Dittmar.

If we aspire for something to ennoble, not mere self, but our fellow men, forget self, *that* is the keynote of our Order. Be kind one to another, and ever generous, giving forth the fragrance of the jessamine.

> Living close to our high ideals,
>   We cannot hold them too high;
> The longer the struggle, the harder the fight,
>   The grander the bye and bye,
> There never was a high ideal
>   But will be the real some day,
> If we follow with practice the paths of love,
>   As the true and only way.

GRAND CHAPTER OF GEORGIA [14]

In accordance with a call of the Most Worthy Grand Patron of the General Grand Chapter, Order of the Eastern Star, a preliminary convention assembled, February 21, 1901, for the purpose of organizing the Grand Chapter of Georgia.

In Brunswick, the beautiful city beside the sea gathered the representatives of five chapters and there laid the foundation for the upbuilding of the Order. It was with feelings of despair; the officers took up their work. The first annual session was held in the hall of Lorraine Chapter at Tennille, May 6, 1902. Peace and harmony prevailed, and each Chapter had taken on new life. They realized that the Grand Chapter had been organized for their mutual development and a better knowledge and a better impression of O.E.S. prevailed. Five new Chapters were organized the first year; the membership was 339. Numbers at that memorable meeting were not great, but all were anxious to do their duty.

The second annual session was held at Fitzgerald, May 5, 1903. In the fitness of things, the time had come when the Order should issue forth from chaos and confusion incident to every new organization. The reports show a healthy, prosperous, growing condition, a few dormant Chapters, but brighter prospects ahead beckoned them on, to place Georgia O.E.S. on a plane as broad, as high, and as grand as the grandest. Little did this faithful band know how well they wrought; chartered Chapters at this session numbered ten; U. D. Chapters, eleven; the membership was 509.

The third annual session convened in Atlanta, the first Tuesday in May 1904, a city possessing the broadening spirit of the fraternal world and all of the fraternal bodies. The membership now numbered 1,218; chartered Chapters, seventeen, with five under dispensation.

---

[14] Organized February 21, 1901. By Mrs. Jennie L. Newman, of Dalton, Georgia, Grand Secretary, 1909 to present.

Thus far the Order had advanced beyond the highest hopes of its most ardent promoters. Many changes had taken place that were consistent with growth and permanency. The great Brotherhood could see that the Order was connected to them by five relations; distinct and separate in organization but the same in the work for uplifting humanity, so long inculcated by the ancient Brotherhood. The question of the Masonic Home was brought before the members at this session; the building was then being erected. New impulses and new interest permeated the members. They needed proper stimulus, direction, and enthusiasm to build an enduring monument that would testify to the earnestness and zeal of the O.E.S. for benevolence.

The fourth annual session convened in Macon, the third Tuesday in May 1905. The members had come to see the beauties of the higher O.E.S. life and had a clearer conception of its mission and a truer realization of the greater possibilities for the Order in Georgia and its advancement for women. There were twenty-three chartered Chapters and three new ones. This was a most prosperous session, the members grasping the aims and objects. For the Masonic Home-work it was decided to furnish the dining-room and to take full charge of the keeping of this beautiful hall; the Chapters voluntarily sending their contributions for the Masonic Home fund. On the wall of the Masonic Home will be found a marble tablet bearing this inscription: "This room is furnished by the O. E. S."

The fifth annual session was held in Rome, May 15, 1906. The order up to this time had been planted deep in life's experiences. Visions of the many beautiful dreams of Georgia O.E.S. could be seen not far distant. Chapters thirty; and six new chapters had been instituted. Each year added strength in greater numbers, power, and influence. The deliberations were characterized by the broad spirit of fraternal love.

The sixth annual session convened at Warrenton, the third Tuesday in May 1907. Recognizing the essential elements of strength and progress, the Order continued to sustain its advanced position and permitted no inroads to be made upon its work. Chartered chapters, twenty-six; new chapters, thirteen; membership, 1,607. It was at this time the Order received official recognition on the Masonic Home board and elected on the board of trustees, October 31, 1906, Sister Senie M. Hubbard. The work of furnishing the dining room was now completed and to have a permanent Home fund was the next proposition presented to the minds of the members. Thirty-five Chapters composing Grand Chapter were enthusiastic, earnest members and they set about to accomplish many beneficial things.

The seventh annual session convened in Atlanta the third Tuesday in May 1908. Having measured from year to year the progress of a rapidly moving Order, it is only when a milestone is reached that the distance advanced can be measured accurately. New conditions rise continuously, and this Grand Body kept its eyes firmly on truth, justice, and wisdom, and did not forget to love one another; the Homework was kept up with care and devotion. One handicap the Order had to contend with was clandestine work, but this was an obstacle that could be overcome. Unconsciously minds reached out for better things. At this meeting, fifty-three Chapters, thirteen new Chapters, and a membership of 2,065. Again, they with renewed courage assumed the work of duties to perform and triumphs to achieve.

The eighth annual session was held in Americus, May 18, 1909. The business of this session was taken up with an earnest purpose. The members had learned to care less for non-essentials and more for the essentials. The advancement of the Order must be conducted by rational educational methods. They knew each other better, were nearer together, the bond of unity stronger. Seventy-six Chapters were reported, and eighteen new ones instituted, with a membership of 2,489. The Order, in the morning of possibilities, was full of promise, silent forces were carrying it forward on its glorious mission.

The ninth annual session met at Cordele on the third Tuesday in May 1910. The Order had grown so rapidly that the system of District Deputy Grand Matrons was adopted to assist the Grand Matron in doing the work of the Grand Chapter. The reports show a marked improvement in all lines of work, general interest increasing over the State. The Masonic brethren of the Grand Lodge of Masons of Georgia regarded favorably the recommendation of the board of trustees of the Masonic Home, making all O.E.S. members in good standing eligible to admission to the Masonic Home. Also, it was this year that Electa Chapter, of Atlanta, conceived the idea of an educational fund for orphan children and they raised a sum of $200 to be a nucleus for a larger and permanent fund for educational purposes. No record of human effort could be more laudable and cannot be too highly estimated as a factor in preparing helpless orphans for positions of greater usefulness; united by a common interest, demonstrating the character of the O.E.S. in the work for the cause of humanity. It was a time for cautious and careful deliberations, with hearts full of gratitude for the united efforts and larger growth. Seventy-six Chapters reported, with a membership of 4,023, and eleven new chapters.

The tenth annual session convened in Augusta the third Tuesday in May 1911. Chapters reported at this time, eighty-six; membership, 4,160; new chapters, fifteen. The slow but sure and steady growth is marked, and the O.E.S. of Georgia feels much pride in its work along all lines. It was at this session that a form for instituting and constituting Chapters was adopted. The Georgia Grand Chapter introduced into the fraternal world an idea no other organization has ever conceived — the O.E.S. educational fund. This idea was born and conceived in the mind and heart of Sister Eva E. Cummings, Past Matron of Electa Chapter No. 6, of Atlanta. The Order in Georgia attained a high plane by this movement and has gradually grown in the estimation of the great Brotherhood. Our standard of helpfulness has been raised higher and many orphan children will rise up and call Eva E. Cummings blessed for making it possible for them to attain a higher education and be self-supporting. This recommendation of Sister Cummings was made at the eleventh annual session which convened in Dublin on the third Tuesday in April 1912. The wisdom of this session cannot be questioned. The noble women of the Order have never tired or shirked duty when opportunity presented itself and the Grand Chapter with great enthusiasm voted to raise $5,000 to be held in trust for the children of the Masonic Home and other needy Masons' children whom the Grand Chapter might deem worthy. Electa Chapter, of Atlanta, pledged itself to raise $1,000 of this sum and the State the remaining sum of $4,000.

The twelfth annual session convened in Macon the 30th of April 1913, with not only an increase in members and Chapters, but fraternal conditions improving.

The thirteenth annual session was held in Atlanta for the third time, and during the years the Order kept pace with the Atlanta spirit. This was the largest and best of all sessions, with 112 chapters.

The Masonic Home was built in 1903-1904 and opened in June 1904. It is located about three miles from the city of Macon on the crest of a beautiful hill, which slopes gradually in all directions a distance of several hundred yards. From the broad veranda of the Home to the west, there is a beautiful view of the Home gardens in the valley, where most of the vegetables used at the Home are raised. Beyond the garden, half a mile away, one catches a glimpse of the Ocmulgee River, which flows grandly on to the sea. From this river the Home receives its water supply, which is furnished by contract with the city.

The Home is maintained by the Masonic Grand Lodge of Georgia making annual appropriations, assisted by the Grand Chapter, O. E. S., which has for its individual work the furnishing and maintenance of the dining-room. The Chapters also contribute delicacies, consisting of boxes of preserves and jellies, canned fruits and vegetables. Chapters also provide technical training for girls and boys becoming of age to leave the Home who wish to take advantage of this opportunity.

The board of trustees is composed of twenty Masons (of which the Grand Master is chairman), including all Past Grand Masters and a few other members of the Grand Lodge, and two ladies from the Grand Chapter, O. E. S., who were selected by request of the Grand Lodge of Georgia, A. F. and A. M., and are both Past Grand Matrons. The trustees realize their great responsibility and plan cautiously and earnestly for the welfare of the Home.

MASONIC HOME, MACON, GA.[15]

There is no school at the Home. The children attend the public schools in the city. Special attention is given children who, have musical talent by Chapters of the O.E.S. and Masonic Lodges. The O.E.S. also have a Christmas Cheer Club, formed by the various Chapters, who send each resident of the Home a present at Christmas time.

The children attend Sunday school and church in the city, and some of the old people also attend when they are physically able. The Home is now full; the family consists of thirty-seven girls, ages four to nineteen, twenty-three boys, ages four to seventeen, nine old ladies, ages fifty to eighty-eight, and one Mason, aged sixty-five.

Many souls, husbands and wives, widows and orphans, have found a haven of rest in this Home, united by the strongest ties of brotherly love, where exists Faith, Hope, and Charity, but the greatest of these is Charity.

The Eastern Star has taken an active interest in the Home since the cornerstone was laid, and never loses an opportunity to do its part towards its maintenance. It is the duty of the O.E.S. trustees to solicit funds for the maintenance of the dining-room and keep it intact, and solicit funds for special educational purposes, such as

---

[15] By Senie M. Hubbard, P.G.M.; Worthy Grand Adah of the G. G. C., 1913-1916.

musical and technical training, and attend all meetings of the board of trustees, and they are vested with the same power exercised by the Masonic trustees.

Those eligible to the Home are Master Masons in good standing in the Masonic Lodge, and their wives, widows, and orphans, and members of the Order of the Eastern Star in good standing.

The two O.E.S. trustees on the Masonic Home board, Mrs. Senie M. Hubbard, P.G.M., and Mrs. Rose M. Ashby, P.G.M., have, through their individual efforts, placed in the Home this year a handsome upright grand Kranich and Bach piano.

Our O.E.S. trustees are elected every two years, one for two years, and one for four years, the one for four years being chairman.

The Home is fortunate in being situated near what is rated as the second healthiest city in the United States.

Grand Chapter of Idaho [16]

In the early history of the world, in Chaldea dwelt astrologers, who cast horoscopes by reading the stars. By claiming to be able to foretell future events, they had been called the "Wise Men."

According to tradition, as the three "Wise Men" were studying the heavens, they were greatly startled by the sudden blazing out of a star or comet. It was the night when a holy messenger had appeared, and with a rush of glory, spoke to some frightened shepherds in the inspiring words, "Fear not, for behold I bring you good tidings of great joy, which shall be to all people. For unto you is born this day, in the city of David, a Savior, which is Christ the Lord." The awe which filled the minds of the shepherds prompted them to leave their flocks, and with all haste they sought and found the Christ-child in a manger as the angel from heaven had revealed unto them. Accordingly, as the "Wise Men" recalled the prophecy, they too started

---

[16] Organized April 18, 1892.

toward Jerusalem, bearing costly gifts, intended as the first offerings of the Gentile world to the infant Jesus. The beautiful Star of the East went before them until they had followed it to the Holy City. Here they asked the people, saying, "Where is He that is born King of the Jews, for we have seen his Star in the East and are come to worship Him."

The State of Idaho first saw His Star in the East at Mount Idaho, May 21, 1880, with Mrs. Belle J. Randall, Worthy Matron; Farring B. King, Worthy Patron; the Chapter being organized by F. B. King, acting as special Deputy of the Most Worthy Grand Patron. After a few years of active work, this Chapter became dormant and the oldest Chapter surviving at the time the Grand Chapter was organized was Hugh Duncan No. 2, organized March 18, 1886, at Salmon City, with Mrs. Mary Kirtley, Worthy Matron; Robert McNicoll, Worthy Patron, and Rev. Hugh Duncan acting as special Deputy for the Most Worthy Grand Patron.

As the principles of charity, truth, and loving kindness, taught by the members of the earlier organized Chapters, became more and more prominently recognized, others wished to enjoy the benefits of this, the greatest organization of Christian womanhood depending upon secret work for its fulfilment. Accordingly, there followed Ruth Chapter No. 3, Pocatello, chartered August 16, 1888; Naomi Chapter No. 4, Albion, charter granted April 25, 1890; Mizpah Chapter No. 6, Idaho City, chartered December 29, 1891; Mountain Gem Chapter No. 7, Lewiston, chartered June 6, 1892; Adah Chapter No. 8, Boise City, chartered March 23, 1893; Ruby Chapter No. 9, Moscow, chartered February 22, 1895; Shoshone Chapter No. 10, Wallace, chartered February 22, 1895; Mountain Queen Chapter No. 11, Grangeville, chartered December 30, 1895; Laurel Chapter No. 13, Lewiston, chartered April 9, 1897; Esther Chapter No. 14, Blackfoot, chartered March 28, 1898; Golden Star Chapter No. 15, Bellevue, chartered January 30, 1899; Miriam Chapter No. 16, Mountain Home, chartered April 13, 1899; Queen Isabelle Chapter No. 17, Montpelier, chartered June 29, 1899; Syringa Chapter No. 18, Harrison, chartered March 19, 1900; Loyante Chapter No. 19,

Weiser, chartered February 28, 1901; Lorraine Chapter No. 20, Payette, charter granted to thirty-four members February 26, 1901; and Henrietta Chapter No. 21, organized at Idaho Falls April 16, 1902, with thirty-three charter members.

Only sixteen of the twenty-one Chapters organized by the General Grand Chapter survived at the time the Grand Chapter was organized at Weiser, April 18, 1892, with Mrs. Laura B. Hart, Most Worthy Grand Matron, acting as Deputy of the Most Worthy Grand Patron, and was recognized by the proclamation issued May 1, 1902, by L. Cabell Williams, Most Worthy Grand Patron. The first officers elected were Mrs. Louisa M. Rhea, Grand Matron, Weiser; Edward L. Liggett, Grand Patron, Wallace; Miss Helen Coston, Grand Secretary, Boise.

The Grand Matron was given exclusive executive authority, including the organizing of Chapters, a duty which usually is given to the Grand Patron, which was changed in 1908, and the Grand Patron was given power to organize Chapters in addition to his position as an advisory officer.

The fee for dispensation for a new Chapter, together with supplies, was fixed at $30; per capita tax, fifty cents. Any member not wearing the badge of membership shall not be allowed to speak on any question without the consent of the Grand Chapter, the badge of membership to consist of a blue ribbon with the letters O.E.S. printed thereon. The minimum annual dues in the subordinate Chapter was placed at $2 and any officer of a subordinate Chapter failing to attend four consecutive meetings without satisfactory excuse could be deprived of office and of any honors which would be included with the office. Any member in arrears for dues for one year or more shall not be allowed to vote at the annual election, nor be eligible to any office.

The first annual communication of the Grand Chapter convened in the Masonic Temple, Pocatello, June 9, 1903. With a band of enthusiastic workers, the work was carried bravely forward to a successful close, notwithstanding the fact that nine Grand Officers were unable to be present, including the Grand Matron and the Grand Patron, whose places were ably filled by the respective Associates. At this meeting, all the old charters issued by the General Grand Chapter were ordered called in and charters of the Grand Chapter of Idaho were given instead. The fraternal building fund was created, with $36.80 as a basis, to which they would add with loving thoughts and willing hands, until in time their ambitions would become a reality.

The second annual session was held at Wall ace, the metropolis of the Coeur d'Alene. It is stated that more than half of the lead consumed in the world is supplied from the mines in this section and the Grand Chapter was given a recess to allow the delegates to accept an invitation to visit the mining camps on Canyon Creek, where the wonderful sight of a mining shaft running down about 2,300 feet was visited at Frisco. The Mammoth mine boasts of a tunnel driven straight into the mountains to a distance of 3,800 feet. The ponderous machinery of the Coeur d'Alene district is propelled by electric power brought over the mountains from Spokane, Washington, its towns and mines being lighted from the same source.

At the third annual session, held at Hailey, June 1905, it was decided to contribute $47.25 for the O.E.S. headquarters at the Portland fair. At this meeting, only seven Grand Officers were present.

The fourth annual session convened in Masonic Hall, Boise, at which time report was made of $255 having been contributed to the California sufferers in response to a circular letter; $100 was appropriated to purchase jewels for the Past Grand Matrons and Past Grand Patrons.

The fifth annual session met at Lewiston in 1907, and there accomplished a grand and effective work under the motto:

> Do something for somebody always
> Whatever may be your Creed.
> There's nothing on earth can help you
> So much as a kindly deed.

The sixth session was held at Coeur d'Alene, June 9, 1908.

> So the world would be purer and better far,
> Because of the work of the Eastern Star.

An invitation from the Grand Lodge of Idaho, to participate in the ceremonies of the laying of the cornerstone of the City Hall of Coeur d'Alene, was accepted. Also, an invitation from the Masons to attend a reception given by them to the members of the Grand Chapter at Fraternal Hall. The State was divided into three districts, and Deputies appointed for two of them, the Grand Matron reserving one of the three for herself to visit, but the year 1909 witnessed the end of the Deputy system.

At the eighth annual session, held at Twin Falls in 1910, upon the recommendation of the Worthy Grand Matron the Grand Chapter adopted the memorial service known as the "Chapter of Sorrow" prepared by Sister Addie C. S. Engle for use in the subordinate Chapters.

A special session of the Grand Chapter was called August 4, 1910, at Pocatello, for the purpose of attending the funeral of Past Grand Matron Anna Dolbeer. At the 1910 session the annual per capita tax was raised to seventy-five cents.

The proceedings of the Grand Chapter of Idaho have been actuated by the spirit of fidelity to right and duty, obedience to the demands of honor and justice, loyalty to God, a trustful faith, and with charity to all.

Grand Chapter of Illinois [17]

The information here given has been taken from the Grand Chapter Proceedings since its organization October 6, 1875, previous to which time the facts as related were obtained from Sister Lorraine J. Pitkin from her own personal experience, for the most of which she possesses documentary evidence. Sister Pitkin is a pioneer worker for the Order in Illinois, having labored early and late, without money and without price, giving her very best endeavors toward the advancement of an Order dedicated to the advancement of "Charity, Truth and Loving Kindness" — and one so closely allied to that great Fraternity acknowledged as the strongest and most influential in all the world—the Masonic Fraternity. As a matter of fact, a history of the Order of the Eastern Star in Illinois would be impossible without frequent mention of the name of her to whom all members of the Order, and especially those of Illinois, owe so much.

Rob Morris originated the Order of the Eastern Star. He was born in Boston in 1818, made a Mason at Oxford, Mississippi, on March 5, 1846, and died in LaGrange, Kentucky, July 31, 1888. He was the second "Poet Laureate" of Masonry. In 1847, with his wife, he received the degree of the "Heroine of Jericho." He was greatly interested but felt that a more simple and heartfelt ritual would attain greater success. In February 1850, he devised the Order of the Eastern Star. He writes of his having "hesitated for a theme on which to build such an order" and of "having dallied over a name and pondered long over the selection of the five-pointed star and pentagon as its chief emblems." His calling it the Order of the Eastern Star was merely a happy coincidence. Morris wanted this society to become a branch of Masonry insofar as to permit women, through their membership therein, to establish a recognition among the Fraternity anywhere,

---

[17] By May Bromley Milroy, P. W. G.M. Membership, last Proceedings, October, 1915, 82,512; number of active Chapters, 651 (of this number 107 are in Chicago); gain in membership at rate of 5,000 per annum.

that would insure them protection by means of their Masonic relationship. His idea excited great opposition and failed.

Morris called these new adoptive lodges, "Constellations." In 1853 he instituted the first Constellation, Purity No. 1, at Lodge, Kentucky. Lexington was the headquarters of the order, and Robert Morris was called the "Grand Luminary." About two hundred Constellations were formed throughout the United States. The ceremony did not find favor with Masons, however, and Morris revised it in 1859, renaming it "Families of the O. E. S." At this time, he began issuing charters to the latter, using the elaborately lithographed charters which were in his hands, showing that the two systems, "Constellations" and "Families," were the same, the latter having superseded the former.

Reports show that many Master Masons in Illinois were clothed with authority from the fountainhead in this country, Rob Morris, to confer the degrees of the Eastern Star as early as 1860, since which time the signs and lectures have not in the main materially changed.

Mrs. Lorraine J. Pitkin, her sister, Mrs. Lucy M. Sherwood, with their brother, David H. Dickinson, and his wife, were invited to be present at a meeting at Mrs. Cynthia Leonard's, on West Lake Street near Leavitt Street, Chicago, on October 6, 1866. Dr. W. Thompson, Grand Lecturer of the Grand Lodge, A. F. and A. M. (one of those who in 1860 had been authorized by Rob Morris to confer degrees), took charge of the meeting and conferred the degrees upon about thirty persons there assembled, for the purpose of organization. The result was the formation of the first Eastern Star Society in Illinois, known as Miriam Family No. 1111.[18] The officers selected at this time were: Patron, D. W. Thompson (elective); Patroness, Mrs. Myra Bradwell; Conductor, J. H. Varnell (elective); Conductress, Mrs. Lorraine J. Pitkin; Treasurer, Walter A. Stevens (elective); Hebe, Mrs. J. H.

---

[18] How long before this the Order had been introduced as organized bodies, it has been impossible to definitely learn, but as 110 lodges must have been formed at various places previous to the above, it must certainly have been some time.

Varnell; Secretary, Simon Quinlan (elective); Thetis, Mrs. Cynthia Leonard; Warder, James B. Bradwell (elective); Areme, Mrs. Chas. T. Wilt: Tyler, John Porter Ferns.

The five high officers being elective, were filled by brothers, who chose their correspondents, the latter being sisters. The Patroness occupied a seat on the left of the Patron in the East and wore a sash, the color appropriate to Adah. The Conductor and Conductress were in the West, the latter wearing a sash appropriate to Ruth. The Patron, Conductor, and Conductress took part only in the initiatory work. The Treasurer, Secretary, and Warder occupied the same positions as now, and their correspondents sat on their left, wearing a sash, the color being appropriate to Esther, Martha, and Electa respectively, their mystical names being Hebe, Thetis, and Areme. The meetings were held the first and third Tuesdays of each month in Blair Hall, located on the present site of McVicker's Theatre and destroyed during the great fire of 1871.

Of more than one hundred "Families" organized between 1860 and 1867 no complete record has been preserved, if one was ever made, and only the following are known and are a matter of record in the office of the Right Worthy Grand Secretary: Rose of Sharon No. 4, Annapolis, Ind., organized January 15, 1861; Plymouth No. 41, Plymouth, Maryland, organized June 25, 1864; Friendship No. 103, Brooklyn, New York, organized January 25, 1866; Sunbeam No. 83, Mt. Vernon, Indiana, organized April 19, 1866; Miriam No. 111, Chicago, Illinois, organized October 6, 1866; Orion No. 112, Rensselaer, Indiana, organized February 27, 1867.

Mrs. Myra Bradwell, the first Patroness, was the first woman to preside over an Eastern Star organization in Illinois. She was the wife of Judge James B. Bradwell, of the Probate Court, and was herself a lawyer of great ability and editress of the Chicago *Legal News*.

The Patron and Patroness of the original Family were sole judges of membership in the Order, although they were compelled to recognize an objection from a member.

Each female member at the time of her initiation was required to select an emblem from the following flowers: violet, sunflower, white lily, pine sprig, or red rose, and the Recorder was required to keep a book in which these selections were entered.

The order of business provided for a banquet with elaborate decorations and ceremony, which was under the supervision of the Treasurer and Warder with a set form for the officers at the table. Letters were cut from pasteboard an inch in height, each one representing one of the initials of the cabalistic motto, which were laid on the right of the plates of the Patron, Patroness, Conductor, Conductress, and Recorder. Bouquets were laid at the left of each plate, together with a very hard and dry biscuit cut in the form of a Star — then followed a long and elaborate ritualistic ceremony.

Their Signet was very similar to the one now in use.

At the first regular election of officers in January 1867, Walter A. Stevens, Worshipful Master of Blair Lodge, was elected Patron, and Mrs. Lorraine J. Pitkin was made Conductress.[19] It was under this administration, in 1867, that Mrs. Elizabeth Butler and Dr. S. A. McWilliams were initiated. Their names appear on the original dispensation asking change of organization, now in possession of Miriam Chapter No. 1, of Chicago.

During the latter part of 1867 a Miss Knapp came to Chicago from Adrian, Michigan, and introduced the "Tatem" or "Michigan Ritual," which was adopted, and Mrs. Lorraine J. Pitkin of Illinois was elected Worthy President September 24, 1867. The manuscript, secret work, with the rituals, etc., are now in the possession of Sister Pitkin. *Tatem's Monitor* contained the ritual of Adoptive Masonry used in the Eastern Star degree, consisting of the initiation or degree work, ceremony for opening and closing, installation services, etc., together with forms and rules for government compiled and

---

[19] Just forty-five years later (in 1912) the daughter of Walter A. Stevens was elected to the degrees and initiated in Miriam Chapter No. 1.

arranged by John H. Tatem, of Adrian, Michigan. This work seemed to be what the members in Illinois thought would be permanent, but after about a year's trial they decided they did not like it as well as the "Family" and they again adopted the latter.

In 1868 Rob Morris, having resolved to give the remainder of his life to Masonic explorations in the Holy Land, turned over to Robert Macoy of New York, his powers and prerogatives in the Eastern Star so far as he was concerned. There were some who intimated that all these powers were self-assumed, but be that as it may, the Order of the Eastern Star of today has become a very large and powerful organization and all who in the early days were instrumental in aiding the Order to reach a permanent standing in the world, should be given a full measure of praise.

The February number of the *Voice of Masonry* for 1869 prints the result of the last election and installation of officers in the original Miriam Family, held on Wednesday evening, December 30, 1868, which was only about two months previous to its reorganization into a Chapter:

Patron, Dr. S. A. McWilliams; Patroness, Mrs. Joseph Butler; Conductor, A. B. Haight; Conductress, Mrs. E. G. Butler; Secretary, E. St. John; Hebe, Miss M. Ferns; Treasurer, Jas. B. Wyman; Thetis, Mrs. A. B. Haight; Warder, Joseph Gallagher; Areme, Mrs. M. A. J. Ogden. About this time, all the Families in existence were being merged into the Chapter form of work under the authority of Robert Macoy, of New York.

On March 4, 1869, Miriam Chapter No. 1, O. E. S., was organized with nine charter members, the charter issued to Miriam Family No. 111 was surrendered and a new one issued to Miriam Chapter No. 1, thereby changing the name of the organization but not the name of the body. The officers elected were: Worthy Matron, Mrs. Elizabeth Butler; Worthy Patron, Dr. S. A. McWilliams; Associate Matron, Mrs. Chas. T. Wilt.

The dispensation for Miriam Chapter No. 1's dated March 4, 1869, although the original book of record says the Chapter was organized on March first. The petition for a *"Warrant"* as they were called in early days was made to "The M. E. Grand Patron of the Supreme Grand Chapter of the Adoptive Rite of the Order of the Eastern Star." A charter was issued in this form signed by Robert Macoy. Following are the nine charter members: Mrs. Joseph Butler, Dr. S. A. McWilliams, Mrs. Chas. T. Wilt, A. B. Haight, Mrs. Sarah Farrar, Mrs. John C. Howell, Mrs. A. B. Haight, Joseph Gallagher, Mrs. Mary J. Ogden.

After its organization, all those who had been members of the Family were notified that if they wished to become members of the Chapter they could, by signifying their desire to do so and paying their dues to that body. Among those who did so was Mrs. Lorraine J. Pitkin, who paid her dues to Dr. McWilliams, thereby becoming a member of the reorganized body, Miriam Chapter. The Chapter form of organization and government became quite popular and up to the time of organizing the Grand Chapter of Illinois, on October 6, 1875, Robert Macoy had formed 178 Chapters in Illinois, the first one being Miriam Chapter, and the last one Tallula Chapter No. 178, organized February 8, 1875.

The original charter of Miriam Chapter dated March 4, 1869, was destroyed in the great fire of 1871 and was duplicated by Brother Macoy in January 1872. This latter charter is the one which was endorsed by the 'Grand Chapter in Springfield in 1876 and became Miriam's legal authority for convening as a Chapter in Illinois. Mrs. Elizabeth Butler, Miriam's first Worthy Matron, subsequently left to organize Butler Chapter and later became the first Worthy Grand Matron of Illinois and the first Most Worthy Grand Matron.

When the call was made for the convention to consider the advisability of organizing a Grand Chapter in Illinois, the representatives of the following twenty-two Chapters, working under the authority of Robert Macoy, met in Chicago at the Commercial

Hotel on Wednesday evening, October 6, 1875. Rob Morris, being present, was invited to preside: Miriam No. 1, Amnesty No. 9, Dorcas No. 22, Minerva No. 23, Lydia No. 28, Wyoming No. 52, Schuyler No. 67, Sta. Maria No. 70, Illiopolis No. 72, Bennett No. 87, Golden Ray No. 88, Continent No. 90, Starlight No. 93, Winifred No. 98, Capitat No. 100, Lady Franklin No. 113, Mary Burns No. 118, Lady Washington No. 158, Greenup No. 169, Egyptian No. 173, Stone Fort No. 176, Tallula No. 178.

Frank Hudson, Jr., was appointed Secretary. Committees (all brothers) were appointed on credentials, constitution, and nomination of Grand Officers, and the Grand Chapter of Illinois was duly organized, and its officers elected — without a single *sister* up to this time having had anything whatever to do with its organization. Further than this, the *Grand Patron* was made the chief executive officer. This is probably not known by the average member today who has not studied the early history. The following from the constitution is interesting:

> Sec. 10. The Grand Matron *shall assist* the *Grand Patron* in the discharge of his duties, *be subject* to the *orders of the Grand Patron* or Grand Chapter, and in case of the death, absence from jurisdiction or inability to act, of her *Superior Officer*, she is to assume and discharge all his powers, duties and prerogatives.
>
> Sec. 16. The elective officers are Grand Patron, Grand Matron, A. G. Patron, A. G. Matron, G. Secy., G. Treas., G. Conductress and *Grand Warder*, who shall be elected by ballot.

Daniel G. Burr, of Paris, was elected Grand Patron and Mrs. Elizabeth Butler, of Chicago, Grand Matron. The Grand Matron did not sign the proceedings, the only signatures being those of the Grand Patron and Grand Secretary.

Brief Histories of the Several Grand Chapters

The second annual session[20] met in the hall of Miriam Chapter No. 1, Chicago, Wednesday, October 4, 1876. Fifteen Chapters were represented by twenty-seven delegates. Only four Grand Officers were present.

Notwithstanding the Constitution provided for the title of Grand Officers, such as Grand Matron, etc., they are entered of record as Right Worthy Grand Matron, etc. — these two words having been prefixed without any apparent authority.

The address of the first Grand Patron (who was a bachelor) contains a high tribute to Woman:

> As our organization has been more properly formed for the benefit of woman, then her mission is peculiar and sublime. There is a work to be done in the fraternal world. There may be some wilderness of nature in the Order to be subdued; its barrenness and deformity, if any, are to be converted to fertility and beauty; nature is to be brought more fully in subjection to the purpose of man; but: some will say, this work rests not on woman. There are new channels of the institution to be opened up, new lines of intercommunication to establish; arts to foster, fields of discovery to explore; social systems to reconstruct; and institutions to regenerate; but the peculiar mission of woman is not here.
>
> To all this we reply, her mission is what the soul is to the body — what the spirit is to the matter which it animates and informs. Woman is emphatically and essentially an educator. Woman is also a reformer; the influence of woman on the order of society is controlling; she wields in society a moral influence which man never can command. Her power makes itself felt, for good or evil, in all the walks of social

---

[20] Presiding officers: Daniel G. Burr, Grand Patron; Elizabeth Butler, Grand Matron; Frank Hodson, Grand Secretary.

life. It is welded into all the ramifications of life and occupies all the recesses of the heart.

Woman is the destroyer or the conservator of the best interests and highest happiness of social man; one way or the other, her influence must be controlling.

All this we suppose to be generally and clearly admitted truth. And in this view, how commanding, how awfully responsible is the position of woman in this Order. Look at the present beauty of our Society and see the end toward which this amazing moral power is to be exerted.

The committee on addresses reported on the Grand Patron's address in part recommending "That this Grand Chapter send a delegate to the Convention to assemble at Indianapolis in November next (1876), for the purpose of considering the propriety of organizing a Supreme Grand Chapter." The report was amended, naming the following delegates: Henry R. Kent, Grand Patron; Mrs. Laura N. Young, Grand Matron; Daniel G. Burr, Past Grand Patron; Mrs. Elizabeth Butler, Past Grand Matron. The records show the membership in thirty-nine Chapters to be 956 brothers, 1,200 sisters, and $67.55 in the Grand Treasury.

The third annual session was held in Chicago.[21] Sixteen Chapters were represented by thirty-two delegates and eleven Grand Officers were present.

The dispensation to organize Queen Esther Chapter with Mrs. Lorraine J. Pitkin as Worthy Matron, was granted at this session. A motion also prevailed that "New Charters be issued to Chapters under the jurisdiction of Illinois and that they be numbered according to the date of the Charter held at "that time which has been issued to Mr. Macoy. . ." Miriam therefore was recorded as No. 1, and the new charter signed by Laura N. Young, Worthy Grand Matron, Henry

---

[21] Presiding officers: Henry R. Kent, Grand Patron; Mrs. Laura N. Young, Grand Matron; Frank Hodson, Jr., Grand Secretary.

R. Kent, Worthy Grand Patron, and Frank Hudson, Jr., Grand Secretary.

The Grand Matron said:

At the beginning of my term of office, when I sought to know my duties, I was duly informed that the office was only an honorary one; that all executive and supervisory duties devolved on the Right Worthy Grand Patron. He might ask my assistance. From his absence from the jurisdiction or from his death, I might be called upon to perform the executive duties; otherwise, I need not trouble myself with the thought that the Right Worthy Grand Matron had anything to do. Is this the sense of the Grand Chapter? In the subordinate Chapters, we are instructed that upon the judgment and discretion of the Worthy Matron rests the government of the Chapter. Shall she reach a higher office only to find her hands tied? I would suggest that it would be but justice to define her duties, if she has any. On you, as Matrons, rests not only the government of the Chapter, but the responsibility of its welfare and progress. You must exact of every officer the duties of the office in which she is installed and be ready at all times to give information which will enable them to do perfect work. To do this, you must be a good workman yourself. Self-poised, with a headful of knowledge and a heartful of love, you will do yourselves honor and be a guiding light in the Chapter. Thus, may you exemplify the teachings of Masonry, and contribute in your own lives to the strength and beauty and usefulness of our Order.

Several amendments to the constitution were presented, but the most important one, which was adopted, made the Grand Matron the executive officer during the session. During the vacation of the Grand Chapter, she was assigned its executive powers, "conjointly with the Grand Patron."

The following resolution was also unanimously adopted:

> *Resolved,* That this Grand Chapter cordially approves of the action of the convention of November 15 and 16, 1876, at Indianapolis, organizing the General Grand Chapter of the O.E.S.[22]

The fourth annual session was held in Chicago,[23] October 1, 1878. Eighteen Chapters were represented by thirty-eight delegates and fifteen Grand Officers were present.

The fifth annual session was held in Chicago,[24] October 7, 1879. Twenty Chapters were represented by forty-one delegates and sixteen Grand Officers were present. Total active Chapters in Illinois at this time were twenty-seven, with a membership of 1,862.

Sister Pitkin advocated at this time the organization of practical charity in Chapters and asked that a certain per cent of the receipts be set aside for a "Charity Fund." In speaking of establishing a "Home" for needy members of the Order of the Eastern Star and their children, she said:

> If our Chapters had something to labor for, some little bare feet to clothe, or poor heart-sick souls to comfort, there would be no time for contention and strife; the seeds of discord would never be sown, and a spirit of harmony and unity would prevail throughout this and other Grand Jurisdictions.

The sixth annual session was held in Chicago,[25] October 5, 1880. Twenty Chapters were represented by thirty-five delegates and members. At this meeting a constitution was adopted and printed in

---

[22] Illinois had been honored by Elizabeth Butler's election as Most Worthy Grand Matron.

[23] Presiding Officers: Mrs. Laura N. Young, Grand Matron; Henry R Kent, Grand Patron; Frank Hodson, Jr., Grand Secretary. Note that the name of the Grand Matron here precedes that of the Grand Patron for the first time as presiding officer.

[24] Presiding officers: Mrs. Lorraine J. Pitkin, Grand Matron; James W. Watson, Grand Patron; Robert Malcolm, Grand Secretary pro tem.

[25] Presiding officers: Mrs. M. Lemon, Grand Matron; Mrs. Laura N. Young, Grand Secretary. (Henry R Kent, Grand Patron, absent.)

the Proceedings and the Grand Matron was made the sole executive officer.

The seventh annual session was held in Chicago,[26] October 4, 1881. No report of committee on credentials is shown and no way of knowing how many chapters were represented. Finances were considerably "tangled." The Grand Treasurer reported $49.90 on hand and $368.50 in the hands of the Grand Secretary. The committee on finance apparently made a desperate struggle to balance accounts and finally made a report "recommending a more complete style of keeping the financial books of the Grand Chapter."

The eighth annual session was held in Chicago,[27] October 3, 1882. Thirty Chapters were represented by fifty delegates and twelve Grand Officers were present.

The Grand Patron evidently had experienced some difficulties with the ballot as the following would indicate:

> I can take but little credit to myself for the work done the past year. To the Worthy Grand Matron, whose untiring industry and extraordinary zeal in the performance of her official duties, rendering much valuable time and assistance to many of the Subordinate Chapters, is entitled the highest commendation for the healthy and prosperous condition in which you find the Order today.
>
> I would respectfully call your attention to that feature of our general By-laws which require the ballot on petition for membership to be unanimous. I consider it a dangerous and unjust delegation of power to one member. One black ball should never be sufficient to keep a good and worthy person out of a Chapter, in defiance of the judgment of all the rest of its members. And yet, it often does. It is the

---

[26] Presiding Officers: Mrs. Jeannette W. Ashley, Grand Matron; James M. Brice, Grand Patron; Mrs. Laura N. Young, Grand. Secretary.

[27] Presiding officers: Mrs. Jeannette W. Ashley, Grand Matron; Alonzo Eaton, Grand. Patron; Mrs. Mary A Beale, Grand Secretary pro tem.

unjust exercise of this power on the part of a few members that creates more discord and disturbs the peace and harmony of our Chapters throughout the State, to a greater extent than all other causes combined. I would recommend that this Grand Chapter forward to the General Chapter, at its next meeting, a Resolution asking that the law in this regard be changed.

The recommendation of the Grand Patron was referred to the General Grand Chapter, asking favorable action.

The ninth annual session was held in Chicago,[28] October 2, 1883. Thirty Chapters were represented and eleven Grand Officers were present. Up to this time the revenue of the Grand Chapter had remained the same as when it was organized, *i.e.*, $10 for dispensation for new Chapter, $1 for degrees at sight, $1 for dispensations of any kind, fifteen cents per capita, and ten cents for each initiation. After consideration and reconsideration, postponement and reference, an amendment to the constitution was adopted at this session to increase the revenue, making the per capita twenty-five cents and each dispensation for new Chapter, including charter when granted, $20.

Rob Morris was present and installed the Grand Officers, with Mrs. Nettie C. Ransford, Grand Matron of Indiana, as Grand Marshal.

The tenth annual session was held in Chicago,[29] October 7, 1884.

Albert Ashley brought to the Grand Chapter a Masonic influence that was felt throughout the State. He sent out a circular letter to each Lodge in the State, setting forth the beauties of the Eastern Star and inviting investigation. He reported that several of the eleven dispensations which he had granted had come through this channel of introduction, he having visited twenty-six Masonic Lodges in the interests of the Eastern Star.

---

[28] Presiding officers: Mrs. Jane F. Cozine, Grand Matron; John F. Dickinson, Grand Patron; Mrs. Mary A. Beale, Grand Secretary.

[29] Mrs. Jane F. Cozine, Grand Matron; Albert B. Ashley, Grand Patron.

Just as the financial question seems to have been mastered, comes an amendment to the constitution to strike out the ten cents for initiations, which was adopted. Past Grand Matron Lorraine J. Pitkin made a short address in favor of the Grand Chapter taking some action and sanctioning the taking of some step toward establishing an Orphans' Home, and resolutions in favor of this project were adopted.

Rob Morris was present and gave an interesting talk, which was printed in the Proceedings, and from which is quoted the following:

In the Chapters I have visited in Illinois the past year I have heard no rumors of the difficulties which a few years since were so rife.

> If there is not the zeal we should like to find, at least there is none of the zeal of hatred and revenge which make so many other societies centers of discord. The orphan is coming into a nearer relationship with Masonic charities through the influence of the Eastern Star. The widow has learned that her claim upon the Brothers of her dead husband is a genuine claim, readily acknowledged. The Masonic Lodges themselves, in many instances, have been purified through female influence, not merely in the removal of dust and cobwebs and the whitening of gloves and aprons, but in the cleansing of the membership, the removal of the vicious, the drunkard, the profane, who by a shameless falsification of truth, had foisted themselves upon the Masonic membership. Nothing but female influence can accomplish such a revolution as this — that no man shall be admitted to the Lodge circles who is not equally fit and welcome in the domestic circle. For myself, I have for forty years adopted this rule: i. e. — never to vote for a man to be made a Mason whom I cannot introduce freely to my wife and daughters.

Except the Lord build the house, they labor in vain that build it — except the Lord build the city, the watchman worketh but in vain.

The eleventh annual session was held in Chicago,[30] October 6, 1885. In her address the Grand Matron said:

We have not added as many Chapters this year as last, but we have other causes for congratulations. The deep-rooted prejudice against our Order, which has existed in some places, has to a great extent been overcome, and year by year we are gaining more friends among the Masonic fraternity.

The twelfth annual session. was held in Chicago,[31] October 5, 1886. Considerable good work was reported at this session showing gratifying progress. In closing his report, the Grand Patron said:

It is now three years since you first honored me with the high office I am now about to restore to your hands. We have now over eighty subordinate Chapters, twenty-nine of which have been added during this period. The completion of this number makes us, I think, the largest Grand Chapter in existence. May we not congratulate ourselves that we have reached this satisfactory position? Let me, however, with a closing word, remind you that with enlarged capabilities come increased responsibilities. If we have reached a leading position, should we not be careful that all our actions be consistent therewith Grand Chapters fewer in numbers and younger in years will look to us as an example worthy of imitation. Let us see to it, therefore, that this example be always such as shall be a credit to ourselves and

---

[30] Mrs. Jennie M. Walker, Grand Matron; Albert B. Ashley, Grand Patton.

[31] Mrs. Jennie M. Walker, Grand Matron; Albert B. Ashley, Grand Patron. Sister Jennie Walker, Past Grand Matron, was called to her heavenly home in January, 1916, and Illinois bas lost a beloved sister who faithfully emulated the teachings of our Order and who endeavored at all times to zealously promote its interests.

an assistance to our dearly loved order wherever the light of Charity, Truth, and Loving-kindness illumines a benighted world.

The position established thirty years ago has never been relinquished, for Illinois today is still the largest Grand Jurisdiction in the world with over eighty thousand members and about seven hundred Chapters, one hundred of which are in the city of Chicago.

The thirteenth annual session was held in Chicago,[32] October 4, 1887. At this session the State was divided into districts and deputy Grand Matrons provided for. The constitution was amended to read: "In case of conflict of opinion between the first two officers of a Chapter, the Worthy Matron's opinion shall take precedence."

Sopha C. Scott was reelected and presided at the fourteenth annual session in Chicago, with W. O. Butler as Grand Patron, October 2., 1888, and again at the fifteenth annual session in the same city, October 1, 1889, with E. L. Palmer as Grand Patron. The Grand Matron issued a circular letter showing the appointment of seventeen Deputies in 1888 and eighteen in 1889 for as many districts, whose reports appear in the Proceedings.

At the fifteenth annual session the constitution was amended to read: "Nor shall any member be eligible to the office of Grand Matron more than two years in succession."

Sue M. Simpson presided at the sixteenth annual session in Chicago, October 7, 1890, with E. L. Palmer as Grand Patron, and again at the seventeenth annual session in the same city, October 6, 1891, with Geo. F. Howard as Grand Patron. At the latter session the Grand Patron recommended that the Grand Chapter take decided steps towards making the Masonic Orphans' Home its special work, which was referred to a special committee, consisting of Lorraine J. Pitkin, Jennie A. Walker, and Sopha C. Scott, whose report, as follows, was adopted:

---

[32] Sopha C. Scott, Grand Matron; John E. Pettibone, Grand Patron.

Your committee earnestly endorses the recommendation of the Grand Patron regarding the Masonic Orphans' Home Association and fully appreciates the responsibility the Masons of Illinois have assumed to care for the Masonic orphans of this jurisdiction. Their by-laws do not protect the children of members of the Order of the Eastern Star or members of the Eastern Star unless they are the widows or orphans of Master Masons.

Your committee does not desire to make any recommendation to this Grand Chapter that would in any way antagonize the best interests of the Master Masons of this State. We do earnestly desire to lend our influence as the representatives of seven thousand members, knowing that such an influence must be effectual. We would recommend that the representatives of this Grand Chapter, i.e., the Grand Patron and Assistant Grand Patron (who are entitled by our two life memberships in said association) attend the annual meeting of the Masonic Orphans' Home in March, 1892, and ask the association in the name of the Eastern Star of Illinois to so amend their by-laws that the orphans of members of the Eastern Star may find a home under the same roof with the orphans of Master Masons, and when this is done, we will pledge the financial aid in every particular that this large membership in Illinois may warrant.

The records show that this proposition was declined by the Masonic association.

Jane M. Ricketts presided at the eighteenth annual session, Chicago, October 4, 1892, with A. H. Wright as Grand Patron, and again at the nineteenth annual session in Chicago, October 3, 1893, with Wm. H. Bartells as Grand Patron. At the latter session the Grand Chapter was satisfied, after a trial of three years, that the District Deputy System was not a wise one and the constitution was therefore amended abolishing the same and the system of schools of instruction was established under the supervision of the Grand Matron. An effort was also made to discontinue the vote in Grand Chapter of Past Matrons and Past Patrons but was not successful. An amendment, however, was adopted, striking out of the constitution the vote of the Associate Matrons which had hitherto been permitted and making the Worthy Matron and Worthy Patron the only representatives.

Due to the unremitting efforts and earnest and zealous interest of Lorraine J. Pitkin, space was allotted to the O.E.S. in the organization room of the Woman's Building during the World's Fair held in Chicago in 1893. Sister Pitkin assumed a great responsibility when she undertook to establish the "Eastern Star Corner" at the great exposition, but this wonderful and capable woman brought all the details of her preparatory arrangements to so successful a termination that the aims and purposes of the Order were more universally understood and respected than years of work could otherwise have accomplished. On "Woman's Day," October 28, 1893, the total registration in the organization room, of all the Societies represented, revealed that during the life of the exposition the Eastern Star had registered second in numbers, the first being the Woman's Christian Temperance Union.

May 16, 1893, was "Eastern Star Day," a courtesy extended by the "World's Congress of Women." It was the "Day of Days" and was perfect from beginning to end. Music, flowers, and speeches characterized the event and at night everyone departed tired but happy. Mrs. Mary C. Snedden, Most Worthy Grand Matron, presided, and General John Corson Smith, Past Grand Master and ex-Governor of Illinois, gave a most interesting address.

The twentieth annual session was held in Chicago,[33] October 2, 1894. A great impetus was given to the progress of the Order during Sister Kenner's administration due to her wonderful capability and

---

[33] Mrs. Nettie C. Kenner, Grand Matron; D. H. Zepp, Grand Patron.

charming personality. She could have received the unanimous vote of the Grand Chapter for reelection, but firmly declined it with thanks, saying that in this fast growing jurisdiction one term was all for which any sister should aspire and that she wished to nominate her associate in office, and hoped that the vote might be unanimous, craving the privilege of casting the vote, which was granted her by the vote of the Grand Chapter. She established the precedent of one term which has since continued.

Thus did the outgoing administration work in perfect harmony with the incoming and the future seemed full of hope for those who were to assume official responsibility. All praise is justly due to Sister Kenner for her generosity and loyalty to the best interests of the Order, believing as she did that the Order was served best by sharing the honors as well as the responsibilities with others, and establishing the precedent that a Grand Matron shall not succeed herself.

The Grand Chapter was at this time composed of 243 Chapters, with a total membership of 14,190.

At the twenty-first annual session, held in Chicago,[34] October 1, 1895, a resolution was presented by Geo. Howison, Past Patron of Miriam Chapter No. 1, and adopted, which was the foundation of our present beautiful and splendid Home at Macon, which has grown from a modest beginning (initial cost being $6,500) to its present noble proportions, representing now an investment of $100,138.

The twenty-second annual session convened in Peoria,[35] October 13, 1896. This was the first time in its history that the session assembled outside of Chicago.

The first report of the Home board was given by Mary A. Bradley, the Secretary, which was adopted. She gave a detailed description of the grounds, receipts and donations of the newly located Home at Macon. The formal dedication of the Eastern Star and Masonic Home

---

[34] Mate L. Chester, Grand Matron; G. A. Edwards, Grand Patron.
[35] May Brown, Grand Matron; Chas. L. Hovey, Grand Patron.

occurred July 7, 1897, at Macon, to "indigent Masons' widows and female members of the Eastern Star and such orphans as the Board deemed wise to admit." The dedicatory ceremonies were conducted by Jennie W. Freeman, Grand Matron. This Home has become an eloquent monument to the labors of the Order in this State.

At the twenty-third annual session[36] an amendment was adopted, raising the per capita tax to thirty-five cents, ten cents of same being ordered paid to the Treasurer of the Home board, and at the thirty-ninth annual session it was again raised to fifty cents, twenty-five cents of which is turned over to the Treasurer of the Home funds.

The work achieved by each of the officers since 1897 has been noteworthy indeed, and each has done her full quota to maintain and still further increase the high standard of excellence which has ever characterized both the spirit and the letter of the noble work done by the Eastern Star in Illinois.

A system of instruction has been adopted in both ritual and floor work called the "Standard Work." The law provides for a "Board of Grand Examiners," consisting of seven members, the Worthy Grand

---

[36] Below is a table showing the names of the presiding officers following the twenty-second annual session:

Annual Session	Held at	Date	Worthy Grand Matron	Worthy Grand Patron	Grand Secreta
23	Chicago	Oct. 5, 1897	Jennie W. Freeman	W. B. Carlock	Sopha C. Scott
24	Chicago	Oct. 4, 1898	Sarah D. Haggard	W. B. Carlock	Sopha C. Scott
25	Chicago	Oct. 3, 1899	May Chapman	J. J. Crowder	Mate L. Cheste
26	Chicago	Oct. 1900	Sadie B. Morrison	F. M. Hocker	Mate L. Cheste
27	Chicago	Oct. 1901	Lottie J. Wiley	D. W. Whittenberg	Mate L. Cheste
28	Chicago	Oct. 7, 1902	Edna C. Wilcox	A. G. Hug	Mate L. Cheste
29	Chicago	Oct. 6, 1903	Mary H. Goddard	Edmund Jackson	Mate L. Cheste
30	Chicago	Oct. 4, 1904	Mary R. Inghram	Harris W. Huehl	Mate L. Cheste
31	Chicago	Oct. 10, 1905	Kate Aull Heath	Fred E. Glenn	Mate L. Cheste
32	Springfield	Oct. 23, 1906	Henrietta B. McGrath	Walter R. Kimsey	Mate L. Cheste
33	Peoria	Oct. 15, 1907	Jennie E. Bell	George J. Kurzenknabe	Mate L. Cheste
34	Chicago	Oct. 20, 1908	E. Mae McRae	Wm. H. Brydges	Nettie C. Kenne
35	Chicago	Oct. 5, 1909	Effie M. McKindley	Milton E. Robinson	Nettie C. Kenne
36	Chicago	Oct. 4, 1910	Amalia Huehl	D. John Forbes	Nettie C. Kenne
37	Chicago	Oct. 3, 1911	Inez J. Bender	Madison Brower	Nettie C. Kenne
38	Chicago	Oct. 1, 1912	Hester M. Smith	Herbert T. McLean	Nettie C. Kenne
39	Chicago	Oct. 7, 1913	Cassie G. Orr	Samuel M. Fitch	Nettie C. Kenne
40	Peoria	Oct. 6, 1914	May Bromley Milroy	Wallace C. Watkins	Nettie C. Kenne
41	Chicago	Oct. 5, 1915	Selma N. Weege	Harry L. Gannett	Nettie C. Kenne

Matron and Worthy Grand Patron, the Associate Grand Matron and Associate Grand Patron being *ex-officio* members thereof, and three members annually appointed by the Worthy Grand Matron. There are only seven copies of the "Standard Work" in existence, one of which is given to each of the seven members of the board during their term of office. About nine or ten State schools are held early in the year (the law requires at least six), under the direct supervision of the Worthy Grand Matron, assisted by the Board of Grand Examiners, and thorough instruction is provided from the "Standard Work" to all representatives in attendance. The schools are located at convenient and accessible points throughout the State, so that all Chapters may benefit therefrom, and uniform work be assured. This system has been operative since 1909 and has proven extremely successful. The law also provides for commissioned Grand Lecturers who, having qualified by hard study and a rigid examination under the Board of Examiners, are granted a commission by the Worthy Grand Matron permitting them to instruct subordinate Chapters throughout the State in all the requirements of the Standard work. All Grand Lecturers must be present or past Worthy Matrons of Illinois. There had been 27 Grand Lecturers commissioned to October 1915. The commissions may be revoked at any time at the discretion of the Worthy Grand Matron. At the annual session of the Grand Chapter the seven copies of the "Standard Work" are turned over to the Grand Secretary who receipts for them, and they are again given out to the newly appointed Board of Grand Examiners.

The voters or delegates at the annual session are the present Worthy Matrons and Worthy Patrons and Past Worthy Matrons and Past Worthy Patrons. The membership July 1, 1915, was 82,512, forming 651 Chapters. As the membership is increasing at the rate of about five thousand per year there will be approximately 88,000 members at the approaching census. The minimum fee for initiation is $3 and ranges from this sum to $15. Annual dues range from $1.50 to $5. Dispensation fee for new Chapters in cities of over 10,000 population is $60; for the same in all other cities, $30. No more than six candidates may be initiated at any one meeting.

The Home is centrally located at Macon, Illinois. There are twenty-three acres of land, and spacious buildings containing seventy-two rooms. There is a well-equipped hospital with a trained nurse, and adequate help is employed to properly maintain such a large establishment. The aim has always been in both management and surroundings to eliminate all idea of an "institution" and cultivate the thought of "home." The Home has been in existence nineteen years, during which time peace and happiness has been brought to many an aching heart. The Home is more than maintained by a per capita tax of twenty-five cents and is under the direction of a board of trustees, seven in number, five of whom are elected for terms of one, two, and three years respectively, the Worthy Grand Matron and Worthy Grand Patron being *ex-officio* members. The funds are kept separate from those of the Grand Chapter, and at the present time are in a very flourishing condition although it has taken years of good management and judicious economy to attain the present position.

GRAND CHAPTER OF INDIANA [37]

> Fair Star, that o'er the manger shone,
> Guiding the Wise Men to his throne,
> That was so humble and unknown,
> All hail 1 All hail, that wondrous Star!
> —*Elvira Adams Atwood.*

The degrees of the Order of the Eastern Star were communicated by its founder, Dr. Rob Morris, in Indiana on a number of occasions,

---

[37] Organized May 6, 1874.

the first having been at New Albany in 1852, and very frequently afterwards.

Lodges of the Adoptive Rite of Masonry were organized at Orland, Salem, Fremont, Butler, and Elkhart, and all used the Tatem ritual. On January 27, 1869, the Grand Lodge of Adoptive Masonry was organized at Elkhart, by representatives of the five Lodges mentioned above adopting regulations for their government similar to that in use by the Grand Lodge of Adoptive Masonry of Michigan. The second and last meeting was held in Orland in October 1869, which closed to meet the following October, and the Lodges composing the Grand Lodge soon became dormant after the Grand Lodge failed to meet.

Robert Macoy chartered a Chapter at State Line City in January 1870, and later charters were issued to the number of twenty-five, but only fifteen were active at the time of organization of the Grand Chapter, at Anderson, May 6, 1874, by representatives of ten Chapters. The organization was effected by the Rev. John Leach, Deputy Supreme Grand Patron. The constitution adopted recognized the Grand Patron as the executive officer, which prevailed until 1877, when the Grand Matron was accorded the recognition of presiding for the first time in any Grand Chapter and was made the executive officer. No provision was made for Grand Officers at the star points, but this was provided for in 1877. The right to vote in subordinate Chapters was given only to sisters, though the brothers were accorded the privilege of the ballot in the Grand Chapter. The right of voting in subordinate Chapters was given to the brothers in 1877.

To the untiring efforts and commendable zeal of the members of this Grand Chapter we are indebted for the activities which resulted in giving to the Fraternity the General Grand Chapter. To the Rev. Willis D. Engle, more than any other person, belongs the credit, and without his splendid work this organization would not have been possible; the benefits to all the members of the Fraternity cannot be estimated.

Sister Nettie Ransford, Past Grand Matron of the Grand Chapter of Indiana and Past Most Worthy Grand Matron of the General Grand Chapter, is the only sister who has been in attendance at every meeting of the General Grand Chapter, and Rev. Willis D. Engle, Past Grand Patron of Indiana and Past Most Worthy Grand Patron of the General Grand Chapter, is the only brother who has attended every meeting of the General Grand Chapter since the organization of that body in 1876. The members of the Order of the Eastern Star are indebted to two members of this Grand Chapter, Sister Ransford and Brother Engle, for much of the legislation that has been the keynote of the success that has marked the progress of this, the greatest organization of women.

The Grand Chapter arranged for a location in Indianapolis in 1879 and with but one exception, has held all its meetings in that city since that date — the exception was in 1899 when it met in Fort Wayne where it celebrated the twenty-fifth anniversary in a manner adapted to the occasion.

In 1892 the Grand Chapter appointed a committee of three to act with a like committee from Masonic bodies to devise ways and means for raising funds for a Masonic Widows, and Orphans, Home. This committee failed to accomplish the intended results, but in 1902 a fund was commenced which accumulated with wonderful rapidity. In 1911 a per capita tax of ten cents was levied for the benefit of the fund and this, with the assistance of the Grand Lodge, was productive of a large addition to the Home fund. In 1909 an Eastern Star Home Association was formed and at the 1910 session, a request was made that the Grand Lodge, A.F. and A.M., permit a special representative of the Grand Chapter, O. E. S., to be heard on the floor of the Grand Lodge, on the question of a Masonic and Eastern Star Home. With the most cordial welcome, this request was granted. The ways and means committee reported that "We believe now is the time, and this is the place for this Grand Lodge, representatives of 53,000 Hoosier Masons, to declare themselves in favor of such an institution," the report being adopted by the Grand Lodge, and a permanent and organized committee was appointed. As a result of their strenuous efforts and the generous assistance and combined work of the members of the Masonic bodies and the encouragement and donations of the members of the Eastern Star, a tract of two hundred and fifteen acres of land was purchased, adjoining Franklin, about twenty-two miles south of Indianapolis. The first building to be erected was the administration building, the cornerstone of which was laid during the meeting of the Grand Lodge, A.F. and A.M., in May 1915. The Masons of Indiana greatly appreciate the cooperation of the Order of the Eastern Star by assisting in a substantial manner in this worthy enterprise. At the time the cornerstone was laid, the O.E.S. donations amounted to the magnificent sum of nearly $32,000. As the work progressed, the interest among the members of the subordinate Chapters increased with many pledges from subordinate Chapters for $100 each, which amount was intended to furnish one room in the building.

The Proceedings of 1898 contained a splendid tribute to those who had been honored by official trust by including the portraits of the Grand Matron and Grand Patron, also sixteen Past Grand Matrons and twenty-two Past Grand Patrons.

In 1901, the "Test Oath" was adopted, and the Grand Secretary was instructed to prepare a form for minutes, code of by-laws, and instructions for the use of subordinate Chapters. The office of Grand Organist was created. The organization of a Past Grand Matrons' and Past Grand Patrons' Association in 1911 has been an added impetus to the zeal and energy of this Grand Jurisdiction in promoting the principles of charity, truth, and loving kindness.

Grand Chapter of Iowa [38]

The Eastern Star, historically, in Iowa is marked by three distinct eras. The first is its introduction when charter was granted by Brother Macoy for a Chapter in Clermont in April 1870, which was followed by fifty-eight others. The second is the reorganization in the State by the General Grand Chapter, of Ruth No. 6, Iowa City, May 9, 1877, which was also the first subordinate Chapter organized by authority of the General Grand Chapter. A Supreme Grand Chapter charter dated November 21, 1871, was surrendered and thus, with John N. Coldren, Patron, and Phila B. Coldren, Matron, the first efforts toward the present widespread organizations were completed when J. Norwood Clark, deputy for the Most Worthy Grand Patron, constituted this Chapter May 16, 1877. Then followed Charity Chapter, Marble Rock, chartered May 14, 1877; Harmony Chapter, Council Bluffs, whose charter was received March 9, 1878, in exchange for their Supreme Grand Chapter charter dated August 26, 1873; Home Chapter, Des Moines, chartered April 29, 1878; Fidelity Chapter, Rockford, chartered May 8, 1878, exchanging their charter of the Supreme Grand Chapter dated December 30, 1873; Excelsior Chapter, Charles City, chartered May 8, 1878; Gem Chapter, Shell Rock, chartered May 8, 1878; Missouri Valley Chapter, Missouri Valley, chartered July 18, 1878.

Mrs. Jennie E. Mathews, Deputy of the Most Worthy Grand Patron, issued the call for the convention to organize the Grand Chapter, which met in Cedar Rapids, July 30, 1878, at which time seven Chapters were represented. A constitution was adopted which made the Grand Patron the executive officer but in 1881 the Grand Matron was given that authority. During the first nine years, the annual dues were twenty-five cents per capita, but after that time were increased to thirty-five cents.

---

[38] Organized July 30, 1878.

In 1879 is was decided that regalia should be worn as follows: "For sisters, a scarf with white ground, six inches wide, the five colors to be worked around the edge. For brothers, a Master Mason's apron, with stars worked in at the two points, and borders of the five colors." Later, the officers' scarves and aprons were ordered made of different colors, and those of the members were white, bordered with the five colors.

In 1893 the State was divided into five districts, with a Deputy Grand Matron in each. In 1894 the Treasurer of the Charity Fund reported $520 on hand, which had been increased until the balance after all charitable work had been deducted, amounted to $854.29 in 1902. The Masonic Library Building voted the use of a "Memorial Case" for the O.E.S. In 1902 Sister Lorraine J. Pitkin, Right Worthy Grand Secretary, gave $6 — the first — toward an Iowa Home; other pledges were made and the sum of $235 was raised. This grand work of love was followed with such zeal that on October 18, 1905, the beautiful brick structure with all modern improvements at Boone was dedicated to the Order as the O.E.S. Masonic Home, a monument to the largest, the best, and the most practical woman's order in the world, at a cost of $13,694.24 for the Home.

By order of the Grand Chapter, the memorial service of Sister Engle is held at each annual meeting and in 1898 the Grand Matron's address incorporated the following extract from the address of the Grand Master of the Masons of Iowa, which was approved by the Grand Lodge:

> My observation is that where Chapters of the Order of the Eastern Star have been established it has added a new zest to Masonry, stimulating its social features, and, indeed, proving itself an active auxiliary to our Order. If this is true, it would follow that it is little for us to do, to so far extend our good wishes and fraternal sympathy as shall afford encouragement. That we may do so, I suggest the adoption of

the following, or some like enactment as a standing regulation:

That the organization known and designated as the Order of the Eastern Star, when composed of Masons, their wives, widows, mothers, sisters and daughters, may occupy Masonic halls for festal and ceremonial purposes.

The Grand Secretary's report in 1909 gave the following:

I must not forget to mention a very pleasant fact, and one which, a few years ago, would have caused some of the good and strait-laced Masonic brethren to hold up their hands in holy horror. When the twenty-first volume of the *Annals of Iowa Masonry* came out it was dedicated to the Wives, Daughters, Mothers, Widows, and Sisters of Master Masons, who though they cannot become members of our Fraternity can and do cooperate with us in their individual capacity and through the Order of the Eastern Star, in directing the charities and toiling in the cause of human progress and aid in the upbuilding of the Fraternity. To the purest, wisest, and noblest of womanhood, we dedicate this, the twenty-first volume (1908-1909) of *Annals of Iowa Masonry*.

Over $900 was contributed to the Galveston flood sufferers and $634 to the Temple of Fraternity at the St. Louis fair. A memorial bookcase was placed in the Masonic Library in memory of T. S. Parvin and a memorial to Thomas R. Ercanbrack, who served as Grand Patron for five years, was placed in the Masonic Home. His widow, Mrs. Harriet A. Ercanbrack, was the first Worthy Matron of Mt. Moriah Chapter, Anamosa, and served as such for fifteen years. In 1886 the Grand Chapter of Iowa elected her Worthy Grand Matron, and for five years she presided over that body, which was then practically in its infancy. In 1889 she was elected Right Worthy Grand Treasurer, which office she held continuously until the time of her death, January 1, 1915.

> Some time, someday our eyes shall see
> The faces kept in memory,
> Someday their hands will clasp our hands
> Just over in the border lands.

GRAND CHAPTER OF KANSAS [39]

The Grand Chapter of Kansas held their twentieth annual session in Kansas City as guests of Mendias Chapter No. 1, at which time Mendias Chapter proudly exhibited their old charter, signed by the illustrious founder of the Order of the Eastern Star, Rob Morris, LL.D., and bearing date of July 28, 1856, which fully established this Chapter as the oldest O.E.S. organization in the State.

Active and zealous work was done by Harmon G. Reynolds, through whose energy and influence eighty-two Chapters had been organized previous to the date when he called the convention to organize the Grand Chapter, at Emporia, October 18, 1876, at which time forty-two Chapters were represented either by official representative members or by their proxies. By the constitution adopted, the Grand Patron was made the executive officer, but this was changed in 1877, since which date the Grand Matron has held this authority.

Though this Grand Chapter was actively engaged in the progressive duties of the Order at the time the convention was called for the organization of the General Grand Chapter, it did not send delegates, but in 1877 delegates were elected, with discretionary powers, and they, for this Grand Chapter, formally pledged allegiance to the General Grand Chapter at its meeting in Chicago in 1878. The delegates were Mary A. Hepler, Worthy Grand Matron, and Willis Brown, proxy for Worthy Grand Patron.

---

[39] Organized October 18, 1876.

The constitution provided that meetings should be held at the same time and place as the meetings of the Grand Chapter of Royal Arch Masons, and the postponement of its meeting from October 1879 to February 1880, resulted in not having any meeting of the Grand Chapter in 1879. The meeting of 1882 decided to hold the annual meetings at such time and place as the Grand Chapter shall designate.

The birthday of Dr. Rob Morris is enthusiastically celebrated each year, and to further the proper observance of the day, an Eastern Star Association was organized by members in Kansas and the western part of Missouri.

In 1891 the following resolution was adopted:

Resolved, That, in token of the high appreciation of her services, the Grand Chapter extends to its first Grand Matron, Mary A. Hepler, a heartfelt welcome, and authorizes the Grand Secretary to draw an order on the Grand Treasurer refunding to her the amount of her expenses incurred in attending this meeting, and this be done annually so long as she remains in this Grand Jurisdiction.

In 1893 the Grand Chapter presented Sister Hepler with a gold watch, inscribed with proper mention of the conditions which prompted the gift, and in 1895 the Grand Chapter appropriated $10 per month to her during the remainder of her life, a beautiful tribute and substantial recognition of' invaluable services and devotion to the Order, and a reward well bestowed upon one most worthy.

This Grand Chapter assumed the care and education of a little girl, Emma Avery, whose dying mother left her in the care of Electa Chapter, and an appropriation of $50 annually was made to Electa Chapter to assist in this work so long as the Chapter had her in charge.

> Thanks for the sympathies that ye have shown,
> Thanks for each kindly word, each silent token,

That teaches me, when seeming most alone,
Friends are around us, though no word be spoken.

The O.E.S. assumed the honor and pleasure of furnishing the Masonic Home dedicated at Wichita, September 10, 1896, and this assistance was thankfully received and appreciated by the Masonic Fraternity.

The Grand Chapter met at Wichita in 1893, at which time an entertainment was given by the children of the Home; a silver shower which followed amounted to $53.65 for the children.

All Chapters have one "Masonic Home Day" and each member is expected to give something which will be presented by her Chapter to the support of the Home. In 1898, the matron of the Home in her remarks at the Grand Chapter meeting said: "We have the only Masonic Home in the world; we meet around the same common Altar; one table, father, mother, our children, grandma's and grandpa's — we are all one family, no institutional discipline."

A donation of $282.45 was made to the Galveston flood sufferers; an appropriation of $186.40 to the Temple of Fraternity at St. Louis. In 1905 $86.80 was donated to the Lewis and Clark Exposition fund.

In 1895 the Grand Chapter, O. E. S., received commendable recognition from Mt. Olivet Commandery, Knights Templar, when invitations were extended to attend a reception and ball given by them. Further courtesy was extended by the Grand Commandery in 1898, in the adoption of the following:

> *Resolved*. That the Grand Commandery of Knights Templar, in annual conclave assembled, hereby extend to the Order of the Eastern Star our knightly and courteous greeting and our sincere wish that their session may be pleasant and harmonious and their legislation wise and judicious.

Masonic recognition and fraternal courtesy have marked the history of this Order whose basic foundation is the greatest benefit to humanity at large, mankind in general, and womanhood in particular, and has greatly assisted their noble efforts to excel in the progress of their undertakings. In 1910 the matron of the Kansas Masonic Home, Mrs. Mary C. Snedden, who is also Past Most Worthy Grand Matron of the General Grand Chapter, in her report of the conditions surrounding the children at the Home, said: "I think our children are receiving a better and higher moral and religious training than nine-tenths of the children in the so-called Christian homes. Twenty-seven of our children have been baptized, and all over thirteen . . . have united with the church, and are trying to lead Christian lives."

In 1911 the first military Chapter was chartered — Maple Leaf Chapter, at Fort Leavenworth. This is the only military Chapter in the world, by reason of which many questions as to jurisdiction arose, which had to be met. It is a well-established Masonic law that a member or officer of the United States army can claim his residence anywhere, and is, therefore, eligible to petition a lodge for the mysteries of Masonry without regard to time. Following the Masonic law, the Grand Patron of Kansas held that the residence of the wife or unmarried daughter of a member of the United States army was the same as that of the husband and father, notwithstanding the law of the Order governing the length of time necessary to gain a residence.

In 1906 the Order of the Eastern Star built a chapel on the Masonic Home Grounds at a cost of $10,000, which structure was a magnificent recognition of the benefits such a building can be to those who are living at the Home. In the additions to the beautiful Home, in the isolation cottage, in the furnishings, in the endowment fund, in the giving of many little comforts and luxuries for the benefit of those who live at the Home, the Order of the Eastern Star has had a substantial part. Wherever a helping hand has been needed, in the many disasters that have come to members of the Order in our sister States, the Grand Chapter of Kansas has ever stood ready and willing to give assistance whenever it was asked or needed.

Today well lived makes every yesterday a dream of happiness and every tomorrow a vision of hope.

GRAND CHAPTER OF KENTUCKY [40]

Kentucky soil has given sepulcher to one whose inspired genius brought forth the Order, its author and founder, the venerable patriarch, Brother Rob Morris, LL.D., who for twenty years preceding his death was a resident of La Grange, Kentucky. Here the lyre of this noted brother was tuned to higher and sweeter strains of melodious songs, and from there his writings have gone forth to millions of people in other lands, telling in accents of joy and gladness, to Masons and their kindred, the peace and profound satisfaction of dwelling together in unity.

In the year 1787, in Cannongate Kilwilling Lodge No. 2, of Edinburgh, Scotland, Worshipful Brother Robert Burns was coronated first Poet Laureate of Freemasonry, which honor he highly prized but modestly wore for nine years, with distinction to himself and pleasure to the Fraternity.

The honorary position of Poet Laureate of Freemasonry having remained vacant since the death of Robert Burns in 1796, a period of nearly eighty-eight years, the leading Masonic bodies and prominent brethren of this country selected Past Grand Master Rob Morris, of Kentucky, for that great honor. He was accordingly coronated second Poet Laureate of Freemasonry in the Masonic Temple, New York City, on December 17, 1884, before a large assemblage of brethren, which honorable position he held until his death almost four years after.

Following the death of Brother Rob Morris in 1888, a period of twenty years, no steps were taken to fill the position of Poet Laureate, made vacant by his death, until Right Worshipful Brother Fay

---

[40] Organized June 10, 1903.

Hempstead, of Little Rock, Arkansas, was coronated third Poet Laureate of Freemasonry on October 5, 1908, in Ravenswood Lodge, No. 777, at Medinah Temple, Chicago, Illinois.

The first Constellation ever organized was Purity No. 1, located at Lodge, Fulton County, Kentucky, which was, at that time, the place of residence of Dr. Rob Morris.

Brother Morris having conveyed the duties incident to the promotion of the Order of the Eastern Star to Brother Macoy, the first Chapter was chartered by him at Lancaster, in August, 1870; and later Queen Esther Chapter, located at Louisville, was chartered January 15, 1879, which charter was exchanged for one from the General Grand Chapter, March 25, 1882, and this being the first Chapter chartered by the General Grand Chapter, was numbered 1. J. W. Hickman, special Deputy for Willis Brown, Most Worthy Grand Patron of the General Grand Chapter, constituted the Chapter April 20, 1882, with Miss Annie F. Kalfus, Matron; Lew Varalli, Patron. This Chapter maintained an existence for a short time, after which it became dormant, but was reorganized by the Rev. H. R. Coleman, Deputy for the Most Worthy Grand Patron, L. Cabell Williamson, April 17, 1902, with thirty-eight charter members.

In all, thirty-nine Chapters were chartered by the General Grand Chapter, but only twenty-two of them survived at the time of the Grand Chapter organization by Mrs. Laura B. Hart, Most Worthy Grand Matron, acting as the Deputy of the Most Worthy Grand Patron.

The Grand Chapter was organized at Louisville, June 10, 1903, at which convention the Most Worthy Grand Matron was ably assisted by Sister Lorraine J. Pitkin, Right Worthy Grand Secretary; Mrs. Kate I. Thomas was elected Grand Matron; R. H. Corothers, Grand Patron; Mrs. Josephine H. Tinder, Grand Secretary.

The address of welcome in 1904 was given by Rob. Morris, son of the founder of the O. E. S., at which time he gave an excellent history of the Order, known to him personally, as he was born one year after the system was wrought out by his honored father, and therefore has lived all his life in the atmosphere and with the absolute knowledge of its growth,[41] The sum of $956.75 was contributed by the several Chapters to the Masonic Widows' and Orphans' Home. In 1905 the Grand Chapter was called off to attend services under the auspices of the Grand Lodge A. F. and A. M. and in the same year, Sister Engle's Chapter of Sorrow was rendered as the memorial service; also, at each annual session since that time.

Mrs. Callie L. Clagett was chosen Grand Matron, with Brother Rob. Morris, son of the founder of the O. E. S., Grand Patron for 1905 and 1906. In this manner Kentucky members of the O.E.S. tendered their appreciation of the father, also of the son, when they gave their sacred charge in the keeping of one who fully realizes that "Woman's heart beats responsive to the same inspiration that prompts man to noble deeds." Many Chapters combined to celebrate the "Festal Day" of the Order and $94.61 was presented to the old Masonic Home at Shelbyville.

In 1909 $500 was appropriated for an Eastern Star dormitory at the Masonic Widows' and Orphans' Home and a fund was commenced which should be used for erecting an Eastern Star Home.

It is a matter for general rejoicing that the Grand Lodge of Kentucky has accorded such cordial recognition to the Order of the Eastern Star. This is the result of a visit to the Grand Lodge when in session, by Mrs. Clara A. Henrich, Grand Matron, who was escorted into the room by the Grand Warden and seated by the Worshipful Grand Master in his chair in the East. She addressed the Grand Lodge, giving a short history of the Order, and benefits to be derived from its teachings and closed by saying that all the Eastern Star wished was the good will of the Masonic Fraternity in Kentucky. An unanimously adopted resolution was conveyed by special messenger from

---

[41] See Dr. Morris's biography as given by his son, page 33.

the Masonic Grand Lodge to the Grand Chapter, O. E. S., in session, in which "heart-felt goodwill" was extended.

In 1913 the Grand Matron was presented with a gavel made by a boy in the Masonic Widows' and Orphans' Home at Louisville, from a tree that had been planted by Henry Clay.

Sister Clara R. Henrich, Past Grand Matron of Kentucky, was honored by appointment as Worthy Grand Warden of the General Grand Chapter, 1913-1916.

GRAND CHAPTER OF LOUISIANA [42]

Sometime in the late eighteen sixties or early seventies, someone whose identity is not established, traveled through the State of Louisiana, initiating persons into what was termed the degrees of the Eastern Star. The extent of his travels is not known, but this is known that the traveler left a picture of Dr. Rob Morris in Alexandria, which picture now hangs in the parlor of the Chapter rooms in that city. This may indicate that the traveler was the person who now is recognized as the founder of the Order. There is no evidence that he granted any charters in the State.

On April 17, 1884, a charter was granted and a Chapter duly constituted by the General Grand Chapter. This was Rob Morris Chapter No. 1, at New Orleans. Miss Anna Prophet was the Worthy Matron; Alfred Shaw, Worthy Patron; Mrs. Lizzie Coulter, Associate Matron. There were twenty-six signers to the application for a charter. Within the five years following its organization, there were eighty-seven initiated by this Chapter; then for some cause, not clearly evident, the Chapter ceased to meet and was suspended.

On the 28th of September 1900, a new charter was granted by the General Grand Chapter to a new Chapter under the same name

---

[42] Organized October 4, 1900. Data by Mrs. Maria Elizabeth Duncan. Grand Secretary, 1907 to 1915.

and number, but in whose membership was included but one member of the old Chapter.

The oldest Chapter with continuous existence from the date of constitution to the present, is Rebecca Chapter No. 2, at Welsh, chartered June 3, 1890, and constituted July 26, 1890, with Mrs. Kate Hewitt, Worthy Matron; L. E. Robinson, Worthy Patron; Mrs. Rosa Kelly, Associate Matron. Subsequently the General Grand Chapter granted charters to Robertsville Chapter, at Robertsville; Mt. Carmel Chapter, at Florien; St. Joseph Chapter, at St. Joseph; Louise L. M'Guire Chapter, at Monroe; Alice Chapter, at Morgan City; Lorraine Chapter, at Opelousa; Harmony Chapter, at Coushatta; Evangeline Chapter, at Farmerville; De Sota Chapter, at Logansport; Electa Chapter, at Franklin; Good Intent Chapter, at Kentwood; Gody Chapter, at Ruston; Jennings Chapter, at Jennings, and Electa Chapter, at Alexandria, making a total of sixteen Chapters, only ten of them active at the time the Grand Chapter was organized.

On October 4, 1900, there assembled at Alexandria a convention at which were represented Rob Morris Chapter, Rebecca Chapter, Louise L. M'Guire Chapter, Alice Chapter, Harmony Chapter, Gody Chapter, Jennings Chapter, and Electa Chapter of Alexandria, at which time and place the Grand Chapter was organized by Mrs. Kate C. Brechner, Deputy of the Most Worthy Grand Patron. Mrs. Maria Elizabeth Duncan was chosen Grand Matron but declined the office.[43]

---

[43] Mrs. Maria Elizabeth Cooke Duncan was initiated by Electa Chapter No. 10, June 29, 1900; Worthy Matron of Electa Chapter, 1900-1901, elected Grand Secretary of the Grand Chapter of Louisiana on June 7, 1907, serving in that office continuously until her death on February 27, 1915.

Her record in office, her devotion to the interests of the Order of the Eastern Star, her character and life, endeared her to all who had the pleasue of coming within the sphere of her influence.

It is with a sense of personal loss that we record the passing of one of the helpers upon this work. She was one of our associates during the General Grand Chapter session in Chicago in 1913 and her interest in the Order was never failing.

There is a stream that we all must cross,

Subsequently Mrs. Mary S. Herring was elected Worthy Grand Matron; John S. Alfred, Worthy Grand Patron; Mrs. Pattie O. Johnston, Associate Grand Matron, and C. R Brownell, Associate Grand Patron. Immediate recognition was accorded by the General Grand Chapter and all other Grand Chapters of the Order. The per capita dues were fixed at twenty-five cents.

Subsequent to the organization of the Grand Chapter, Mt. Carmel and Evangeline Chapters gave their allegiance and received charters from it. The other Chapters chartered by the General Grand Chapters as above mentioned, had become extinct. The returns from the several Chapters showed that at the date of the organization of the Grand Chapter there was a total membership of 392, apparently all of them energetic in their efforts to further the best interests of the Order, each in her or his position giving of their best in this great service for humanity.

In 1908 the State was divided into districts. The Grand Chapter has met annually and the returns from Chapters indicate a steady growth, with new Chapters instituted by the Grand Chapter to the number of ninety-nine. Forty-three dollars was contributed to the Order's headquarters known as the Temple of Fraternity at the St. Louis fair.

According to the Grand Lodge laws of Louisiana only Masonic bodies are permitted to meet in Masonic halls, and in consequence the Eastern Star cannot meet in these halls, but an exception is made in the city of New Orleans.

The legislation of the Grand Chapter has been conservative, and it is believed that nothing has been enacted that is not common to

---

The River of Human Years;
Now lying calm in the summer's light,
Now splashed with the rain of tears;
Out from the hill of God it flows,
And on to the shoreless sea,
Where the noontide sun no shadow throws,
And time is eternity.

all Grand Chapters of the Order. The Grand Chapter owns a library of eleven hundred volumes, including the Proceedings of the several Grand Chapters, most of them bound and cased. Funds belonging to this Grand Chapter have been invested to the amount of $4,878.74, of which $3,378.74 is a Relief Fund. In 1908 a resolution was adopted looking to the accumulation of a fund to furnish a Masonic Home, should one be erected, failing which it should be used for the erection of an Eastern Star Home, and liberal contributions have been made to this fund.

GRAND CHAPTER OF MAINE [44]

Brother Robert Macoy chartered a Chapter at South Berwick, Maine, in May 1870. The first Chapter chartered by the General Grand Chapter was Adah No. 1, located at Biddeford, April 3, 1888, which was closely followed by Overcome Chapter No. 2, Bowdoinham, chartered June 13, 1888. By request of the members of this Chapter, who wished the name changed, Jefferson S. Conover, Most Worthy Grand Patron, on January 5. 1889, authorized the name of Overcome Chapter No. 2, to be changed to Electa Chapter No. 2, which action was approved by the General Grand Chapter on September 26, 1889.

Charter was granted December 9, 1889, by the General Grand Chapter for Mizpah Chapter No. 3, Saccarappa, and organization completed January 7, 1890, by E. M. Forbes of Winchester, New Hampshire, Deputy of the Most Worthy Grand Patron. There were forty-three petitioners and the first officers were Arthur M. Ricker, Worthy Patron; Mrs. Anna D. Phinney, Worthy Matron.

Kineo Chapter No. 3, Old Town, was chartered July 2, 1890, and organized September 10, 1890, by J. E. Haynes, Deputy of the Most Worthy Grand Patron, having forty-one signers to the petition.

---

[44] Organized August 24, 1892.

Beulah Chapter No. 5, at Westbrook, was chartered March 30, 1891, and organized by A. H. Burroughs on April 29, 1891, having fifty-three signers to the petition. Mount Moriah Chapter No. 6, Denmark, was chartered July 10, 1891, and organized by A. H. Burroughs on July 24, 1891, with thirty petitioners.

Pleiades Chapter No. 7, located at Patten, was granted a charter July 29, 1891, and organized August 18, 1891, by John E. Haynes, Deputy of the Most Worthy Grand Patron, having forty-nine names upon the petition.

Charter was granted to 210 petitioners for Golden Rod Chapter No. 8, located at Rockland, December 18, 1891, and organization was completed February 11, 1892, by C. D. Blanchard, Deputy of the Most Worthy Grand Patron.

Charter was granted to forty-eight petitioners for Jonathan Hunt Chapter No. 9, located at Herman, on December 22, 1891, and organization was completed on February 4, 1892, by C. D. Blanchard, Deputy of the Most Worthy Grand Patron.

Queen Esther Chapter No. 10, located at Hallowell, was chartered January 11, 1892, and organized January 26, 1892, by Hadley O. Hawes, Deputy of the Most Worthy Grand Patron, having upon the petition forty-four names.

Pioneer Chapter No. 11, Lisbon Falls, received its charter from the General Grand Chapter April 6, 1892, in response to the prayer of fifty petitioners and was organized by F. Kossuth Jack, Deputy of the Most Worthy Grand Patron, on April 30, 1892.

The convention to organize the Grand Chapter was called by Golden Rod Chapter No. 8, Rockland, and met in Rockland August 24, 1892. Seven of the eleven Chapters in the State were represented and allegiance to the General Grand Chapter was declared; a constitution was adopted which made the Grand Matron the executive officer, and all Past Matrons and Past Patrons permanent members of the Grand Chapter. It was further provided that, in addition to the three principal officers, a Chapter of over fifty members should be entitled to one additional representative, also to one additional representative for each additional fifty members, but the provision for representation other than the three principal officers was abolished in 1894. The by-laws adopted provided "That any member who shall report outside of the Order, the name of a rejected candidate, shall be subject to the penalty of suspension, and in order that no member shall plead ignorance of this provision, it shall be so stated to the Chapter immediately after each rejection."

In 1895 the Grand Matron was authorized to make one official visit to each Chapter at the expense of the Grand Chapter, and in 1896 the State was divided into five districts with a Deputy Grand Matron in each, and schools of instruction have been held annually since the division was effected. The number of districts has been increased as the growth of the Order required.

An appropriation of $136.60 was made for the relief of the Galveston flood sufferers, and $733 for the relief of sufferers from the San Francisco disaster, and $60.95 given as a free will offering to assist in maintaining O.E.S. headquarters at Portland, Oregon.

In 1902 the work was exemplified with the aid of colored lights, stereopticon illustrations, and vocal music, which added much to the impressions made upon those witnessing the work.

By recommendation of the Grand Patron, an amendment to the constitution was adopted in 1905 limiting the number of Rituals in each Chapter to not more than ten, also that upon the request of the Grand Matron, $5 shall be paid to the Grand Secretary if copy of *Ritual* be lost, also the same amount for copy of *Secret Work* if lost.

The amount in the charity fund in 1913 was $3,527.87.

Since the organization of the Grand Chapter of Maine in 1892, it has gathered from its hilltops and its valleys, yea, from its rockbound coast of the broad Atlantic, strong and able minds, tender and loving hearts of its best citizens; closely allied with an institution which stands second to none — that great Order of Masonry — representing the highest ideals of manhood, truth, honor, virtue, and

Grand Chapter of Maryland [45]

The Most Worthy Grand Patron of the General Grand Chapter issued a charter for Alpha Chapter No. 1, located in Baltimore, in exchange for a charter which had been issued by the Grand Chapter of New York, dated September 15, 1879. This, the first Chapter which formed a part of the Grand Chapter, was organized by Brother James M. Thomas, of Baltimore, Deputy for the State of Maryland.

On March 7, 1881, the Most Worthy Grand Patron received a petition signed by ten members of the Order in Baltimore, praying for a charter under the name of Excelsior Chapter No. 2, but Alpha Chapter No. 1 refusing to recommend the petition, the charter was refused June 25, 1881.

Maryland Chapter No. 2, Baltimore, was chartered May 20, 1895, with forty-two petitioners and organized by John E. Becker, Deputy of the Most Worthy Grand Patron for Maryland.

Queen Esther Chapter No. 3, Hagerstown, was chartered February 19, 1896, and constituted March 3, 1896, by Harry B. Pearson, with twenty-eight charter members.

Baltimore Chapter No. 4, Baltimore, was chartered February 25, 1896, and constituted March 3, 1896, by John A. Becker, with fifteen charter members.

Concordia Chapter No. 5, Baltimore, was chartered February 24, 1897, and constituted March 2, 1897, by Chester B. Hayes, with fifty-six charter members.

---

[45] Organized December 23, 1898.

Pentalpha Chapter No. 6, Savage, was chartered February 27, 1897, and constituted March 6, 1897, by C. F. Stewart, Deputy of the Most Worthy Grand Patron, with thirty-three charter members.

Ruth Chapter No. 7, Hyattsville, was chartered April 9, 1897, and constituted April 21, 1897, by E. C. Register, with forty-two charter members.

Monumental Chapter No. 8, Baltimore, was chartered April 9, 1897, and constituted May 25, 1897, by Fred W. Lantz, with eighteen charter members.

Mizpah Chapter No. 9, Fredericksburg, was chartered June 26, 1897, and constituted July 9, 1897, by H. W. Nicholson, with sixty-one charter members.

Martha Washington Chapter No. 10, at Lonaconing, was chartered December 20, 1898, and organized December 22, 1898, by J. H. Graham, Deputy, with twenty-three charter members.

The Grand Chapter of Maryland was organized December 23, 1898, by Mr. L. Cabell Williamson, Deputy of the Most Worthy Grand Patron, when seven of the ten Chapters in the State were represented. When the motion to organize the Grand Chapter was put to a vote, six Chapters voted for and one against, and upon the announcement of the vote, the representatives of the dissenting Chapter withdrew from the convention. The constitution adopted made Past Matrons and Past Patrons permanent members of the Grand Chapter, the Grand Matron the executive officer. The first Grand Matron was Mrs. Margaret Meganhardt, first Grand Patron William T. Lechlider, and the first and only Grand Secretary, R M. Coombs. The Grand Matron-elect and Grand Patron-elect each volunteered to advance $100 to pay the necessary expenses, which offer was accepted. Following the illustrious example of the District of Columbia, the constitution provided for two stated meetings each year — the annual in January and the second in June, but the June meeting was discontinued in 1901. It was further provided that a majority of the Chapters of the State should constitute a quorum. At the first annual meeting, January 25, 1899, the records show five Chapters represented and five not represented. However, the Grand Chapter proceeded with the regular business, because a proclamation had been issued, declaring Concordia Chapter No. 5, Baltimore, clandestine, which action was prompted by the refusal of its presiding officer to take cognizance of the Grand Chapter, or recognize any of its Grand Officers as such. In January 1900, the Chapter having reconsidered its action and submitted to the authority of the Grand Chapter, it was reinstated.

The sum of $25 was set aside annually to create a sinking fund, to be applied as a majority of the members may decide for an O.E.S. Home, this dating from the meeting in 1901; the same year $71 was sent for the relief of the Galveston sufferers. At the June meeting in 1901 a day to be known as "Widows' and Orphans' Home Day" was requested to be celebrated by each Chapter, and they were requested to provide some feature of entertainment, the receipts for same to be given to the Home fund. In 1904 a resolution was passed that no member of the O.E.S. in Maryland shall be allowed to associate with or become a member of the White Shrine of Jerusalem.

In 1908 over 200 well filled baskets were given to the poor at Christmas time and from 500 to 600 children were given Christmas tree pleasures at Hepsatophe Hall, where toys and candy were distributed at an expense of nearly $250, borne by the Chapters of the jurisdiction.

This Grand Chapter appointed in Baltimore, and also in Cumberland, a committee on Christmas entertainment and charity. The Baltimore committee reported the distribution of 225 baskets of edibles, each weighing approximately forty-five pounds. These baskets were filled with poultry, vegetables, meats, fruits, puddings, and other foods. An entertainment for the children was given where Christmas cheer was tendered these dear little pilgrims for eternity in the form of music, moving pictures, and a Christmas tree. The distribution of gifts included 450 dolls, 425 games, 450 books, 475 toys,

550 pounds of candy, and 1,000 oranges. The baskets and gifts aggregated a value of 647.77. The Cumberland committee consisted of twenty and was ably assisted by the two Masonic Lodges of the city. They also distributed baskets with toothsome edibles, fruits, toys, and candy for the children. This work is highly commendable, and these practices of charity and loving kindness cannot be too highly commended. It is a good rule for the individual, in his daily routine of life, to look up at the high and noble things, and not down to the least beautiful conditions which surround us. The greatest joy which this world holds is the pleasure resulting from unselfish action.

Grand Chapter of Massachusetts [46]

Harmony Chapter No. 1 was organized at Shelbourne Falls, March 1869, by virtue of a charter granted them by Brother Robert Macoy — the first Chapter in Massachusetts. Just three weeks previous to the organization of the General Grand Chapter, a meeting was held for the purpose of considering the expediency of forming the Grand Chapter of Massachusetts, which council met on October 23, 1876, at which time six Chapters were represented. It was decided to issue a call for a convention to organize a Grand Chapter at Worcester, December 11, 1876 (a little less than one month after the General Grand Chapter had been organized), when organization was affected by representatives from five of the eight Chapters in the State.

By the constitution adopted, the Grand Patron was made the executive officer, with power to appoint all of the appointive officers, including a Deputy Grand Patron, who was the second officer, there being no provision for an Associate Grand Patron. All present and Past Matrons, Patrons, and Associate Matrons, and such other persons as the Grand Chapter shall elect, were made members, but the latter clause was removed in 1882. The Grand Patron was given

---

[46] Organized December 11, 1876.

jurisdiction over the approval of by-laws, decisions of appeals, and formation of new Chapters. At a later meeting a penalty of $25 was fixed for any Chapter violating the jurisdiction laws.

The Grand Chapter declared its sympathy with the General Grand Chapter and elected Brother Thomas M. Lamb delegate to the second session, at which time he served as Most Worthy Grand Patron *pro tem*, and was elected to that exalted office to serve from 1878 to 1880.

Brother Lamb said at the meeting for organization of the Grand Chapter of Massachusetts, with reference to the ritual then in use, that "its histories are too lengthy and untrue, its symbols double-tongued, and their teachings inconsistent; as a specimen of English composition, it is unworthy of the Order."

On the motion of Brother Lamb, it was ordered that a committee of five be appointed to make a thorough revision of the ritual. The chairman of this committee, Brother Lamb, reported in 1877 that he had made suggestions to the ritual committee of the General Grand Chapter as to the changes desired, and recommended that the Grand Chapter await the action of the general body. The Grand Chapter, having declared allegiance to the General Grand Chapter, elected Brother Lamb as a representative to it. The ritual committee appointed consisted of Thomas M. Lamb, John M. Mayhew, and the Rev. Willis D. Engle. In 1878 the Grand Chapter voted unanimously to acknowledge allegiance to the General Grand Chapter and a special meeting of the Grand Chapter was held January 27, 1879, for the purpose of exemplifying the work according to the new *Ritual*.

In 1880 the duties of the Grand Matron were greatly enlarged and in 1894 she was made the executive officer. In 1892 the State was divided into districts and a Deputy Grand Matron appointed in each. The Grand Patron's address in 1897 stated: "Our Chapters are as near perfection in the rendition of the ritualistic work as are those in any other jurisdiction . . . but I would say that while perfection in ritualistic work is very desirable, and necessary, true perfection is not gained until with perfect work is blended a complete and thorough knowledge of the jurisdiction of our Order."

This Grand Chapter entertained the General Grand Chapter at Boston, August 29-30, 1895, and each Chapter was requested to contribute for this purpose, the sum realized amounting to $1,664.13; of this amount a balance of $84.90 remained, which was placed in the Grand Chapter treasury.

A sinking fund, looking toward the accumulation of $50,000, was established in 1903 and the amount realized the first year was $1,329.20, this fund to be used for the erection of an O.E.S. Home. Contributions were made to the Galveston flood sufferers, $491; Temple of Fraternity at St. Louis, $128.60; to the San Francisco sufferers from the earthquake and fire, $7,756.

A Past Matrons' and Past Patrons' Association was formed in 1904 for the purpose of promoting friendship, etc., and has existed since that time.

At the 1901 meeting it was stated that all printed copies of the *Secret Work* had been recalled and destroyed, then replaced by copies of same in cipher. The same year a native Japanese received the degrees in a Chapter in South Boston. This Grand Chapter imposed a fine upon a Chapter of $25 for conferring the degrees upon a candidate when release of jurisdiction had been denied by a sister Chapter, a fine of $10 is regularly imposed for loss of *Secret Work*, and of $5 for loss of *Ritual*, the fine to be paid by Chapter.

In 1909, business was suspended to receive a committee from the Grand Lodge, who came for the purpose of speaking on the subject of the Masonic Home of Massachusetts. Both the Masons and Stars were very enthusiastic over the project of building a Home. The Home fund, O. E. S., was then $9,712.67. In 1913 the Home was completed and together the two Orders are conducting same with great satisfaction to all. The spirit of cooperation of the Masonic and Eastern Star members in their efforts to promote this trust is everywhere apparent; the Grand Lodge established it on a firm basis, and with the help of the Order of the Eastern Star, it must be a success.

GRAND CHAPTER OF MICHIGAN [47]

At Cooper, Michigan, an organization of the "Constellations" was formed in 1860, and a number of active Masons had given much attention to the "Eastern Star" as early as 1851. At Rochester, Michigan, a "Lodge of the Adoptive Rite of the Eastern Star" was organized by J. V. Lambertson, of Caro, on December 15, 1866, but without the authority of a charter. Brother Lambertson was a self-constituted Worthy President; Jonathan Hale, Worthy Vice-President; Sister H. H. Gillette, Secretary; Sister J. V. Lambertson, Treasurer; Sister Andrews, First Patron; Sister Roberts, Second Patron; Sister Robinson, Third Patron; Sister Carleton, Fourth Patron; Sister Halem, Fifth Patron; Brother Andrews, Sentinel. The ritual was formulated by J. V. Lambertson and printed at his own expense.

As early as 1854, John H. Tatem, later a student in the department of law of the University of Michigan, knew of the O.E.S. degrees and organized a Lodge of the Adoptive Rite at Adrian some time previous to 1867.

Sister Purinton, of Coldwater, states that on April 18, 1867, a meeting was held in Coldwater, consisting of Masons and their wives, to talk about organizing a Lodge of the Adoptive Rite. Committees were appointed and on April 26, 1867, the organization was completed.

A convention was held on October 20, 1867, in the city of Adrian for the purpose of organizing an "Eastern Star Grand Lodge of Adoptive Masonry." Sixty-nine delegates from fifteen subordinate Lodges participated: Rochester, Adrian, Bronson, Palmyra, Medina, Osseo, Fairfield, Jackson, Manchester, Coldwater, Sturgis, Constantine, Burr

---

[47] Organized October 30, 1867, as "Grand Lodge of Adoptive Masonry."

Oak, Jonesville, and Morenci, representing a membership of 873. Different rituals were exemplified and, after considering all, that of John H. Tatem (*Tatem's Ritual*), with some changes, was adopted.

The Grand Worthy President (equivalent to Grand Matron) was given the powers of executive officer, including the granting of dispensations for the organization of new lodges. Mrs. Martha G. Lindsay, of Constantine, was elected first Grand Worthy President; David Bovee, of Coldwater, Grand Vice-President. A committee was clothed with authority to procure regalia for the Grand Officers. In 1868 a revised ritual was adopted with added ceremonials, including opening and closing prayers. The State was divided into nine districts with a District Lecturer in each.

In 1869 a revision of the ritual included forms for funeral ceremony, but complaint having been made by Robert Macoy that the form adopted was his property, in 1871 a funeral service was prepared by Brother H. E. Rehklaw and adopted by the Grand Lodge. In 1876 a revised edition of the ritual was published under the name of the *Michigan Ritual* and was in use until 1878 at which time the General Grand Chapter *Ritual* was adopted.

In 1878 the Grand Lodge of Adoption adopted a resolution that "We acknowledge the jurisdiction of the General Grand Chapter of the Order of the Eastern Star, and conform our work to its ritual," and a committee was appointed to make the necessary revision of the constitution and laws. When completed, in 1879, the change was made and this the oldest Grand Chapter became a constituent part of the General Grand Chapter. In the records of the General Grand Chapter of May 9, 1878, it is shown that on motion of the Rev. Brother John Leach, it was

> *Resolved*, That in the event of the Grand Lodge of Adoptive Masonry of the State of Michigan conforming to the General Grand Chapter, the Past Grand Presidents and Past Grand Vice-presidents of the Grand Body shall be entitled

to membership in this Grand Body on the same footing as Past Grand Patrons and Past Grand Matrons.

July 21, 1877, Acacia Chapter, Rockford, surrendered its charter issued by the Supreme Grand Chapter and dated March 30, 1870, and was given a charter from the General Grand Chapter September 7, 1877, Unity Chapter, Sand Lake, Michigan, surrendered a similar charter dated March 30, 1876.

In 1881 a resolution was adopted as follows:

Whereas, The time has come in the temperance work when every person and society ought to take right grounds and show their true colors everywhere; therefore,

Resolved, That we believe in and will practice total abstinence from all that will intoxicate and will use our most earnest endeavors to totally abolish all drinking customs and suppress the liquor traffic by the use of all moral and legal measures practicable.

In 1886, a communication from Dr. Rob Morris was spread upon the minutes after adoption:

The Eastern Star: The Star of Bethlehem once guided three wise men to the place where the infant Jesus lay. But the Eastern Star is this hour guiding fifty thousand *women* to the highest plane of earthly merit and usefulness. May the rays of light we cherish continue to guide us through middle life, through old age, and even through the darkness of the tomb to those green meadows by the crystal river, where the tree of life grows, and where faith is lost in sight, and hope ends in fruition.

At the request of the Past Grand Matrons, Sister Addie C. S. Engle wrote "The Vocal Star." It was rendered by them in 1890 for the first time and has been given a number of times since.

In 1894 jewels were purchased by the Grand Chapter for the use of its officers that were more than ordinary, an elegant set, being made of sterling silver, gold plated, bearing the name of the State and of the Order emblems combined with beautifully enameled portions.

The State was divided into districts in 1901 and the system of schools of instruction adopted. In 1903 the Grand Matron recommended that county associations be formed with annual meetings, which have been done in more than thirty of the counties. Though Past Matrons and Past Patrons were made members of the Grand Chapter in 1889, they were denied this privilege in 1892 and are not now members of the Grand Body.

Grand Officers, Past Grand Matrons, Past Grand Patrons, and one member from each subordinate Chapter are each allowed $2 per day for each day in attendance and six cents per mile, one way.

The Masonic Fraternity of Michigan established a Masonic Home in 1890 and the Chapters of the O.E.S. responded to the request of the Grand Matron, lending their assistance and hearty cooperation in promoting a State Masonic Fair for its benefit. This netted more than $7,000, and since that date the Chapters have contributed very liberally to its support.

A beautiful and well-equipped Masonic Home, the gift of Mr. Ammi W. Wright, is a worthy addition to the work of the Order there and has received the donations of the O.E.S. in its efforts to relieve distress.

The only O.E.S. Temple in the world was formally dedicated in Detroit, Michigan, on March 18, 1915, with a beautifully arranged program. Sister Emma C. Ocobock, Right Worthy Associate Grand Matron, as representative of Sister Rata A. Mills, Most Worthy Grand Matron of the General Grand Chapter, was present and gave an address. The evening ceremonies were conducted by the officers of the Temple Association and by the Most Worshipful Master of A. F. and A.M., William M. Perrett, assisted by the Grand Officers of the Grand Chapter of Michigan, O. E. S.

The Order of the Eastern Star has taught the institution of Masonry that its notion of universality was an error. Masonry extends from east to west, and from north to south, but it did not embrace within its enfolding arms the better half of humanity known as womankind, and the institution was a great loser thereby. In the last twenty years more progress has been made in Masonic Temples and Halls than in scores of years previous when the Order of the Eastern Star had not given such support as now. What man could not do alone, woman's assistance has made possible and through the Order of the Eastern Star, she has taught Masonry the beauty of charity. God grant that the walls of this magnificent monument to O.E.S. devotion and endurance may hear only the accents of faith, these halls echo only the promises of hope, these precincts see only acts of human charity such as will delight mankind.

Grand Chapter of Minnesota [48]

The first Chapter organized in Minnesota was Crystal Lake No. 1, at Hokak, in October 1869. The Most Worthy Grand Patron appointed Brother Leonard Lewis, of Minneapolis, special Deputy for the State of Minnesota in 1878. Through his efforts, the organization of the Grand Chapter was affected at Minneapolis, June 27, 1878, when five of the nine active Chapters in the State were represented by seventeen delegates. Allegiance to the General Grand Chapter was declared, and the constitution adopted made Past Matrons and Past Patrons members of the Grand Chapter. The Grand Matron was given authority as the executive officer and the per capita dues were fixed at fifteen cents.

The first Grand Matron, Mrs. Sarah B. Armstrong, less than a year after election, April 14, 1879, was called in death. The Grand Chapter did not meet in 1880; in 1882 the State was divided into three districts with a Deputy Grand Matron in each. In 1883, the Grand Patron criticized the work as exemplified in Minneapolis

---

[48] Organized June 27, 1878.

Chapter No. 9, which was an attempt to dramatize the work as is given in the *Mosaic Book*, but not nearly so elaborately. The jurisprudence committee recommended, and its report was adopted,

> That so much of the Grand Patron's address as refers to the peculiar exemplification of the work in Minneapolis Chapter No. 9, be not entered on the Grand Chapter records — from our knowledge, we deem it not as an ignoring, nor any infraction of the recognized ritual of the Order, but simply as an enlargement, or perhaps, an enriching of the work, rendering it more attractive and impressive. While we do not recommend its adoption by other Chapters, we see nothing inappropriate in this practice, if any Chapters desire to adopt it.

In 1884, the Grand Matron in her address referred to the work of Minneapolis Chapter No. 9 as being an innovation on the ritual, which part of her address was referred to a special committee. This committee made a special report, and pending a motion to receive and adopt the report, a motion was made to adjourn the Grand Chapter *sine die*. In spite of the protests of several members and in violation of the rules of order which provide that same could not prevail except by unanimous consent, the motion was entertained and the Grand Chapter adjourned without electing officers or arranging for the next place of meeting.

On March 30, 1885, the Grand Matron declared Minneapolis Chapter No. 9 suspended until the next regular meeting of Grand Chapter. This action was without authority, as was also the appointment of a Grand Secretary to fill the vacancy which the Grand Matron declared to exist because the Grand Secretary elected, being a member of the suspended Chapter, was, by the action toward the subordinate Chapter to which she belonged, suspended from membership.

At a regular session of the Grand Chapter held in October 1885, the action of the Grand Matron was approved, and the charter of

Minneapolis Chapter No. 9 was arrested. The Grand Chapter continued its work, holding regular meetings and transacting such business as would properly come before this body; five Chapters were represented in 1886, six in 1887, eight in 1888, eight in 1889, ten in 1890, eight in 1891, seven in 1892, seven in 1893, while in 1894 the consolidation of Grand Chapter No. 1 and Grand Chapter No. 2 was effected and reorganization of the Grand Chapter of Minnesota completed on May 10, 1894.

Representatives of Chapters working under Grand Chapter No. 2 applied for admission in 1889, but upon the refusal of the Grand Chapter to admit representatives from three of the Chapters, all declined to enter. After further consideration it was decided to admit all representatives, with the provision that the Grand Patron should fully concur in this decision. Through the many long years of struggling with conditions almost unsurmountable, the true loyalty and cordial support of those whose hearts were in the work is a commendable example of fidelity to convictions of right and duty.

Action of the General Grand Chapter, at the meeting in Columbus, Ohio, in 1892, left the burden of adjustment with the organizations in Minnesota. Comprehending the situation in its broadest sense, and with a sincere desire to promote the greatest good of the Order, a special meeting was held May 9, 1894, with nine Chapters concurring by sending their representatives. After conferring with representatives of Grand Chapter No. 2, the following resolution was adopted:

Whereas, It is desirable that the two Grand Chapters Order of the Eastern Star, existing in the state of Minnesota, be united;

Resolved, That the Grand Chapter now in session in St. Paul is invited to meet this Grand Chapter at the Masonic Temple in St. Paul at three o'clock this day to perfect such union, to be known as the Grand Chapter Order of the Eastern Star of the state of Minnesota, which organization shall be upon this basis: The preservation of the Eastern Star status of all officers and members of all subordinate Chapters. Also, that all charters of all subordinate Chapters be preserved, subject to revisal wherein conflict in names or numbers exist.

Resolved, That the seal of the Grand Chapter shall contain the inscription: "Grand Chapter of the Order of the Eastern Star, Minnesota, 1878-1886. United May 10, 1894." Also, the signet.

Thus, a union was at last formed, which gives every member of the former bodies all the rights and privileges of the Order. It is a just and honorable ending of a most unfortunate affair which caused continued agitation and was a constant source of disturbance for thirteen years. By action of the General Grand Chapter, officers of both organizations are recognized upon an equal basis and harmony again restored. Attention should not be given to these matters except to profit by the lessons to be drawn from it, and thus be more mindful of the solemn obligation and the words of the Golden Rule.

Grand Chapter No. 2 Minnesota

At the beginning of the difficulty which caused so many years of disturbance and retarded the advancement of the best interests of the Order in Minnesota, seventeen Chapters were actively engaged in the work of the Order. Of this number, six became discouraged and later dormant, six remained loyal to the original organization known as Grand Chapter No. 1, five joined Grand Chapter No. 2, one subordinate Chapter divided into two Chapters, one remaining with No. 1, and the other joining No. 2, each believing itself right and each desiring to act for the best interests of its members.

The Most Worthy Grand Patron of the General Grand Chapter, having withdrawn recognition of the Grand Chapter of Minnesota on

August 11, 1885, the General Grand Chapter, at its meeting in the city of St. Louis in September 1886, approved his actions.

The convention to organize Grand Chapter No. 2 met May 12, 1886, when six Chapters were represented, and the State was divided into five districts with a Deputy Grand Patron in each.

After having entered into the work of the Order with earnestness and zeal, this Grand Chapter, enthusiastic with the ambition of one whose hopes are very bright, adopted the Chapter of Sorrow by Sister Addie C. S. Engle, in 1889, further set apart July 31st, the day of Dr. Rob Morris's death, "as the day for holding such Chapter of Sorrow throughout this jurisdiction." This recognition of their grief at the loss of our illustrious founder has been held by the Grand Chapter frequently.

The Order increased in strength. Five Chapters were added in 1891 by organization and one by the affiliation with Grand Chapter No. 2 of one of the Chapters formerly in harmony with No. 1. In 1892 two more were added from No. 1 and ten were organized, showing an increase of twelve for the year; in 1893 thirteen Chapters were organized; and in 1894 fifteen were organized, making a total of sixty-four Chapters working under charters from No. 2 at the date of uniting the two Grand Chapters of Minnesota.

GRAND CHAPTER OF MINNESOTA (REORGANIZED)

On May 10, 1894, the two Grand Chapters of Minnesota met and formed a united Grand Chapter. Mrs. Mary C. Snedden, Most Worthy Grand Matron, Deputy for the Most Worthy Grand Patron, presided. The Most Worthy Grand Matron invited the Worthy Grand Matrons and Worthy Grand Patrons from both Grand Chapters, to seats in the East, and the work was supported by two corps of Grand Officers. Sixty Chapters were represented, and the following resolution was unanimously adopted:

Resolved, by the two Grand Chapters, now jointly assembled, that the proposed union is hereby declared to be effected, and the Grand Chapter resulting from said union is declared to be the Grand Chapter, Order of the Eastern Star of the State of Minnesota.

Through the untiring efforts of many faithful workers, and especially to Brother Alexander Gearhart, Grand Patron, this reconciliation was reached; that judgment which knows no one, in the settlement of differences, except God's justice and Masonic charity, finally triumphed and peace and harmony prevailed.

In 1897 the Grand Matron divided the State into fifteen districts, with conventions in each that were productive of such benefits that the Grand Chapter decided to continue the work upon this plan. A committee on Masonic and O.E.S. Home reported in 1900 and interest in this branch of the Order's duties was manifested.

In 1899 the Grand Matron decided that it would not be lawful to repeat the obligation to a Catholic lady who wishes to know the obligation she would be obliged to take, *before* joining. A code of etiquette has been adopted, including the customs and rules, for the guidance of subordinate Chapters.

This Grand Chapter has contributed large amounts to charitable and benevolent purposes; to the sufferers from the Galveston flood, $630.92; to assist in the Temple of Fraternity at St. Louis, $388.45; to the O.E.S. headquarters at Portland Exposition, $85.81.

In 1914 the requirements of the Order demanded thirty-four District Deputy Grand Matrons, and twenty schools of instruction were held:

> Dream constantly of the ideal,
> Work ceaselessly to perfect the real.

Members will never rise above their individual ideals. If one know the value of a member, one must know what her or his ideals are. Talent is not enough; thousands were intended to be aeolian harps but want of energy and ideals found them at the end of life's journey only tuneless fiddles.

> We are building for time and eternity,
> Building from without and within.
> Our bodies we build with the salts of the earth
> Cell upon cell from the time of our birth.
> For our souls we build with virtues fair,
> Truth upon truth, a beautiful stair —
> Upon which, when time for us shall cease,
> And the soul thereby finds its release,
> Leaving behind this body and sin,
> We shall mount to the arms of Divinity.

The charitable work of the Order in this Grand Jurisdiction has been concentrated upon the one great object of providing a Home for its loved ones, who may find it to their interest to use it. To this end, a committee was appointed to confer with representatives of the Grand Lodge, relative to cooperating in the erection of a Masonic Home, the Grand Lodge having accumulated more than thirty thousand dollars for that purpose. Favorable action resulting, a ten cent per capita tax was decided upon and a committee appointed to collect and manage the Home fund. The Grand Chapter accumulated a sum which, in 1914, amounted to $15,981.82 toward building a Home, and a Masonic Home Association was incorporated, with Mrs. Mary C. Taylor, Past Grand Matron and Grand Secretary, as one of the directors. The plans include the building of a Home as soon as $100,000 has been raised, $50,000 of which is to be used as endowment.

Grand Chapter of Mississippi [49]

In April, 1870, the first Chapter was organized at Starkville, by authority of a charter issued by Brother Macoy, and though it is claimed and we believe the claim is founded upon facts that the idea of a State Grand Chapter was originated in this State, yet the date of organizing the Grand Chapter gives Mississippi the third place.[50] This organization took place at Rienzi, December 15, 1870, by representatives of five of the seven Chapters that had been organized in the State.

Brother John L. Powers was commissioned by the Supreme Grand Council on May 26, 1870, as Deputy for Mississippi, and served as Grand Patron during the entire existence of the Grand Chapter, from 1870 to 1881, at which time they voluntarily surrendered their organization to the authority of the General Grand Chapter, giving the territory into that jurisdiction.

The very early history of the Order is given authoritatively by quoting from the address of Brother Powers, delivered at the Grand Chapter session in 1873:

> It is well known to us, and it may as well be known to others, that the first idea of a State Grand Chapter originated in this State. Chapters of the Order have, for many years, existed in the Eastern and Western States, deriving their authority and charters from a sort of self-constituted Supreme Grand Council located in the East, that place of all light, Masonically. It was from this Supreme authority your Grand Patron received his commission on May 26, 1870. On the 15th of December, following, Chapters numbered 2, 4, 5, 6, and 7 held a convocation at Rienzi, and organized the third Grand Chapter on this continent. On the 3rd of the

---

[49] Organized December 15, 1870.

[50] New Jersey Grand Chapter was organized July 18, 1870; New York Grand Chapter was organized November 30, 1870.

previous month, a Grand Chapter was formed in New York, but the correspondence of this office for 1870 attests that the brethren and sisters of the Empire State acted upon suggestions from this Grand Jurisdiction in organizing their Grand Chapter.

In 1873 the Supreme Council was recognized as the official head and was pledged the cooperation of the Grand Chapter. This recognition was withdrawn at the regular session held in Tupelo, July 15, 1875, and resolutions adopted which would recognize efforts that might be made to form a lawful General Grand Body. The following is taken from the Proceedings of this meeting:

Whereas, We deem uniformity of Ritual and lectures essential to the present and future prosperity of the Order; therefore, we respectfully recommend that a committee, consisting of seven members of this Grand Chapter, of which committee the Grand Patron and Grand Matron shall be members, shall be appointed to confer with like committees that may hereafter be appointed by other Grand Chapters of the Order in the United States, or elsewhere, whose duty it shall be to take under advisement, and present, if practicable, some feasible and judicious plan for the organization of a Supreme Grand Chapter; which said Supreme Body shall, when organized and recognized by two-thirds of the Grand Chapters in the United States, have absolute and supreme control over the Ritual and lectures of the Adoptive Rite. We also recommend that said committee shall be the accredited delegate from this Grand Jurisdiction to a convention of the Order wheresoever and whensoever convened, and they shall have all power and authority to do any and all acts necessary and lawful to be done in the premises; and they shall report their doings to this Grand Chapter at each Annual Grand Convocation.

Thus will it readily be learned that the work of the Rev. Willis D. Engle, directed toward the formation of the General Grand Chapter, was heartily cooperated in by Mississippi.

Previous to the organization of the General Grand Chapter, the Grand Chapter of Mississippi had assumed jurisdiction over two Chapters in Florida — one of which had been chartered by Brother Macoy and the other by the Grand Chapter of Mississippi April 22, 1876, at Cedar Creek, Florida. Mississippi recognized the legality of the General Grand Chapter and cheerfully surrendered all territory beyond the limits of the State over which the Grand Body had assumed control.

The last meeting of this Grand Chapter was held in 1877, at which time ten Chapters were represented, seventeen reported to the Grand Chapter, and up to that date forty-one Chapters in all had been organized by the Grand Chapter. During the year 1878 the yellow fever, spreading sickness, suffering, sorrow, and death throughout the State, prevented the annual meeting of the Grand Chapter, and the year following, 1879, dread of another outbreak prevented a meeting. Failing to meet again in 1880, early in the year of 1881 the Grand Patron decided that it would be best to surrender the territory to the General Grand Chapter, which he did on June 11, 1881.

For almost four years, the Right Worthy Grand Secretary, the Rev. Willis D. Engle, earnestly and persistently tried to effect a meeting of this Grand Chapter, but without material results. On April 23, 1895, the Most Worthy Grand Patron issued the following edict withdrawing recognition from the Grand Chapter of Mississippi, for reasons therein stated:

> *Whereas*, The Grand Chapter of the Order of the Eastern Star of the State of Mississippi, has held no meeting since the year 1877 and
>
> *Whereas*, The Grand Patron, J. L. Powers (being the executive head of said Grand Chapter), on June 11, 1881, did,

Brief Histories of the Several Grand Chapters

so far as he had power to do, transfer the Order in that state to the care and control of the General Grand Chapter; and

Whereas, The various efforts that have since been made to revive the said Grand Chapter have proved ineffectual; and

Whereas, It seems to be the desire of those in that state who have an interest in the success of the Order, that proper action should be taken with a view of securing renewed interest and future prosperity in that jurisdiction;

Therefore, With a hope and desire of producing such results, I, R. C. Gaskill, Most Worthy Grand Patron of the General Grand Chapter, do hereby declare that the Grand Chapter of the Order of the Eastern Star of the State of Mississippi no longer exists, and that the General Grand Chapter has, and does assume full and complete jurisdiction over all matters and persons relating to the Order in that state, and I do hereby invite the cooperation of all persons in that state who are members of the Order, or those who may desire to become such, in the formation of new Chapters, and the revival of old ones, thereby making it possible for the speedy establishment of a new Grand Chapter that shall place the Order in a position of honor and influence in that state.

The work of the Order remained very inactive in this State for ten years. August 30, 1895, thirty petitioners were granted a charter for Winnie Davis Chapter No. 1, Brookhaven. In all, sixteen Chapters were organized previous to the date on which the call was issued by the officers of the General Grand Chapter for the convention to reorganize the Grand Chapter, which was held at Meridian, May 29, 1906. Mrs. Madeleine B. Conkling, Most Worthy Grand Matron, special deputy of the Most Worthy Grand Patron, presided.

A constitution was adopted, granting to the Grand Matron the powers of the executive officer, membership was accorded Past

Matrons and Past Patrons, fee for charter was fixed at $25, and the minimum fee for the degrees was made $3, while that for special dispensation was $2. Annual per capita dues were made fifty cents, ten cents of this to be set aside for a Home fund. No Chapter was permitted to work, either under dispensation or charter, until it had provided furniture, etc., necessary and proper to give due effect to the solemn ceremonies of the Order.

On June 24, 1907, the cornerstone for the Masonic Widows' and Orphans' Home at Meridian was laid, with a most interesting and entertaining program, and the Grand Matron urged the members of the O.E.S. to use all their available strength to assist the Masons in making this an ideal Home. The Order is represented by three members of the board of trustees of the Masonic Home and has contributed liberally towards its support. At the 1909 meeting, it was decided to work for the erection of a hospital in connection with the Masonic Home. The children attend the public schools and are not uniformed nor required to wear any distinguishing marks to make them appear conspicuous; they are all happy and well provided for. In 1913 the Grand Lodge, A. F. and A. M., presented a resolution expressing their appreciation of aid already rendered by the Order of the Eastern Star by donations to the Home, and that they had now signified their purpose to donate a building to be known as the Eastern Star Chapter House, to be used as an assembly room.

In 1909 the Grand Commandery, Knights Templar, sent a representation to the Grand Chapter and a joint social reception was held. The Grand Chapter room presented a scene of magnificence, beautiful women handsomely gowned, surrounded by rich decorations in the colors of the Order, rare and beautiful flowers, and the gorgeous regalia of the Chapter. By order of the Grand Matron the doors were opened, admitting a corps of Sir Knights in full dress uniform, who bore the most cordial fraternal greetings from the Grand Commandery to the Grand Chapter, O. E. S., and further offering the assurance that cooperation is tendered the O.E.S. in bringing about the universal doctrine of the brotherhood of man and the Fatherland of God, and disseminating the principles of the O.E.S. — charity, truth, and loving kindness.

In 1910 all Past Grand Masters who were members of the O. E. S., were elected Honorary Past Grand Patrons and in 1911 the various Masonic bodies which were in session at the same time, in a distant city, united in sending fraternal greetings by telegram.

> Our lives are songs, God writes the words,
> And we set them to music at pleasure;
> And the song grows glad or sweet or sad
> As we choose to fashion the measure.
> We must write the music, whatever the song,
> Whatever the rhyme or meter;
> And if it is sad we can make it glad,
> Or sweet, we can make it sweeter.

GRAND CHAPTER OF MISSOURI [51]

Brother Macoy issued charters for several Chapters in Missouri, the first in October 1869, at Graham, followed by the organization of Queen Esther Chapter, at Hannibal, December 1871. The growth of the Order was marked, there having been Chapters organized to the number of 144 previous to the date of the call for a convention. This call was issued by Thomas C. Ready, Provisional Grand Patron, and the convention met in Masonic Hall, St. Louis, October 13, 1875. Sixty-five representatives were present, from forty-five Chapters. The work accomplished was done mainly through the devotion of Harmon G. Reynolds and one Provisional Grand Patron assisted by two Deputy Grand Patrons. A constitution was adopted, which differed greatly from any other Grand Chapter in that provision was

---

[51] Organized October 13, 1875.

made for triennial meetings instead of annual meetings, also for a corps of Grand Officers numbering seventy-seven, seven of whom were elective and seventy appointive: Grand Patron, Deputy Grand Patron, Grand Matron, Deputy Grand Matron, Associate Grand Matron, Deputy Associate Grand Matron, Grand Treasurer, Grand Secretary, Grand Conductress, Deputy Grand Conductress, Associate Grand Conductress, Deputy Associate Grand Conductress, five Grand Chaplains, Grand Marshal, five Assistant Grand Marshals, Grand Lecturer, Grand Adah, three Assistant Grand Adahs, Grand Ruth, three Assistant Grand Ruths, Grand Esther, three Assistant Grand Esthers, Grand Martha, three Assistant Grand Marthas, Grand Electa, three Assistant Grand Electas, Grand Warder, Assistant Grand Warder, Grand Sentinel, and thirty District Deputy Grand Patrons. A board of commissioners, consisting of seven members, was given authority to conduct the affairs of the Grand Chapter, except legislative, during the recess of the Grand Chapter, and this board was authorized to meet annually in the intervening years. Past Matrons and Past Patrons, with the usual Chapter representation, and the Grand Officers formed this Grand Chapter.

The Grand Chapter of Missouri, at its session in St. Louis, October 9, 1876, resolved to accept the invitation of the Grand Chapter of Indiana, and to appoint a committee of seven to represent the Grand Chapter in the proposed meeting at Indianapolis, November 16, 1876.

The committee consisted of the Rev. Dr. John D. Vincil, Mary J. Wash, Mattie A. Yost, Frances F. Holden, Thomas C. Ready, P. D. Yost, and John R. Parsons, all of whom attended the convention to which they were appointed except Brothers Holden and Ready.

A revision of the constitution in 1876 rendered it more nearly in conformity to the laws and regulations as adopted by sister Grand Jurisdictions. The State was divided into districts and a Deputy Grand Matron appointed for each. Allegiance was acknowledged to the General Grand Chapter, and such regulations adopted as would conform to the requirements of that body, and the broad field for work revealed was entered into with willing hearts and ready hands.

The State was divided into districts. In 1900 there were fifty-four districts with a Deputy Grand Matron in each. The office of Deputy Grand Matron having been abolished, in 1902, Deputy Grand Lecturers were appointed for each of the fifty-five districts. The Deputy Grand Matron system was reestablished in 1913 and fifty-nine were appointed. In 1906, while visiting Chapters, the Grand Matron found two working under the Macoy charters, Corinthian Chapter, Gallatin, where charter was dated October 7, 1875, and Florence Chapter, Brookfield, where charter was dated August 30, 1875. Both charters were signed by Robert Macoy, Most Eminent Grand Patron, and Robert Morris, Grand Secretary. Subsequently approved charters were issued.

This Grand Chapter contributed $732.39 to the Temple of Fraternity at the St. Louis fair, and a voluntary collection amounting to $32 was given to purchase tickets for the Masonic Home children to attend the World's Fair; the call for aid to the sufferers from the San Francisco disaster received a contribution of $500 and $50 was appropriated for the relief of the Galveston flood sufferers; $83.75 was given toward the support of O.E.S. headquarters at Portland, Oregon.

Funds for the establishment of an O.E.S. Home were early accumulated, each year finding something to be added, but it was not until 1888, when the efforts of the Masonic Fraternity assumed definite action that the contributions of the Grand Chapter reached large proportions. After the Masonic Home was established, the O.E.S. proposed to build a chapel at the Home, which movement was begun in 1894 and the building completed in 1897. The twenty-third annual session of the Grand Chapter was held in this chapel October 22, 1897. It was dedicated by the Grand Master, October 21, 1897, in the presence of the members of the Grand Chapter, many of its members having prominent parts on the program. The building is a splendid monument to the devotion and fraternal love and energy of the Order in this Grand Jurisdiction, by whose enterprise and untiring labors it has been erected at a cost of $3,500. All of this was appropriated by the Grand Chapter and the subordinate Chapters of the State, except a contribution of $339.95 donated by the children of the Home. This amount was earned by the children by singing. Sufficient money was earned in the same manner, with which the little pilgrims toward useful manhood and womanhood purchased the Eastern Star window that adorns the east end of the chapel. On the right of this window is a picture of Christ blessing little children, the gift of Ascalon Commandery, Knights Templar; on the left, one of the Repose in Egypt, the gift of Molah Temple, Mystic Shrine. Other windows have been given which represent one of each of the Heroines of the Order, the Ascension, the Guardian Angel, etc., showing that this effort to provide for those who are in need is the pride and glory of every member of the Order in Missouri. The grand work that is now being done there, that has been done there in the past and will be accomplished in the many years to come, to aid the helpless orphan, the aged fathers and mothers, is a Christ-like labor of love and devotion. The Masonic Fraternity realized, as never before, the value of the cooperation of their wives, daughters, mothers, and sisters in this great work. In 1903 the Grand Chapter appropriated $657.74 to be used in improvements upon the Chapel and at each session donations have been made of from $50 to $100 to be used to furnish Christmas cheer.

In 1902 the Masonic Home directors adopted a resolution, whereby widows who are O.E.S. members, and orphans of deceased members, are eligible for admission to the Home. With this magnificent monument to the sincerity of their devotion to the principles of the Order, they truly have built for eternity.

> Build thee more stately mansions, O my soul,
> As the swift seasons roll!
> Leave thy low-vaulted past!
> Let each new temple, nobler than the last,

Shut thee from heaven with a dome more vast,
Till thou, at length, art free,
Leaving thine outgrown shell by life's unresting sea!
— *The Chambered Nautilus*

GRAND CHAPTER OF MONTANA [52]

At evening time, it shall be light!
When slowly closes in the night,
While gleaming searchlights paint the sky,
One shining STAR leads all on high;
Light of the world since life began,
Guide to the BROTHERHOOD OF MAN,
Watch o'er thy earthly children far,
O Lamp of Love! O Blazing Star.
— *Mrs. Elvira Adams Atwood*

The first Chapter in Montana, Miriam No. 1, at Helena, was chartered by the Most Worthy Grand Patron of the General Grand Chapter December 20, 1880, and organized January 10, 1881, by Cornelius Hedges, special deputy. The first officers were Mrs. Edna L. Hedges, Worthy Matron, and John Stedman, Worthy Patron.

Ruth Chapter No. 2, Butte City, was chartered March 19, 1881, and organized by John Stedman, special deputy, on April 15, 1881, and Esther Chapter No. 3, located at Townsend, was chartered May 22, 1888. Lily of the Valley Chapter No. 4, located at Bozeman, was chartered March 20, 1890, and organized the following April by Charles E. Lancaster, Deputy of the Most Worthy Grand Patron, with thirty-two petitioners. A charter was granted to seventeen petitioners for Yellowstone Chapter No. 5, located at Glendive, on June 30,

---

[52] Organized September 24, 1800.

1890, and organization was completed on August 27, 1890, by N. Fretz, Deputy of the Most Worthy Grand Patron.

The Grand Chapter was organized at Livingston by representatives of all five Chapters, September 24, 1890, at which time a carefully prepared constitution was adopted. This constitution, also the by-laws, was modeled after Michigan, with some changes which were desirable, making this a most excellent and exemplary Grand Chapter. The Grand Matron was made the executive officer and was clothed with the privilege of granting dispensations for new Chapters. In 1892 this authority was given to her exclusively, also to organize new Chapters. In 1897 authority was granted for the election of proxies to serve if the three principal officers could not attend the meetings of the Grand Chapter. In 1895 the Grand Secretary was instructed to keep at least 100 copies of Grand Chapter Proceedings to be sold at not less than twenty-five cents each, the proceeds to go to the traveling expenses of the Grand Matron.

Recognizing fraternal ties, Grand Chapter was called off in 1895 to allow Helena Lodge, A. F. and A. M., to attend the funeral services of a brother in the Temple, and in 1902 the sum of $50 was appropriated toward the purchase of a monument for a deceased member who had formerly served as Grand Secretary.

In 1904 an interesting and instructive program was rendered during a recess which had been declared for the purpose, celebrating the crystal anniversary of the Grand Chapter.

Generous contributions were made as follows: For maintaining O.E.S. headquarters at the Portland fair, $49.35; to the sufferers from the San Francisco disaster, $372.

This Grand Chapter has assisted the Masonic Fraternity in erecting and furnishing the Masonic Home, having contributed annually to a fund that was created in 1898. The cornerstone of the Home was laid December 20, 1906, and completed within the. following year. The furnishing of the Home was the work of the O.E.S. and in 1912 the Home was reported so well equipped that no calls had been made upon the O.E.S. during the year.

The work of the Order in this State is directed toward the progress, uplifting, and betterment of the human race, its members striving in their own daily lives to exemplify the work of charity, truth, and loving kindness.

Grand Chapter of Nebraska [53]

> Wise men in far Judea,
>   Saw in the sky,
> Lo, there the STAR appears,
>   Glowing on high.
> Bring now the myrrh and gold,
>   For they the sign behold,
> That leadeth them afar;
>   Lo! there the Star!
>   — *Mrs. Elvira Adams Atwood*

Twelve Chapters were chartered in Nebraska by Brother Macoy previous to the organization of the Grand Chapter. Queen Esther Chapter No. 1, at Nebraska City, Adah Chapter No. 2, at Brownsville, and Bellevue Chapter No. 5, at Bellevue, were all organized before the close of 1872.

Bellevue Chapter No. 5 was organized by Edwin Davis, Deputy of the Supreme Grand Patron, assisted by Major G. Stevenson. The first officers were Mrs. Jane E. Leach, Worthy Matron; James Campbell, Worthy Patron; Stephen D. Bangs, Secretary; David Leach, Treasurer. Of this number, all have passed to the joy and peace and rest of a higher plane of life except Mrs. Jane E. Leach, who is now an honored member of Rosebud Chapter at Bonesteel, South Dakota.

---

[53] Organized June 22, 1875.

Bellevue Chapter had but a few years of activity when it became dormant and the charter together with other property was relinquished. Of the twelve organized, only two have had a continuous existence, Vesta No. 6, Omaha, and Electa No. 8, Lincoln.

The convention to organize the Grand Chapter met in the parlors of the Commercial Hotel, Lincoln, June 22, 1875, nine Chapters being represented by nineteen delegates. The constitution adopted made the Past Matrons and Past Patrons members without the right to vote, but in 1892 the full privileges of representation were accorded and the right to vote established. The Grand Patron was made the executive officer and continued to hold that position until 1888 when, by vote of the Grand body, this authority was given to the Grand Matron.

The convention called by the Rev. Willis D. Engle and others of the Grand Chapter of Indiana for the organization of the General Grand Chapter was sanctioned by Nebraska, and in 1876 delegates were elected to that convention, but none were in attendance though the recognition was made, and allegiance declared in 1877, and dues were paid. In 1880, at the General Grand Chapter assembly, two Past Grand Matrons, one Past Grand Patron, the Grand Patron, and Associate Grand Patron were all present and were recognized by appointment to various responsible positions, Mrs. H. C. Smith, Past Grand Matron, receiving the appointment as Worthy Grand Martha and Marshall Smith, Grand Patron, as Worthy Grand Marshal.

Proceedings of 1879, 1880, 1881, and 1884 were not published and no meetings were held in 1882 and 1883, hence authentic records are not readily available, but much good was accomplished, though with many trials for the true and earnest members who so loyally braved disappointments that success might result. In 1894 the solemn and beautiful "Chapter of Sorrow," by Sister Addie C. S. Engle, was exemplified by Harvard Chapter.

In 1895 the beautiful, instructive, and elegant public service as arranged by Sister Helen M. Stires for use at Christmas time was adopted. In 1898, the Grand Matron, Mrs. Helen M. Stires, was one of the O.E.S. executive committee for the Trans-Mississippi Exposition. At this exposition the Order had a splendid display, Nebraska contributing for that purpose $345. Contributions have been made to various sufferers from disaster: $84 to the Nebraska cyclone sufferers; $200 for the San Francisco sufferers; $284 to the Galveston flood sufferers; for the benefit of the Temple of Fraternity at St. Louis $115 was donated, and $56 for maintaining O.E.S. headquarters at the Portland Exposition.

In 1900 the Grand Matron was authorized to appoint a committee of three as the Eastern Star and Masonic Home board whose duty it shall be to invest such sums as may come into the hands of the Grand Chapter for the purpose of establishing a Home. In 1903, $1,500 was appropriated for Masonic Home purposes, the Masonic Home being located at Plattsmouth. In 1904 a splendid work was accomplished: four Chapters united and furnished the dining-room at a cost of $150, one Chapter furnished the kitchen at a cost of $100, another Chapter gave $65 toward furnishing a room, and by a vote of the Grand Chapter, Dr. Rob Morris's birthday, August 31st, was set aside as an Eastern Star Masonic Home Day. In 1909 a resolution was adopted authorizing the building of a hospital in connection with the Masonic Home at Plattsmouth, to be known as the Eastern Star Hospital. This is a beautiful edifice and monument of perseverance in the discharge of duty. In 1913 the balance in the Home fund was $10,834.12.

In 1908 the floral work and drill was given and at the close the Grand Matron was presented with the American Beauty roses used in the drill, which were presented to her by Mrs. Lorraine J. Pitkin, Right Worthy Grand Secretary, the author and composer of this beautiful addenda and the guest of the Grand Chapter.

A Past Grand Matrons' Club was organized in 1909, which meets annually, and in 1910 Achoth Sorority, to which only members of the O.E.S. are eligible, was organized at the University of Nebraska.

The Eastern Star in Nebraska has assumed the care of the needy children of the members of the Masonic and Eastern Star fraternities. The help is extended to the children who are in need, though one of the parents may be living but unable to properly care for the child, hence the term orphans does not wholly apply.

In 1915 the Masons of Nebraska purchased a forty-acre tract of land near Fremont, upon which they erected a beautiful brick and stucco cottage, which is occupied by girls. In 1916 they built a similar structure upon the same grounds for the use of the boys.

Each of these cottages is built to care for twelve to fourteen children comfortably and was erected at a cost of about $12,000. It is the intention to build more cottages as needed and as each is opened for use, a matron is placed in charge and the children are under her direct guidance and training, supervised by one superintendent who has charge of all the cottages.

The annual dues to the Grand Chapter are fifty cents from each member, half of which is appropriated for the use and maintenance of the Eastern Star Homes in this Grand Jurisdiction.

The girls and boys from the Home attend the public schools. The Freemasons appropriate the amount necessary to clothe the children of the Masons, and those children of Eastern Star parentage only are clothed from an Eastern Star source.

The girls are each assigned a part of the housework and are trained in the practical and useful occupations. The boys are each furnished a set of tools which are used in connection with their manual training and practical work incident to duties assigned to them in the conducting of the work of the Home.

Grand Chapter of Nevada [54]

The history of the first gleams of the Eastern Star in Nevada is lost in a haze of uncertainty. Some Chapters under the *Macoy Ritual* were organized but lasted only a few years. One existed in Virginia City for quite a period, and some of the members still have in their possession the white aprons and gloves which were worn, and also beautiful collars of the emblematic colors, trimmed with gold fringe. There are also some *Rituals* bearing date of 1866 which have been treasured by these early members of the Eastern Star. After a few years these Chapters ceased to exist, and we have no authentic record of any that were Macoy Chapters.

The first Chapter organized by authority of a charter issued by the General Grand Chapter, was Friendship Chapter No. 1, at Elko. The charter was dated November 25, 1879, and the Chapter had a total membership of twenty-nine. This Chapter became dormant in 1882 and surrendered its charter June 8, 1883.

Electa Chapter No. 2, at Austin, next shone in the Eastern Star constellation and from the date of its organization in 1882 it has been shining bravely; often its light has been almost extinguished, but the loyal members have struggled on through all these years. The greater number of them live out of town and must come a distance of twenty and some as far as thirty miles, and frequently one officer must fill two or more stations, but the work is carried forward with brave hearts and willing hands to do the very best that conditions will permit. There is but one meeting each month. These brave sisters and brothers deserve great credit for their faithfulness, and "Well done, thou good and faithful ones" applies to Electa Chapter No. 2.

---

[54] Organized September 19, 1905. Data furnished by Mrs. Mary E. Talbot, Grand Secretary, 1912 to present.

Esther Chapter No. 3, at Carson, was organized in 1886. The same year Adah Chapter No. 4 was chartered in Reno; this is now the banner Chapter of the State, with a membership of over 250.

In 1894, by request of the three Chapters — Electa, Esther, and Adah — they were annexed to the jurisdiction of California. From 1894 to 1900 inclusive, Nevada was under the jurisdiction of the Grand Chapter of California and District Deputy Grand Matrons from California visited and instructed the Chapters.

Martha Chapter No. 5, at Sparks, was organized in 1901; Silver State Chapter No. 6, at Wannemucca, and Argenta Chapter No. 7, at Virginia City, Iphigenia Chapter No. 8, at Eureka, were organized this same year. Sabra Chapter No. 9, at Delamar, organized in 1900, lasted only until 1904 when its charter was surrendered.

From 1900 to September 1905, the Chapters in Nevada were again under the immediate jurisdiction of the General Grand Chapter, and during this period Turquoise Chapter No. 10, at Tonopah, Ruth No. 11, at Lovelock, and Myrtle Chapter No. 12, at Fallon, were added.

The vicissitudes of the Chapters of Nevada have been many, as the records of the General Grand Chapter will reveal, but there was hope and zeal in the hearts of the sisters and brothers and with a unanimous vote of all the Chapters expressing a desire for a Grand Chapter, William F. Kuhn, Most Worthy Grand Patron, commissioned Mrs. Madeleine B. Conkling, Most Worthy Grand Matron, to organize the Grand Chapter of Nevada, which was most ably done on September 19, 1905.

Since then, the following Chapters were organized: Nevada Chapter No. 13, at Reno; Ely Chapter No. 14, at Ely; Gold Nugget Chapter No. 15, at Goldfield; Naomi Chapter No. 16, at Yerrington; Elko Chapter No. 17, at Elko, and South Gate Chapter, No. 18, at Las Vegas.

There are sixteen Chapters in Nevada, but they are scattered over an extensive territory and for the Grand Matron to visit them all would require her to travel the length and breadth of the State — over 2,500 miles — on her visitations. The membership is 1,505 but make up in zeal and enthusiasm for their small numbers. There is a true understanding of the real objects and teachings of the Order, and its principles are put into practice: The members are earnest, whole-hearted, helpful, and faithful to their obligation.

If there is any one object to which the Order is sacredly pledged, it is to provide for the widow and orphan, and Nevada is working along these lines for a Home fund, which was started in 1911 with cash donations amounting to about $12. Now there are $1,800 in this fund, the result of "gleaning here a little and there a little to provide for the infirmities of age." A "Home Fund Day" has been established in November, at which time each Chapter contributes what it can and in any way, it wishes to this cause. The result so far has been very gratifying for it has meant self-denial and earnest work in many small struggling Chapters. The one great object in the jurisdiction is to hasten the day when there can be erected the greatest of all monuments, the Eastern Star Home in Nevada.

GRAND CHAPTER OF NEW HAMPSHIRE [55]

Brother Macoy chartered four Chapters in New Hampshire. Olive Branch Chapter No. 3 was constituted March 16, 1870, with a Macoy charter, under which it worked until June 15, 1888. On this date the Macoy charter was exchanged for a charter from the General Grand Chapter under whose jurisdiction it remained for three years. It became Olive Branch Chapter No. 1, on May 12, 1901, when the Grand Chapter of the State of New Hampshire was organized and constituted at Lancaster.

Eureka Chapter No. 2, located at Colebrook, was granted a charter on January 1, 1890, and the Chapter was organized March 5, 1890,

---

[55] Organized May 12, 1891. Data by Mrs. Bessie P. Norris, Grand Secretary.

by Frank Spooner, with twenty-three petitioners. This Chapter was chartered September 23, 1889, but for some reason the first charter issued was never received and a new charter was issued upon a new petition without any charges for same.

Ransford Chapter No. J, located at Derry Depot, was granted a charter October 7, 1890, and organized the same date by R. C. Huntress, Deputy of the Most Worthy Grand Patron, with sixty-three petitioners.

Excelsior Chapter No. 4, at Whitefield, was granted a charter December 5, 1890, and organized by J. C. Trickey, Deputy of the Most Worthy Grand Patron, on February 5, 1891, with twenty-eight petitioners.

Mount Hope Chapter No. 5, located at Ashland, was granted a charter February 8, 1891, and organized by Frank Spooner, March 3, 1891, with fifty-six charter members.

Martha Washington Chapter No. 6, located at Goffston, was chartered April 10, 1891, and organized April 28, 1891, by Frank E. Shaw, Deputy for the Most Worthy Grand Patron, with nineteen petitioners.

All of the six Chapters were represented in the convention at the organization of the Grand Chapter. The constitution adopted made Past Matrons and Past Patrons members of the Grand Chapter and the Grand Matron the executive officer. The first officers elected were Mrs. Mary D. M. Quimby, Grand Matron; Dr. Frank Spooner, Grand Patron; J. Sullivan Chase, Grand Secretary. In addition to the three principal officers, Chapters were allowed one representative each by resolution adopted in 1895. A board of finance consisting of three members passes on all bills and allowances. The annual per capita dues are twenty-five cents, and mileage is allowed at the rate of five cents per mile one way.

The Chapters make annual contributions to the Masonic Home. This donation has been voluntary, but an amendment is now awaiting the action of the Grand Chapter to the effect that each Chapter shall contribute ten cents per member to a Masonic Home fund, one-half of which is to be paid each year to the trustees of the Masonic Home and one-half to be kept as a Masonic Home fund to be used only upon vote of the Grand Chapter.

The response to all emergency calls has been prompt and generous, liberal gifts having been made to those who may have met with misfortune through floods, fire, or other forms of disaster.

Sister Mary Herbert of The Weirs, New Hampshire, was initiated into the Order of the Eastern Star in a class of fifteen, by Dr. Rob Morris in 1858, at Newburg, Vermont, and so far as is known, she enjoys the distinction of the longest membership of any person now living.

GRAND CHAPTER OF NEW JERSEY [56]

Seven years before the organization of the General Grand Chapter, the Order of the Eastern Star was established in New Jersey, when Brother Robert Macoy chartered the first Chapter at Keyport, March 25, 1869. Two other Chapters were organized, and the Grand Chapter was formed at Newark on July 18, 1870, by representatives from all three Chapters. One of the three — Eureka, No. 2, located at Elizabeth port — is still active.

On October 20, 1870, a constitution and by-laws were adopted for the government of the Grand body, by virtue of which the Grand Matron was made the presiding officer and all Past Matrons and Past Patrons members of the Grand Chapter. The conduct of the affairs of the organization having been such that disfavor was aroused in the midst of the Fraternity, Brother Macoy declined to further participate in the workings of the Order in that State, which fact was made known at the meeting in June, 1871; however, in 1873, Brother Macoy was present in a friendly and fraternal spirit, commending highly

---

[56] Organized July 18, 1870.

the attainments of this Grand Chapter, its approved progress and material advancement.

In 1874 the Grand Chapter of New York formally recognized the Grand Chapter of New Jersey, but the legality of the organization was questioned by Brother Macoy at a later period, in his report as chairman of the committee on correspondence. The use of the *Macoy Ritual* was begun, but the new *Ritual* was adopted in 1876.

On October 13, 1875, five delegates were selected to represent the Grand Chapter at any meeting or convention that might be called for the purpose of organizing a Supreme Grand Chapter of the Order of the Eastern Star.

At its session October 11, 1876, the resolutions of the Grand Chapter of Indiana were received, the invitation accepted, and the following delegates were elected: John M. Mayhew, Grand Patron; Mrs. E. D. Tilden, Grand Matron; Mrs. Anna M. Mayhew, Past Grand Matron; George Haskins, W. V. W. Vreeland, Mrs. F. A. Graul, and Mrs. M. C. Dobbs.

Of the above number, John M. Mayhew and W. V. W. Vreeland were in attendance at the organization of the General Grand Chapter at Indianapolis, November 15-16, 1876, and Brother Mayhew was elected the first Right Worthy Grand Treasurer. Sister Anna M. Mayhew received appointment as Worthy Grand Esther, Brother W. V. W. Vreeland was appointed Worthy Grand Marshal, and Sister. Vreeland Worthy Grand Warder. John M. Mayhew, Thomas M. Lamb, and Willis D. Engle were the committee appointed by the Most Worthy Grand Patron to formulate the first ritual issued by the General Grand Chapter, printed in 1878.

The Grand Chapter of New Jersey was most cordially received in the incipiency of the General Grand Chapter and the delegates who represented it were given positions of honor and trust, and to them the Order is, in a measure, indebted for the present *Ritual*. Strange as it may seem, within two years from the date of issuance of the first *Ritual*, this Grand Chapter withdrew allegiance to the General Grand

Chapter in 1880. At the meeting of 1881 this action was rescinded, and the Grand Chapter retained its allegiance to the General Grand Chapter until 1887, when it permanently withdrew and appointed a committee to prepare a ritual.

During the month of June 1883, Mrs. Lorraine J. Pitkin, Most Worthy Grand Matron, visited five of the Chapters in New Jersey, officially, and in her address to the General Grand Chapter said:

> The Chapters in New Jersey presented me with beautiful floral offerings as token of their appreciation of my visits. Who does not love flowers? They delight the eye, gratify the sense, and are eloquent teachers of purity and love. As I received these tokens, a silent prayer went up from the deepest recesses of the heart, that the admonitions silently given me by the emblematic flowers, should serve to inspire me to greater fidelity, constancy, purity, hope, and fervency. We acknowledge this as the oldest Grand Chapter included in our constituent number, and their representatives are here at this meeting.

At the annual meeting in 1888, the mover of the resolution, who was then Grand Patron, said the withdrawal was an illegal act, committed inadvertently, and asked that the Grand Matron declare the same null and void, but action was not taken upon this recommendation. In 1889 a new committee on ritual was appointed, which reported in 1890 in favor of adopting the *Macoy Ritual*. This report was not adopted, and it was ordered that the General Grand Chapter *Ritual* be continued in use and a committee be appointed to translate it into the German language. In 1890 the Grand Patron stated that he had visited every Chapter and that the ritualistic work was almost perfect; that not in one instance during the series of official visits did a regular officer of a subordinate Chapter perform her or his work from the book.

In this Grand Jurisdiction, a sister, to be eligible to the office of Worthy Matron, must have served in the office of Associate Matron or Conductress. Emergent sessions of the Grand Chapter are held for the purpose of instituting, also for constituting Chapters; four to twelve sessions almost every year. The charter is the special charge of the Worthy Matron, and it is understood that she shall keep it constantly in her charge, not framing and hanging in Chapter room. In 1903 the Grand Matron decided that the appointive officers may be installed by proxy; also recommended that no one but a member of the O.E.S. shall be permitted to hold the office of Worthy Patron.[57]

In 1903 the ritual question was again considered. Action was postponed for two years, but at the end of one year this action was rescinded and the revised General Grand Chapter *Ritual* adopted in 1904. This was in use until 1907, at which time the General Grand Chapter approved the following upon the recommendation of the Most Worthy Grand Patron:

> New Jersey was one of the Grand Chapters which joined in the formation of the General Grand Chapter, and, after a few years, alleged to withdraw therefrom, but still continued to use the ritual of the General Grand Chapter. In the opinion of your committee and from the record which we would here reaffirm, the Grand Chapter of New Jersey is bound morally and legally to loyally obey all the acts, rules and regulations of the General Grand Chapter to which they gave assent during the time of their unchallenged fealty, one of which was the non-mutilation of the ritual. Therefore, the sale of rituals to the Grand Chapter of New Jersey is hereby interdicted from this date, September 5, 1907.

In 1908 the Grand Patron recommended the adoption of the New York *Ritual*, which was not concurred in, and in 1910 a committee appointed for that purpose presented the New Jersey *Ritual*, which is materially a reprint of the General Grand Chapter Revised, with the

---

[57] The New Jersey Grand Chapter, following the New York law, admits all Master Masons in good standing, obligating them to secrecy only, and the office of Worthy Patron bas been filled by one, not a member of the Order.

addition of ceremonies for instituting Chapters under dispensation and constituting under charter, and for draping the altar. The principal variations are that a brother's presence is necessary to open a Chapter; the ballot box must be placed upon the altar; no requirement is made as to floor star and point emblems; the Matron is escorted to the East by both Conductresses; a password is collected from the women present, while the Patron vouches for the men as Master Masons; the Chaplain, Marshal, and Organist have responses in the opening ceremony and no provision is made for omitting any portion of it.

In 1897, a committee was appointed to visit the General Grand Chapter at its meeting in Washington in 1898. This committee reported in 1899, that a proposition had been made, comprehensive in its character, which would render it both practical and advantageous for them to rejoin, but action on the question was laid over for one year, and in 1900 it was postponed for another year. In 1902 a motion to rejoin failed of adoption.

In 1882 the office of Associate Grand Patron was created, abolished in 1890, and reestablished in 1902 upon the recommendation of the Grand Patron. In 1904 the office of Grand Instructor was abolished.

A fund is maintained whereby they are enabled to offer relief to any member of the Order of the Eastern Star in New Jersey, in good standing, who may need assistance. Such a person may, by applying through the proper channels, be allowed a sum not to exceed fifty dollars in any one year.

The Grand Chapter was incorporated in 1908; the fee for charter was raised from $10 to $25 in 1909 and the minimum fee for the degrees is $3.50.

Contributions to the amount of $54 were made to the Temple of Fraternity at St. Louis, $251 for the relief of sufferers in the San Francisco disaster, and much attention is given to charitable work in general.

Grand Chapter of New Mexico [58]

We must love one another as life's burdens we bear
To the orphan and distressed lend a listening ear;
We must aid, we must comfort, and ever protect,
All grief-stricken Sisters — no call reject.

The first Chapter organized in New Mexico was Queen Esther No. 1, at Raton, chartered November 5, 1888, with eighty-two petitioners. Following this there were nine more Chapters organized, previous to the organization of the Grand Chapter: Ransford No. 2, at East Las Vegas, chartered July 29, 1891; Silver City No. J, Silver City, chartered February 10, 1893; Georgetown No. 4, at Georgetown, chartered March 10, 1893; Adah No. 5, Albuquerque, chartered September 22, 1894; Ruth No. 6, at Deming, chartered December 11, 1897; Rio Arriba No. 7, at Chama, chartered May 16, 1901; Clayton No. 8, at Clayton, chartered March 26, 1902; Magdalen Chapter No. 9, at Socorro, chartered March 19, 1902; Roswell Chapter No. 10, at Roswell, chartered April 10, 1902, and organized by Mrs. Laura B. Hart, Most Worthy Grand Matron.

Five of the ten Chapters participated in the organization of the Grand Chapter at Albuquerque April 11, 1902, Mrs. Laura B. Hart, Most Worthy Grand Matron, presiding as Deputy for the Most Worthy Grand Patron. While organizing the Grand Chapter, Sister Hart was invited to attend an open meeting of the G. A. R. territorial encampment and escorted to the platform where she was saluted with military honors. Thus, was exemplified a portion of the softening influence of the Eastern Star upon the bitterness of that great struggle represented by the military organization.

---

[58] Organized April 11, 1902.

By the constitution adopted, Past Matrons and Past Patrons were made permanent members of the Grand Chapter. The State was divided into districts and a Deputy Grand Matron and Deputy Grand Patron appointed for each. The minimum fee for the degrees was fixed at $3 and the charter fee at $30. The Grand Matron was given all authority, even to the conferring of degrees, but her deputies were allowed to call a brother to their assistance if they so desired. It was made the duty of the deputies to inspect the laws and records and correct the same in accordance with the Grand Chapter's rulings.

At the third annual session, the Grand Matron was prevented from attending by illness in her family and the Associate Grand Matron assumed all her powers and prerogatives.

The revised by-laws adopted in 1905 require that the election of the Grand Officers shall be the special order of business immediately following the opening of the Grand Chapter on the afternoon of the first day. New Chapters could be instituted only by the Grand Matron or her Deputy, but this was changed in 1909, and this duty given to the Grand Patron.

Liberal contributions were made: $136 to the San Francisco fire sufferers; $11 to the Temple of Fraternity at St. Louis fair; $149 was sent to the Grand Chapter of Ohio for the relief of those who suffered loss from the floods; $10.90 for O.E.S. headquarters at Lewis and Clark Exposition.

This State is now reaping benefits to its people because of the effect of this organization with its lofty ideals and teachings which emulate in thought and deed the life of the Perfect One.

GRAND CHAPTER OF NEW YORK [59]

The degrees of the Eastern Star were first conferred in lecture form, in New York City, in 1853, and frequently thereafter were used

---

[59] Organized November 30, 1870.

in the social gatherings of the Masonic Fraternity as a special feature of attraction and conferred upon large audiences composed of persons entitled to receive them.

The first known periodical published in the interests of the Order was a bi-monthly publication styled the organ of the American Adoptive Rite, in the month of August 1855. The second number did not appear until January 1856, and this was the last number published. Dr. Rob Morris was the editor, though his name is not used as such in the publication, which was published by John W. Leonard & Co., American Masonic Agency, No. 383 Broadway, New York City.

Friendship Family No. 103, Brooklyn, chartered January 25, 1867, is regarded by many as the oldest Eastern Star organization in the State, and is now known as Esther Chapter No. 2, Brooklyn.

In 1863 and 1864 the project of the Masonic Hall and Home was agitated by the Masonic Fraternity, and the brethren, realizing the advantage of cooperation of the ladies in such work, invited their interest and influence in this direction. This was probably the main factor which influenced the desire to promote an organization through which the ladies could continue the charitable work thus well begun.

The members of the Masonic Fraternity had purchased the French church, located on the corner of Grand and Crosby Streets, which they wished to remodel and utilize for their purposes. To raise funds for the promotion of this work, a fair was held in this church through the entire month of December 1886, and about $60,000 was realized. The ladies who were thus brought together in assistance to the Fraternity, formed friendships so cordial and sincere that deep regret was expressed that the closing of the fair would terminate their meetings and that this work of advancement along worthy lines could not be continued. A suggestion was made, almost immediately after the closing, that the ladies connected with the fair form an organization to continue the work so agreeably begun, and if possible to so arrange that the result of such efforts be in the interests of the Masonic Hall and Home fund.

In harmony with this idea, Brother Joseph F. Waring, of Enterprise Lodge No. 228, at the request of members of the Masonic Fraternity, invited the ladies who were connected with the Masonic fair to meet in the board of relief room, Odd Fellows Hall, corner of Grand and Center Streets, on Monday, January 21, 1876, at 3 o'clock P. M., for the purpose of organizing a society of the Sisters of the Eastern Star.

The day upon which this meeting was arranged proved to be very stormy and a full attendance was not secured, but a sufficient number was present to effect an organization. Mr. Waring presided, explained the purpose of the meeting, and under his directions the society was organized, by-laws were adopted, and the organization was named Alpha Sisters of the Eastern Star. The society, from its formation, took an active interest in every effort intended to promote the hall and asylum fund and a reception was given by them at Irving Hall, March 7, 1867, which netted $973. In order to make the donation to the fund $1,000, the society drew from its treasury $27.

Alpha Chapter No. 1, New York City, was the first Chapter organized in the State, as well as having the great distinction of being the first Chapter ever organized. Mrs. Christiana Buttrick, for twenty-one years the Grand Secretary, occupying this exalted office until her death, February 5, 1900, just a few weeks before her death gave an interesting account of the organization of Alpha Chapter No. 1. She was a member of sterling worth and faithfully served the Order, and this account as she has recorded it is given below:

> Mrs. Maria A. Warner was one of the original charter members of Alpha Chapter No. 1, which held informal meetings once or twice a month at different members' houses, doing a good charitable work, which was the purpose of the organization. Finally, one afternoon, it was suggested that it would make the meetings more interesting

if they were formal; if we had some ceremonies for opening and initiation of members. Robert Macoy had previously attended the meetings, and on October 21, 1867, conferred the degrees in lecture form; these meetings were usually held at 16 Vandam Street, the residence of Mrs. Frances E. Johnson.

The result of the discussion of the aforesaid afternoon was that a committee was appointed to call on Mr. Macoy, and to ask him if he could prepare an initiation ceremony. Mrs. Warner and Mrs. Barnes were two of the committee; I do not recall the third member. They called on Mr. Macoy at his place of business, corner of Broome and Crosby Streets. He was absent and the committee waited for a brief time, then left; when walking a short distance from the building, met Mr. Macoy, and when they approached him Mrs. Warner stated the object of their visit. She reported back to the next meeting that Mr. Macoy had something of the kind in his mind, which he would put forth in due time.

After that, until the work was completed, and from time to time, he would drop into the meetings at Mrs. Johnson's, and report how the work was progressing. When ready he selected, at her home, the different officers for the several points. The degrees were read to us from a manuscript, but when first conferred (October 9, 1868, at 594 Broadway), all the officers read their parts from a printed copy.

On December 28, 1868, at a meeting held in the afternoon at 594 Broadway, the first meeting as a chartered Chapter, the degrees were conferred for the first time, Mrs. Eliza A. Macoy being the first candidate. Aside from the records, I remember the event distinctly, as it left a great impression on me.

On the same day the installation of officers took place, I, being the secretary, felt the importance and responsibility of the position. The following is the record of the officers at the time, viz: Robert Macoy, Patron; Mrs. Frances E. Johnson, Worthy Matron; Mrs. Maria A. Warner, Associate Matron; Mrs. C. Asten, Treasurer; Mrs. C. Buttrick, Secretary; Mrs. S. L. Vickers, Conductress; Mrs. E. L. Chipman, Associate Conductress.

As previously stated, Friendship Family No. 103 is recognized as the first organized body of the Eastern Star, the charter of which is dated January 25, 1867. The first meeting under the "Family" charter was held February 6, 1867, in Andrew Young's room, corner Court and Joralemon Streets. Later meetings were held in the parlors of the members until May 29th. Thereafter a room was secured and used by the "Family" until reorganized as a Chapter in June 1869, when by vote of the members, the name of Esther Chapter No. 2 was decided upon for the new organization.

Twenty Chapters were chartered, including Alpha No. 1 and Esther No. 2, previous to the organization of the Grand Chapter at New York City, November 30, 1870, by representatives of fourteen Chapters, five of them being proxies who were not members of the Chapters they represented. A constitution was adopted which made the Grand Patron the executive officer and all Past Matrons and Past Patrons members of the Grand Chapter; also requiring that proxies must be members of the Chapter which they represent, and that sisters and daughters, if unmarried, must have attained the age of eighteen years to be eligible to the degrees.

Prior to 1885 the Grand Patron was the highest officer, but at the meeting in 1884 this authority was given to the Grand Matron, who conducted the affairs of the Grand Chapter as its executive officer and at the session in 1885 presided as such. The Grand Matron has retained this position since that date.

In 1873 the Grand Chapter was honored by the presence of Dr. Rob Morris, who delivered an address. In 1874 the Grand Chapters of New Jersey, Vermont, California, Indiana, and Massachusetts were formally recognized, sisters were exempted from dependence upon the standing of the Mason through whom they obtained membership, and the addition of the burial service, which had been previously printed in pamphlet form, was decided to be included in the ritual.

Misunderstandings, jealousies, and diversions from the principles of the Order, precipitated a difference which remains, as yet, unsurmounted between Brother Macoy and the members of the Grand Chapter of New York and the General Grand Chapter. The conditions as they have existed are better forgotten and the present work of this Grand Chapter accepted as magnificent contributions to the tenets of our Order.

In 1883 Mrs. Lorraine J. Pitkin, Most Worthy Grand Matron of the General Grand Chapter, was cordially invited as a guest of this Grand Chapter and accorded the fraternal courtesies, invited to a seat in the Grand East and welcomed as becoming to her most exalted position, which was the first time such honors had rested upon the Most Worthy Grand Matron.

Early in the spring of 1888, the Most Worthy Grand Patron of the General Grand Chapter received a request for a charter for a Chapter at Lockport, New York, but declined to grant same, referring the brother to the Grand Secretary of the Grand Chapter of New York as the proper person to whom application should be made, believing that the General Grand Chapter should never, in any case, invade the jurisdiction of a Grand Chapter not owning allegiance to the Grand body.

Responding to the invitation of the Right Worthy Grand Secretary, representatives from New York were present at the meeting of the General Grand Chapter in 1898, at which time resolutions were agreed upon which when accepted by this Grand Chapter, looked to the uniting of the Grand Chapter with those composing the General Grand Chapter, but were not deemed acceptable.[60]

---

[60] The following, taken from the Proceedings of the General Grand Chapter, tells the story:

CONFERENCE

James B. Merritt, from the Committee on Conference, submitted the following report, which, together with the recommendations, were concurred in.
To the Officers and Members of the General Grand Chapter:
Your committee appointed to confer with the representatives of the Grand Chapters of New York, Connecticut and New Jersey, would respectfully report the following:
A meeting of the committees was held with a full representation, as follows: Mrs. Eleanor Burton, Mrs. Rachel L. Stiefel, and Mrs. Eliza M. Demarest, of New York; Mrs. Frances L. Boone, Wm. C. Brown and Mrs. Anna Garabrant of New Jersey; Chas. L. Fowler and Mrs. Ida M. Fiske of Connecticut. The Chairman of the Committee from New York, Mrs. Eleanor Burton, submitted the following written statement, which is hereto attached and made a part of this report.

New York: City, Sept. 27th, 1898.
To the Most Worthy Grand Matron, Officers and Members of the General Grand Chapter,
 Order of Eastern Star, United States.
Esteemed Members in Session — Greeting: As the Grand Chapter of New York has been fraternally invited to unite with the General Grand Chapter, and as we are here as delegates from the Grand Chapter of New York, we can frankly say that the purpose or work of this body is not understood by a large majority of the members of the Grand Chapter of our State; unfortunately they have not taken the opportunity to inform themselves, and the grand representatives have not kept themselves nor the Grand Chapter posted, and we feel that owing to these conditions, we of New York might be misjudged or made to appear antagonistic to the General Grand Chapter, when such is not the case.

It is true we use the Macoy ritual, because it was the original work of the Order, and one under which many of the chapters now throughout the United States first found the light of the Eastern Star. As it is the desire of the General Grand Chapter for a standard ritual, we think the time has come for the entire Order to have a secret uniform work, and as united action can end in success, it may be that a universal ritual, compiled or revised by good ritualists of the Order at large. can work together for the advancement and elevation of the combined associations.

We, the committee, appointed by the Grand Chapter of New York, to see what arrangements can be made for affiliating with your body, are here for the purpose of ascertaining all possible facts, whereby we may make a full report at the next annual session to be held in June, 1899, at which time final action will be taken.

But before uniting with the General Grand Body there are a few important questions to be considered.

First: We have bought at an expense of one thousand dollars the copyright of the Macoy ritual; we have had it printed; it is in use in all our chapters, and any change of ritual would entail a heavy expense upon our Grand Chapter, as well as every chapter of our State.

Second: It has always been the custom of our State to admit Master Masons to our assemblies, and after obligating them to secrecy, permit them to witness our work. In the majority of eases these Masons become impressed with the Order, and bring in the petition of a daughter, wife, sister or mother. Masons in New York have so many orders of their own, for example, the lodge. chapter, council, commandery, and the shrine, that they do not care to Join the Eastern Star, but they are willing that the female members of their families should become members, and they give us their friendly and financial support, and we feel that we have their good will.

Third: We have in our work a Floral Ceremony, which was first brought out in Stella .Chapter No. 29, on May 5th, 1875, and since then has become part of our ceremonies. It is beautiful and instructive, and capable of being made a source of pleasure to candidates and visitors alike. Our Grand Chapter has adopted this ceremony as a part of the standard work, and the members would not be willing to give it up.

Fourth: We have several chapters that work in the German language, and they have our ritual translated, and this at their own expense; if we make a change they must be considered, and provision made to care for them.

In presenting these facts, we, as delegates, would like a friendly and fraternal discussion as to what arrangements can be made in reference to the first question, the ritual. Surely you as a great body of intelligent members would not expect that we should be put to the expense of so great a change without some compensation as to the money expended on our work.

And we would in a fraternal manner ask the question: "What would this grand body do in re-imbursing us for the expenses of a change?" In view of the fact that Master Masons (not members of the Order) are admitted to our meetings, but are obligated to secrecy, how can we reconcile that with the laws of the General Grand Chapter, or would you be willing to grant us time to bring about the change?

As to the third, our floral degree, we learn that mand of the states of the West are beginning to use it as an addendum, an we think that when its beauties are fully known, that it will be adopted by all the states. that it will be a source of pleasure to all our members, and therefore feel that this matter may be left in your hands with safety. This leaves but the consideration of the German chapters, and now, brothers and sisters, having placed these facts of our Grand Chapter before you, we ask your kindly consideration of them, and trust that your decision will be such that it may bring harmony and good feeling to all grand bodies now affiliated with you, and that we can look forward to the day when your wise judgments wilt make us one grand, united body, whose only aim will be "who best can work, and best agree."

LANDMARKS OF STATE OF NEW YORK GRAND CHAPTER

Those eligible to membership are master masons in good standing in their lodges: Wives, sisters, daughters, mothers, and widows.

Fraternally submitted,
MRS. ELEANOR BURTON.
MRS. RACHEL L. STIEFEL.
MRS. ELIZA M. DEMAREST,
Committee.

Your committee carefully reviewed the reasons given, why these Grand Chapters have not deemed it wise to become our constituents. The discussion was protracted, free and full. From the above statement, together with the information gained from conversation with the representatives of New York, New Jersey and Connecticut, the real matters in controversy appeared to be reduced to two: namely, the Macoy ritual and the admission of Master Masons to the meetings of the Order, without a regular initiation.

Connecticut expresses a fear that they would lose their independence and be compelled to contribute to the financial support of the General Grand Chapter. They also have the so-called "higher degrees," and were uncertain whether a union would be affected in any manner by this fact.

Your committee do not consider these matters of any vital importance. It is to be hoped — nay — presumed, that the wisdom of the General Chapter will so handle its finances that no assessments wilt ever be necessary, and at most that the demand upon the Grand Chapters will be nominal.

As to the "higher degrees" — they are entirely outside the province of this General Grand Chapter, and the Most Worthy Grand Matron has in her address, at this session, ably stated the position of this General Grand Chapter in that matter.

In regard to the ritual and the admission of Master Masons, your committee feel that the General Grand Chapter ought to be generous and forebearing. Both these questions are of great importance to New York and New Jersey.

While this General Grand Chapter desires to hold out the welcoming hand, believing that a union of all the Grand Chapters would tend to strengthen the Order and to promote truth and love, unity and peace, yet we cannot entirely sacrifice uniformity of ritual, and of qualifications for membership, the establishment and perpetuation of which is one of the principal objects of the existence of the General Grand Chapter.

In addition to the officers that are common to all Grand Chapters, New York has three Associate Grand Marshals, three Grand

---

We have, therefore, formulated a proposition, which, we hope, will be acceptable, both to the General Grand Chapter and to the Grand Chapters of New York, New Jersey and Connecticut.

Resolved: That in the event of a decision on the part of the Grand Chapter of New York, to become a constituent of this General Grand Chapter.

This General Grand Chapter will present to the Grand Chapter of New York five hundred copies of our ritual, and further; will exchange, copy for copy, all rituals sent by the Grand Secretary of New York to our Right Worthy Grand Secretary.

That the Right Worthy Grand Secretary be authorized to have a translation of our ritual made into the German language, and to furnish as many copies thereof as shall be desired as a part of the five hundred rituals to be presented, and to exchange ritual for ritual, such copies of the German ritual of New York, as may be sent to our Right Worthy Grand Secretary, by the Grand Chapters of New York and New Jersey.

Provided, That should a revision of the ritual be ordered at this session of the General Grand Chapter, then the exchange shall be made after the promulgation of the revised ritual.

Furthermore, That the Grand Chapter of New York destroy the plates of the Macoy ritual now in their possession. or place the same in the hands of our Right Worthy Grand Secretary.

That a period of three years be allowed, during which time the Grand Chapters of New York and New Jersey shall conform their regulations in the matter of the admission of Master Masons to those of the General Grand Chapter.

Provided, That nothing herein contained shall confer the privileges of visiting Chapters outside of the Grand Chapters of New York and New Jersey upon any Master Mason, who shall not have been regularly initiated into the Order.

Further, That the Past Grand Officers of the Grand Chapters of New York, New Jersey, Connecticut and Vermont, be entitled to the rights and privileges of membership in this General Grand Chapter.

                Respectfully submitted,
                        JAMES B. MERRITT, California.
                        L. CABELL WILLIAMSON, District of Columbia.
                        MRS. JENNIE E. MATTHEWS, Iowa.
                        MRS. NETTIE RANSFORD, Indiana.
                        MRS. LORRAINE J, PITKIN, Illinois.
                        NATHANIEL A. GEARHART, Minnesota.

The representatives from New York, New Jersey and Connecticut were then introduced and made appropriate remarks indicative of their pleasure at the happy result of the conference.

Chaplains, a president of Hall and Home Association, Historian, and Grand Lecturer.

In 1901, the true fraternal spirit was indicated when funeral services were conducted for a sister from Arizona who died in a New York hospital.

In 1903, the scarf worn by Sister Eliza A. Macoy, Grand Matron in 1876 and who was the first candidate to receive the degrees of the Order after the Chapter form was arranged by Brother Robert Macoy in 1868, was presented to the Grand Chapter and this scarf is treasured by the Grand Chapter for its historic association. Sister Macoy was the wife of the man to whom all owe a debt of gratitude for the beautiful arrangement of the beloved Chapter system.

Contributions have been made to the various charitable purposes for which call has been made: $100 to the Temple of Fraternity at the St. Louis Fair, $2,000 to the sufferers from the San Francisco disaster; $510 to the relief of Galveston flood sufferers, and in 1913 $1,024.81 was sent for the relief of the sufferers from the Ohio flood.

As stated in the original organization of the women of the Masons' families in New York State, as early as 1863-1864, their object was for charitable purposes, especially as they wished to promote the establishment of a Masonic Hall and Home and work for the maintenance of same after it was fully established. This spirit has remained and has dominated their ideas throughout the existence of the Order. In 1890 a committee, composed of one member from each Chapter, was appointed, to arrange for an entertainment in New York and Brooklyn to raise a fund to form the nucleus around which they all could work, with the end in view to provide a Home for deserving members of the Order. The services of the Order were tendered the Grand Lodge and accepted by them, to furnish one room in the Masonic Home at Utica, when completed, which might perhaps be set aside for the use of deserving members of the Order, and later $200 was appropriated for this purpose. In 1892 an Eastern Star Home Association was organized. Great interest was manifested in its undertakings and assistance was freely and generously rendered by the Fraternity. In 1901 an Eastern Star fair was held, in which all the Chapters in the jurisdiction participated. This continued for two weeks and netted the Home Fund a profit of $12,685.51 and that same year $500 was paid into the Home Fund from the Chapters. In 1903 a circular letter sent to the Masonic Lodges brought responses amounting to $4,000 for the Hall and Home Association fund. The fund continued to grow with the wonderful rapidity that surely must result from the united efforts of so many earnest and untiring workers, until in 1907 it amounted to $67,102.25 and a committee was appointed to select a site for the Home. On June 20, 1908, the new Eastern Star Home was dedicated.

The Grand Chapter purchased a beautiful estate, located at Waterville, to be used for a home for indigent sisters of the Order of the Eastern Star. The substantial building was well suited for this purpose, with spacious grounds surrounding it, and the restful and picturesque location and the farm in connection make this an admirable place for the O.E.S. Home. The building was remodeled and fitted up in a splendid manner, giving a haven of refuge to the few who need care and protection. The sisters of this jurisdiction are to be congratulated upon the fact that there are only a few who have needed their kind care, and further that for those who are there they are given a home in the truest sense, where may be enjoyed every comfort and convenience. Attractive sun parlors with delightful outlook furnish comfort and enjoyment through the winter months, while the spacious grounds and ample verandas prove enticing during the warm weather. Plentiful food, wholesome and well cooked, and a well-stocked library, satisfy physical and mental desires, and an infirmary fund is maintained that will ensure the sisters proper medical and surgical attention when needed.

In 1909 the Grand Patron in his address, speaking of the O.E.S. Home at Waterville, said:

Up to the present time, it has been necessary that we have a President of the Hall and Home Association, whose particular duty it has been to secure funds by soliciting from Chapters and otherwise, said funds to be used for the benefit of the Home. The time is now at hand when the per capita tax will provide such funds as are necessary for the care and maintenance of the Home, and it is no longer necessary that these solicitations should continue.

In 1910 an appropriation amounting to $715 was given to the educational fund for the children at the Masonic Home at Utica, to be used in preparing the little ones for useful vocations in life.

A board of relief has been organized, which occupies a field entirely distinct and separate from the work of the established Masonic Home and O.E.S. Home, its object being to assist members in times of special stress and enable them to pass through crises of trouble or misfortune to better days. This work is done privately in the true Masonic manner.

In 1912, Sister Julia Thayer, Grand Matron, said: "Those who do not look upon themselves as a link connecting the past with the future, do not perform their duty to the world."

> The easy path in the low grounds hath little of grand or new,
> But the toilsome ascent heads on to a glorious view;
> Peopled and warm is the valley, lonely and chilly the height,
> But the peak that is nearest the storm cloud is nearer the Stars of light.

GRAND CHAPTER OF NORTH CAROLINA [61]

In February 1869, a charter was issued by Brother Macoy for a Chapter at Kingston. The State remained open territory for the Order

---

[61] Organized May 20, 1905. Data by the Superintendent Masonic and Eastern Star Home, Brother L. M. Clymer, Past Grand Secretary and Past Grand Patron.

of the Eastern Star until the General Grand Chapter issued a charter for Hope No. 1, at Boone, April IS, 1882, which Chapter only remained in active work for a short time. Later, a charter was granted to Center Grove and this new Chapter received a charter issued July 30, 1890, and was given the number, 1. After a short time Center Grove Chapter ceased activity and the oldest Chapter doing active work is Mt. Vernon No. 2, Ore Hill, chartered April 30, 1903. Twelve Chapters had been given charters but only seven were active at the time of the organization of the Grand Chapter.

On Saturday, May 20, 1905, in the Masonic Hall, Asheville, a convention of six Chapters, O. E. S., assembled for the purpose of organizing a Grand Chapter. The convention was called to order by J. A. Gorman, Worthy Patron of Esther Chapter No. 12, and was composed of eighteen representatives from Mt. Vernon No. 2, Lois No. 8, Silver City No. 9, Grace No. 10, Clay No. 11, and Esther No. 12.

The Most Worthy Grand Matron of the General Grand Chapter, Mrs. Madeleine B. Conkling, was made chairman. Following the election of officers, they were installed by the Most Worthy Grand Matron, who was presented with a loving cup and upon motion she was elected an honorary member of the Grand Chapter of North Carolina.

Past Matrons and Past Patrons are members of the Grand Chapter. Annual dues are fifty cents per capita, fifteen cents of which are to be set aside as an O.E.S. charity fund. No Chapter is to begin work under dispensation or charter, until it shall have provided all furniture, implements, or other things necessary and proper to give due effect to the solemn ceremonies of the degrees of the Order. The privileges of visitation, Chapter relief, or Chapter burial are denied to anyone who voluntarily remains a non-affiliate more than twelve months.

Following the recommendation of the Grand Matron in 1906, a committee was appointed to visit the Grand Lodge, A. F. and A. M., to secure recognition from that body, which recognition was cordially granted.

The Grand Officers began their work with energy and enthusiasm, but owing to many so-called Chapters throughout the State which did not accomplish the work expected or send dues to the Grand Chapter during the first five years it was difficult to forward the work of the Order. Those who were active gave their hearty support to the Masonic Orphanage at Oxford, which institution is now caring for 336 children. Training is there offered that will surely result in the molding of these little children into men and women who will prove of great value to the State. Many have left this home to be honored men and women, who lead the most worthy and useful lives.

The month of November has been set apart for benefits to be donated to the orphans at Oxford.

The Grand Matron is assisted in her work by Deputy Grand Matrons, having appointed twelve in 1912.

The movement for an O.E.S. Home was instigated in 1905, and in 1910 the Eastern Star Grand Chapter and the Masonic Grand Lodge united their efforts in the erection of the Masonic and Eastern Star Home. On a beautiful site of about twenty-five acres, donated by J. Van Lindley and his son, Paul Lindley, Masons of the city, just outside of Greensboro may be seen the Masonic and Eastern Star Home, recently built and equipped at an approximate cost of about $30,000. Many of the Chapters and Lodges in the State of North Carolina have furnished rooms. One of the most conspicuous pieces of furniture in the dining-room is a china closet, donated by the Grand Chapter, O. E. S., of the State of New York. The Stars of North Carolina have a very tender feeling for the New York State membership, as this represents the only gift so far received from outside the State. The time of architects and builders was donated by members of the craft, and today may be seen a beautiful finished structure — a happy home for Masons and their wives and Eastern Star members who are unable to care for themselves.

Brother John J. Phoenix, the capable secretary of the Home board, is untiring in his efforts to promote the welfare of this institution and its residents. The Home will accommodate seventy-five residents. There are now about a score of happy men and women enjoying the comforts of this beautiful Home.

Grand Chapter of North Dakota [62]

Silently one by one in the infinite meadows of heaven,
Blossomed the lovely Stars, the forget-me-nots of the angels.

• • • • • • • •

Numberless torrents, with ceaseless sound, descend to the ocean,
Like the great chords of a harp, in loud and solemn vibrations.
Spreading between these streams are the wondrous, beautiful prairies,
Billowy bays of grass ever rolling in shadow and sunshine,
Bright with luxuriant clusters of roses and purple amorphas.
Over them wandered the buffalo herd and the elk.

During the territorial days of Dakota — 1861 to 1889 — Brother Macoy granted a charter for a Chapter at Vermillion in July, 1871, but it became dormant and our Star was not seen in Dakota Territory again until the General Grand Chapter granted a charter for Queen Esther Chapter No. 1, at Mitchell, February 4, 1882.

Preceding the Act of the United States Congress, dividing the Territory of Dakota into the States of North and South Dakota, eleven charters for Chapters had been granted. Only one of these was located within the boundary limits of North Dakota—Lady Washington

---

[62] Organized June 14, 1894.

Chapter No. 8, at Jamestown, chartered August 29, 1887, and organized by J. W. Cloes, special Deputy of the Most Worthy Grand Patron. It was later given the number, 1, it being the oldest organization in the newly formed State.

Logan Chapter No. 2, Oakes, was chartered February 15, 1890; Wapeton Chapter No. 3, Wapeton, December 23, 1890; Woodbine Chapter No. 4, Valley City, February 19, 1891; Mecca Chapter No. 5, Fargo, February 2, 1893; Mizpah Chapter No. 6. Grafton, February 21, 1893; Prairie Chapter No. 7, Sanburn, May 30, 1893; Adah Chapter No. 8, Ellendale, December 21, 1893; Queen Esther Chapter No. 9, Mandan, March 7, 1894; Ceres Chapter No. 10, Tower City, March 23, 1894; Bismarck Chapter No. 11, Bismarck, May 7, 1894; Acacia Chapter No. 12, Grand Forks, May 1, 1894; Fidelity Chapter No. 13, Hope, May 7, 1894.

Pursuant to an invitation issued by Thomas N. Ritchie, the convention of all of the thirteen Chapters (represented by forty-one delegates) working under charters granted by the General Grand Chapter, assembled in the Masonic Hall at Valley City, June 4, 1894, for the purpose of organizing a Grand Chapter, O.E.S. Mrs. Lorraine J. Pitkin, Right Worthy Grand Secretary, Deputy of the Most Worthy Grand Matron and Most Worthy Grand Patron, presided over the convention. A constitution was adopted making the Grand Matron the executive officer and similar to that of other Grand Chapters with reference to representation, per capita dues, etc.

The Grand Lodge, A. F. and A. M., then in session at Valley City, extended an invitation to the representatives of the several Chapters at the convention to attend the installation of the Grand Lodge officers. Mrs. Lorraine J. Pitkin, Right Worthy Grand Secretary of the General Grand Chapter, accepted an invitation to sit in the Grand East during the installation, this being the first time that a lady had ever received such distinguished honors at the hands of any Masonic body. In her report read at the eighth triennial session of the General

Grand Chapter held in Boston, Massachusetts, 1895, the Right Worthy Grand Secretary expressed her sincere appreciation:

June 14, 1894, the representatives of the several Chapters in North Dakota, met in convention at Valley City to organize a Grand Chapter. Through the courtesy of those present, it was my pleasure to preside during the organization. Thomas N. Ritchie, a zealous and earnest worker, who had rendered valuable service as Deputy of the Most Worthy Grand Patron in extending the Order, was wise in the selection of the time and place for holding this meeting.

The "Grand Masonic Bodies," were in Annual Session during the week, and each vied with the other in extending every kindness to all who had gathered in the interests of the "Eastern Star."

The very atmosphere was permeated with enthusiasm, and the representatives of the "Masonic Bodies," throughout that Northern Jurisdiction, seemed to cover us with an "Arch of Steel," as we completed our labors — and surely the "Order of the Eastern Star," in that far away State must be founded upon a "Rock," when such "Ancient Builders" assist in placing the foundation stone."

A magnificent and elaborate social session followed the joint installation of Grand officers, at which time a reception and banquet was given in honor of the officers and delegates of the Grand Lodge of A. F. and A. M., Royal Arch Masons, Knights Templar, and Order of the Eastern Star, which was attended by over three hundred enthusiastic guests.

The floral work has been twice rendered before the Grand Chapter, the first time in 1895, and in 1900 the district school of instruction, under the supervision of district Deputies, was inaugurated with marked success. In 1900 a resolution was adopted making all delegates who took part in the organization of the Grand Chapter, permanent members. The recognition thus extended included twenty-four who were not otherwise permanent members. A ceremony for constituting Chapters was adopted. The second Sunday of September was designated as "Memorial Day" and each Chapter requested to hold a Chapter of Sorrow in memory of deceased members of the Order. In 1901, all Past Grand Matrons and Past Grand Patrons were constituted a permanent committee on jurisprudence.

Contributions for charitable purposes have been made frequently; $82.60 was given for the Temple of Fraternity at the St. Louis Exposition; $42.26 to be used in maintaining O.RS. headquarters at the Portland fair; a circular letter in 1905 resulted in contributions from Chapters amounting to $126.50, which formed the nucleus around which has grown a fund that will soon give this Grand Jurisdiction an O.E.S. Home. In 1909 it was resolved that the several Chapters set apart a day in each year to be known as Masonic and Eastern Star Day, and devote the day to the raising of money for the Home Fund. In 1912 the fund amounted to $1,236.10.

At the 1914 session, Mrs. Lorraine J. Pitkin, Right Worthy Grand Secretary of the General Grand Chapter, was present and was elected to honorary membership in the Grand Chapter of North Dakota. This was especially fitting, as she had organized the Grand Chapter twenty years previously.

GRAND CHAPTER OF OHIO [63]

The development of unfavorable resolutions and antagonism of a marked character, from the Grand Lodge of Masons in Ohio, greatly retarded the initial efforts of the O.E.S. in Ohio as will be evident by the following passed by the Grand Lodge in 1868:

> *Resolved*, That the said degrees, otherwise called Adoptive or Androgynous Masonry, are not legitimate Masonic degrees, and do not entitle the recipients thereof to any of

---

[63] Organized July 24, 1889.

the rights or benefits of Masonry; that the conferring of said degree on women is calculated to deceive and mislead them, and is, therefore, improper.

Resolved, That the Lodges of this Jurisdiction are forbidden, under any pretense whatever, to permit their halls to be used for the purpose of conferring said degree.

Rollin C. Gaskill, Most Worthy Grand Patron, on October 9, 1883, appointed S. C. Chorlton Deputy for the State of Ohio, and through his untiring efforts, Lorraine Chapter No. 1, located at Columbus, was chartered by the General Grand Chapter on November 13, 1883, and organized December 6, 1883, by Brother Chorlton.

Pearl Chapter No. 2, located at Cleveland, was chartered December 4, 1886, and organized by S. C. Chorlton, who had been reappointed Deputy for Ohio. Bucyrus Chapter No. 3, at Bucyrus, was chartered January 20, 1887; Ruby Chapter No. 4, Chardon, April 27, 1887; Iona Chapter No. 5, Eaton, March 18, 1889. All of the five Chapters were organized by Dr. Chorlton.

The officers of the General Grand Chapter called a convention to organize a Grand Chapter, which met in the Knights of Pythias Hall, Cleveland, on July 24, 1889, the Most Worthy Grand Patron, Jefferson S. Conover, presiding. All of the five Chapters were represented, there being present thirteen delegates. A deep gloom was cast over the assembly because of the death of Dr. Chorlton, which occurred a few weeks previous to the date of organization. The constitution adopted made the Grand Matron the executive officer.

Owing to refusal of Masonic recognition, the Order found it difficult to advance as rapidly as in jurisdictions where Masonic influences are favorable. In 1891 a committee asked permission from the Grand Lodge to hold meetings in Masonic Lodge rooms, but it was not until 1892 that the Grand Lodge decided that, with the consent of the Grand Master and the unanimous consent of all Masonic bodies occupying Masonic halls, their use might be granted to Chapters for festival and ceremonial purposes. The result was that the number of Chapters increased from seventeen in 1894 to thirty-seven in 1895, this growth being directly attributed to the advantages gained by change in the attitude of the Grand Lodge.

In 1895 the State was divided into districts, with a Deputy Grand Matron in each, and annually a detailed report is submitted as to the condition of each Chapter. The laws require that each Chapter receive a visit and inspection annually, a law that would be greatly to the advantage of subordinate Chapters if all Grand Jurisdictions would adopt a similar one. In 1915 it required twenty-five Deputy Grand Matrons to properly conduct the work of inspecting the twenty-five districts.

In 1895 a communication was received from the Grand Master, A. F. and A.M., in which he expressed himself as being in sympathy with the O. E. S., and that he was willing to do anything in his power to further the cause. In 1897 the Grand Lodge ordered that Chapters might meet in Masonic halls by obtaining the consent of Masonic bodies using the same. This opened the way for the rapid extension of the Order which a review of the succeeding years reveals.

In 1901 the Grand Chapter, O. E. S., arranged to cooperate with the Grand Lodge in an effort to improve the Masonic Home at Springfield and a beautiful and commodious hospital building was erected at a cost of $15,200.94. In 1904 a special train carried the members of the Grand Chapter from Columbus to Springfield to participate in the laying of the cornerstone of the hospital building, and on May 10, 1905, the magnificent O.E.S. Memorial Hospital, which stands on a knoll on the Masonic Home Farm, was dedicated with appropriate ceremonies. In 1910 an addition was completed at a cost of $6,548.58.

Appropriations have been made to charitable work: To the Temple of Fraternity at St. Louis, $100; to the Galveston flood sufferers, $50. The Grand Patron in 1913 received and expended about $5,000 for the relief of their own sufferers in the disastrous flood that swept their domain during that year.

In 1898 the *Sedgwick Monitor*, for use in connection with stereopticon views, was indorsed, and the following year the superintendent of the Masonic Home and his wife were elected to receive the degrees, which were conferred, the *Sedgwick Monitor* lectures being given by the author, Brother Sedgwick. The memorial service has been rendered several times as has also the floral work and mystic tie.

In 1907 the Grand Chapter set apart the last Sunday in the month of June of each year as a memorial day for the O.E.S. in the jurisdiction of the State of Ohio.

In 1912 the O.E.S. Hospital Circle was organized in the twentieth district and is composed of the Worthy Matron and three members from each Chapter, whose purpose is to administer to the sick in the various hospitals and homes, distributing flowers and good cheer to ill and ailing members of the Order of the Eastern Star or Masons, or to their wives, mothers, daughters, or other relatives. It is maintained by voluntary contributions from the various Chapters, O. E. S., and from the twenty-one Masonic bodies represented, the latter looking upon this circle with very great favor.

In 1914 the Grand Chapter appropriated $100 to the Red Cross Society to assist in the great work they are doing in Europe.

Grand Chapter of Oklahoma [64]

Through the efforts of Joseph S. Murrow, Grand Master of Masons of the Indian Territory, who also was the Deputy of the Most Worthy Grand Patron of the Order of the Eastern Star, the first Chapter was organized at A-to-ka, Choctaw Nation, and chartered by the General Grand Chapter February 25, 1879, having for its first Matron,

---

[64] The history of the present Grand Chapter of Oklahoma necessarily includes that of the Grand Chapter of Indian Territory (organized July 11, 1889) and the Grand Chapter of Oklahoma Territory (organized February 14, 1902). The present Grand Chapter of the State of Oklahoma was organized April 27, 1915.

Mrs. C. Bond, and first Patron, Joseph S. Murrow. It was christened *O-ho-yo-hom-ma* (Red Woman's) No. 1. Thus, this noble Mason, in his efforts to be practical, to do good, to benefit mankind, assist the weak and to give them substantial cause to be thankful that there is such an institution as Masonry with its lessons of light shed through symbols, established an Order which has become an institution of permanent benefit throughout the Territory.

Antak-Homa Chapter No. 2, McAlester, Choctaw Nation, was chartered May 31, 1881, with Lalla R. Zimmerman, Worthy Matron, F. H. Doyle, Worthy Patron, and constituted June 14, 1881, by A. Frank Ross, Deputy of the Most Worthy Grand Patron.

Puc-caun-la Chapter No. 3, Colbert, Chickasaw Nation, was chartered by the General Grand Chapter February 9, 1882, and organized by Rev. J. S. Murrow, March 18, 1882, with Mrs. Morning T. Gooding, Worthy Matron, Henry F. Murray, Worthy Patron.

Savanna Chapter No. 4, Savanna, Choctaw Nation, was chartered February 22, 1886, and constituted by Rev. J. S. Murrow on March 11, 1886, with Agnes Cameron, Worthy Matron, and Emmett A. Berry, Worthy Patron.

Naomi Chapter No. 5, Prairie City, was chartered September 19, 1887.

The call for the convention to organize the Grand Chapter was issued by O-ho-yo-hom-ma Chapter No. 1. The convention met at Atoka, July 11, 1889, with representatives from six of the Chapters in the Territory. Allegiance to the General Grand Chapter was declared, the Grand Matron was made the executive officer, and dues were fixed at twenty-five cents. Mrs. Mary E. M'Clure was elected the first Grand Matron; John Lennie, Grand Patron; and Edmond H. Doyle, Grand Secretary.

By the Act of the United States Congress, Oklahoma Territory was set off from Indian Territory, following which the question of jurisdiction arose. This question remained in controversy until settled by the General Grand Chapter at its meeting at Columbus, Ohio, in 1892, at which time the following was adopted:

In the matter of jurisdiction over the territory of Oklahoma, we find that on July 11, 1889, a Grand Chapter was organized for the Indian Territory, which then embraced the geographical domain since set apart by the U. S. Government as the territory of Oklahoma.

Subsequent to the organization of said Grand Chapter this body formally recognized it and thereby surrendered to it all the government and control of the Order in said territory, and we find no law whereby this General Grand Chapter can regain government and control over the Order in that territory, or any portion thereof, unless it be voluntarily surrendered, or the Grand Chapter of Indian Territory ceases to exist; and, in our opinion, said Grand Chapter still has exclusive jurisdiction, and can exercise all the rights of sovereignty therein until, by arrangements mutually satisfactory to the Chapters in the two territories, it may surrender a portion thereof.

Any other action, it seems to us, would give rise to many complications, and bring controversies into the General Grand Chapter, instead of leaving the settlement of details where they properly belong and can be most satisfactorily adjusted with the Order in that jurisdiction.

· · · · · · · ·

We have no right, and certainly it is not expedient for us to assume it, to attempt to declare what portion of the Order in any given jurisdiction, that may be divided by the action of the civil government shall retain, and what portion shall surrender the rights they have in a grand body of which they are coordinate members. We, therefore, submit the following:

Resolved, That the Grand Chapter of Indian Territory is entitled to retain jurisdiction over the entire original geographical territory for which it was organized until, by its own action, it may surrender same, either to this General Grand Chapter or to a Grand Chapter that may be organized for the territory of Oklahoma.

Contributions to the amount of $56.50 toward an Orphans' Home were reported at the 1894 meeting. In 1896, the first business was to confer the degrees upon five candidates, with the purpose in view of organizing Chapters at their respective places of residence, they each residing where no Chapters existed; only two of the five succeeded in effecting organizations. One of the candidates, Brother Armstrong, was the newly elected Grand Master of Masons, also the last Chief of the Wyandotte, an honored and respected Mason; another was the Grand Commander of the Knights Templar.

In 1900 a petition was presented bearing the signatures of representatives of eleven Chapters in Oklahoma, asking that Chapters within that Territory be allowed to withdraw and organize a Grand Chapter, but a resolution granting the petition was laid upon the table. The following year a similar petition was granted, and separation effected in 1901.

The Grand Lodge of Masons, at their meeting in 1900, fully endorsed the Order of the Eastern Star, not as a part of Masonry, but as a powerful adjunct to Masonry in its great work, it being composed of Master Masons, their wives, widows, sisters, and daughters, and recommended the Order to all Masons.

A resolution to the same effect was presented to the Masonic Grand Lodge of Oklahoma and was most heartily endorsed by that body. In 1902 the Masonic Grand Lodge reported that the Masonic Orphans' Home fund had reached the $10,000 mark and solicited the cooperation of the Grand Chapter, O. E. S., in making a real home for helpless children.

The last session of the Grand Chapter of Indian Territory was opened on February 9, 1909, at South McAlester, after a successful career of twenty-one years. The Grand Matron and Grand Patron read addresses in which they each called attention to the solemn purpose of this final meeting; when this session ended, the Grand Chapter of the Order of the Eastern Star of Indian Territory ceased to be. Its work and its progress passed into history. By act of the United States Congress, Oklahoma and Indian Territories together became a State, and the object of this meeting was to merge the Order of the East and the Order of the West into one Grand Chapter. After the reports of the Grand Secretary and Grand Treasurer were read, the Grand Chapter closed and was dissolved the following day at Guthrie. The members, together with those of the Grand Lodge, were transported in Pullmans during the night, the Grand Lodge very generously having appropriated $700 toward the transportation of the Grand Chapter members to Guthrie where the Grand Chapter of the Indian Territory and the Grand Chapter of Oklahoma were to be merged. Upon arriving at Guthrie, the Grand Lodge, A. F. and A.M., which was in session at Guthrie, was at the station in a body to meet the Indian Territory Star members and acted as their escort to the Temple where the sessions were to be held. Rev. Joseph S. Murrow, who was the special Deputy who constituted the first Chapter, who was instrumental in effecting the organization of the Grand Chapter, was present and helped dissolve, as well as organize, the Grand Chapter.

The Grand Chapter of Indian Territory at its annual session held at Durant, August 15-16, 1901, released from its jurisdiction the constituent Chapters located in Oklahoma Territory, as the latter Territory desired to be organized into a separate jurisdiction. The General Grand Chapter then assumed jurisdiction and granted four dispensations to Chapters, viz: Watonga, located at Watonga, January 16, 1902; Billings Chapter, at Billings, January 16, 1902; Mizpah Chapter, Cheyenne; Lawton Chapter at Lawton, February 3, 1902. All the above Chapters were organized previous to the date of organizing the Grand Chapter, but charters were not issued, or numbers given these Chapters until the Grand Chapter of Oklahoma was organized February 14, 1902, the dispensations having been granted by the General Grand Chapter to meet the emergency existing.

This Grand Chapter was peculiarly honored at its birth, there being present many Stars of the first magnitude, the Most Worthy Grand Matron, Mrs. Laura B. Hart, acting as the Deputy of the Most Worthy Grand Patron, presiding. Sister Hart was assisted in the duties of organization by Right Worthy Associate Grand Matron, Mrs. Madaline B. Conkling; Right Worthy Associate Grand Patron, Dr. William F. Kuhn; and the Worthy Grand Marshal, Mrs. M. Alice Miller. All these distinguished officers delighted and instructed the membership of the new Grand Chapter by appropriate and eloquent addresses. There is nothing so eminently helpful to the success of a Grand Chapter as to have present at its organization distinguished and experienced members of the General Grand Chapter, who by their counsel, advice, and encouragement can inspire the members of the new body to greater devotion and to higher ideals.

The convention embraced twenty Chapters holding charters from the Grand Chapter of Indian Territory and the four organized by the General Grand Chapter after the surrender of Oklahoma Territory by the Grand Chapter of Indian Territory, making a total of twenty-four, with eighty-two votes.

The constitution adopted made all Past Matrons and Past Patrons members. All Grand Officers shall be sisters, except the Grand Patron, Associate Grand Patron, and Grand Chaplain, the Grand Matron being the executive officer. The annual dues were fixed at fifty cents, twenty-five cents of which are to be turned over to the Masonic Home fund. From the laws prepared for the government of subordinate Chapters the following is worthy of mention: "That any member who violates the secrecy of the ballot by stating how he or she voted on any question, or by endeavoring to ascertain how any member voted, or if he or she be aware and mention to any member, shall thereby render themselves liable to severe censure, and for a second offense, to expulsion from the Order."

In 1904 a donation was made to the Temple of Fraternity amounting to $64.55 and in 1905 $100 was given to the Masonic Home fund. The memorial service and floral work were frequently exemplified and rendered with solemnity and impressiveness.

The seventh annual session convened at Guthrie, February 11, 1909, with Sister Ella Simmons Washburn, Most Worthy Grand Matron; Sister M. Alice Miller, Right Worthy Associate Grand Matron; and Sister Lorraine J. Pitkin, Right Worthy Grand Secretary, as guests of honor; also all Past Grand Matrons were present as distinguished guests.

By a unanimous vote it was decided, "That upon adjournment of the Grand Chapter, Order of the Eastern Star of Oklahoma Territory tonight, that said adjournment should be without date, and the members of this Grand Chapter shall go immediately into convention with the members of the Grand Chapter, Order of the Eastern Star of Indian Territory for the purpose of forming the Grand Chapter Order of the Eastern Star of the State of Oklahoma."

After the Territories of Oklahoma and Indian Territory had attained statehood, the Grand Chapters of these jurisdictions agreed upon a plan of consolidation and called a convention of the representatives of those Grand Chapters to meet in Guthrie, Oklahoma, February 12, 1909, for the purpose of carrying into effect the proposed consolidation.

Mrs. Ella Simmons Washburn, Most Worthy Grand Matron, acting as Deputy of the Most Worthy Grand Patron, presided over the deliberations, assisted in the work by Mrs. M. Alice Miller, Right Worthy Associate Grand Matron. Mrs. Lorraine J. Pitkin, Right Worthy Grand Secretary, was appointed Secretary, with Mrs. Kitty Lee M'Clain, Past Grand Matron, assistant. The plan for the merging of the two Grand Chapters having been outlined and accepted, the two hundred Chapters represented proceeded with the necessary steps to complete organization, adopt measures for government, etc. The molding together of the hopes, the aims, the cherished plans for the future, the treasured history of the past, of two such strong and active Grand Chapters, was no light or frivolous undertaking, and this new Grand Chapter of Oklahoma appears as a great lighthouse built upon the rock of Freemasonry with their opportunities, aspirations, and future efforts merged into one magnificent body.

The Masonic Fraternity having purchased a tract of thirty-two acres of land, containing a number of buildings, at Atoka, with plans that it shall be the location of a Masonic College, the O.E.S. appropriated $1,000 for a library in connection.

This Grand Jurisdiction is justly proud that one of their number, Mrs. M. Alice Miller, was elected Most Worthy Grand Matron of the General Grand Chapter, and this great honor conferred has done much to inspire the workers to renewed efforts in the great work of the Order.

At the fifth annual session the Grand Chapter reported having under construction a chapel for the Masonic Home and at this session in 1913 the O.E.S. representative on the Masonic Home board reports the Home in a prosperous condition.

Mrs. M. Alice Miller accepted an invitation to address the assembly at the laying of the corner-stone of the Eastern Star Chapel, September 16, 1913, at the Masonic Home, Darlington, Oklahoma. This beautiful brick chapel, costing $10,000, built by the Grand Chapter, Eastern Star of Oklahoma, is another monument to the interest manifested in Masonic homes by our Order.

GRAND CHAPTER OF ONTARIO [65]

The seeds of charity, truth, and loving kindness were planted in Ontario during the administration of Sister Lorraine J. Pitkin as Most Worthy Grand Matron. The records of the General Grand Chapter held in San Francisco in 1883 show that Alexander Gardner, of Toronto, was appointed Deputy by Willis Brown, Most Worthy Grand Patron, and that he organized Chapters in Toronto, Stratford, London, Eden Grove, and Chatham.

The Grand Chapter of Ontario was organized May 3, 1882, with Alexander Gardner, Grand Patron; Mrs. Mary A. Robertson, Grand Matron; and W. J. R. Haywood, Grand Secretary. In June, 1882, it was reported to the Most Worthy Grand Matron of the General Grand Chapter that the Eastern Star in Canada had been organized under the direct supervision of the Grand Lodge of Ontario. The Rev. Willis D. Engle, Right Worthy Grand Secretary at that time, replied to the communication from the Most Worthy Grand Matron regarding the facts connected with the O.E.S. work in Ontario, that the Most Worthy Grand Patron and himself would settle it as "it was a fight for jurisdiction." At the following session of the General Grand Chapter, Sister Lorraine J. Pitkin, Most Worthy Grand Matron, reported as follows:

> As I understand the matter, the Grand Lodge of Canada is the only Grand Lodge recognized as a sovereign body by consistent Grand Lodges and consequently fully occupies the Province of Ontario, Canada, and if so, is the only authority under whose protection the Eastern Star can thrive in harmony and prosperity.

At a meeting of Stella Chapter No. 29, Brooklyn, New York, June 16, 1883, the Grand Matron of New York, Mrs. Kate E. Hopper, read a letter from Grand Patron Alexander Gardner, attested by the Grand

---

[65] Organized April 27, 1915.

Secretary, Miss Martha J. Fennel, requesting the installation of Mrs. Lillie Rowland, the newly elected Grand Matron of Ontario, as she was absent when the other officers were installed. As Sister Pitkin, Most Worthy Grand Matron, was present at Stella Chapter on that occasion, she installed Mrs. Lillie Rowland, with Mrs. Eleanor Burton as Grand Marshal.

At the San Francisco meeting, Miss Mary Engle was given a seat in the General Grand Chapter, she having been reported by the credentials committee as representing the Grand Chapter of Ontario as proxy for the Grand Patron.

The Grand Chapter of Ontario not having been organized under the Masonic influence to insure its permanence, became dormant and two sessions is all that is recorded.[66]

There were no more Chapters organized in any of the Canadian Provinces until June 8, 1899, when Alpha Chapter was chartered in Rossland, British Columbia, by Nathaniel A. Gearhart, Most Worthy Grand Patron.

The growth of the Eastern Star in all the Canadian territory during the administration of William H. Norris, Most Worthy Grand Patron, 1907-1910, was phenomenal and resulted in extending the Order into the provinces of New Brunswick, Quebec, Ontario, Saskatchewan, and Alberta.

Victoria Chapter No. 1 was organized at Windsor, Ontario, on June 1, 1910; Blackburn Chapter No. 2, Sombra, March 25, 1909; Maple Leaf Chapter No. 3, St. Thomas, May 27, 1909; Windsor Chapter No. 4, Windsor, June 31, 1910; Florence Nightingale Chapter No. 5, Brockville, June 6, 1910; Sarnia Chapter No. 6, Sarnia, chartered February 12, 1913; Queen City Chapter No. 7, Toronto, chartered May 31, 1913; Bethel Chapter No. 8, Walkerville, chartered July 11, 1913; Connaught Chapter No. 9, Fort Williams, chartered July 11, 1913; Argyle Chapter No. 10, Port Arthur, organized September 12, 1913, by

---

[66] See General Grand Chapter Proceedings, Fourth Session, 1883.

the Rev. Willis D. Engle, Most Worthy Grand Patron, but charter was not granted until the next term, January 3, 1914, to twenty-nine charter members.

Harmony Chapter No. 11, Toronto, was organized January 14, 1914, by Mrs. Lorraine J. Pitkin, Right Worthy Grand Secretary, with sixty-four charter members. Charter was granted April 18, 1914.

Corinthian Chapter No. 12, Toronto, was organized January 15, 1914, by Mrs. Lorraine J. Pitkin, Right Worthy Grand Secretary, with seventy-five members. Charter granted April 18, 1914.

Forest City Chapter No. 13, London, was organized January 17, 1914, by Mrs. Lorraine J. Pitkin, Right Worthy Grand Secretary, with twenty-six charter members. Charter granted April 16, 1914.

Alexandria Chapter No. 14, Windsor, was organized May 29, 1914, by Manly B. Squire, Deputy of the Most Worthy Grand Patron, with forty-seven charter members and charter was granted July 6, 1914.

Areme Chapter No. 15, Vienna, was organized August 19, 1914, by C. L. Cottingham, of St. Thomas, Ontario, with twenty-two charter members. Charter was granted August 29, 1914.

The Most Worthy Grand Patron, Dr. George A. Pettigrew, called the convention to organize the Grand Chapter of Ontario, on April 27, 1915. The organization of the present Grand Chapter of Ontario is not a revival of the old one nor in any way connected with the former Eastern Star organizations in Ontario. On April 27, 1915, representatives from all of the fifteen Chapters in Ontario, met in the city of St. Thomas. The organization of a new Grand Chapter while always interesting and hopeful, in this particular case was an unusually noteworthy occasion because of the fact that it was the first time in the history of the General Grand Chapter that the Most Worthy Grand Matron, the Most Worthy Grand Patron, and the Right Worthy Grand Secretary were all able to participate in its ceremonies. Dr. George A. Pettigrew, Most Worthy Grand Patron, of Sioux Falls, South Dakota, presided, and was ably assisted by Mrs. Rata A. Mills,

Most Worthy Grand Matron, of Bradford, Pennsylvania, and Mrs. Lorraine J. Pitkin, Right Worthy Grand Secretary, of Chicago, who acted as secretary.

Every Chapter of the fifteen in Ontario was represented, with a total of eighty-three votes and the delegates held an enthusiastic meeting which was most gratifying to the officers in attendance.

Grand Chapter of Oregon [67]

An effort was made to introduce the Order in Oregon as early as 1870 when Robert Macoy chartered a Chapter at Oregon City. Later, three others were chartered by him, none of the four remaining active, and the present status of the Order in that State is based upon the work of the General Grand Chapter.

Alpha Chapter No. 1, located at Ashland, was chartered February 24, 1880, by the Most Worthy Grand Patron of the General Grand Chapter and organized by William S. Moses, special Deputy of the Most Worthy Grand Patron.

Eugene City Chapter No. 2, located at Eugene City, was chartered April 13, 1880, by the General Grand Chapter and organized by F. W. Osburn, special Deputy of the Most Worthy Grand Patron.

Adarel Chapter No. 3, Jacksonville, was chartered May 27, 1880, and organized by W. H. Atkinson, special Deputy of the Most Worthy Grand Patron, assisted by members of Alpha Chapter No. 1, of Ashland.

Cottage Grove Chapter No. 4, Cottage Grove, was chartered June 26, 1880, and organized by F. W. Osburn, special Deputy of the Most Worthy Grand Patron, assisted by members of Eugene City Chapter No. 2.

---

[67] Organized October 3, 1889.

Oriental Chapter No. 5, located at Lakeview, was chartered April 19, 1883, by the General Grand Chapter and organized June 2, 1883, by J. Frankl, special Deputy of the Most Worthy Grand Patron.

Beulah Chapter No. 6, at Coquelle City, was chartered June 2, 1883, and organized by Charles Olive, special Deputy of the Most Worthy Grand Patron.

Independence Chapter No. 7, Independence, was chartered July 27, 1885, and organized by the Rev. Robert W. Hill, special Deputy of the Most Worthy Grand Patron.

Roseburg Chapter No. 8, located at Roseburg, was chartered December 10, 1885, and organized January 27, 1886, by T. G. Reamer, special Deputy of the Most Worthy Grand Patron.

St. Mary's Chapter No. 9, Corvallis, was chartered by the General Grand Chapter May 18, 1886, and organized by W. P. Conaway, special Deputy of the Most Worthy Grand Patron.

Forest Grove Chapter No. 10, located at Forest Grove, was chartered by the General Grand Chapter January 24, 1887. Esther Chapter No. 11, located at Baker City, was chartered June 1, 1888.

Six of the eleven Chapters organized in the State were represented at the convention called by the General Grand Chapter at the request of Roseburg Chapter No. 8, which met at Roseburg, October 3, 1889. With the necessary changes, the constitution of the Grand Chapter of California was adopted, making all Past Matrons and Past Patrons members of the Grand Chapter and providing further that in the event that any of the three principal officers of a Chapter could not attend the Grand Chapter meeting, the Chapter could elect representatives to act in the premises. The Grand Patron was made the executive officer, but in 1891 a resolution was adopted making the Grand Matron the executive officer, and she has retained this position since that date. Petitions for dispensation are signed by both the Grand Patron and Grand Matron. By invitation, the installation ceremonies were witnessed by the members of the Blue Lodge, A. F. and A. M. in 1891. Charters granted by the General Grand Chapter were replaced without charge. In 1893 a resolution was adopted, "That officers regularly elected and installed be not allowed to resign."

The most cordial relations exist between the Masonic Fraternity and the Order of the Eastern Star and in 1892 a letter was adopted and presented to the Grand Lodge in which it was stated that "We come to you as your mothers, wives, daughters, widows, sisters, sons, and brothers would come to you, and ask that we be allowed to assist you in carrying forward the grand work."

To this greeting the Grand Lodge replied, "The Grand Lodge will be glad of your cooperation in the fraternal and charitable work of the Masonic Order, and when the members of this Grand Lodge go back to their several homes, they will endeavor to do all in their power toward furthering the interests of the Order of the Eastern Star among Masons and their families."

Similar greetings were exchanged in 1896 and the same year it was unanimously adopted "That we adopt the custom of standing whenever our National Air 'The Star Spangled Banner' is sung on public occasions, and that the National Flag be displayed in the Grand Chapter Room at each annual communication." The practice of veiling the candidate was discontinued in 1896 by recommendation of the Grand Patron.

In memory of their Past Grand Matron, Mrs. Julia Abraham, a Grand Chapter of Sorrow was held in Portland November 7, 1897, and each Chapter that had been called upon to mourn the loss of a member responded with flowers and brief remarks as the roll call designated their loved ones gone. Annually since that time, the Grand Chapter has conducted a similar ceremony, it having been adopted as the form to be used by the members of the Order when assembled as a Chapter of Sorrow, and the uniform code of by-laws provides for its use after the death of any member.

In 1898 the meeting was held in Commandery Hall, Masonic Temple, Portland, at which time the Worthy Matrons from the several Chapters of the city, dressed in the emblematic colors of the

Order, laden with appropriate flowers, approached the East and welcomed the Grand Chapter with touching and eloquent remarks, afterwards presenting the flowers to the Grand Matron.

Annually since the initial exchange of greetings in 1892, the exchange of courtesies between the Grand Chapter, O. E. S., and the Grand Lodge, A. F. and A.M., have been extended, their meetings being held at the same time and place, each body appointing a committee to convey messages of good will to the other, the committee from the Grand Chapter usually having in its membership at least one lady. Cooperation of the two Grand bodies in accumulating funds for charitable work has been maintained through many years of earnest effort. The result of their efforts is given in the report of the board of trustees of the O.E.S. Home Fund in 1909:

> It is very satisfactory to report that at the communication of the Grand Lodge A. F. and A.M., held this year, the report of its special committee on Masonic Home appointed in 1908, was adopted, and which report finds that the sentiment of the Masons of Oregon is that it would be well to establish a Masonic Home for the old and helpless Masons, the widows and orphan children, and recommends the appointment of a committee to receive donations and subscriptions for the purpose of the institution of a Masonic Home, and to request of the Masonic Lodges of the State, information and offers of what they consider as suitable sites for location of such a Home.

In 1898 the Grand Chapter elected five trustees to promote the work of establishing a Masonic Home and appropriated $300 to the fund. Their offer of assistance was cordially accepted by the Masonic Lodge and in 1899 the subordinate Chapters contributed $133 and the Grand Chapter appropriated $100. The object of their ambitions is now almost at hand when they may commence the actual work of building.

The charitable work of the Order has been carefully and conscientiously developed. Donations have been generous and frequent: $351.75 was given to the Galveston flood sufferers; $820.10 to the San Francisco fire sufferers; $211.55 appropriated for the Temple of Fraternity at St. Louis; $500 appropriated toward maintaining O.E.S. headquarters at the Lewis and Clark Exposition, Portland; and $3,000 worth of stock was purchased by the Grand Chapter, O. E. S., in the Portland Masonic Temple. In response to an appeal by the Grand Matron, the subordinate Chapters contributed $1,360 for the relief of members of three Chapters who were sufferers from a disastrous fire, many of the sisters and brothers having been left homeless and some were destitute. They seem to have lived in such a manner that they have protected the widow and orphan, sympathized with the sorrowing, aided the unfortunate, and their ideals are based upon a constant effort to attain the height of their privileges in the Order.

GRAND CHAPTER OF PENNSYLVANIA [68]

Brother Rob Morris, though he was by no means the first to write a manual giving the wives, daughters, mothers, sisters, and widows of Master Masons the benefit of an association which would guarantee them the protection and support of all good Masons, was, nevertheless, the true founder of the Order of the Eastern Star, and the glory of the grand achievement, through ages to come, will be his alone. It will be seen that all the chapters in the State of Pennsylvania were organized under the General Grand Chapter, using the General Grand Chapter *Ritual*.

It was at the beginning of the year 1888 that the Order was introduced into this State. On February 3d, of that year, Wyoming Chapter No. 1, located at Pittston, was granted a charter by Jefferson S. Conover, Most Worthy Grand Patron. The petition bore the names

---

[68] By Mrs. Rata A. Mills, M.W.G.M.

of fifty-nine petitioners. Mrs. Annette Gorman, Worthy Matron, Samuel A. Fear, Worthy Patron, were the first officers. The Reverend Daniel W. Coxe, a Past Grand Patron of another jurisdiction, acted as Deputy and constituted the Chapter.

Keystone Chapter No. 2, located at Duke Center, was granted a charter containing thirty-five names, by Jefferson S. Conover, Most Worthy Grand Patron of the General Grand Chapter, John V. Brown, Duke Center, being deputized to conduct the constituting ceremony. Mrs. Rebecca Brown, Worthy Matron, Phineas L. Golden, Worthy Patron, were its first officers.

Martha Washington Chapter No. 3, located in Scranton, with a petition bearing eighty-three names was granted a charter by Benjamin Lynds, Most Worthy Grand Patron of the General Grand Chapter, on March 10, 1892, Samuel Fear of Pittston being deputized to constitute the Chapter, with Mrs. Genevieve Fellows, Worthy Matron, and Frank J. Powell, Worthy Patron.

Under date of October 26, 1892, St. John's Chapter No. 4, located at Philadelphia, was granted a charter containing seventy-nine names, by James R. Donnell, Most Worthy Grand Patron of the General Grand Chapter, deputizing John C. Becker of Baltimore, Maryland, to constitute the Chapter, with Mrs. Kate M. Dierkes, Worthy Matron, George W. Crouch, Worthy Patron.

Canawacta Chapter No. 5, located at Susquehanna, with thirty-nine charter members, was granted a charter by James R Donnell, Most Worthy Grand Patron, General Grand Chapter, who deputized Orin T. Smith to constitute the Chapter. Mrs. Adell Outwater, Worthy Matron, George W. Gleason, Worthy Patron.

The five chapters located in the State of Pennsylvania and subordinate to the General Grand Chapter, being desirous of forming a Grand Chapter for the State of Pennsylvania, petitioned the General Grand Chapter for that purpose, and under date of November 1, 1894, the Most Worthy Grand Patron, Brother James R. Donnell, issued a call for a meeting to be held in the city of Scranton, on Wednesday,

November 21, 1894, for the purpose of organizing the Grand Chapter of Pennsylvania, Order of the Eastern Star. At this time there were 441 members in the State.

In the absence of representatives from the necessary number of Chapters (there being but three Chapters represented) requisite to form a Grand Chapter, the meeting adjourned until Thursday, November 22, 1894, at which time, in a Masonic Hall, at Scranton, the Most Worthy Grand Matron, Sister Mary C. Snedden, being present and presiding, the five regularly constituted chapters being represented by their proper officers or duly constituted proxies and in accordance With the wishes and instructions of the members of the several Chapters, proceeded to organize the Grand Chapter of Pennsylvania and to adopt a constitution and general regulations. The committee appointed on framing a constitution was as follows: Brother B. Holmes, No. 3; Sister Rata A. Mills, No. 2; Brother George W. Gleason, No. 5; Sister Sarah J. Wintersteen, No. 1; Philip C. Shaffer, No. 4.

The election of the first board of Grand Officers resulted in the following choice: Sister Annette Gorman, No. 1, Worthy Grand Matron; Brother Philip C. Shaffer, No. 4, Worthy Grand Patron; Sister Rata A. Mills, No. 2, Worthy Associate Grand Matron; Brother Andrew B. Holmes, No. 3, Worthy Associate Grand Patron; Brother George W. Gleason, Grand Secretary; Sister Elvira A. Fear, Grand Treasurer.

The Order had no easy task in its efforts to exist and prosper in the Keystone State. Philadelphia, it is claimed, was the first resting place on this continent of the great Brotherhood of Freemasonry, and what more appropriate place could have been chosen to celebrate the first anniversary of the Grand Chapter. A prerequisite for membership requires that the Order be indissolubly connected with the magnificent and ancient Fraternity of Freemasonry, the while the Fraternity in this jurisdiction was not only hostile, but threatened its very existence. It required all the fortitude and patience portrayed in the life of Electa to survive the frowns and aspersions that were cast upon the Order. The pioneers in the work had obstacles to overcome that are not comprehended by those who enter the cultivated fields. To secure successful results to a purpose so important and laudable it was necessary that the members of the Order should apply its rules in a rigid sense; carefully maintain its landmarks; affiliate into its sacred bonds only those who were well calculated by temperament and principle to understand and appreciate its exalted teachings; to preserve the beauty and dignity of the Ritual and to work out patiently and untiringly its commendable designs. They were determined to do their full share in attaining desirable results.

Two years slipped away after the organization of the Grand Chapter before another subordinate chapter was constituted. In the city of Pittsburgh, on October 23, 1896, Guyasuta Chapter No. 6 was constituted by Brother Andrew B. Holmes, Worthy Grand Patron, and Sister Rata A. Mills, Worthy Grand Matron, this being the first Chapter organized under the jurisdiction of the Grand Chapter of Pennsylvania. In this same year the original charters were cancelled and the five Chapters were granted charters by the Grand Chapter of Pennsylvania. From this time on the Order continued to grow and prosper until in 1914 there were 175 Chapters with a membership of 20,000.

Looking toward the fulfillment of the tenets of our Order — charity and loving kindness — a noble effort is being put forth to raise funds for the purpose of erecting a Home. The Grand Chapter has a Home Fund and the O.E.S. Home Association has accumulated $5,000, being a nucleus with which to begin the establishment of an Eastern Star Home.

In looking back over the records which have to do with the work of the Order since 1888 one is brought face to face with the fact that the Order in Pennsylvania has marched through the wilderness of privation and sacrifice, yet it has been so skillfully managed and so nobly supported that success and progress has marked its history. It is well for an Order to have a struggle. The Order that knows no struggle knows no strength. There is more honor in leading a struggling enterprise on to success than there is in winning a victory with mighty forces. The story of the work of twenty years has been merely hinted at, but to the man of vision the light lies on the farther hills and by the favor of God this Eastern Star has her face set toward the sunrising.

A tribute to the retiring president of the O.E.S. Home Association of Pennsylvania, Mrs. Emma C. Robinson, by Mrs. Margaret K. Griffith:

> Today we dream of an earthly "Home"
>   For those who are dear to us all,
> An Eastern Star Home, a house built with hands,
>   Where those in misfortune may call.
> We long for the day when our hopes we attain
>   And our service of love be complete,
> With songs of rejoicing and loving acclaim,
>   We lay our gift at the Saviour's feet
>
> Today we dream of a Heavenly Land,
>   Where the weary of earth may find rest.
> Of a mansion so fair, not built with hands,
>   A "Home" with the redeemed and blest;
> Where we shall walk with Him in white,
>   And the King in His beauty shall see.
> No more pain; no more tears; but where all is bright,
>   And the Lamb is the light thereof.
>
> So, today, may we like the Shepherds of old
>   And the Wise Men who traveled afar,
> When we all reach the Home, we the face will behold,
>   Of our beautiful "Eastern Star."

> When with loved ones we will meet
> And in the Chapter above shall greet,
> "For we have seen His Star in the East
> And have come to worship Him."

GRAND CHAPTER OF PUERTO RICO [69]

The first Chapter of the Order of the Eastern Star in Puerto Rico was Juanita Chapter No. 1, located at San Juan, organized December 30, 1913, by Dr. W. Fontaine Lippitt, Grand Master of the A. F. and A. M. Grand Lodge of Puerto Rico and Deputy of the Most Worthy Grand Patron, Dr. George A. Pettigrew. There were thirty-four charter members to whom charter was issued on January 20, 1914.

Dr. George A. Pettigrew, Most Worthy Grand Patron, made a personal visit to this beautiful island in the interests of the Order and during his stay there organized four subordinate Chapters previous to the organization of the Grand Chapter, as follows: Aurora del Porvenir Chapter No. 2, Mayaguez, organized February 10, 1914; with thirty-two petitioners; Esperanza Chapter No. 3, located at San German, organized February 11, 1914, with twenty-two petitioners; Electa Chapter No. 4, located at Yauco, organized February 12, 1914, with fifteen petitioners; Caridad Chapter No. 5, located at San Juan, organized February 17, 1914, with nineteen petitioners. The charters for these Chapters were issued just previous to the organization of the Grand Chapter of Puerto Rico.

The convention to organize the Grand Chapter was called by Dr. Geo. A. Pettigrew, Most Worthy Grand Patron, met at San Juan February 17, 1914, and was presided over by Dr. Pettigrew. It was attended by a large number of the important personalities of the island, and the Grand Chapter was organized with great faith and enthusiasm. The meetings were attended by very distinguished

---

[69] Organized February 17, 1914.

ladies and great interest was taken in the study and practice of the duties of the Order in their efforts to spread the benefits of the beautiful organization.[70] The officers of the Grand Chapter elected were: Mrs. Ana M. Degetau, Grand Matron; Dr. W. Fontaine Lippitt, Grand Patron; Mrs. Maria Skerret de Gutierrez, Grand Secretary.

The selection of Sister Ana M. de Degetau as Worthy Grand Matron placed the Order under the direction of one who discharged the duties with devotion to the principles of the Order she had agreed to support. Her high ideals of purity, nobility of purpose, love for mankind, and devotion to right and duty, spread a halo of reverence wherever the light of the Star shone in this infant Grand Jurisdiction.

The Most Worthy Grand Patron caused a translation of the *Ritual of the General Grand Chapter* to be published in the Spanish

---

[70] The proclamation was issued as follows:

OFFICE OF Tat MOST WORTHY GRAND PATRON,
Sioux Falls, South Dakota, March 10, 1914.

To all Members of the order of the Eastern Star, GREETING:

Whereas, Representatives of the five Chapters of the Eastern Star in Porto Rico being convened upon the call of the Most Worthy Grand Patron, and presided over by him, in the City of San Juan, on the 17th day of February, A. D. 1914, did adopt a constitution for the government of the Order in said Puerto Rico, and thereunder selected a full corps of officers who were duly installed; and the proceedings of said representatives appearing to be in accord with the Constitution of the General Grand Chapter;

Now, therefore, we do make PROCLAMATION:

That the Grand Chapter of Puerto Rico, thus organized, is recognized as a constituent part of the General Grand Chapter, having exclusive jurisdiction over the Order of the Eastern Star in Porto Rico, subject only and always to the Constitution of the General Grand Chapter of the Order of the Eastern Star.

In testimony whereof we have hereunto set our hands and caused these presents to be attested by the Seal of the General Grand Chapter of the Order of the Eastern Star the day and year first above written.

GEORGE A. PETTIGREW,
Most Worthy Grand Patron.
RATA A. MILLS,
Most Worthy Grand Matron.

Attest: LORRAINE J. PITKIN,
Right Worthy Grand Secretary.

language for the use of the Spanish speaking Chapters in Puerto Rico and in other territory where same may be preferred.

> God lays a little on us every day;
> And never, I believe, on all the way
> Will burdens bear so deep,
> Or pathways lie so threatening and so steep,
> But we can go, if by God's power,
> We only bear the burden of the hour.

GRAND CHAPTER OF RHODE ISLAND [71]

Responding to the call of eighty-three petitioners, Providence Chapter No. 1, located at Providence, was chartered by the General Grand Chapter December 3, 1890, and organized by Frank E. Shaw of Boston, Massachusetts, Deputy of the Most Worthy Grand Patron, with S. Penrose Williams, Worthy Patron; Mrs. Emogene Williams, Worthy Matron; and Mrs. Hattie E. Davis, Associate Matron.

Brother S. Penrose Williams, Deputy of the Most Worthy Grand Patron for Rhode Island, organized Chapters that were chartered as follows: Queen Esther Chapter No. 2, at Central Falls, chartered February 2, 1893, with 105 charter members; Woonsocket Chapter No. 3, at Woonsocket, with 102 charter members, chartered December 28, 1894; Hope Chapter No. 4, located at Hope Valley, chartered February 14, 1895, with sixty-three members and Ruth Chapter No. 5, Riverpoint, chartered April 6, 1895, with seventy-nine members.

The Most Worthy Grand Patron of the General Grand Chapter issued the call for the convention to organize the Grand Chapter, which met in Providence August 22, 1895, all five Chapters in the State being represented. Mrs. Mary C. Snedden, Most Worthy Grand Matron, presided, and there were present a number of distinguished

---

[71] Organized August 22, 1895.

guests who were enroute to Boston to attend the meeting of the General Grand Chapter. The usual constitution was adopted, making Past Matrons and Past Patrons members of the Grand Chapter. The Grand Matron was made the executive officer, representatives of a majority of the Chapters, or a majority of the members of the Grand Chapter was declared to constitute a quorum, and per capita dues were fixed at twenty-five cents. In 1897 the "Test Oath" was adopted and in 1898 a form for opening and closing the Grand Chapter, for official visitations and for constituting new Chapters; an amendment also adopted permitting a collective ballot, with provisions for separate ballot if negative votes appear. This was rescinded in 1905. Duplicate charters are permitted, that the original may be kept in a place secure against its loss by fire; the charter of a Chapter cannot be surrendered as long as three members desire to retain it. In 1910 the number of *Rituals* were limited to five in any one Chapter, and they must remain the property of the Chapter.

The Grand Chapter appropriated $25 for the relief of the Galveston flood sufferers and the subordinate Chapters added to this amount a sufficient sum to make the total $103; $11 was donated to assist in maintaining O.E.S. headquarters at the Portland Exposition.

This Grand Chapter was organized with only five Chapters in the State and the number has increased until in 1913 twelve Chapters had been organized. Owing to the short distances necessary to travel, it has become an established custom for the Grand Matron, assisted by the Grand Patron and Grand Marshal, to preside at each election in the subordinate Chapters and to install their officers. This jurisdiction has had a committee on appeals and grievances, but the committee has never found any work to be done, as fraternal harmony has existed continuously during its activities.

> How little it costs if we give it a thought,
> To make some heart happy each day;
> Just a kind word or a tender smile,
> As we go on our daily way.

Grand Chapter of Saskatchewan

Mizpah Chapter No. 1 was organized at Moosejaw, Province of Saskatchewan, on August 4, 1909, and charter was granted by the General Grand Chapter on August 12, 1909, with forty-one members at time of organization.

North Battleford Chapter No. 2 was organized at North Battleford by the Rev. Willis D. Engle, Most Worthy Grand Patron, on July 16, 1912, and charter granted by the General Grand Chapter on October 9, 1912, with fourteen charter members at date of organization and twenty-three at the time the charter was granted.

Saskatoon Chapter No. 4, located at Saskatoon, was organized March 4, 1914, by John L. Gessell, Deputy of the Most Worthy Grand Patron, with thirty-seven charter members. The Charter was granted by the General Grand Chapter March 27, 1914.

Humboldt Chapter No. 5, located at Humboldt, was organized April 27, 1914, by Brother John L. Gessell, of Saskatoon, Deputy of the Most Worthy Grand Patron, with thirty charter members. Charter was granted by the General Grand Chapter May 12, 1914.

Maple Leaf Chapter No. 6, located at Semans, was organized February 18, 1915, by Brother John L. Gessell of Hanley, with fourteen charter members, and chartered by the General Grand Chapter March 29, 1915.

Eight Chapters had been organized previous to the call issued by Dr. George A. Pettigrew, Most Worthy Grand Patron, to organize the Grand Chapter. Delegates were present from Mizpah Chapter No. 1, Acacia Chapter No. 3, Saskatoon Chapter No. 4, Maple Leaf Chapter No. 6, Regina Chapter No. 7, and Assiniboia Chapter No. 8. North Battleford Chapter No. 2 and Humboldt Chapter No. 5 were unable to send representatives, but were included in the organization.

The convention to organize met at Saskatoon, May 16, 1916, with Dr. George A. Pettigrew, Most Worthy Grand Patron presiding, assisted by Mrs. Emma C. Ocobock, acting Most Worthy Grand

Matron. Mrs. Flora Trick was elected Worthy Grand Matron and Norman J. Bellamy, Worthy Grand Patron.

Grand Chapter of Scotland [72]

Previous to the organization of the General Grand Chapter, the Order of the Eastern Star was introduced in Scotland by Brother Robert Macoy when he issued a charter for Victoria Chapter No. 1, located at Glasgow, on September 30, 1874, and later chartered three others, only Victoria Chapter No. 1 maintaining a continued existence.

The organization in Scotland of Chapters of the Order of the Eastern Star, represents the facing of the conservatism which characterizes all Masonic action in the countries under the jurisdiction of the Grand Lodge of England. They view with alarm any attempt at innovation to a remarkable degree. That the O.E.S. could so commend itself to Scottish Masons that they are willing to welcome it in connection with their Masonic work is driving a wedge that must eventually appeal to their best judgment.

"Masonry of Adoption," the general name in the old country for that branch of Masonry to which women were admitted, was a different institution, with different aims and objects from those of the Order of the Eastern Star, and accounts of their workings would indicate that, at times, their privileges were not well improved and the craft did not receive a great amount of credit by reason of the "Lodges of Adoption." The O.E.S. is of a different character, and its objects must appeal to all who are imbued with the true principles of Craft Masonry; the charitable and kindly tendencies of English, Irish, and Scotch Masonry would readily recognize the laudable objects of our Order.

---

[72] Organized August 20, 1904.

John Crombie was at one time an active Mason and held the office of Grand Warder of the Grand Lodge. He published a Blue Lodge *Ritual*, which he was directed to recall, but refused to do so. This refusal was deemed a just cause for the action taken by the Grand Lodge when orders were issued for his suspension from the Fraternity. Following this, Mr. Crombie published rituals for other rites, including the Eastern Star, and assuming the right to do so, under the authority and title of the Supreme Council of Rites, issued charters for Chapters, first in Aberdeen and later at other points, but only one at Aberdeen is known to have remained active.

The officers of the General Grand Chapter issued a charter for Dundee Chapter No. 1, located at Dundee, on May 28, 1901, with twenty-four charter members. Organization was completed by Alonzo J. Burton, of New York City, Deputy of the Most Worthy Grand Patron.

Immediately upon learning that the General Grand Chapter had exercised its right to organize Chapters, officers of Victoria Chapter, which used the *Macoy Ritual*, made an effort to revive the other three Chapters, then dormant, that had been chartered by Macoy and had used the *Macoy Ritual*. In this they were successful with two, and on January 24, 1903, representatives of the three Chapters met in a convention and organized a governing body which they named the "Supreme Grand Chapter of the Order of the Eastern Star of Scotland," requesting recognition from the Grand Chapters in this country.

Although this body was not recognized by the officers of the General Grand Chapter, and not being conversant with the fact that only three Chapters were included in the organization and also that the General Grand Chapter claimed jurisdiction in Scotland and deemed the organization irregular, some of the Grand Chapters, acting through their Grand Matrons, recognized it by appointing Grand Representatives near the same; and the Grand Chapter of California, by resolution, recognized the Grand Chapter of Scotland, but many of them withdrew the recognition when advised of the facts in the case.

On December 1, 1902, the General Grand Chapter issued a dispensation for a Chapter at Glasgow, Scotland, and Fidelity Chapter No. 2 was given its charter on February 7, 1903, with fourteen charter members; organized by John Healy Fash, Deputy of the Most Worthy Grand Patron.

Alexandra Chapter No. 3, located at Glasgow, received a dispensation from the officers of the General Grand Chapter on December 18, 1903; was organized January 15, 1904, by Matthew Richmond, Deputy of the Most Worthy Grand Patron, with sixteen members, and chartered March 10, 1904.

Pollok Chapter No. 4, located at Pollokshaw, was granted a dispensation on March 22, 1904, and organized by Matthew Richmond, Deputy of the Most Worthy Grand Patron, with twenty-four charter members, the charter having been granted on August 15, 1904.

Laura Chapter No. 5, located at Glasgow, was organized August 20, 1904, by the Most Worthy Grand Matron, Mrs. Laura B. Hart, acting as the Deputy of the Most Worthy Grand Patron.

With five regularly chartered and active Chapters, working by authority of charters granted by the General Grand Chapter and using the *Ritual* issued by that body, the time had arrived when it was deemed expedient to organize the Grand governing body. The situation was complicated by the conditions existing in that country, with three divisions of the Order. In order to take such steps as might be for the best interests of the Order and harmonize the forces the General Grand Chapter, by its principal officers, placed the matter in the hands of the Most Worthy Grand Matron, Sister Laura B. Hart, who, exercising all the authority vested in her by the constitution of the General Grand Chapter and as the Deputy of the Most Worthy Grand Patron, clothed with his authority also, assembled representatives of all the Chapters and organized the Grand Chapter of Scotland on August 20, 1904. A concordat was entered into with the representatives of all three factions whereby they are to use the *Ritual* as established by the General Grand Chapter, and they are to have jurisdiction over the British Empire, excepting such portions as are on the continent of America, with the privilege of organizing a Supreme Grand Chapter as soon as a sufficient number of Grand Chapters are organized in the territory to make it expedient to do so.[73]

Though the constitution adopted differs some from that usually adopted in the States, the same spirit and earnestness of effort for the advancement of the Order prevails. Following the opening of the Grand Chapter, the Grand Matron invites the Grand Patron to preside, which has been done regularly. The grand committee, consisting of all grand office bearers, hold meetings previous to the annual meeting of the Grand Chapter, at which time questions to be brought before the Supreme Grand Chapter are discussed, grand office bearers for the ensuing year are selected, and upon the recommendation to the Supreme Grand Officer, were appointed, following the laws of the Grand Lodge of England.

In 1910 it was decided that the Grand Chapter of Scotland should meet twice each year, and special dispensations were granted to two prominent Freemasons in the Transvaal and New Zealand respectively, to confer the degrees and establish the Order in those countries; petition blanks were ordered to have the following appended: "The Order of the Eastern Star is purely a Christian Order, and this matter should be pointed out to applicants for admission."

In 1912 a lengthy discussion as to whether the star should have one point upward or two points upward resulted in the new Constitution establishing that the star shall have two points upward. Three negative votes are necessary to reject a petitioner. In 1908 an organization termed "Lady Freemasons" was declared a clandestine body and recognition denied members of the so-called 'Women Freemasons."

---

[73] See Concordat with Scotland elsewhere in this volume, pp. 129-131.

At the annual meeting of the Grand Chapter of Scotland, held in Glasgow, March 21, 1914, the following motion by Brother A. F. Mennie, Worthy Patron, was carried unanimously:

That Grand Secretary be instructed to communicate with (a) each chapter of the order in the British Dominions, (b) the General Grand Chapter which exercises jurisdiction over America and elsewhere, and (c) each grand chapter in the United States of America, and inform them that a number of persons styling themselves "Thistle Chapter" or "Aberdeen Chapter, No. 1, Eastern Start and who meet as a chapter in Aberdeen, Scotland, are not recognized by the Supreme Grand Chapter of Scotland, and point out to the member of chapters under the Supreme Grand Chapter of Scotland that, in countenancing in any way the said chapter in Aberdeen, they are liable, not only to expulsion from the order, but to have their names erased from the books of their chapter and from the roll of the Supreme Grand Chapter; inform all the above chapters that the only regular chapter of the O.E.S. in Aberdeen is "Alexandria" Chapter, No. 5, under the Supreme Grand Chapter of Scotland; and respectfully request each of the aforesaid chapters (General Grand, Grand, and subordinate) to engross this communication in their minutes.

It has been ascertained that among members of this illicit body, known as "Thistle Chapter," are a number of renegade members of the Order of the Eastern Star. This illicit body have a ritual of their own in use, but, in addition, they are making an incorrect use of the ritual of the Order of the Eastern Star. They are in possession of all the necessary information for testing members to the Eastern Star, and admit members to their body who are not in any way related to Master Masons.

It has been stated that the members of this illicit body intend to visit the subordinate chapters of the Supreme Grand Chapter of Scotland, especially those situated in Glasgow, and I have been instructed to request that the chapters exercise the greatest care in admitting visitors to the chapter room, especially before opening, and to require from visitors from Aberdeen production of documentary evidence of a satisfactory character.

I have further to request that the subordinate chapters report to me without delay any applications for admission by "Thistle Chapter" members, and that this circular be read in open chapter, and engrossed in the minutes, all with the view of giving the matter the greatest publicity.

The Grand Chapter is maintained by a graded per capita tax, according to the rank of its members; the dues of the Grand Matron and Grand Patron are £1 1s; each Associate Grand Matron and Associate Grand Patron 10s; and for members of the Grand Chapter 2s each.

> Then let us pray that come it may,
> As come it will for a' that,
> That man to man, the world o'er,
> Shall brithers be, an' a' that.

GRAND CHAPTER OF SOUTH CAROLINA [74]

The Grand Chapter of the Order of the Eastern Star in South Carolina was organized June 1, 1907, at Greenwood. Previous to this, Brother Macoy had granted a charter to a Chapter at Charleston some time during the month of April, 1873, but it soon became dormant and no further activity is recorded until the General Grand Chapter issued a charter for Gate City Chapter No. 1, at Florence, March 31, 1893. After five years this charter was surrendered February 25, 1898.

---

[74] Organized June 1, 1907. Data by Mrs. Ila Leonard Willson, Grand Secretary.

Vances Chapter No. 2, at Vances, was chartered October 8, 1895, and was instituted December 5, 1895, with twenty-seven charter members; Lily of the Valley Chapter No. 3, Orangeburg, was chartered July 6, 1896, and instituted July, 1896, with forty-two charter members; Greenwood Chapter No. 4, Greenwood, was chartered April 26, 1897, and instituted May 1, 1897, with eighteen charter members; Charity Chapter No. 5, located at Elloree, was chartered October 22, 1897, and instituted November 3, 1897, with thirty charter members; Electa Chapter No. 6, Greenville, was chartered August 7, 1899, constituted January 16, 1900, with thirty-nine charter members and surrendered its charter September 29, 1906; Esther Chapter No. 7, Columbia; chartered August 16, 1900, and organized October 17, 1900, with forty-four charter members; Electric City Chapter No. 8, at Anderson, was chartered September 11, 1900, and organized September 21, 1900, with ninety-six charter members; Ruth Chapter No. 9, Newberry, chartered November 19, 1902, with thirty-eight charter members; Palmetto Chapter No. 10, at Mullins, was organized April 19, 1905, with twenty-four charter members and charter granted May 1, 1905; Esscon Chapter No. 11, at Marion, chartered July 27, 1905; Fort Mill Chapter No. 12, at Fort Mill, chartered July 6, 1906; Seneca Chapter No. 13, at Seneca, chartered December 19, 1906; and Adah Chapter No. 14, at Laurens, chartered November 14, 1906.

Of the fourteen Chapters chartered, only six were active at the time of organization of the Grand Chapter, and all united in the request sent to the Most Worthy Grand Patron, W. F. Kuhn of Farmington, Missouri, who appointed the Most Worthy Grand Matron, Mrs. Madeleine B. Conkling, as his Deputy to meet with the representatives of the several Chapters at Greenwood, June 1, 1907, at which time and place the Grand Chapter was organized.

From this center has radiated beneficent influences that can never die; this is the home of the *first* Grand Matron of South Carolina, Sister Mary Pickney Ouzts, whose sweet face is enshrined in the hearts of all who knew her. She is the pioneer of the Order in this

State; her husband, Brother D. A. G. Ouzts, gave her aid, sympathy, and encouragement, and they, together, "Scattered the literature of the Order, its history and meaning, the beauties enfolded in its teachings by pen and tongue" and planted the seeds which have responded to the touch of the Master's hand and brought forth good fruits. To the faithfulness and loyalty of these two enthusiastic members, the Grand Chapter owes its existence. Sister Ouzts served as Grand Matron from 1907 until 1909, retiring to the rank of Past Grand Matron at her own request, carrying with her the love and esteem of the entire membership. She was honored in the General Grand Chapter at Milwaukee in 1907, being appointed Worthy Grand Martha, 1907-1910, for the General Grand Chapter, which convened for the first time in a southern city in 1910 at Jacksonville, Florida. On February 16, 1910, the spirit of this beloved sister was wafted "to mansions in the skies" and she heard the Master's plaudit, "Well done." She sleeps sweetly in her native soil in the cemetery at Marshall, Texas.

Brother Henry P. Boggs was the first Worthy Grand Patron of South Carolina, and ably assisted the Worthy Grand Matron in establishing the work on a firm foundation. He is a teacher of recognized merit and has a splendid home school for boys at Glenn Springs, South Carolina. The second Worthy Grand Patron, W. L. R. Cahall, served one term, 1908-1909; the following year his fraternal relations were dissolved.

At the Grand Chapter session in Spartansburg, June 16, 1909, Sister Annie Lee Anderson, of Blacksburg, became the second Worthy Grand Matron. Brother D. A. G. Ouzts, of Greenwood, was elected the third Worthy Grand Patron, serving for three years, 1909-1912. During these years, Brother Ouzts did much effective work. He wrote an article, "What the Eastern Star is doing for Masonry," emphasizing the assistance that the Order has given to help mankind to a higher sphere of happiness and usefulness and giving aid and comfort to dependent loved ones. This has received favorable comment and his compilation of statistics on what each State has done for Masonic and Eastern Star Homes, Orphanages, and Hospitals, has added greatly to the value of our Order as a means of furthering charity, truth, and loving kindness among the members. Requests for this pamphlet are received quite often.

The third Worthy Grand Matron, Sister Tallulah L. Cudd, of Spartanburg, was elected at Sumter, June 22, 1910; she served faithfully 'and efficiently for two years, 1910-1912, joining the ranks of Past Grands with the assurance of the love and confidence of her sisters and brothers in this great work — the advancement of fraternal love and brotherly kindness — leaving all the Chapters in the State harmoniously working together. Inheriting a love for the principles of Freemasonry from her beloved forefathers, this sentiment was emphasized by the intimate relationship with the sainted Sister Ouzts and she was imbued with an enthusiasm like unto her own; this dear sister feelingly referred to Sister Cudd in the last address she made to the Grand Chapter at Spartanburg in 1909 in these words: "I love all my sisters and brothers and all our Chapters, but there is *one* that is dearer than all, for it so happened, when the darkest day came and I felt 'What is the use, nobody seems to care! A letter full of cheer and good report came from that Worthy Matron about her Chapter and the good work it was doing." Sister Cudd treasures a personal letter which contains this sentiment expressed to her. When the honor came to her of filling the station of Worthy Grand Matron, it seemed as if the "mantle had been cast on her shoulders" by this dear friend, asking her to take up this noble work which she had begun, and, like Elisha of old, she carried the work forward earnestly.

On July 21, 1910, Sister Cudd[75] received the appointment of Worthy Grand Martha from the Most Worthy Grand Matron, Sister

---

[75] Sister Tallulah Leonard Cudd, Past Grand Matron of South Carolina, died at Spartanburg, South Carolina, August 3, 1915. God said, "Come with Me, my child."

Ella S. Washburn, of the General Grand Chapter, to fill the chair made vacant by the death of Sister Mary Pickney Ouzts.

Sister Cudd and Brother Ouzts felt that their successors should be elected at Florence in 1912 and the fourth Worthy Grand Matron, Sister Nancy L. Bennett of Keystone Chapter No. 24, Greer, was elected; she served two years and declined the nomination for a third term.

Brother W. C. Davis, an eminent lawyer of Manning, was elected fourth Worthy Grand Patron. He and Sister Bennett had two successful terms, 1912-1914; the growth and prosperity of the Order during that time revealed unmistakably that the hands at the helm steered the "Craft" successfully.

The fifth Worthy Grand Matron was elected at Clio, June, 1914, and Sister Leilah F. Attaway of Saluda Chapter No. 8, Saluda, fill this position.

Brother Kenneth Baker, of Mary Pickney Ouzts Chapter No. 1, Greenwood, is the fifth Worthy Grand Patron.

When the history of the year 1914-1915 is written in the annals of the Order of the Eastern Star, there will be the record of much good accomplished. May those who follow continue to scatter the seed with one hand while the other gathers in the hearts, making each life better, each home dearer, and each heart purer, giving to all a deeper love and more tender care over those who need loving and uplifting, that by the works we do, others may know us to be members of the beautiful Order of the Eastern Star.

In 1909, the Grand Chapter voted to unite with the Grand Lodge, cooperating in their efforts to establish a Home, and donations amounting to more than $500 have been made by the Grand Chapter for the use of the Masonic Grand Lodge for charitable purposes. The O.E.S. has a charity fund; also the Mary Pickney Ouzts memorial

---

She could not say nay; so, taking His hand, she turned from the loved ones around her and trustfully followed her Savior to the New Jerusalem, that city not made with hands.

fund, the latter to be used for a Masonic Hospital when same may be erected.

The following beautiful poem is from the pen of Past Grand Matron, Sister Mary Pickney Ouzts, written June 15, 1909:

The Eastern Star

May it shine on the mountain,
    Cast its spell on the vale,
And its mystical radiance
    On all hearts prevail;

For sweet is the truth, on the Ritual's page,
    Seen by the rays of that magical Star,
Open to those of all clime and age,
    Who living and loving its clasp will debar.

Glorious Star! Whose beautiful light,
Scatters the darkness and illumines the night,
May the glow of its rays in all hearts be cast,
'Til its truth and beauty are understood at last.

GRAND CHAPTER OF SOUTH DAKOTA [76]

In the spring of 1871, there was instituted in the village of Elkpoint, Dakota Territory, an Eastern Star Chapter, chartered as Violet Chapter No. 2. The charter was granted June 22, 1871, and was signed by Robert Macoy and Edward O. Jenkins. No record has been obtainable of the first Chapter chartered in the Territory, but legend has it that Robert Macoy organized the first Chapter at Vermillion in 1871.

---

[76] Organized July, 1889. Data by Mrs. Angie L. Williamson, Grand Secretary O.E.S. and P. W. G.M.

Pioneer life was not conducive to fostering the Chapter, when both mental and physical efforts were utilized to cope with drought, grasshoppers, floods, and disease, so the little Chapter died.

About 1878 the Macoy charters were recalled and exchanged, but in some way the charter and signet of Violet Chapter No. 2, Dakota Territory, were overlooked and have remained intact for forty-five years in the home of the first Associate Matron, Mrs. Margaretta Blair.

During the life of the Chapter Mrs. Henry Schumaker died and was buried with Eastern Star rites, the first funeral of its kind on Dakota soil.

At the present writing (1916) there are six survivors of this early Chapter: Mr. and Mrs. C. W. Beggs, of Chicago, and Mesdames Mary Northrup, Clara Wixson, Martha Wallace, and Margaretta Blair, all of Elkpoint, South Dakota. By special dispensation, granted by the Grand Chapter, O. E. S., of South Dakota, June 8, 1916, Wynoka Chapter No. 107, O. E. S., of Elkpoint, was granted permission to recognize Violet Chapter No. 2, Dakota Territory, and affiliate the members within her jurisdiction. On June 28, 1916, with the floral affiliation work, these four elderly ladies, with ages ranging from seventy-two to seventy-six years, were received into Wynoka Chapter. The old charter and the signet, both in their old frames, have been presented to Wynoka Chapter and are hung in the Chapter room.

Early history tells us that Robert Macoy organized the first Eastern Star Chapter in South Dakota, at Vermillion in June, 1871. This chapter only survived a short time.

In February, 1882, Queen Esther No. 1 was organized at Mitchell as the first to receive a charter under the General Grand Chapter. Black Hills No. 2 was organized at Rapid City, January 22, 1883. Evergreen No. 3 at Madison, April 16, 1883. Vesta No. 4 at Watertown, March 15, 1884. Beulah No. 5 at Flandreau, September 24, 1884. Howard No. 6 at Howard, March 16, 1885. Lois No. 7 at Webster, May

12, 1887. Crescent No. 9 at St. Lawrence, February 11, 1888. Minerva No. 10, at Aberdeen, March 16, 1888. Madison No. 11, Madison, February 18, 1889.

Queen Esther, Black Hills, Evergreen, and Howard gave up their charters and Evergreen was reorganized as Madison, No. 11, February 18, 1889. There were then six live Chapters. Delegates from these met at Watertown in July, 1889, and there organized the Grand Chapter of South Dakota.

At this meeting a constitution and by-laws were adopted, the Chapters renumbered, and Brother J. H. Baldwin elected Grand Patron, Sister May Monks Grand Matron, and Mrs. A. M. McCallister Grand Secretary, which position she held until her death. At the second meeting at St. Lawrence 401 members were reported. Sister Monks was not able to preside at this meeting but sent her address to be read. She had been honored by the appointment of Worthy Grand Warder of the General Grand Chapter.

The third session opened at Webster with three new Chapters added. The first report of foreign correspondence was printed in this year's Proceedings, eighteen States being reviewed. Brother Geo. A. Pettigrew presided as Grand Patron for the first time.

The fourth session convened at Madison and Madison Chapter exemplified the work for the Grand Chapter. At the next session in Flandreau, Beulah Chapter exemplified the work. The Grand Secretary was instructed to keep on hand the necessary supplies for the Chapters. Fifty dollars was appropriated for the use of the Grand Matron and the same amount for the Grand Lecturer. The Grand Secretary's salary was raised. This Grand Chapter was called upon to mourn the loss of its Associate Grand Conductress, Sister Estella Baldwin, who had been killed in an accident a short time before the session convened.

The sixth annual meeting was held at Aberdeen with Sister Mary Brown in the East. She recommended that the Grand Chapter meet at the same time and place as the Masonic Lodge, so it might be possible to get reduced railroad rates. A resolution was presented at this session asking that a "Pass" be granted for the use of the subordinate Chapters, which resolution was lost.

DeSmet was the next place of meeting. This year was the first time a delegate had been sent to the General Grand Chapter. Sister Sarah J. Clark was elected. Sister Clark gave a very fine report of her visit at the next session of the Grand Chapter which met at Brookings. Brookings Chapter exemplified the work and also the floral work at this meeting.

The next session met at Sioux Falls. A reduction of railroad fares for the first time. Six U. D. Chapters reported. The tenth annual met at Redfield. The Home fund was started at this session, Sister Sarah J. Clark giving $5 and the Grand Chapter appropriated $100. Regular memorial services were held for the first time. Sister Clark received the appointment of Very Worthy Grand Chaplain of the General Grand Chapter. For the first time the Grand Matron's address was read before the Grand Patron's. Sister Mary E. Partridge, Most Worthy Grand Matron, was an honored guest at this session.

At the close of this decade there were forty-five Chapters with a total membership of 2,035; the jurisdiction had received two appointments from the General Grand Chapter, revised the constitution and by-laws twice, and elected ten Grand Matrons and eight Grand Patrons to preside in the East.

Many things happened in the next decade, which would make a good sized history if everything of moment could be recorded. Both the Stars and Masons met together at Yankton, the first year of this decade. At the next session at Aberdeen, greetings were exchanged with the Masonic brothers for the first time and this courtesy has passed down to the present day. The next year memorial services were held for Sister Jennie Shirk who passed away November 7, 1900. This was the first time death invaded the ranks of the Past Grand Matrons. Sister Pettigrew was elected delegate to the General Grand Chapter and Brother Robert Kerr received the appointment of

Worthy Grand Sentinel. They brought back a very fine report of that meeting. The next year the card index was installed.

Brother Marshall Brown, during his term of office as Grand Patron purchased some very beautiful jewels for the Grand Officers, a very desirable acquirement to the Grand Chapter belongings. At the seventeenth annual session steps were taken to incorporate the Grand Chapter. Brother Albert Coe, Past Grand Patron, passed away during this year after a long illness.

At the eighteenth session three of the Senior Grand Matrons were presented with Past Grand Matron's jewels. Sisters Lurancy Norton, Mary Brown, and Sarah J. Clark were the recipients. This custom has been kept up until all Past Grand Matrons have jewels, and now one is given each year to the outgoing Grand Matron.

The next year was the saddest in the history of the Order in South Dakota, for the ever faithful, competent Grand Secretary, Sister McCallister, "passed beyond" February 9, 1907, after a long and serious illness. The whole State was in mourning as she was endeared to everyone who knew her. She had served eighteen years, ever since the Grand Chapter was organized. Her husband was appointed to finish out the year's work and Sister Angie L. Williamson was elected Grand Secretary at the next session, which was held in the city of Lead, and the Grand Chapter had Sister Madeleine Conkling, Most Worthy Grand Matron, as its honored guest. This was the second time the State had been honored by a visit from the Most Worthy Grand Matron. She gave many delightful talks and all were benefited by her presence. Sister Angie Williamson was appointed Worthy Grand Adah by Sister Conkling. A Past Grand Matrons' and Patrons' Association was organized here.

Sister Linnie Ketcham brought a fine report from the General Grand Chapter at Milwaukee, where a large delegation of voting members were present from South Dakota. Now comes the end of this decade and at the city of Watertown the twenty-first birthday was celebrated. The Grand Chapter was welcomed by the same gentleman, D. C. Thomas, who accorded the welcome at the first session twenty years previously. Sister Mary Brown gave a history of the Grand Chapter up to this time. This session will long be remembered as one of our most interesting meetings together. At the end of this second decade there were ninety-four Chapters and a membership of 6,609. Total in Home fund, $3,818.49.

The next session met at Pierre, the home city of the Grand Matron, Sister Lumley. The next session met at Chamberlain where the Order was again honored by a visit from the Most Worthy Grand Matron, Sister Alice Miller, and Geo. A. Pettigrew, who held the position of Right Worthy Associate Grand Patron. Sister Morse was delegate to the General Grand Chapter.

The next session met in the city of Deadwood, where there are many interesting attractions for visitors. The constitution and by-laws were revised. The next year brought the twenty-fifth anniversary, which was celebrated at Yankton at the same time the Masonic brethren were celebrating their fiftieth anniversary. It was a great pleasure for the two Grand bodies to be together at this time. Four Past Grand Patrons, Brothers Pettigrew, Alfred Poznansky, Frank A. Brown, and Joseph A. Poznansky, were presented with buttons in honor of their service as Past Grand Patrons of the Order. This custom was adopted and is to be carried out until all have received a button. The second time the Grim Reaper invaded the ranks of the Past Grand Matrons and Sister Anna Lumley answered the summons to come up higher. Her death caused universal sorrow throughout the State. Sister Doherty was elected delegate to General Grand Chapter at Chicago and she had a full quota of voting members with her. Doctor Geo. A. Pettigrew was elected Most Worthy Grand Patron to the satisfaction of all. Sister Jessie G. Harris received the appointment of Worthy Grand Martha.

The next session met at Sioux Falls and at this time the Grand Chapter was called upon to mourn the death of Sister Sarah J. Clark, who died in Quincy, Massachusetts, March 10, 1915.

In 1915 the deputy system was adopted. The State divided into three districts and a Deputy Grand Matron appointed for each. Sister Susan B. Warring, Grand Matron, instituted a system of schools of instruction that proved very successful and her plans for conducting the same were officially adopted at the 1916 session. The same year recommendations of Grand Patron Richard Norman Axford were adopted requiring the obligation to be repeated by the Chapter immediately preceding balloting.

Three of our Past Grand Matrons have "passed on," eighteen reside in the State, and six in other States. Twenty Past Grand Patrons still live in South Dakota, one has "passed on," and three reside in other States. Those present form a true and faithful band of workers who stand shoulder to shoulder for the advancement of the Order of the Eastern Star in South Dakota. There are 117 Chapters with a membership of 9,962; the Home fund amounts to $11,454.09.

Grand Chapter of Tennessee [77]

The very earliest history of Tennessee, as connected with O.E.S. work, begins with the chartering of three Chapters by Brother Macoy, one at Nashville in 1874, but none has endured to the end, and we may properly date the active work from the granting of charters by the General Grand Chapter.

East Fork Chapter No. 2 was chartered April 30, 1880, by the General Grand Chapter and was organized by J. C. Bruice, special Deputy, while Esther Chapter No. 1 was not chartered until July 16, 1880. Fayetteville Chapter No. 3, located at Fayetteville, was chartered December 29, 1881, and was organized by Brother Ewan Burney, Deputy for Tennessee. Again, all Chapters became dormant. In consequence, the charter granted March 6, 1893, to thirty-six

---

[77] Organized October 18, 1900.

petitioners, to form a Chapter at East Nashville, was given the number, 1, and was organized by John B. Garrett, Deputy.

Chattanooga Chapter No. 2 was chartered December 5, 1893, and organized by Loren Mitchell, Deputy of the Most Worthy Grand Patron, with 106 charter members.

McKinnon Chapter No. 3 was chartered June 18, 1894, in response to the petition of thirty-four charter members at Erin, and was organized at that place by D. L. Willatt, special Deputy of the Most Worthy Grand Patron.

Wayland Springs Chapter No. 4, located at Wayland Springs, was chartered on December 8, 1894, with twenty-four members and organized by Rev. S. A. McMackin, Deputy of the Most Worthy Grand Patron for that purpose.

Esther Chapter, located at Bagdad, was reorganized December 21, 1895, and wishing to retain their former charter, which had been granted as Esther Chapter No. 1, on July 16, 1880, the Most Worthy Grand Matron endorsed the same, but gave them No. 5 on said charter instead of No. 1.

Olive Leaf Chapter No. 6 was chartered October 12, 1896, and was constituted at Dickson, October 30, 1896, by J. T. Spaulding, with twenty charter members.

Rock City Chapter No. 7, located at Nashville, was chartered February 15, 1897 and constituted February 19, 1897, by A. S. Williams, with twenty-six charter members.

Hurricane Chapter No. 8, Hurricane, was chartered June 22, 1897, and constituted June 26, 1897, by J. J. Sanders, Worshipful Master of Geo. Hillman Lodge No. 431, with fifty-two charter members.

Elmwood Chapter No. 9, Elmwood, was chartered June 28, 1897, and Amanda Chapter No. 10, Crossville, was chartered in February, 1898.

Bethpage Chapter No. 11, Bethpage, was chartered May 27, 1899, and constituted August 27, 1899, by W. C. Nimmo, Deputy, with thirty-eight charter members.

Kingston Chapter No. 12, Kingston, was chartered August 26, 1889, and was organized September 11, 1889, by J. B. Goodwin, Deputy, with thirty members.

Of the twelve Chapters organized only six were active and participated in the organization of the Grand Chapter at Nashville on October 18, 1900. The convention to organize was presided over by Mrs. Kate C. Brechner, Deputy of the Most Worthy Grand Patron. The constitution adopted made Past Matrons and Past Patrons members, and together with Associate Matrons they were made eligible to any office in the Grand Chapter: "That the office should seek the person and not the person the office. It is unwise and undignified to solicit votes for an office and the practice has a tendency to create ill-feeling and dissension among the membership of the Grand Chapter. It is, therefore, an offense against the Order, and members guilty thereof shall be subject to discipline."

In 1901 an amendment was adopted empowering the Grand Chapter to receive petition, ballot, and confer the degrees upon applicants not located convenient to chartered Chapters, for the purpose of extending the Order, conveying upon the person membership in good standing but not the privilege of a vote until affiliated with a chartered Chapter. Twelve persons were thus received at the meeting in 1901.

In 1903 $11.60 was donated by one Chapter to form a nucleus for an endowment fund for the Masonic Home. This fund has increased each year and the O.E.S. has contributed in various ways, to the amount of about $5,000, to the Masonic Home, located five miles from Nashville, and has a representation upon the Home board. In 1909 the O.E.S. furnished the Old Women's Building; in 1910 installed electric lights; in 1911 installed a heating plant; in 1913 and 1914 built an infirmary in connection with the Home which stands as a monument to their untiring devotion to the charitable work of the Order, and are looking to the erection of an O.E.S. Home in the near future.

In 1905 Brother Rob. Morris, Past Grand Patron of Kentucky, was present as an honored guest and made an address, and in 1912 he was made an honorary member of the Grand Chapter as a tribute to the son of the founder of the Order.

A resolution adopted in 1915 unanimously elected the Grand Secretary, Sister Mary R. Reeves, an Honorary Past Grand Matron, as a recognition of the many long years of faithful service which the recipient had rendered to the Order.

Grand Chapter of Texas [78]

The lessons of fidelity to convictions of right, faithfulness to the demands of honor and justice, loyalty to kindred and friends, trustful faith and hope of immortal life, and heroic endurance were first introduced into Texas by Brother Robert Macoy when he sold five charters for Chapters therein in 1870.

Brother Thomas M. Lamb, Most Worthy Grand Patron of the General Grand Chapter, appointed Brother Loron Mitchel, of Dallas, special Deputy for the General Grand Chapter, under whose influence Friendship Chapter No. 1, Dallas, was chartered June 22, 1877, and organized July 24, 1877, with Henry Boll, Worthy Patron, Jane Austin, Worthy Matron, Anna Pearson, Associate Matron.

Chico Chapter No. 2, Chico, was chartered December 9, 1879, with Mrs. Emma J. Blanton, Worthy Matron, Theodore Merriman, Worthy Patron, and Mrs. Feno Dickenson, Associate Matron, and organized by Theodore Merriman, Deputy for the Most Worthy Grand Patron.

Cecelia Chapter No. 3, Clarksville, was chartered June 26, 1882, and organized July 11, 1882, by W. L. Burdett, special Deputy, with

---

[78] Organized May 5, 1884. Data furnished by Mrs. Cassie C. Leonard, Grand Secretary.

Mrs. M. L. Hazzard, Worthy Matron, James H. Cheatham, Worthy Patron, Mrs. Sue B. Cheatham, Associate Matron.

Samuel Long Chapter No. 4, Paris, surrendered its charter, granted by the Supreme Grand Chapter and dated May 28, 1879, and received a charter from the General Grand Chapter dated October 30, 1882.

Esther Chapter No. 5, San Antonio, was chartered December 12, 1882, and organized March 11, 1883, by Nathan H. Gould, special Deputy. Mrs. Mary Shardein, Worthy Matron, A. H. Boyd, Worthy Patron, Mrs. Lily Ryan, Associate Matron.

Queen City Chapter No. 6, Queen City, was chartered April 20, 1883, and organized by George H. Salmon, Deputy.

Hadassah Chapter No. 7, Georgetown, was chartered June 18, 1883.

Fort Worth Chapter No. 8, Fort Worth, was chartered January 28, 1884 and organized February 23, 1884, by Wm. L. Holt, Deputy.

Mt. Moriah Chapter No. 9, Kildare, was chartered January 28, 1884, and organized March 6, 1884, by the Rev. Perry Hawkins, Deputy.

Jonesboro Chapter No. 10, Jonesboro, was chartered March 4, 1884, and organized March 22, 1884. Cedar Bayou Chapter No. 11, Cedar Bayou, was chartered April 29, 1884. Liberty Hill Chapter No. 12, Liberty Hill, was chartered May 19, 1884, fourteen days after the Grand Chapter had been organized, but before same had been recognized by the General Grand Chapter. May 22, 1884, a charter was issued by the General Grand Chapter to New Hope Chapter No. 13, Gibtown, seventeen days after the organization of the Grand Chapter.

The call for the convention to organize the Grand Chapter was issued by members of Fort Worth Chapter No. 8 and the meeting was held at Fort Worth May 5, 1884. Sister Elmira Foley, Past Most Worthy Grand Matron, who at that time was a member of Fort Worth Chapter No. 8, as Deputy for the Most Worthy Grand Patron organized this Grand Chapter, but the action having only representation from four Chapters, it was not recognized by the General Grand Chapter until July 20, 1884, when the action of the convention had been endorsed by an additional Chapter.

The Grand Chapter membership was made to include not only Past Matrons and Past Patrons but also Past Associate Matrons.

Starting out under circumstances having features of discouragement because of so few Chapters entering the work of the Grand Chapter, the meetings were not well attended. Irregularities in records, with imperfect statistics regarding number of members and the finances also, resulted in a chaotic condition prevailing for several years. In 1888 only a sufficient number were present to constitute a legal quorum and in 1889 only two of the Grand officers were present, even the Grand Secretary being among the absent ones and having only submitted a skeleton report, lacking the necessary statistics and the names and addresses of the Secretaries of active Chapters.

Though difficulties were present, with spirits undaunted the brave workers struggled along, obtaining the necessary information from the best available sources. In 1889 only six Chapters were represented, but the conditions were bravely faced and this heroic band adopted effective steps to put the Order upon a firm foundation.

At the 1892 session the State was divided into forty-five districts, but the number was reduced to ten in 1896. Previous to 1895 the Grand Patron had been the executive officer, but on that date the Grand Matron was clothed with that authority.

A committee of the work was given full authority to communicate the secret work and in 1894 all copies of the work then in the hands of Chapters were called in. Instruction was to be given the delegates to Grand Chapter by the committee entrusted with that duty.

In 1895 a test oath was adopted, the form for same having been presented by Sister Ree Alford who is now Past Grand Matron. The State having been invaded by persons who communicated the degrees without authority, it became necessary for the Grand Secretary to issue a circular letter of warning against such practices which were termed the work of "Masonic Pirates."

In 1898 the Grand Chapter donated $185.65 to the Masonic Widows' and Orphans' Home fund, this being ten per cent of the receipts that year. The Grand and also the subordinate Chapters have made liberal donations each year to both the Masonic Orphans' and Aged Masons' Homes.

The committee on work examines applicants in the secret work and grants certificates of proficiency at each meeting of the Grand Chapter, and copies of the secret work are given out only to members of this committee, the four principal Grand officers, and to each District Deputy.

In 1908, by resolution of Brother E. J. Hosey, now Past Grand Patron, Grand Chapter appointed a graduating committee whose duties are to locate the graduates from the Masonic Home in such employment and home surroundings as will best fit them for a useful and Christian life.

In 1911, Sister Edith Findlater, Grand Matron, in behalf of the Grand Chapter, donated $300 to the Home for Aged Masons, to be used for furnishings.

The Home Fund Movement

In April, 1900, Sister Laura B. Hart, Past Grand Matron and Grand Secretary, Brothers Ludlow and Atchison, Past Grand Patrons, memorialized the Grand Commandery, Knights Templar, of Texas, through Sir Knight Robert L. Ball, requesting a donation of $100 as a nucleus for a Grand Chapter Eastern Star fund, to provide a home for aged and indigent Masons. This movement was successful and the $100 was contributed by the Grand Commandery.

This suggestion had been offered by Grand Master Samuel R. Hamilton for the reason that the Masonic Home, which had been recently established at Fort Worth, Texas, provides only for the widows and orphans of Texas Masons; no provision whatever having been made by the Grand Lodge of Texas for the general care of their own aged and indigent members.

In September, 1900, by resolution of Sister Kate M. Bryan, now Past Grand Matron, and Brother F. H. Shumate, $500 was donated to the Galveston flood sufferers from the general fund of the Grand Chapter; there was also offered a resolution, signed by Sister Laura B. Hart and Brother A. C. McDaniel, appropriating $500 for a permanent charity fund; and providing further that in the future twenty-five per cent of the gross receipts should be appropriated for this purpose. This resolution was carried.

On October 10, 1901, Brother P. S. Park, chairman of the board of trustees, reported $4.50 interest accrued on the $100 donation from the Grand Commandery, this being the first interest ever earned by Grand Chapter funds.

In October, 1902, Brother McDaniel, then the Grand Patron, recommended to the Grand Chapter in his annual address that the purpose of the charity fund be changed to provide a home and refuge for old people of the O.E.S. not eligible to the Masonic homes; and also, for any members, regardless of sex, who might choose to select this prospective home instead of the Masonic homes.

It might be well to state here that only the widows and orphans of Texas Masons in good standing are eligible to the protection of the Home already established in Fort Worth; thus leaving a large membership of the Eastern Star entirely without protection for their aged unmarried women and widows and daughters of Masons not registered in Texas. After most strenuous efforts with the finance committee, which had previously recommended the rescinding of the twenty-five per cent appropriation, Brother McDaniel secured a recommendation that five per cent of the gross revenues of the Grand Chapter be set aside for the purpose named in his report.

The committee also recommended that the Grand Commandery be advised of this change of purpose; and if the same were not agreeable to the wishes of that Grand Body, then the $100 which had been previously received was to be returned to them. It was later reported to the Grand Chapter that such change was not agreeable to the Grand Commandery, and the $100 was returned. The fund derived from the above-mentioned five per cent appropriation was to be placed in the hands of three Grand Chapter trustees.

In 1906, Brother McDaniel, then Past Grand Patron, prepared a full and complete resolution for the trustees' report, providing that the number of trustees be increased from three to five, with terms of service of five years each; they to serve without bond, the Grand Treasurer being made the custodian of the fund. In this resolution, five trust companies were designated as depositories, to-wit: San Antonio Loan and Trust Company, of San Antonio; Bankers Trust Company, of Houston; Texas Bank and Trust Company, of Galveston; Dallas Trust and Savings Bank, of Dallas; and the Continental Bank and Trust Company, of Fort Worth.

In 1909, a new constitution was adopted, at which time the Home fund was placed under constitutional protection, and the trustees given specified duties relating thereto. The State was at this time divided into five districts, each to be represented by one grand trustee, they to be, as before, elected in rotation for five-year terms and to serve without bond or remuneration of any kind. The fund at present amounts in round numbers to $57,000 and is invested with the above trust companies at five per cent and six per cent interest compounded semi-annually.

This splendid accumulation has been brought about by the appropriation of five per cent of the gross revenues of the Grand Chapter, together with the surplus of the general fund each year over and above the necessary running expenses of the body. At the meeting in October, 1912, Brother McDaniel and other members of the board of trustees presented a resolution which provided that the fund should be further augmented by the payment, by each member of the Order, of $1 per capita, for five years; this payment to be in the nature of a freewill offering, and no penalty for non-payment was attached thereto. This resolution further provided that when $75,000 should have been accumulated, the trustees should advertise for bids for the land location of the Home; but that they should not proceed to build until a permanent endowment of $100,000 had been secured, and enough additional funds for building purposes. At this date, about one-seventh of the Texas membership. Have paid the $1 per year as specified.

At the 1913 meeting, it was moved by Sister Edith Findlate, Past Grand Matron, that the children of O.E.S. members be admitted to the Home, which was unanimously carried.

Brother McDaniel has served continuously as a member of the board of trustees since 1906, and, with the exception of one year, has been the chairman of said board. The trustees have carefully directed and guarded all investments, and strenuously opposed and prevented any diversion of the fund from its original purpose.

The enactment of the Eastern Star Home resolution as recommended by the board of trustees has resulted in added interest among the members and a decided increase in the growth of the Order.

Grand Chapter of Utah [79]

> Nineteen hundred years ago
>   The Star in the East first shone;
> In the light of that Star
>   Lie the ages empearled,
> And that song from afar

---

[79] Organized September 20, 1905. Data by Mrs. Frances G. Shields, Grand Secretary.

Has swept over the world.

We rejoice in the light,
 And we echo the song
That comes down through the night
 From the heavenly throng.
Aye we shout to the lovely evangel they bring,
And we greet in His cradle, our Savior and King.

The light of His Star in the East was first visible to those within this State when Lynds Chapter No. 1 was chartered June 6, 1892, in Salt Lake City. This was followed by Mountain Chapter No. 2, Park City; Valley No. 3, Provo; Queen Esther No. 4, Ogden; Mizpah No. 5, Salt Lake City, chartered September 20, 1905.

By the organization of Mizpah Chapter No. 5, effected by Mrs. Madeleine B. Conkling, Most Worthy Grand Matron, on September 20, 1905, in Salt Lake City, assisted by Mrs. Lorraine J. Pitkin, Right Worthy Grand Secretary, there was then in existence the constitutional number of Chapters in Utah to form a Grand Chapter. The call having been issued by Dr. W. F. Kuhn, Most Worthy Grand Patron, the Grand Chapter was organized September 20, 1905, by Mrs. Madeleine Conkling, Most Worthy Grand Matron, Deputy of the Most Worthy Grand Patron, assisted by Mrs. Lorraine J. Pitkin, Right Worthy Grand Secretary. All Chapters were represented, there being fifty members present. The constitution adopted fixed the annual dues at fifty cents per capita, but it was found necessary to advance the annual dues to seventy-five cents per capita, which was done in 1908. Each Chapter was accorded three votes — one for the three principal officers and two additional votes to represent the collective votes of Past Matrons and Past Patrons.

At the first annual session, held in Salt Lake City, the Grand Matron recommended that a beginning be made toward some charitable and benevolent work, urging that the social aspect of the Order must not overshadow its higher opportunities.

The Chapter of Sorrow, by Addie C. S. Engle, was impressively rendered in 1906, also in 1909, and the memorial service, by Sister Elvira Adams Atwood, was impressively rendered at the meeting in 1911. Through the recitation of the vocal star at the 1909 meeting, the well-beloved symbols as they were recorded in the rituals of the *Mosaic Book* and *Adoptive Masonry*, Sister Addie C. S. Engle's conception of their application in this connection was beautifully presented to those in attendance at the Grand Chapter meeting.

A special session was called in 1908 for the purpose of receiving Sister Ella S. Washburn, Most Worthy Grand Matron, and listening to her broad-minded and helpful talks upon the value of concentrating the efforts upon the charitable work made possible through the members uniting in one common line of action. At this time, the "Home Fund" was started, with love and goodwill toward all.

In 1910 the ceremonies for instituting and constituting Chapters were adopted and the floral work exemplified. A special session was called for the instituting of Ivy Chapter at Mt. Pleasant, June 8, 1911; also for instituting Corinne Chapter at Corinne, February 16, 1912, and again for the purpose of instituting Radiant Chapter at Salt Lake City, January 13, 1914.

Responding to a request from the Grand Matron, $217 was raised by the subordinate Chapters for the purpose of helping to lift the mortgage on the home of a widowed sister who held her membership in Montana.

> Charity is the cornerstone of our Order,
>   The key to our structure grand;
> And he who would enter our portals
>   Should bear it in his hand.
> And none is worthy to enter
>   Who envy or malice feel;

For each should work for the other
To promote our Order's weal.

GRAND CHAPTER OF VERMONT [80]

Bright Eastern Star, though years have fled
    Adown Time's swiftly flowing stream,
The holy light thy clear rays shed
    Yet mark the way with steady gleam,
Still lead thou weary steps along
    The narrow path; it lonely seems,
Though cheered anon by angel's song,
    To find Him of our hopes and dreams.
                      — J. E. H. Boardman.

In tracing the progress of the Order of the Eastern Star, we find it was very early introduced into Vermont and Chapters were organized as early as 1869. The records show that a charter was issued by Brother Macoy, dated December 21, 1869, for Mt. Anthony Chapter No. 1, located at Bennington, which Chapter is in active existence at the present time — an enviable record of duty well done for a period of forty-six years and an active Grand Chapter of forty-three years.

Six Chapters having been organized, Electa Chapter No. 6, located at Brandon, invited all the Chapters to meet in convention with a view to the formation of a Grand Chapter. Accordingly, November 12, 1873, representatives of five of the six Chapters of the State met in convention at Brandon and there organized the fifth Grand Chapter, adopting the constitution of the Grand Chapter of New York with such changes as were necessary to comply with the best interests of the newly formed Grand Chapter.

---

[80] Organized November 12, 1873.

At various times committees have sought to improve the work of the Order by investigating the feasibility of the adoption of a ritual giving uniformity of work. Such a committee reported in 1876 that they recommended the use of the Adoptive Rite ritual as used in the State of New York. This report was concurred in by the Grand Chapter and 100 copies ordered to be purchased, but the *Macoy Ritual* had been issued at a date just previous to the time when purchase was to be made and instead the question was reconsidered and the *Macoy Ritual* adopted.

In 1879 a resolution was adopted authorizing the appointment of a committee of three with duties defined, "To consider the propriety of revising our ritual, and to recommend such work, as in their judgment, is best calculated to promote the good of the Order."

The following year the committee reported that both the *Ritual* of the General Grand Chapter and the *Macoy Ritual* possessed merit, and further stated that the matter concerned each individual Chapter and was of too great importance to be decided upon the recommendation of the committee. A resolution was then adopted that the matter of ritual be postponed until the next meeting with the request that the subordinate Chapters instruct their representatives as to their wishes with a view to thus gain the expression of all members. The following year, 1881, upon bringing the matter before the Grand Chapter, a motion to adopt the General Grand Chapter *Ritual* was lost, though there were many zealous and ardent friends of the General Grand Chapter among the sisters and brothers of Vermont. The question of cooperation with that body had been a fruitful topic for consideration at the annual meetings, and while there may have been a disposition to precipitate the issue and declare in favor of allegiance to the General Grand Chapter, it was deemed best that the spirit of unity be preserved and await the time when harmonious arrangements could be reached.

In 1888 dissatisfaction was expressed that the *Macoy Ritual*, at that time the only ritual used, could not be purchased except copies that contained the Queen of the South ritual also. This degree not having been adopted by the Grand Chapter of Vermont, the Grand Secretary was instructed to request that no *Rituals* be sold within the jurisdiction unless the request for same be under seal of the Grand Chapter or one of its subordinate Chapters.

In 1891 the Grand Patron, in his address to the Grand Chapter, recommended that the time had come for the Grand Chapter of Vermont to have a ritual of its own, and that a committee be appointed to prepare and present the same, combining the *Macoy Ritual* and the General Grand Chapter *Ritual*. For financial reasons, this recommendation was not concurred in and further consideration of the matter was deferred until the financial condition of the Grand Chapter might warrant further action. However, in 1892 it was brought to the attention of the Grand Chapter that the only *Macoy Rituals* obtainable contained the Queen of the South and the Amaranth degrees, and that same were publicly sold in bookstores, etc., with the misrepresentation that they were the original and only Eastern Star manual. It was then resolved that a committee be appointed with full power to arrange for the printing of a ritual for the use of the Grand Chapter and its subordinate Chapters, separate from those containing the objectionable degrees, and if unable to do so, that they have power to prepare and print a ritual for the use of the Grand Jurisdiction of Vermont.

The following year, 1893, the report of the committee was concurred in, which report was that:

> We recommend that if suitable and satisfactory arrangements can be made with the General Grand Chapter, that purchases of rituals for all new Chapters be made from the General Grand Chapter; that permission be granted to any Chapter to substitute the General Grand Chapter ritual for the Macoy, and that until some definite action as to the adoption of a ritual by this Grand Chapter, other than the one heretofore adopted, any of the Chapters within this

Jurisdiction may use either the Macoy or General Grand Chapter ritual as they may determine, or may use the ritual of the General Grand Chapter, except as to the history of the five degrees, and, as to that, may, if they desire, substitute our present ritual.

The selections, by Chapters, of either ritual, continued until 1901, when the amendment to the constitution was adopted, declaring allegiance to the General Grand Chapter.

In 1895 the Chapters in the State were divided into districts and it was made a compulsory duty on the Deputy of each of the several districts to appoint district conventions, to be held once each year, if possible.

In 1896, upon the recommendation of the Grand Matron, it was adopted that hereafter "no hats" shall be the rule in Grand and subordinate Chapter meetings. Each district, in addition to the District Deputy Grand Matron, also has a District Deputy Grand Patron and both make reports to the Grand Patron, who is the executive officer and presides at all convocations of the Grand Chapter, grants special dispensations, receives all reports, and exercises the authority usually vested in the Grand Matron's office.

At the twenty-ninth convocation of Vermont, held at Newport, June 5, 1901, an amendment to the constitution, which had been proposed in 1900 and action deferred until 1901 in order that all the members might fully understand its import before taking action, was adopted, Vermont thereby declaring itself in favor of becoming a constituent member of the General Grand Chapter. By virtue of this action, notice of which was duly sent to the Most Worthy Grand Patron, that officer, together with the Most Worthy Grand Matron and Right Worthy Grand Secretary, recognized the Grand Chapter of Vermont as a constituent member of the General Grand Chapter. By the provisions of the constitution as amended, the Grand Patron and Grand Matron are granted coordinate powers, with the provision that, wherever they may fail to agree upon points of coordinate power, the matter must be submitted to the Grand Chapter for decision. In case of the death, absence, or disability of the Grand Patron, the Grand Matron is to assume his powers and prerogatives. The Grand Patron's address takes precedence. The Grand Warder is included with the elective officers.

In 1906, upon the recommendation of the Grand Patron and concurred in by the Grand Chapter, the Grand Matron was made the presiding officer and official head, and in 1906 the Grand Matron presided but the Grand Patron's address takes precedence.

In 1907 the Grand Lodge, A. F. and A.M., passed a resolution conveying permission to Masonic Lodges to grant Chapters of the O.E.S. the privilege of meeting in Lodge rooms, providing the members of the Lodge were agreed. In 1909 it was decreed that members of the O.E.S. shall not become members of either the Amaranth or the White Shrine of Jerusalem, and providing a penalty for those who ignore this decision.

Though repeated recommendations have been made that the Grand Chapter of Vermont adopt the plan of all other jurisdictions except California, that the Grand Matron be made the executive officer with her duties defined, the recommendation has not been concurred in. The Grand Matron presided in 1906, 1908, 1911, 1912, and 1914, not by rights conferred by the constitution, but by the courtesy of the Grand Patron. These two States — California and Vermont — still retain this practice, though provisions to the contrary are made by the ritual.

The most cordial relations have always existed between the Masonic Fraternity and the Order of the Eastern Star, and harmonious work for the Masonic and O.E.S. Home fund has been carried forward continuously since 1904; $176.45 was contributed to the Galveston flood sufferers.

The total membership in 1914 was 7,527.

In 1914 a committee was appointed to confer with the Grand Lodge, A. F. and A. M., at its annual session, with a view to determining the intent and purpose of the Home fund, whether or not it is desirable that the funds be retained as jointly accumulated or separate Homes be established.

In 1912, by a rising vote of the Grand Chapter, Sister Ruby Hawley, Grand Lecturer for eight successive years, was made honorary Past Grand Matron, with all the rights and privileges of an active one.

In 1914 recognition was extended to a former resident of Vermont, one who had been made a Mason within the State, Dr. George A. Pettigrew, Most Worthy Grand Patron of the General Grand Chapter, and Past Grand Patron of South Dakota, by electing him an honorary member. A Past Grand Matrons' and Past Grand Patrons' Association was formed; also a State Secretaries' Club.

GRAND CHAPTER OF VIRGINIA [81]

> Have you found the heavenly light?
>   Pass it on.
> Souls are groping in the night,
>   Daylight gone.
> Hold thy lighted lamp on high,
> Be a *Star* in some one's sky,
> He may live who else would die,
>   Pass it on.

During the month of January, 1872, a charter was granted for a Chapter at Portsmouth, Virginia, by Brother Macoy, and the first charter issued by the General Grand Chapter in this State was for Alpha No. 1, located at Woodstock, on March 30, 1896, to twenty-two petitioners. This Chapter was constituted April 16, 1896, by R. G. Alexander, Worshipful Master of Union Lodge No. 27, acting as Deputy of the Most Worthy Grand Patron, but became dormant in 1899, and

---

[81] Organized June 22, 1904.

the oldest surviving Chapter is Alpha No. 2, located at Petersburg and working by authority of a General Grand Chapter charter issued April 17, 1896. This Chapter was constituted June 11, 1896, by D. S. R. Jones, Wor. Master of Stark Lodge No. 124, Powhatan, Deputy of the Most Worthy Grand Patron, with thirty-seven charter members. Charter was granted sixteen petitioners for Milnes Chapter No. 3, located at Shenandoah, dated August 14, 1896, and the Chapter was constituted September 10, 1896, by Chester B. Hayes, Deputy of the Most Worthy Grand Patron.

Botetourt Chapter No. 4, located at Gloucester Court House, was granted a charter November 20, 1896, and constituted December 8, 1896, by John B. Donovan, Deputy of the Most Worthy Grand Patron, with twenty-six charter members.

Electa Chapter No. 5, located at Luray, was granted a charter on February 10, 1897, and constituted February 24, 1897, by J. H. Morrison, Deputy of the Most Worthy Grand Patron, with twenty-nine charter members.

Blackwater Chapter No. 6, at Zuni, was granted a charter July 27, 1897, with thirty charter members, and constituted September 1, 1897, by Frank L. Snipes, Deputy of the Most Worthy Grand Patron.

Magdalene Chapter No. 7, at Stanley, was chartered November 13, 1897, and constituted November 19, 1897, by A. S. Harmon, Deputy of the Most Worthy Grand Patron.

Ruth Chapter No. 8, at Richmond, was granted a charter June 22, 1899, organized June 24, 1899, by Charles A. Nesbitt, Deputy of the Most Worthy Grand Patron, with twenty-four charter members.

Tidal Wave Chapter No. 9, at Port Norfolk, was organized June 6, 1902, by Charles N. Nesbitt, Deputy, with thirty-one charter members; chartered August 22, 1902.

Urbana Chapter No. 10, at Urbana, was organized January 20, 1903, by Charles A. Nesbitt, Deputy, with thirty-nine charter members; chartered February 11, 1903.

Blair Chapter No. 11, at Williamsburg, was organized February 19, 1903, by Charles A. Nesbitt, Deputy, with fifty-one charter members; charter granted March 12, 1903.

Liberty Chapter No. 12, at Bedford City, was organized December 1, 1903, by George S. Spencer, Deputy, with thirty-two charter members; charter granted January 25, 1904.

Chesapeake Chapter No. 13, at New Market, was organized December 28, 1903, by John Hardy, Deputy of the Most Worthy Grand Patron, with twenty-two charter members; charter granted January 13, 1904.

Pocahontas Chapter No. 14, at Pocahontas, was organized June 10, 1904, by John M. Newton, Deputy of the Most Worthy Grand Patron, in response to the prayer of twenty-eight petitioners; charter was granted June 14, 1904.

The Grand Chapter of Virginia was organized in Richmond, June 22, 1904, by the Most Worthy Grand Patron, L. Cabell Williamson, assisted by the Most Worthy Grand Matron, Laura B. Hart; and the Right Worthy Grand Secretary, Lorraine J. Pitkin, and was recognized by proclamation of the General Grand Chapter. Only nine of the fourteen Chapters were active at the date of the organization of the Grand Chapter, six of which were represented. The first officers selected were: Mrs. Annie L. Huber, Grand Matron; Charles A. Nesbitt, Grand Patron; Mrs. Mary E. Nesbitt, Grand Secretary. Past Matrons and Past Patrons were made members of the Grand Chapter; the dues fixed at twenty-five cents per capita, but in 1906 were changed to fifty cents.

The memorial service used at the 1914 session was arranged by Sister Evelyn Wardwell Heath, Grand Matron, and dedicated to the subordinate Chapters, O.E.S. of Virginia, by the author. Instructions were given for balloting, opening and closing of the Bible, presenting of Grand Officers, and the rules for a model Chapter.

In the city of Richmond is the first building erected on the American continent devoted exclusively to Masonry. At Fredericksburg is located Masonic Lodge No. 4, in which our first President, George Washington, was initiated in 1752. The original record sheets, and the Bible on which he took his obligation are still in existence and are prized by this Chapter as priceless treasures.

Wherever the principles of our Order are practiced, they lift the burden from the tired heart; they place a smile on the face of care; they wipe the tears from sorrow's eyes and touch the earth with the kiss of God; sympathies are more extensive, purposes ennobled, and lives made better. Among the manifold expressions of the wonderful skill of God, the great architect of the universe, none appeals more strongly to our senses than the firmament, studded with stars, with their brilliant light when the world is dark after the sun disappears. Significant of His loving kindness was the Star of the East, proclaiming the birth of the Savior, whose life is the light of our lives, bringing "Peace on earth, good will to men." His advent was the emancipation of women; how fitting then that this, the greatest fraternal organization of women, should have for its inspiration, the Star of Bethlehem!

GRAND CHAPTER OF WASHINGTON [82]

If you will look upon your map, you will find the State of Washington 'way up in the northwest part of the United States, called by some the "jumping off place." It is 500 miles east and west and 350 miles north and south. Little notice was given it until the Northern Pacific undertook to build a railroad across the Cascade Mountains. One of the greatest engineering feats accomplished was the building of the great Stampede tunnel, two miles long, at a cost of over two million dollars. At its completion a three days' jubilee was held in Tacoma, July 4, 5, and 6, 1889. People came from all parts of the

---

[82] Data furnished by Libbie J. Demorest, Grand Secretary, June, 1892, to June, 1914.

United States. A great many remained, others invested and returned later to make it their home.

It seems strange that the first Eastern Star Chapter should have been planted in the little village of Goldendale, far remote from a railroad, in the south part of the State, when larger villages and towns existed along the river and railroad. But Peter Gunn and wife were enthusiastic members and formerly belonged to a Chapter at Dixon, California, taking their dimit when they moved to Washington in 1887 and settled as pioneers seven miles from the village of Goldendale. The comforts and pleasures of other years were denied them in this new country and nothing but hardships and privations prevailed at that time. Longing for the pleasures of the Eastern Star, after a two years' residence they began to talk among the handful of Masons upon the subject of starting an Eastern Star Chapter. This finally resulted in the organization of Evergreen Chapter No. 1, which received its charter from the General Grand Chapter November 12, 1881. As a Chapter Evergreen No. 1 has had its share of hardships, such as all pioneers encounter. Twice the demon fire wiped everything away, but the little Evergreen had become so firmly rooted that on each occasion it sprang up larger and more thrifty than before. They now have a fine brick building in which to hold their meetings and in 1908 there was great rejoicing when the last spike was driven in the railroad which connected them with the outer world.

The following eight Chapters were organized by the General Grand Chapter: Evergreen Chapter No. 1, Goldendale, chartered November 12, 1881; Rainbow Chapter No. 2, Dayton, chartered May 9, 1883; Chehalis Chapter No. 3, Chehalis, chartered April 16, 1885; Washington Chapter No. 4, Colfax, chartered March 31, 1886; Silver Spray Chapter No. 5, Cheney, chartered June 12, 1886; Lorraine Chapter No. 6, Seattle, chartered October 18, 1886; Fern Chapter No. 7, Tacoma, chartered March 7, 1887; Henrietta Chapter No. 8, Sprague, chartered January 23, 1888.

At a meeting of Fern Chapter No. 7, Tacoma, held March 9, 1888, a resolution was introduced asking the eight Chapters in the State (then a Territory) to send delegates to Port Townsend during the annual session of the Grand Lodge, and to petition the General Grand Chapter to delegate some suitable person to constitute them as a Grand Chapter at that time. As a result of this communication the Grand Chapter was organized at Port Townsend July 11, 1888. All Chapters were represented, with twenty-three members present; the membership at that time was 367.

It was quite an undertaking to launch a Grand Chapter in this vast territory, so thinly populated and with so small a membership, where prejudice and opposition to the Order on the part of the Masons was strong and when women, with a lack of experience as to what was really necessary to any organization where obstacles existed, shrank from assuming office.

It was fortunate that a most enthusiastic Mason was the first Grand Patron, Brother J. M. Taylor, who at that time was the head of the Order. One of the greatest difficulties he had to contend with was the delay of nine months over a trivial matter before the General Grand Chapter would release jurisdiction and proclaim the Grand Chapter of Washington organized.

At the first annual session held in Olympia there were eight Grand Officers present and twenty members. At the second annual session held in Ellensburg only four Grand Officers were present and sixteen members. It was quite discouraging to find that at this session a less number were present than when they were organized, but the Territory was new to O.E.S. work, distances were great, money scarce, Chapters remote from place of meeting, and objections not yet removed. But by perseverance, faithful waiting, and earnestness on the part of all interested the prejudice was overcome, Chapters allowed to meet in Masonic halls, and great success has come. The State has grown in population, so has the Eastern Star increased in the number of members, until now few cities have halls large enough to accommodate the Grand Chapter meetings. The membership in June, 1914, was 14,215. Electa Chapter No. 20, in Spokane, is 'the second largest Chapter in the world; membership January 1, 1914, 746.

In 1891 the Grand Matron was made the official head of the Order, Helen E. Edmiston being the first woman to preside as such and it is gratifying to know all her official acts were approved.

With hearts united in the one desire of doing their duty, the O.E.S. of Washington entered into a task of love, pleasure, and cooperation with the Masons. As a result of their combined efforts, there has been erected a beautiful Masonic and Eastern Star Home, situated on the hillside overlooking the beautiful Puyallup Valley and city. To the east is the city of Sumner and to the west in the distance the city of Tacoma and Puget Sound. There are two electric lines, giving good connections with Tacoma and Seattle, and about sixty trains a day on the steam railroad passing within sight of the place. The original site consisted of twenty acres, the funds being raised principally by voluntary donations of Pierce County Masons. There were an eight room house, a four-room house, and two barns on the grounds, which were repaired and the Home opened with a few inmates, in January, 1912. John Thomas, born in Nazareth, Palestine, December 26, 1828, who was made a Mason in Glasgow, Scotland, over fifty years ago, was the first one admitted to the Home.

The following year twenty-two city lots were purchased adjoining the Home grounds and later on two more acres and a section in Woodbine cemetery. On February 12, 1913, just one year from the day the Home was opened in the temporary quarters, the cornerstone of a new building was laid. The grounds and buildings cost about $40,000. It is the intention to erect cottages throughout the grounds, and a separate building for children. In 1915 there were in the Home three old ladies, nine children, and nineteen men. Great interest is taken in the Home by the Chapters and individuals. Many Chapters have furnished rooms and maintain them thereafter. Over

$23,000 was raised by the Grand Chapter for the Home. At the twenty-fifth anniversary of the Grand Chapter a silver offering was taken for the Home which amounted to $1,039.85.

When the news of the great earthquake that wrecked San Francisco, April 18, 1906, was received in Washington, the Chapters did not wait for an appeal from the Grand Matron but sent to the stricken Chapters financial aid immediately, several Chapters contributing $100 each. Thus, it is shown that true generosity is the priceless coinage of the noblest form of sympathy.

Grand Chapter of West Virginia [83]

Devotion to the great moral principles which the Order of the Eastern Star represents, and the desire to promulgate these principles, teaching respect to the binding force of a vow, devotion to religious principles, fidelity to kindred and friends, undeviating faith in the hour of trial, charity and courage with patience and submission even under the wrongs of persecution, were some of the forces which combined to prompt the twenty-seven petitioners to ask for a charter for the first Chapter to be formed in West Virginia.

In response to their request, charter was granted by the General Grand Chapter under date of April 20, 1892, for Miriam Chapter No. 1, Wheeling, and organization was completed May 3, 1892, by Joseph Hall of Wheeling, Deputy of the Most Worthy Grand Patron, with Mrs. Annie Waterhouse, Worthy Matron, Joseph Hall, Worthy Patron, Mrs. F. Lizzie Peterson, Associate Matron.

Alpha Chapter No. 2, at Ceredo, was chartered by the General Grand Chapter February 25, 1896, with thirty petitioners. This Chapter was instituted March 7, 1896, by James McQuin, Deputy of the Most Worthy Grand Patron. Officers were Miss Maggie Walton,

---

[83] Organized June 28, 1904. Data by Miss Etta M. Barnes, Grand Secretary.

Worthy Matron, Samuel Ferguson, Worthy Patron, Mrs. Maggie Harrington, Associate Matron.

August 30, 1897, a charter was issued by the General Grand Chapter for Augusta Chapter, at Mason, with Mrs. Augusta Sehon, Worthy Matron, P. L. Clifton, Worthy Patron, and Mrs. Sarah E. Carriens, Associate Matron, with twenty-four petitioners. However, the original charter was returned to the Most Worthy Grand Patron and the Chapter was never organized, but requested the return of the charter fee.

Athens Chapter No. 3, Athens, was granted a charter November 14, 1899, and organized December 2, 1899, by W. C. Hedeick, Deputy of the Most Worthy Grand Patron, with twenty charter members. Officers: Mrs. Mamie Gore, Worthy Matron, D. H. Thornton, Worthy Patron, Mrs. Mamie Fortney, Associate Matron.

Esther Chapter No. 4, at Welch, was chartered February 15, 1901, with twenty-nine petitioners, and organized by W. O. Perry, Deputy of the Most Worthy Grand Patron. Officers: Mrs. Jennie Payne, Worthy Matron, W. Burbridge, Worthy Patron, Mrs. Ada Greenawalt, Associate Matron.

Silver Leaf No. 5, at Hinton, was chartered March 7, 1901, and the Chapter was organized March 28, 1901, by H. C. Hedrick, of Athens, Deputy for the Most Worthy Grand Patron, with thirty charter members. Officers: Mrs. Alice L. Pope, Worthy Matron; T. O. Flannagan, Worthy Patron; Mrs. Minnie L. Cox, Associate Matron.

Augusta Chapter No. 6, at Mannington, was chartered by the General Grand Chapter July 5, 1901, and organized by Henry Bostock of Pendleton, Indiana, Deputy for the Most Worthy Grand Patron, with thirty-two charter members. Officers: Mrs. Delia H. Huey, Worthy Matron; James B. Marr, Worthy Patron; Mrs. Minerva C. Debendarfer, Associate Matron.

Ruth Chapter No. 7, at Middlebourne, was chartered April 16, 1902, and organized May 5, 1902, by W. W. Chrisley, Deputy of the Most Worthy Grand Patron, with twenty-four charter members.

Brief Histories of the Several Grand Chapters

Charter was granted May 13, 1902, with Miss J. Dora Carter, Worthy Matron; Dr. M. M. Reppard, Worthy Patron; Mrs. Mary Grim, Associate Matron.

Huntington Chapter No. 8, at Huntington, was granted dispensation October 27, 1902, organized October 30, 1902, by J. H. Williams, Deputy of the Most Worthy Grand Patron, with forty-five charter members. The charter was granted December 30, 1902. Officers: Mrs. Mary J. Wallace, Worthy Matron; J. M. Hawkins, Worthy Patron; Mrs. Elizabeth W. Dickey, Associate Matron.

Lorraine Chapter No. 9, at Cameron, was granted dispensation June 2, 1903, and organized June 5, 1903, by James B. Marr, Deputy for the Most Worthy Grand Patron, with thirty-six charter members. The charter was granted June 24, 1903. Officers: Mrs. Lizzie Howard, Worthy Matron; Harry Burkley, Worthy Patron; Mrs. Margaret Shaner, Associate Matron.

Alkire Chapter No. 10, at Keyser, was granted a dispensation on December 8, 1903, and the Chapter was organized January 14, 1904, by W. E. Heskitt, of Westernport, Maryland, Deputy for the Most Worthy Grand Patron, with twenty-eight members. The charter was granted January 22, 1904, with Mrs. Carrie B. M'Neill, Worthy Matron; George T. Carskadon, Worthy Patron; Mrs. Ella L. Parsons, Associate Matron.

The Grand Chapter of West Virginia was organized June 28, 1904, at Wheeling, by the Most Worthy Grand Matron, Mrs. Laura B. Hart, acting as Deputy of the Most Worthy Grand Patron, assisted by the Right Worthy Grand Secretary, Mrs. Lorraine J. Pitkin. The five Chapters represented at the organization of the Grand Chapter were: Miriam No. 1, Wheeling, with twelve votes; Augusta No. 6, Mannington, four votes; Huntington No. 8, four votes; Lorraine No. 9, Cameron, four votes; Algire No. 10, Keyser, three votes. The two Chapters not represented were Silver Leaf No. 5 at Hinton, and Ruth No. 7, at Middlebourne.

The constitution adopted made the Grand Matron the presiding officer and all Past Matrons and Past Patrons members of the Grand Chapter. Per capita dues were fixed at twenty-five cents, but in 1906 were raised to thirty-five cents. In 1905 it was decided to pay the expenses of Grand Officers to Grand Chapter meetings out of the Grand Chapter treasury. In 1906 it was decided to allow two cents per mile to all Grand Chapter Officers, Past Grand Matrons, Past Grand Patrons, and one representative from each subordinate Chapter to be taken from the Grand Chapter treasury, when attending Grand Chapter meetings. Also, that the Grand Patron or his Deputy be allowed $7.50 for each Chapter organized. Also, that the Bible be opened at the second chapter of Matthew, which refers to the Star of in the East. Also, that the expenses of one of the representatives to the General Grand Chapter be paid — the Grand Matron, if she attends, if not, her proxy.

In 1908 the floral work was exemplified before the Grand Chapter, and this year the memorial service was given for the first time.

The same year Sister Minnie Hart M'Cowan composed and dedicated "To Our Beloved Worthy Grand Matron, of West Virginia, Mrs. Minerva C. Derbendarfer," a song, the words of which are given below:

OUR BETHLEHEM STAR

May the light from that Star
So illumine our heart,
That every day
We may do our part;
And do all we can to lighten the way
Of some struggling pilgrim every day.

Bethlehem Star, My Eastern Star,
Your colors will my zeal inspire,

And lead us to that choir above,
Where all sing in harmony and love,
"We praise Thee, our Father, who giveth a home."

The ancient were guided
   By the bright ray,
Why should not we
   In this latter day?
And if we but follow thy bright light
It will always guide us in the right.

Bethlehem Star, My Eastern Star,
Your colors will my zeal inspire,
And lead us to that choir above,
Where all sing in harmony and love,
"We praise Thee, our Father, who giveth a home."

The Grand Jurisdiction was divided into five districts, by counties, and shortly after the closing of the session of 1908, the Grand Matron duly appointed five District Deputies in the newly formed districts.

St. John's Day, June 24th, is designated as an Eastern Star Recreation Day, and Dr. Rob Morris's birthday, August 31st, as Founder's or Festal Day. The subordinate chapters are required to pay the expenses of any Grand Officer, Deputy, or other person requested to visit them for the purpose of instruction.

At the Grand Chapter meeting, 1911, the home fund was given much careful consideration, the Grand Matron stating in her address that "If there is any one object above another to which the Order of the Eastern Star is pledged, it is the protection of the widow and orphan. . . Almost all Jurisdictions have established homes or have home interests, West Virginia being the only state in the Union that has no official mention of a home fund. The brightening of the lives of our aged and helpless sisters and brothers, and the care of our innocent children will prove that we are indeed 'worthy of the support and protection of all good Masons'." Early in her work she had sent out letters urging that the interest and work during her administration should be directed to this worthy and eminently Masonic effort, which formed the nucleus around which the Home fund has been so tenaciously twined, and has enlarged until in 1914 the accumulated fund amounted to $2,191.74, all of which has been accumulated by voluntary contributions.

Following the recommendation of the Grand Matron, the Grand Chapter in 1910 set aside $100 annually for charitable purposes. During the year of 1913-1914 the first school of instruction was held, which consisted of five very interesting sessions, with all Grand Officers present and a Deputy from each one of the districts.

One of the Past Grand Matrons, Mrs. Minerva C. Derbendarfer, served as Worthy Grand Warder of the General Grand Chapter from 1910 to 1913. West Virginia now has sixty-eight chartered Chapters, and one U. D. Chapter, and a membership of 5,100. Though there are no definite plans for the Eastern Star Home, interest is growing throughout the State and the earnest work that has been done along this line will bear fruit in a visible home at the earliest practicable date.

GRAND CHAPTER OF WISCONSIN [84]

Those who have known our beautiful Order only as it is today, will find it difficult to understand conditions as they existed in the very early period of its existence. The Grand Master of Masons in Wisconsin, in his annual address in 1875 made the following recommendations to the Grand Lodge, A. F. and A. M., which were unanimously adopted by that body:

---

[84] Organized February 19, 1891.

In July, 1874, the Masters of several of the subordinates applied to me by letter for advice and directions, stating that they had received printed circulars addressed to their lodges from a person whose name I omit here, as he has since died, notifying them that he would visit their lodges on certain days designated, in order to organize what he termed Chapters of the Eastern Star. I gave the matter immediate attention and thorough investigation. I found that an organization under a somewhat different name had existed and had been tolerated by the Grand Orient of France during the last century, but that it had decayed and died there. In somewhat different shape it appeared to have been revived in this country, and the effort was to import it into this Jurisdiction, in order that the projector might put money into his purse. A personal interview with him brought from him the open — and, as it seemed to me, the dishonest — avowal that his object in disseminating it was to enable him the better and more conveniently to sell books, etc., that he was engaged in retailing. He stated that he cared nothing for it, but that meeting the brethren assembled together in one place and at their lodge rooms to hear him lecture and receive this new Order, he was enabled thereby to sell his wares more conveniently, and that he was thus saved the time and trouble of calling on each one separately. In short, his object at the bottom was to sell his goods, to spend his evenings pleasantly at the profit of $30.00 for each charter granted, which charter signed in blank, he carried with him; and this he proposed to do in the name of and as an attachment or appendage of Freemasonry. I at once stated to him that his project could have from me, only disapproval and discountenance; that I believe the sentiment of the Grand Lodge was against any such concern, and that our constitution and standing regulations positively prohibited it. He assured me that he would abandon the business in this Jurisdiction, but, feeling no especial confidence in any promises made by any man so unworthy as I was satisfied he was, I caused a circular to be issued to all subordinates calling their attention to the fact that by the constitution the conferring of honorary or side degrees in any lodge is entirely forbidden.

The action of the Grand Lodge was justly taken against one who would trample the principles of the Masonic Order, as well as those of the O.E.S. so thoroughly beneath the status which they should occupy. A Deputy who would lose sight of the grand and noble intentions of his mission should not be tolerated and the Grand Master had the support of the Masonic Fraternity in his decision against the work as conducted under the auspices of the Supreme Grand Chapter. But this action of the Grand Lodge effectually closed all avenues and the Order was not accepted in Wisconsin until the conditions and sentiment changed.

At the annual communication of the Grand Lodge of Wisconsin, held at Milwaukee, June 10, 1890, the Grand Master, Myron Reed, spoke as follows:

> During the past year I have received a large number of communications from Lodges all over the State, asking if our Lodge rooms could be used for meetings of an Order known as "The Eastern Star." This is an independent Order claiming to be closely allied to our Masonic Order, and aims to give practical effect to Masonry's beneficent purpose, to provide for the families of Masons. It is an Order composed of Masons and their wives, daughters, widows, mothers and sisters. It is not a new organization, but has been in existence for several years and is quite strongly established in several States of the Union. I lay before you such information as I have to aid you in determining this question.

The special committee to whom was referred this portion of the address, reported as follows:

> Your committee, to whom was referred such of the Grand Master's address as related to the Order of the Eastern Star, begs leave to report: Your committee recommends that in all cases when the Grand Master shall deem it expedient to grant dispensations to enable the Order of the Eastern Star to bold its Chapter in a Masonic Lodge room, that such dispensation be granted without charge.

This report was adopted and without exception, all requests from Chapters for the privilege of meeting in a Masonic lodge room have been granted.

Following the above action of the Grand Lodge, the General Grand Chapter officers granted a charter to Honor Chapter No. 1, on July 10, 1890, for the first Chapter, located at Sturgeon Bay, to thirty petitioners. This Chapter was organized on July 17, 1890, by F. J. Hamilton, Deputy of the Most Worthy Grand Patron. Then followed Milwaukee Chapter No. 2, located at Milwaukee, charter granted November 13, 1890, by the General Grand Chapter in response to the prayer of 167 petitioners. This Chapter was organized November 20, 1890, by A. H. Wright, Deputy of the Most Worthy Grand Patron, with Mrs. Mary Hendee, Worthy Matron, John W. Laflin, Worthy Patron. Miriam Chapter No. 1, of Chicago, responded to an invitation to go and exemplify the work, which they did, at their own expense. This was done because of their zeal in the work, prompted also by the fact that A. H. Wright was the Associate Grand Patron of Illinois.

Orient Chapter No. 3, located at Mazo Manie, was chartered January 13, 1891, and organized the same date by John W. Laflin, Deputy of the Most Worthy Grand Patron, with seventy-two petitioners.

Queen Esther Chapter No. 4, Lodi, was granted a charter January 14, 1891, and organized the same date by John W. Laflin, Deputy of the Most Worthy Grand Patron, with thirty-nine charter members.

Mizpah Chapter No. 5, located at Star Prairie, was granted a charter January 17, 1891, and organized the same date with thirty-two charter members, by A. P. Swanstrom, Deputy of the Most Worthy Grand Patron.

Tomah Chapter No. 6, Tomah, was chartered January 24, 1891; and organized the same day with twenty-nine charter members by John W. Laflin, Deputy of the Most Worthy Grand Patron.

Mineral Point Chapter No. 7, Mineral Point, was chartered February 12, 1891, and organized the same day with 111 charter members, by A. P. Swanstrom, Deputy of the Most Worthy Grand Patron.

Relief Chapter No. 8, located at Maiden Rock, was chartered February 14, 1891, and organized the same day by John W. Laflin, Deputy of the Most Worthy Grand Patron, with twenty-seven charter members.

Naomi Chapter No. 9, located at Wonewac, was chartered February 10, 1891, and organized the same day by John W. Laflin, Deputy of the Most Worthy Grand Patron, with twenty-six charter members.

Rob Morris Chapter No. 10, Eagle, was chartered February 11, 1891, and organized the same day by John W. Laflin, Deputy of the Most Worthy Grand Patron, with twenty-nine charter members.

On February 9, 1891, one day less than eight months after the date upon the first charter that was granted in the State, the Milwaukee Chapter extended an invitation to all Chapters in Wisconsin to meet with them and consider the advisability of organizing a Grand Chapter. The call was responded to and the organization was effected at Milwaukee on February 19, 1891, with representatives present from eight of the ten Chapters, comprising a membership of 605 active and zealous workers.

The constitution adopted did not differ from the usual laws, granting membership to all Past Matrons and Past Patrons, but the constitution was changed rescinding their membership in 1897, clothing the Grand Matron with executive authority, and fixing the per capita dues at twenty-five cents which was increased to thirty cents in 1901. Dispensation fee fixed at $20 and for charter $5. Mrs. Nettie Ransford, Most Worthy Grand Matron, was present at the organization and installed the first board of officers. In 1894 the State was divided into districts and district Chapters held in each.

In 1899 the State was divided into fifteen districts, but this arrangement did not long prevail and in 1904 the State was again divided into ten districts with nine District Deputy Grand Matrons, the tenth district being reserved for the Grand Matron. These were abolished and a Grand Lecturer, for whom a salary was provided, was substituted in 1905. During the life of the District Deputy system, the expense of the schools of instruction were paid by the Grand Chapter; the expenses of the Deputies to be paid by the Chapter visited.

In 1898 an aged widow of a Master Mason and formerly member of the O.E.S. was placed in a home for old ladies through the efforts of the Grand Chapter. The same year a beautiful silk flag was presented the Grand Chapter by some of the Past Grand Matrons and Past Grand Patrons, and as the "Star Spangled Banner" was rendered, the flag was accorded Grand Honors.

In 1899 a tornado almost entirely destroyed the town of New Richmond, and the Grand Matron, realizing the value of help at the time of disaster and with the true fraternal spirit as her guide, issued an appeal for the relief of those who were sufferers from the storm. Contributions of bedding, clothing, etc., were made, also cash to the amount of $1,192.76 as well as quantities of food. Annually, an appropriation of $50 has been made that life may be made more comfortable for one of the sisters in need of assistance. Unsolicited donations were made from Chapters to the amount of $21.50 for the Temple of Fraternity at St. Louis, and $100 was appropriated by the Grand Chapter.

This Grand Chapter has a permanent home in Milwaukee in the commodious building erected by Wisconsin Commandery No. 1, Knights Templar, for the very reasonable rent of $100 per year, this amount providing an office also a hall for the Grand Chapter meetings. The General Grand Chapter was entertained in 1907 at a cost to the Grand Chapter in money of about $1,500. The result was a gain of many times this amount in the cultivation of that much desired gift, the real O.E.S. spirit which Wisconsin sisters possess in superabundant supply. They are ever ready and willing to welcome members of the Fraternity with that true hospitality which so impresses the guest at every moment that all are glad to have the opportunity of a stay among them.

In 1893 a committee was appointed to consider the advisability of establishing an O.E.S. Home, but progress was not marked until 1901 and 1902. In 1902 it was resolved to erect a Home as soon as sufficient funds were raised to establish and maintain the Home without levying a tax upon the Masons or Eastern Stars. Later, arrangements were completed whereby the Scottish Rite Home agreed to care for dependents upon the O.E.S. for a stipulated sum that would be the actual cost of maintaining the person, not to exceed $3.50 per week; this arrangement to obtain until such time as the funds were sufficient to have the desired buildings, etc., of their own. In 1914 the report of the treasurer of the Masonic Home fund shows almost $20,000 accumulated and all invested in good mortgages or other securities.

Grand Chapter of Wyoming [85]

Alpha Chapter No. 1, located at Laramie City, in Albany County, was chartered by the Grand Chapter of New York on December 24, 1879, but it surrendered its charter and was rechartered by the General Grand Chapter on August 5, 1880. The rechartered Chapter was organized by J. H. Hayford, Grand Master A. F. and A. M., Special

---

[85] Organized September 14, 1898.

Brief Histories of the Several Grand Chapters

Deputy of the Most Worthy Grand Patron, with Mrs. Nancy M. Gavitt, Worthy Matron; Ira I. Williamson, Worthy Patron.

This was the only Chapter until fourteen years had passed, when Naomi Chapter No. 2 was chartered March 3, 1894, by the General Grand Chapter with thirty charter members, and organized by J. F. Hoop, Deputy of the Most Worthy Grand Patron.

The General Grand Chapter granted a charter to forty-one petitioners for a Chapter at Lander, to be known as Olivet Chapter No. 3, which was organized by F. G. Burnett, Deputy of the Most Worthy Grand Patron.

Fort Casper Chapter No. 4, located at Fort Casper, was chartered November 16, 1894, with sixty members and organized by J. A. J. Stewart, special Deputy of the Most Worthy Grand Patron.

Electa Chapter No. 5, Sundance, was chartered July 22, 1895, by the General Grand Chapter, with thirty-seven charter members. This Chapter was organized by Alfred J. Pozhansky, Past Grand Patron of South Dakota and special Deputy of the Most Worthy Grand Patron.

Oak Leaf Chapter No. 6, Cheyenne, was chartered May 17, 1897, and instituted May 26, 1897, by A. S. Harman, Past Worthy Patron of Alpha Chapter No. 1, with twenty-five charter members.

Wyoming Chapter No. 7, located at Rawlins, was chartered November 19, 1897, and instituted December 9, 1897, by A. S. Harman, with thirty-seven charter members.

Mystic Chapter No. 8, Green River, was chartered August 11, 1898, with twenty-three members and instituted August 20, 1898, by Dr. E. P. Rohrbaugh, Grand Master A. F. and A. M., special Deputy of the Most Worthy Grand Patron.

The convention to organize the Grand Chapter was called by the Most Worthy Grand Patron, and met in the Masonic Hall, Casper, September 14, 1898, with representatives present from six of the eight Chapters then organized. The constitution adopted provided for the meeting of the Grand Chapter at the same place and the day preceding the meeting of the Grand Lodge, A. F. and A.M.; made the

Grand Matron the executive officer, and fixed the per capita fees at twenty-five cents, which were increased to fifty cents in 1906. Past Matrons and Past Patrons were made permanent members of the Grand Chapter and the three principal officers representative members.

In 1901 it was decided to permit Chapters to hold special elections to fill vacancies at their pleasure, but revoked in 1902. In 1904 it was decided that subordinate Chapters include in their by-laws the provision that any member of the O.E.S. engaging in any manner in the sale of intoxicating liquors should forfeit his membership in the O. E. S.

The early efforts in this Grand Jurisdiction were attended by many discouraging features, but are therefore more truly recognized as sincere and all the more highly appreciative of their responsibilities and true loyalty to advancement of the Order. One Grand Matron visited fifteen of the sixteen Chapters in the jurisdiction in 1905 and in making these visits she traveled twenty-five hundred miles by rail and four hundred and fifty by stage or private conveyance, and had she visited one Chapter not visited, it would have required a further trip of two hundred and thirty miles by rail and a stage ride of three hundred miles. All the Chapters are doing good work, and some members travel as far as twenty miles to attend meetings, making the drive with the thermometer registering almost twenty degrees below zero, while a candidate once drove sixty miles to be initiated. In 1903 the Grand Chapter met in the extreme northeastern part of the State and it was necessary for a number of the representatives to travel long distances to reach the meeting. A few went the entire length of the State, several hundred miles in Nebraska, and across a part of South Dakota, at an expense for railroad fare alone of more than fifty dollars, with faulty. railroad connections and waits. New York could have been reached in a shorter number of hours. Truly it is inspiring to comprehend the energy and faithfulness of these pilgrims toward a blessed eternity.

At their first session, a public installation of the Grand Officers was held in connection with the installation of the Grand Officers of the Masonic Grand Lodge, and this harmony of the members of the two bodies has prevailed continuously; each year a joint social function has been courteously tendered by the local Lodge and Chapter. In 1908 the Grand Master of the Grand Lodge, A. F. and A. M., presented Mrs. Ella Simmons Washburn, Most Worthy Grand Matron, with an armful of flowers in recognition of her position and as the guest of honor of the Grand Chapter. All Chapters hold their meetings in Masonic Halls and this cordial and friendly exchange of fraternal sympathy has remained unbroken.

This Grand Chapter has responded generously to the benevolent work, having donated $25.63 to the O.E.S. headquarters at Portland Exposition; $50 to the sufferers from the San Francisco fire; and in 1908 a per capita tax of ten cents was levied for the benefit of the Masonic Home fund.

> In life, not death —
> Hearts need fond' words to help them on their way,
> Need tender thoughts and quiet sympathy;
> Caresses, pleasant looks, to cheer each passing day.
> Then hoard them not until they useless be;
> In life, not death.

In 1909 an edict was issued declaring "All Orders, or so-called Orders, which base their membership, in whole or in part, upon membership in the Order of the Eastern Star, which have or may hereafter invade the jurisdiction of this Grand Chapter, are hereby declared to be clandestine, and all Eastern Star members holding membership in said Order, or so-called Order of 'The True Kindred of Masonry,' are hereby required to cease membership therein within sixty days from the date hereof, or be subject to expulsion for conduct unbecoming a member of this Order, in refusing or failing to obey the above mandate of this Grand Body."

Chapters under the Immediate Jurisdiction of the General Grand Chapter

The General Grand Chapter maintains exclusive jurisdiction over all unorganized territory, where no Grand Chapter exists, as prescribed by article VI, section 3, of the constitution, which is designed to include all territory not included in the jurisdiction of the fifty-two Grand Chapters on this continent, the Grand Chapter of Scotland, and the Grand Chapter of Porto Rico.

ALASKA

The first Chapter in Alaska was Alaska Chapter No. 1, Nome; organized June 28, 1907, by Mrs. Hattie Day Delkin, Deputy of the Most Worthy Grand Patron, with thirty-four charter members; the charter was granted August 1, 1907.

Nugget Chapter No. 2 was organized August 23, 1909 by W. H. Norris, Most Worthy Grand Patron, with thirty-three charter members. This Chapter is located upon Douglas Island, just across the bay from Juneau, the capital of Alaska.

Aurora Chapter No. 3 was organized at Ketchikan by the Rev. Willis D. Engle, Most Worthy Grand Patron, on August 1, 1911, and charter granted October 30, 1911.

Cordova Chapter No. 4 was organized at Cordova by John Orchard, special Deputy, on January 30, 1913, and charter was granted September 1, 1913.

Valdez Chapter No. 5 was organized at Valdez by John Orchard, special Deputy, on February 17, 1913, and charter was granted September 1, 1913.

Midnight Sun Chapter No. 6 was organized at Fairbanks, September 29, 1913, by Captain John Rex Thompson, of Seattle, Washington, Deputy of the Most Worthy Grand Patron, with thirty-five charter members. Following in the order regularly adopted in the establishment of a new Chapter, the charter was granted November 24, 1913. This Chapter has the distinction of being the farthest north of any Chapter of the Order of the Eastern Star in the world. The first formal installation of elected officers was April 17, 1914, at which time a pleasing musical program followed the impressive services of installation.

Juneau Chapter No. 7 was organized at Juneau, Alaska, December 15, 1915, by Brother John Orchard of Ketchikan, Alaska, Deputy of the Most Worthy Grand Patron, with thirty charter members, and charter was granted April 13, 1914.

CANAL ZONE — PANAMA

Orchid Chapter No. 1 was organized at Gorgona by the Rev. Willis D. Engle, Most Worthy Grand Patron, on October 25, 1911, with fifty-one charter members. The charter was granted by the General Grand Chapter February 1, 1912, which was the date that the Eastern Star shone for the first time in the land of the Southern Cross.

The abundant growth of orchids in Panama suggested this name for the Chapter, and perhaps the best known variety is the *Spiritus Sanctus*, which has a white bell enclosing a stamen formed like a dove and is commonly known as the "Holy Ghost" orchid. White, yellow, and purple predominate in the colors. Formerly the orchids were very difficult to gather, as the rarest ones grow in the tops of the highest trees, but as the waters of Gatun Lake began to rise, it was possible to go out in row-boats and launches and take them from the branches. In the autumn of 1913 the town of Gorgona was so nearly submerged by the waters of Gatun Lake that the site had to be abandoned and consigned again to tropical flora as Nature made it. The

Chapter was then moved to Empire, and when activities of canal construction ceased there, the Chapter was again moved, this time to Balboa at the Pacific entrance to the canal, where by chance. Of fate, the Chapter holds its meetings in the same hall in which it was instituted, thirty miles away. In addition to the fifty-one charter members, thirty-seven were initiated the first year, twenty-eight the second, and twelve the third year, with two affiliations.

Though the Masonic Fraternity did not regard the establishment of Eastern Star Chapters in a favorable light, and opposition was offered by some of the Masons, the field that has been opened has a firm footing and at this early date many of those who were listed among the opponents have learned more of the purposes of the Order and now look upon the work as a complement to Masonic influences.

Hawaiian Islands

The first Chapter was Hawaii Chapter No. 1, located at Hilo; charter was granted March 15, 1899, to thirty-four petitioners and the Chapter organized June 30, 1899, by John U. Smith, Deputy of the Most Worthy Grand Patron of the General Grand Chapter. The first Worthy Matron was Mrs. Nova J. Galbraith, who had seen the light of the Star in Oklahoma Chapter No. 10, U.S. A.; Philip Peck, Worthy Patron.

Leahi Chapter No. 2, located at Honolulu, was chartered by the General Grand Chapter February 26, 1901, in response to the petition of sixty-two persons, and was organized by C. A. Galbraith, Deputy of the Most Worthy Grand Patron, with Mrs. Emily Elizabeth Grant, Worthy Matron; Louis Theodore Grant, Worthy Patron.

Lei Aloha Chapter No. 3, Honolulu, was organized December 12, 1905, by Philip Peck, of Hilo, Deputy of the Most Worthy Grand Patron, with forty-six charter members, with Mrs. Margaret Moore, Worthy Matron; Clarence M. White, Worthy Patron. The charter was granted by the General Grand Chapter May 3, 1906. Harmony Chapter No. 4 was organized at Honolulu by Carrie B. Riley, special Deputy of the Most Worthy Grand Patron, on May 6, 1911, and a charter was granted on October 30, 1911.

At the earnest solicitation of the Chapters in the Hawaiian Islands, the Most Worthy Grand Matron, Sister M. Alice Miller, officially visited all the Chapters in the Islands and found them in flourishing condition and working in harmony. During her stay of two months, excellent work of instruction was given, first at Honolulu, Island of Oahu, Territory of Hawaii, at which place seven schools of instruction were held in the Masonic Temple. The Most Worthy Grand Matron presided at a public installation of officers of Leahi Chapter on January 2, 1913, and true fraternalism reigned in each heart.

At Hilo, on the Island of Hawaii, three schools of instruction was held in the splendid Masonic Temple. The Worshipful Master of the Masonic Lodge was initiated during the visit of Sister Miller, with the work rendered word perfect, and good music. As the guest of the Chapter, the Most Worthy Grand Matron visited the world-famed volcano, Kilauea, during a period of active operation, when the great fire-pit of molten, yellow-red lava, seething and tossing, with fountains of fire playing high in the air, presented a most wonderful and awe-inspiring sight.

Leahi Chapter No. 2 has organized a Past Matrons' and Past Patrons' Club that meets each month, also a "Golden Circle Sewing Club," the former based upon furthering the social and fraternal advancement of its members, the latter an organization for securing funds for charitable purposes of the Order. In 1915 Mr. and Mrs. Johnson (Mrs. Johnson is a Past Grand Matron of Minnesota) were elected honorary members of Leahi Chapter No. 2, which recognition was a marked courtesy worthy of emulation.

Charity has received much attention in the O.E.S. work of the Islands. Leahi Chapter No. 2 for several months maintained a bed in one of the hospitals in Honolulu, where a number of Masonic and Eastern Star members were cared for.

The Most Worthy Grand Matron, in 1913, in accordance with the wishes of all concerned, granted concurrent jurisdiction over Eastern Star material in the other Islands of the group as follows:

> It is hereby ordered by the Most Worthy Grand Matron and the Most Worthy Grand Patron, attested by the Right Worthy Grand Secretary, of the General Grand Chapter, Order of the Eastern Star, that a Special Dispensation be and is hereby granted to the Chapters of the Order in the Hawaiian Islands — Hawaiian Chapter No. 1, located at Hilo, Hawaii; Leahi Chapter No. 2, Lei Aloha Chapter No. 3, and Harmony Chapter No. 4, located in Honolulu, Oahu, Territory of Hawaii, permitting said Chapters to hold and exercise concurrent jurisdiction over Eastern Star material in the Islands of Maui, Kauai, Molokai, Niihau, Lanai and Kaula, for the purpose of extending the Order of the Eastern Star in these Islands, residence of six months, immediately preceding the presentation of petitions of persons eligible to the degrees, being required.

Philippine Islands

Mayon Chapter No. 1, located at Manila, was granted a charter by the General Grand Chapter on January 11, 1905, and was represented at the thirteenth triennial assembly of the General Grand Chapter by Brother Milton E. Springer, Worthy Patron.

Canada

The prejudice against the Order among Masons, some of them influential members, high in authority, in the Provinces of Ontario, Manitoba, and Saskatchewan, is a feature that has retarded the progress of the work there. In some instances, they forbid a Mason to vouch for the eligibility of petitioners either in writing or personally. Though this condition existed in the States during the earlier days of the Order, it has almost entirely disappeared in consequence of the efficient work of the Fraternity, and those who formerly were opposed to it, now have become its most earnest advocates and it is reasonable to anticipate a like result in the Canadian territory.

Manitoba

Queen Winnipeg Chapter No. 1 was organized at Winnipeg, Province of Manitoba, on August 2, 1909, and chartered by the General Grand Chapter on August 12, 1909.

On April 28, 1914, the Star Club was organized, having for its purpose, the raising of funds with a view of helping any sister or brother in distress and to furnish a bed in one of the city hospitals. During the brief months of its existence it has been a potent factor in promoting good fellowship, as well as the added interest of a nucleus for the charitable work of the Chapter.

Electa Chapter No. 2, located at Portage La Prairie, Province of Manitoba, was organized May 20, 1914, by Brother Samuel R. M'Kee, of M'Clusky, North Dakota, with twenty-five charter members, and chartered by the General Grand Chapter July 6, 1914.

New Brunswick

Victoria Chapter No. 1 was organized at Woodstock, Province of New Brunswick, on March 23, 1909, and chartered by the General Grand Chapter on April 28, 1909.

Sunrise Chapter No. 2 was organized at Upper Mills by the Most Worthy Grand Patron, the Rev. Willis D. Engle, on June 2, 1911, and chartered by the General Grand Chapter June 24, 1911.

Celestial Chapter No. 3 was organized at Fredrickton, Province of New Brunswick, by the Rev. Willis D. Engle, Most Worthy Grand Patron, on June 5, 1911, and chartered by the General Grand Chapter on June 24, 1911.

Quebec

King Edward Chapter No. 1 was organized at Coaticook, Province of Quebec, on September 21, 1908, and chartered by the General Grand Chapter October 13, 1908.

Maple Leaf No. 2 was organized at Frelighsburg on February 15, 1909, and chartered by the General Grand Chapter February 25, 1909.

Unity Chapter No. 3 was organized at Cookshire by the Rev. Willis D. Engle, Most Worthy Grand Patron, on May 30, 1911, and charter was granted by the General Grand Chapter on June 24, 1911.

Connaught Chapter No. 4 was organized at Richmond by the Rev. Willis D. Engle, Most Worthy Grand Patron, on September 18, 1912, and chartered by the General Grand Chapter on September 1, 1913.

In 1914 the Chapters observed August 31st in a manner suited to the proper observance of the natal day of our much revered founder, Brother Rob Morris. After greetings were exchanged a program, including a biographical sketch of Brother Morris, also a brief history of the founding of the Order, was rendered.

Cuba

The General Grand Chapter granted a charter to Mercedes Mora Chapter No. 1, located at Havana, Cuba, on April 18, 1914. Chapter was organized by Brother F. Figueredo, Grand Master of the Masonic Order in Cuba, and Deputy of the Most Worthy Grand Patron, Dr. Geo. A. Pettigrew, of Sioux Falls, South Dakota. The organization of this Chapter with thirty-two charter members signalized the progress of the principles of charity, truth, and loving kindness in this beautiful island and with the Spanish *Ritual* now ready for those who care to use it, Chapters will no doubt be added in the near future.

DELAWARE

As a result of earnest effort and untiring zeal, a Chapter of the Order of the Eastern Star has been organized in Wilmington, Delaware. The Most Worthy Grand Matron, Mrs. Rata A. Mills, being deputized by the Most Worthy Grand Patron, Dr. Geo. A. Pettigrew, visited Wilmington on March 10, 1914, and duly instituted Delaware Chapter No. 1, with 128 charter members, which Chapter was chartered by the General Grand Chapter, April 18, 1914.

The opening ceremonies were performed by the following distinguished officers: Mrs. Rata A. Mills, Most Worthy Grand Matron; Walter M. Jones, Past Grand Patron of Pennsylvania, as Most Worthy Grand Patron; Mrs. N. Luella Jackson, Worthy Grand Matron of Pennsylvania, as Right Worthy Associate Grand Matron; T. Roberts Bright, Worthy Grand Patron of Pennsylvania, as Right Worthy Grand Secretary; Mrs. Martha E. Gelston, Worthy Grand Marshal, as Worthy Grand Organist, and all other offices filled by Past Matrons or Past Patron.

The instituting ceremony was impressively conducted, and was followed by the exemplification of the ritualistic work by officers chosen from Excelsior Chapter No. 38, of Philadelphia, Pennsylvania, who performed their respective duties in a highly meritorious manner.

The officers of the newly organized Chapter were installed by the Most Worthy Grand Matron, assisted by the Worthy Grand Marshal, Chaplain, and Organist.

With Delaware in line, the circuit is complete. Every State in the Union now has the Order of the Eastern Star established therein and the right hand of fellowship is most cordially extended to Delaware Chapter No. 1.

INDIA

Pioneer Chapter No. 1 was organized at Benares, India, by T. E. Madden, special Deputy of the Most Worthy Grand Patron, Nathaniel E. Gearhart. This Chapter in the far-a-way British possessions was chartered October 30, 1899, in response to the petition of eight eligible members, and organization completed on March 12, 1900, having for the first officers Mrs. Laura Elizabeth Madden, Worthy Matron; Travers Edward Madden, Worthy Patron.

The New Century Chapter No. 2, located at Calcutta, India, was granted a dispensation by the General Grand Chapter on October 15, 1901, and the Chapter was organized December 14, 1901, by Sarbotosh Bose, Deputy of the Most Worthy Grand Patron, with twenty charter members. Charter was granted February 26, 1902, and the first officers were Mrs. Edith Mathilde Jackson, Worthy Matron; Atul Krishna, Worthy Patron.

By the terms of the Concordat with Scotland, Section B, adopted by a convention of all the Chapters of the Order of the Eastern Star in Scotland held in Glasgow on August 20, 1904, and adopted by the General Grand Chapter September 20, 1904, the territory of India was released to the Grand Chapter of Scotland. By its terms, the "Grand Chapter of Scotland shall have supreme and exclusive jurisdiction over Great Britain, Ireland and the whole British dominions (excepting only, those upon the Continent of America) and that a Supreme or General Grand Chapter of the British Empire shall be formed as soon as Chapters are instituted therein and it seems expedient to do so."

Mexico

Owing to the unsettled condition of Masonry in Mexico, where there is only one legitimate Grand Lodge, "The Grand Lodge de Valley of Mexico," and even this one has not been accorded recognition by all the Grand Lodges of the United States, the organization of O.E.S. Chapters has not been encouraged by the General Grand Chapter.

A petition for a Chapter at Cananea, Sonora, signed by Americans who lived there, was recognized and a dispensation granted by the General Grand Chapter for Cananea Chapter No. 1. This Chapter was organized on April 17, 1905, by Mrs. Bessie H. Grosetta, of Tucson, Arizona, Deputy of the Most Worthy Grand Patron, with forty-six charter members. The charter, which was granted May 3, 1905, named Mrs. Carrie E. Talbot, Worthy Matron; F. E. Beecher, Worthy Patron.

Owing to the multiplicity of disturbances resulting from the grave political strife within Mexico, on July 31, 1913, Cananea Chapter No. 1 voted to surrender its charter, paid all dues, and demits were issued to thirty-five members. It being the wish of the Chapter to turn the funds remaining in their hands over to the Masonic Lodge for use in caring for destitute Masonic families, that have been or may be brought to that condition by the war then waging in the country of which Cananea is the storm center, the request was made that they be permitted to use the funds in that manner rather than to pay them to the General Grand Chapter. Sister M. Alice Miller, Most Worthy Grand Matron, recognized the justice of the appeal, and knowing something of the strain and stress that country had been laboring under, and the great need likely to obtain, the rights of the General Grand Chapter were waived and permission granted to retain the funds for the purpose named.

Yukon

Yukon Chapter No. 1, located at Dawson was organized August 3, 1906, by Mrs. Rosetta West, Deputy of the Most Worthy Grand Patron, with twenty-one charter members and was chartered by the General Grand Chapter on November 1S, 1906.

Thank you for buying this Cornerstone book!

For over 30 years now, we've tried to provide the Masonic community with quality books on Masonic education, philosophy, and general interest. Your support means everything to us and keeps us afloat. Cornerstone is by no means a large company. We are a small family-owned operation that depends on your support.

Please visit our website and have a look at the many books we offer as well as the different categories of books.

If your lodge, Grand Lodge, research lodge, book club, or other body would like to have quality Cornerstone books to sell or distribute, write us. We can give you outstanding books, prices, and service.

Thanks again!

Cornerstone Book Publishers
1cornerstonebooks@gmail.com
http://cornerstonepublishers.com

www.ingramcontent.com/pod-product-compliance
Lightning Source LLC
LaVergne TN
LVHW041654060526
838201LV00043B/428